PATRICK
THE PILGRIM APOSTLE
OF IRELAND

Including

ST PATRICK'S *CONFESSIO* AND *EPISTOLA*

Edited and Translated

with Analysis and Commentary by

Máire B. de Paor, PBVM

ReganBooks

An Imprint of HarperCollins*Publishers*

Also by Máire B. de Paor

Banfhundúirí Átha Cliath

Tadhg Gaelach Ó Súilleabháin

This book was originally published in Ireland in 1998 by Veritas Publications.

PATRICK. Copyright © 1998 by Máire B. de Paor. All rights reserved. Printed in the United States of America. No part of this book may be used or reproduced in any manner whatsoever without written permission except in the case of brief quotations embodied in critical articles and reviews. For information address HarperCollins Publishers Inc., 10 East 53rd Street, New York, NY 10022.

HarperCollins books may be purchased for educational, business, or sales promotional use. For information please write: Special Markets Department, HarperCollins Publishers Inc., 10 East 53rd Street, New York, NY 10022.

FIRST U.S. EDITION

Printed on acid-free paper

Library of Congress Cataloging-in-Publication Data has been applied for.

ISBN 0-06-000902-0

02 03 04 05 06 RRD 10 9 8 7 6 5 4 3 2 1

CONTENTS

Confessio: Parts I & V

A
Patrick, the nobleman's son and heir
Patrick, the illegal alien slave
Prologue
Humilitas mea, my lowliness
There the Lord opened my mind to an awareness of my unbelief

A'
Epilogue
Donum Dei, the gift of God
Renewal of baptismal covenant

B   To exalt and confess his wondrous deeds
B'   I testify in truth and in exultation of heart

C   Patrick's Creed, quoting Romans 8:16-17
C'   Patrick's Doxology, quoting Romans 8:16-17
Patrick's prayer for God's own people
Patrick's desire for martyrdom
Christ, the true Sun

D   Trust in God, quoting Psalm 50 (49):15
D'   Trust in God, quoting Psalm 55 (54):22

E   Lord I am not worthy
E'   And I was not worthy

F   The mouth which lies destroys the soul
F'   I do not lie

X   The *Apologia*
1,1' Patrick's hesitation about writing his *Confessio*
Pseudo-Christians and pseudo-prophets
Patrick's fear of adverse criticism
Patrick, the chosen fool
Patrick's adversaries *seem* to be wise
Cultural adaptation
Patrick's knowledge of the Gaelic language
That with humility and truthfully I might serve them
Patrick's understanding of his mission
Patrick's legacy
The Lord's eternal consolation

CHAPTER TWO

Introduction
Ceretic (Coroticus) of Wales
Ceretic Guletic (Coroticus) of Ail-Cluaide
The Irish proto-martyrs
Patrick's first *Epistola*
Patrick's second *Epistola*
Structure, Content and Biblical Context of Second Epistola:

Paragraph I

Prologue: A sojourner and a refugee for the love of God
Divine call to Irish mission
An ambassador of Christ
Mission to barbarian, pagan Irish
I live for my God
The despised teacher of pagans
Christian fellow-citizens
Fellow-citizens of demons
A living death

Paragraph II

Patrick's divine inheritance
The tyranny of Coroticus
Repent, do penance
Free the slaves of God
Greed
What does it profit....?
The wages of sin....
Eternal death....

Paragraph III

A slave in Christ
A despised mission
Divine adoption
One God as Father
Coroticus, betrayer of Christ and Christians
Numberless Christians massacred or reduced to slavery
The Church grieves for her slaves and martyrs
The greed of Coroticus and his accomplices
A gift of poison
Damnation for both instigator and collaborator
Christians of Roman Gaul contrasted with British Christians

Paragraph IV

THEMES ON THE EPISTOLA

FOREWORD

This volume is the result of a labour of love extending over many years. It explores St Patrick's pilgrimage of faith as revealed in his writings. The format follows that of the *Confessio* and comprises a prologue, five chapters, and an epilogue.

The prologue contains sketches of the historical Patrick, fifth-century Ireland, and Patrick the writer. The first three chapters cover an analysis of Patrick's term of slavery and escape, his vocation and mission; the fourth chapter deals with his rejection and betrayal; chapter five looks at the historical context, structure and content of his *Epistola* to Coroticus; the epilogue draws together the main threads of the work, presents parallel Latin and English versions of the texts, and a comprehensive list of scriptural quotations and allusions used by Patrick in his writings.

Though belonging to the confessional genre, the *Confessio* incorporates many strands, one being an *apologia pro vita sua* aimed against opponents of his mission to Ireland. The author argues that the need to answer those critics was the principal cause of his writing – as Kingsley's accusations were the immediate occasion of Newman's *Apologia*. But, as with Newman and Augustine, the immediate occasion did not prevent Patrick's work becoming something greater in the writing. It provided an opportunity for his genius to expand into the much larger theme presented in part three of the *Confessio*, namely, a magnificent canticle of gratitude to God who made him what he was and enabled him to achieve what he did. Patrick tells us that he cannot stay silent, nor is it fitting that he should, about the great favours and graces he has had from the Lord in the land to which he first came as captive. At the outset he admits that he 'long ago thought of writing', but had 'hesitated until now' for fear of what critical tongues would say about his literary limitations.

St Patrick's *Epistola* to Coroticus and his soldiers is in fact one of excommunication. Though very moving in its expression of grief and its denunciation of the fierce wolves that attacked his Christian flock, the *Epistola* stands up in idiom and structure as a very fine official document, carefully composed by a confident and experienced churchman.

The layout of the texts of Patrick's writings used by Máire B. de Paor is an adaptation from that of Dr David Howlett who, in his recent work, *The Book*

1

of Letters of St Patrick the Bishop, presents an analysis of the texts which indicates that, far from being 'a barely literate rustic', Patrick was 'both an artist of astounding literary skill and a man of great spiritual depth'.[1]

The Latin used by Patrick was that spoken in everyday life, a colloquial Latin that varied from region to region in the Roman Empire. The term used to describe the quality of this colloquial Latin was *rusticitas*, rusticity, hence Patrick's description of himself in the *Confessio* as *rusticissimus*. The author points out that such self-deprecatory qualifications were commonplace 'within the literary climate of his era'.[2] What Máire B. de Paor, David Howlett and a growing number of scholars now maintain is that the writer of the *Confessio* and *Epistola* to Coroticus is clearly a person of intellectual stature.[3] From the pages of this book Patrick emerges as a man with deep and intimate familiarity with Holy Scripture, a man concerned with faith as life in Christ, a man whose purpose was to share with others that life in Christ, a man whose own life and lifestyle were first and foremost pastoral, missionary and spiritual.

I feel confident that one effect of this scholarly work will be to deepen its readers' faith as a lived reality and intensify their desire to confess 'that Jesus Christ is Lord and God, in whom we believe and whose coming we look for soon....' (*Confessio,* 4).

✠ Thomas A. Finnegan
Bishop of Killala

---

1 Howlett, *BLSPB*, 4
2 *Infra*, 19.
3 See also *St Patrick's Letters; A Study of their Theological Dimension*, edited and presented by Dr Patrick Bastable, together with Thomas Finan, Maurice Hogan, Thomas Norris, and Pádraig Ó Fiannachta of St Patrick's College, Maynooth, An Sagart, Maynooth, 1993.

ACKNOWLEDGMENTS

It is a joy and a privilege to thank all those who helped me in my exploration of Patrick's writings. Dr Breandán Ó Doibhlin and the late Cardinal Tomás Ó Fiaich suggested and consistently encouraged the undertaking. Unfortunately I did not pluck up enough courage to set out on this perilous journey until after Tomás Ó Fiaich's untimely death. Since then Breandán Ó Doibhlin and David Howlett have, with invariable patience, kindness and generosity, guided me over many thorny patches on Tóchar Phádraig; my heartfelt gratitude to both of them agus gur móide glóir shíoraí Thomáis i radharc na Tríonóide.

I am deeply grateful to Srs Elizabeth Starken and Wyona Engles PBVM, Congregational Leaders, and Srs Emmanuel Campion and Frances Crowe, Provincial Leaders, who commissioned this book, and who provided the facilities and the leisure to write it; Most Rev Tomás A. Ó Finneagáin, Bishop of Killala, in whose diocese Silva Focluti, Fochoill, is reputedly situated, for his sustained interest in the progress of this work, and for graciously taking the time to write the Foreword; Most Rev Seosamh Ó Dufaigh, Bishop of Clogher, for reading the manuscript, Charles Ó Dochartaigh, UCD, for reading the historical section, and for their valuable insights and wise suggestions.

My indebtedness to the following for their wisdom, advice, encouragement, constructive criticism, and numerable kindnesses is not easy to calculate: Most Rev Diarmad Ó Clúmháin, Archbishop of Cashel, Professors Dónal Ó Conbhúir, Pádraig Ó Fiannachta, Thomas Finan, Thomas Marsh and the staff of Dámh an Oideachais, Coláiste Pádraig, Máigh Nuad; the late Richard Dudley-Edwards, UCD; Donnchadh Ó Corráin, UCC; Dr Anthony Harvey, RIA; my sister, Margaret Power-Carr; the Cistercian monks Eoin de Bhaldraithe, Patrick Coughlan, Nivard Kinsella, Alberic Moran and M. Philip Scott; Séamus Ó Cearnaigh, Donal Connelly, Derry O'Donnell and Breandán Ó Conaire and colleagues, Comhdháil an Chraoibhín, the Douglas Hyde Summer School; Dr Peter O'Dwyer, OCarm; Very Rev Edward Dowling, PP, VF, An Mhuine Bheag; the Kiltegan and SMA communities, Máigh Nuad; my parents, family, relatives, friends and neighbours; my teachers, the late Déaglán Ó Cuilliú, Diarmad Ó Drisceoil and Mícheál Ó Foghlú; Sr Xavier Ní Mhathúna and the late Sr Madeleine Ní Bhroin of Presentation College, Ballingarry, who faithfully and courageously transmitted

St Patrick's legacy; my colleagues and students in Portlaoise, Baile Chonglais and An Cheathrú Rua who kept urging me to write; the bibliography indicates the extent of my indebtedness to the published works of saints and scholars.

I wish to thank Carmel Hanahan, Carlow County Library, Siobhán Ó Raifeartaigh RIA and the staff of the Royal Irish Academy, Dublin, for graciously providing me with copies of the manuscripts of Patrick's writings, the Dublin Institute of Advanced Studies, the Italian Institute, the National Library of Ireland, the libraries of An Mhuine Bheag, Carlisle, Carlow, Dumbarton, Edinburgh, Maynooth College, Trinity College, Dublin, University College Galway, and the Computer Centre, Maynooth College, for their generous assistance and courtesy.

No small measure of appreciation is due to the following who helped me with the field work in preparation for this book, as well as many other kind people whom I met along the way: Christina ffrench of Stockholm, Fr Frank Fahey of Ballintubber Abbey; Donna Brewster, the Burford family, Fr David Conroy, Dr Peter Hill and the staff of The Dig at Candida Casa, Scotland; Canon Mark Diamond and Paddy Lavin of Silva Focluti; Sr Mercy RSM, my enlightened and gracious guide at Downpatrick, Saul, Sliabh Pádraig, and Struell Wells; the Sisters of Mercy in Cookstown, Belfast and Downpatrick, the Presentation Sisters in Belfast, Dungarvan and Portadown; Sr Sheila Flood SSL, with whom I explored Brú na Bóinne, Tara and the Hill of Slane; the Sisters of St Clare, Newry, who took me to Sliabh Mis for the first time; the late Cairdinéal Tomás Ó Fiaich, and John Ward, who uncovered for me the Patrician treasure of Ulster with such knowledge, perception and enthusiasm, beginning at Eamhain Mhacha; Gareth and Lynnwen Pierce, with whom I explored many of the Celtic and Roman treasures of Wales and England, in particular Caerleon, Caerwent, Chedworth, Bath and Glastonbury; Elizabeth Banerjee of Carlise, the staff of Carlise Tourist Office who arranged my 'pilgrimages' to Birdoswald, Hadrian's Wall, Lindisfarne, Whitby, Dumbarton and the Antonine Wall; Fr Aidan D'Arcy and all the kind people who came to my assistance *en route* to, and at, all those historic places; Robert Hughes and Martin Nevin for their untiring efforts to get this book into print; Anne McParland, Carmel Ryder, and Liam Fennelly for so much patient assistance with typing, charts and word processing; Fiona Biggs and Elaine Campion, my patient and painstaking editors; Barbara Croatto, my equally painstaking typesetter; and last, but not least, my own communities at Máigh Nuad and An Mhuine Bheag, and Presentation Sisters, Bríd Burke, Pius Coughlan, and Yvonne Jennings for so much help and support in bringing this book to publication.

Go gcúití Dia bhur saothar libh go léir agus i líontaibh Dé go gcastar sinn.

Máire B. de Paor PBVM
Clochar na Toirbhearta
An Mhuine Bheag,
Co. Ceatharlach, Éire
7 Feabhra 1998

DEDICATION

Do Phobal Pádraig i ngach aon tír faoi íor na spéire.

To Patrick's children in the faith in every nation under every heaven.

Dóchas linn Naomh Pádraig, Aspal mór na hÉireann.

INTRODUCTION

And so, 'according to the measure of the faith' of the Trinity it is my duty,
without fear of the censure [I may incur]
to make known 'the gift of God'
and his 'eternal consolation';
without fear
faithfully to expound everywhere the Name of God,
so that even 'after my death' I may leave behind a legacy
to my brethren and children,
whom I have baptized in the Lord, so many thousands of people (C 14:71-78).

ST PATRICK'S LEGACY TO HIS CHILDREN IN THE FAITH

St Patrick is known to many as Apostle of Ireland; as first Romano-British missionary bishop, beyond the pale of Roman civilisation, he is known to a few; but as a littérateur of stature and genius and a spiritual thinker of great depth and originality, he is relatively little appreciated. In the 1950s Ludwig Bieler published the standard edition of Patrick's extant writings, i. his *Epistola to the Soldiers of Coroticus* (E), and his *Confessio* (C). That eminent Patrician scholar could say, even at that late date, that those compositions had been almost completely neglected by students of Latin language and literature.[1] Yet, in Patrick's writings we have two unique, personal, spiritual documents from the darkest of the Dark Ages, fifth-century Northern Europe. Indeed, they are the only personal documents that can be claimed by either the Church in Britain or the Church in Ireland from that troubled century.

We had to wait twelve more centuries before Aodh Mac Aingil (1571-1626), one of Patrick's successors in the see of Armagh, produced a kindred personal document. It came in the form of a Christmas poem, *An Naí Naomh*, 'The Holy Child', in early modern Gaelic. In this poem the Franciscan poet tenderly contemplates the Word made Flesh and, with touching, male simplicity of heart, shares with us his personal response in twenty-seven syllabic, four-lined stanzas.[2]

In *The Book of Letters of Saint Patrick the Bishop* David Howlett has, however, amply rectified the sad neglect of the compositions of our national apostle, to which Bieler referred, by challenging 'the modern consensus that Patrick was a barely literate rustic struggling with a sense of his inadequacy in a language he could not master'. Dr Howlett's impressive analysis 'suggests instead that

---

1 Bieler, *LE I*, 5.
2 Ó Dúshláine, *ELG*, 175ff.

Patrick was both an artist of astonishing literary skill and a man of great spiritual depth'.[3]

It was fascinating to discover that Ludwig Bieler further claimed that the ideal form of presentation of ancient texts such as Patrick's writings would be a division *per cola et commata*, 'by clauses and phrases'.[4] I am therefore deeply grateful to Dr Howlett for graciously allowing me to adapt his arrangement of the texts in that form so that the units of Patrick's thought might be revealed.[5]

We Irish are, moreover, the only nation who have the great privilege of treasuring the writings of our Father in the faith about his founding of the Christian Church in our country. Conscious of the unique Christian heritage bequeathed to us by our national apostle who has left such an indelible impression on his people, I have attempted a modest literary and spiritual exposé of his writings to mark the fifteenth centenary of his death.

PATRICK'S PILGRIMAGE OF FAITH

In his *Epistola*, the saint writes: *peregrinatio mea in vacuum non fuit*, my pilgrimage has not been in vain (E 17:172). The aim of this exposé is to explore Patrick's pilgrimage of faith, in particular, in order to gain a deeper insight into the mind and heart of this indomitable sojourner and captive for Christ (cf. C 59:20; E 1:4) as he reveals himself to us in his own writings, but more particularly in his *Confessio*.

As we join Patrick on his pilgrimage of faith, therefore, it might be useful to provide ourselves with a very simple outline 'map' of the ground which we hope to cover. Let us begin by briefly examining the literary genre and structure of the *Confessio*, to enable us to grasp its spiritual content more fully. 'Only by apprehending the mechanical structure of Patrick's thought and prose can we begin to hear the tenor of his explicit statements and the undertones and overtones of his implicit resonances.'[6]

Of the two texts the *Confessio* is the more personal and important document. Patrick has told us that it is his *exagalliae* or 'spiritual legacy' (C 14:77) to us, believers (C 62:1), his children in the faith, in every nation which is under every heaven (C 3:10-11). In the event, we shall also find that in structure and content the *Epistola* has many elements in common with that of the *Confessio*.

The historical context of both writings is briefly sketched for the benefit of readers who may not be familiar with this particular period in history. Thus, an awareness of the quality of soil in which Patrick so firmly planted the seed of God's Word will, it is hoped, help all of us to appreciate both the true

---

3   Howlett, *BLSPB*, jacket copy.
4   Bieler, op. cit., 44.
5   Howlett, op. cit., 12.
6   Ibid., 12.

greatness of this missionary-bishop (E 1:1; C 26:2) and the unprecedented harvest which he reaped in the teeth of enormous difficulties.

A
PATRICK THE WRITER

WHAT IS A *CONFESSIO*?

The *Confessio* is a literary genre, of which two major extant examples in ancient literature are the *Confessions* of St Augustine, written about AD 400 when he was a comparatively young man, and the *Confessio* of St Patrick, written during the fifth century, possibly some short time before his death (C 62:12). In ecclesiastical Latin the term *confessio* has a threefold significance: *confessio peccati, confessio laudis* and *confessio fidei,* i. the penitential discipline, the praise of God, and the confession of faith of the martyrs before a tribunal.[1] *Confessio* in this third context was also termed *depositio*, or deposition, and the confessors were those who made a deposition or, in other words, subscribed to the faith during the persecution of Christians in the early centuries of the Church.[2] It has been argued cogently by Botte that the word, in the sense of 'subscribing to the faith', was extended in the fourth and fifth centuries to denote those who defended it against heresy, and that Augustine used it in this sense.[3]

But, while a refutation of both the Arianism of the fourth century and the Pelagianism of the fifth are implicit in Patrick's *Confessio*, it does not appear to be its overt purpose; nor would Patrick have considered himself qualified for such an undertaking. He was not, after all, a professional theologian, nor did he claim to be a philosopher. As priest and bishop he was pre-eminently a good shepherd, a contemplative in action, and, like his great model, St Paul, 'whatever he wrote was dictated by the responsibilities of his episcopal office'.[4]

His *Confessio*, therefore, defines itself by its own title. It is not an autobiography in the strict sense, because the saint does not tell the story of his life in chronological order and plain narrative, nor is this his sole or main purpose. Neither, as some scholars suggest, is it merely a *defence* of himself against false accusations, an *apologia pro vita sua*.[5] While his initial inspiration

---

1 Solignac, *LCA,* 1 ff; Bieler, *SLH* (1952), 11, 85-88.
2 Chadwick, *ASCC,* 24.
3 Chadwick, ibid., 24-5.
4 Bieler, *LE* I, 5.
5 Chadwick, *ASCC*, 25; Ó Raifeartaigh, *EP*, 3.

9

may well have been the refutation of certain allegations made by his enemies against him and his mission, it evolved into something greater, something more timeless and universal, in the process. This 'record of the inner spirit wrung from the heart of a man of powerful and deep-seated religious conviction'[6] is, like St Augustine's, a magnificent, threefold *Confessio* of repentance, praise and faith as a lived reality.[7] This threefold *Confessio* evolves out of a retrospective, contemplative reflection on the events of Patrick's life. Here the whole of his life – including his failures – is recaptured. What he has experienced is now, in his old age, understood as a single spiritual entity. It all fits together and relates to past and future in, as it were, an eternal present where time and eternity intersect.

BIBLICAL ROOTEDNESS OF THE *CONFESSIO*

True to its genre, Patrick's *Confessio* has its tap-root in Sacred Scripture. It evokes the great Old Testament Psalms of repentance, praise and thanksgiving. Indeed, Bieler has established that Patrick quotes from the Psalms more than from any other book of the Old Testament.[8] It is also reminiscent of the great biblical Canticles such as *The Prayer of Azariah* and *The Song of the Three Jews*, so dear to the Céile Dé reform-movement of the eighth century, as well as the *Magnificat*, the *Benedictus*, and St Paul's many Blessings.

Written some time before Patrick's death, it is also in the tradition of the great biblical Farewell Speeches, those of Jacob (Gn 49) and Moses (Dt 32-33), to name two of the seven from the Old Testament; Christ's Farewell to his disciples at the Last Supper (Jn 13-17) and Paul's to his friends at Miletus (Ac 20:7-36) in the New. It is no coincidence that Patrick quotes Paul's unrivalled pastoral testament at Miletus six times in his writings, three in the *Epistola* (E 5, 10, 12), and three in the *Confessio* (C 43, 48, 55).

And finally, its content, but not its form, might be compared with the impressive *Eucharistikon* of Paulinus of Pella, written in 459 in his eighty-third year, as a thanksgiving to God for ordering and directing his life.[9]

PATRICK'S CONVERSION

Such a *Confessio* presupposes the experience of conversion which, for some people, is a profound, soul-shaking encounter with Christ, like Paul's on the road to Damascus (Ac 9, 22, 26). Patrick's experience was not, perhaps, quite as dramatic and sudden as Paul's, but it was no less dynamic and transfigurative in its lasting effects.

The depth of Patrick's consciousness of the vast abyss between himself and

6   Ó Raifeartaigh, ibid., 3.
7   Malaspina, *PAL,* 223; Bieler, *LL*, 36; Carney, *IER*, 97, 1962, 148-58; Conneely, *TLSP*, 131-50.
8   Bieler, *DB*, 239; Hanson, *OC*, 154.
9   Chadwick, *PLG*, 123 ff.

the total Otherness of the All-Holy God, after his experience of conversion, is one of the twin pillars on which his *Confessio* hinges. He expresses it in the prologue in two simple words: *humilitas mea*, 'my lowliness' (C 2:23). The second pillar is complete dependence on, and total surrender to this All-Merciful God. This humble trust finds laconic expression in *donum Dei*, 'the gift of God' (Jn 4:10; Ac 8:20), in the epilogue (C 62:10).

Patrick's primary purpose as a writer is to make a *retributio* or 'repayment' (C 3, 11, 12, 57) for all that God has done for him, and through him, and in him. The exultant expression of his gratitude and praise, which is rooted in a faith that is almost vision, is the joyful leitmotif which pervades the *Confessio* from beginning to end. It is what gives his work of art its unity and cohesion. In it is captured something of the freshness, the optimism, and the hope of the early spring of Christianity in fifth-century Ireland. And if Patrick were to choose a theme-song for his pilgrimage of faith it might be *Gloria in Excelsis Deo*. This joyful, eucharistic, Trinitarian canticle captures the true spirit of his *Confessio* because the joy of the Holy Spirit is one of the biblical signs of the Messianic era. And that heavenly joy was always welling up in Patrick's great heart and soul (C 34:6-14).

As a work of Christian faith, then, the *Confessio* is best read by believers who share or, at least, desire to share that faith. As a pastoral testimony, it demands that Patrick's disciple be one whose constant aim is fraternal and apostolic Christian charity in imitation of Christ himself.[10]

DRAMATIC STRUCTURE OF THE *CONFESSIO*

Looked at as 'a pilgrim's progress' from youth to old age, Patrick's *Confessio* can be shown to be structured in the manner of a classical drama. It begins with a prologue and ends with an epilogue; it is divided into the classical five parts – exposition, development, nouement, crux and denouement – with the crux at the centre. There is, moreover, a perfect caesura between the crux and the denouement (C 33:1).[11]

Its fivefold division would also suggest the fivefold arrangement of the Pentateuch and the Book of Psalms of the Old Testament, and Matthew's Gospel in the New. The literary format of these biblical books may well have been the definitive influence on Patrick's literary construction of his *Confessio*.

Considered, however, as a retrospective, contemplative reflection on the events of his whole life, David Howlett has discovered once more that the *Confessio* and the *Epistola* are in fact highly-worked, symmetrical compositions, in which parallel and concentric or chiastic patterns can be traced. These literary patterns enable us to enter ever more deeply into the subtle and profound depths of meaning hidden in Patrick's writings. Readers who are

---

10 Solignac, op. cit., *LCA*, 14.
11 de Paor, *FFTO* (July 1990), in *CAC*, 1990, 1992, 49-76, the dramatic structure of the *Confessio*.

not yet familiar with them will find that even an elementary grasp of them will be of help as we begin our pilgrimage of faith in the company of our great national apostle. Let us begin with parallelisms.

PARALLEL PATTERNS IN PATRICK'S WRITINGS

A 'parallelism' in literature is a balanced construction of a verse or sentence, where one part repeats the form or meaning of the other. A clear example of this antiphonal statement and restatement is in Luke 21:23-24, which is as follows:

A   Woe to those who are pregnant
A'   and to those who are nursing infants in those days!

B   For there will be great distress on the earth
B'   and wrath against this people;

C   they will fall by the edge of the sword
C'   and be taken away as captives among all nations.

Patrick makes judicious use of this form of biblical style in his writings, particularly in chapters twenty-three, twenty-four and thirty-four of his *Confessio*.

THE CONCENTRIC OR CHIASTIC STRUCTURE OF PATRICK'S WRITINGS

Concentric structure in literature 'consist in disposing the elements in the pattern A B C N C' B' A' with thematic and verbal correspondences, the central element – N – being stressed'.[12] A 'chiasmus' or 'contrast by parallelism in reverse order', on the other hand, properly refers to only two lines where the themes are reversed in the second, such as Mark 2:27:

A   **B**
The sabbath was made for man,
B   **A**
not man for the sabbath.

If lines were drawn connecting the A's and B's, the lines would form an X, which is the Greek letter *chi*, hence chiasmus. 'Concentric structure' or 'inverted parallelism' is therefore used in this work in preference to 'chiastic structure' as being more appropriate to indicate the use of inversion as the overall pattern of Patrick's *Confessio* and *Epistola*, the pattern of their component parts, as well as certain segments of those parts. In *A Virgin Called Woman*[13] M. Philip Scott OCSO demonstrates the overall concentric structure of St Mark's Gospel thus:

12 Schokel, *LMBW*, 87; Drijvers, *TP*, 21 ff; Howlett, *CLTBS*, 1 ff.
13 Scott, *AVCW* (1986) 52-76, its concentric structure, the key to Mark's Gospel.

(1:2)   A   *An angel witnesses* to his coming
(1:11)   B   You are *my Son*
(2:7)   C   *Who can forgive sins but God alone? (ei me eis ho Theos)*
(3:29)   D   The guilt of *the scribes*
(3:33)   E   Who is *my mother...?*
(3:35)   F   The primacy of doing *God's will*
(4:40)   G   *Who is this* that the winds ... *obey him?*
(6:3)   H   Jesus is called *the Son of Mary*
(8:27)   L   *Who do you say that I am?*
(8:31)   M   Prophecy of *rejection, passion, resurrection*
(9:7)   N   This is my Son, the Beloved, listen to Him
(9:30)   M'   Prophecy of *betrayal, passion, resurrection*
(10:18)   L'   *Why call me good? No one is good but God alone (ei me
                                            eis ho Theos)*
(10:47)   H'   Jesus is called *Son of David*
(11:28)   G'   *By what authority* do you do these things?
(12:30)   F'   The primacy of *God's commandment of love*
(12:37)   E'   How is Christ *David's Son?*
(12:40)   D'   A judgment on *the scribes*
(14:61)   C'   Are you *the Christ the Son of the Blessed God?*
(15:39)   B'   Truly, this man was *the Son of God*
(16:6)   A' *An angel witnesses* to his going

Here Mark presents us with contrasting stories which he has arranged antiphonally with thematic and verbal correspondences (italicised). The writer expects us to begin with what we term 'antiphon' *A* from the first story and then pair it off with 'antiphon' *A'* from the last story; similarly, antiphon *B* is followed by antiphon *B'* and so on, until the crux or central element is reached at *N*, which has no corresponding antiphon. It is noteworthy that the biblical crux is at the centre, as in classical drama and in many Gaelic poems, and not at the end, as in modern literature.

When the pairs of related antiphons are placed side by side the thematic and verbal correspondences become clearer. Thus:

(1:2)   A   *An angel witnesses* to his coming
(16:6)   A' *An angel witnesses* to his going.

(1:11)   B   You are *my Son*
(15:39)   B' Truly, this man was *the Son of God.*

(2:7)   C   *Who can forgive sins but God alone? (ei me eis ho Theos)*
(14:61)   C' Are you *the Christ the Son of the Blessed God?*

(3:29)   D   The guilt of *the scribes*
(12:40) D' A judgment on *the scribes*

(3:33)   E   Who is *my mother...?*
(12:37) E' How is Christ *David's Son?*

(3:35)   F   The primacy of doing *God's will*
(12:30) F' The primacy of *God's commandment of love*

(4:40)   G   *Who is this* that the winds ... *obey him?*
(11:28) G' *By what authority* do you do these things?

(6:3)   H   Jesus is called *the Son of Mary*
(10:47) H' Jesus is called *Son of David*

(8:27)   L   *Who do you say that I am?*
(10:18) L' *Why call me good? No one is good but God alone (ei me eis ho Theos)*

(8:31)   M   Prophecy of *rejection, passion, resurrection*
(9:30)   M' Prophecy of *betrayal, passion, resurrection*

(9:7)   N   This is my Son, the Beloved, listen to Him.

The central element is usually reinforced by relating it specifically to the flanks of the structure, A and A'. The theophony at the centre of Mark's Gospel, for example, is heralded by angelophanies at the flanks:

(1:2)   A   *An angel witnesses* to his coming
(9:7)   N   *This is my Son, the Beloved, listen to him.*
(16:6) A' *An angel witnesses* to his going.

There is also a 'point of turning' just past the centre of the structure: the phrase '*et statim*', 'and suddenly' (Mk 9:8), in this instance. This point of turning introduces a crucial new element in the lower half of the overall pattern that resolves or completes the first half, thus in Mark:

Et statim // *circumspicientes neminem amplius viderunt nisi Iesum tantum secum* (v 8) And suddenly // *when they looked around, they saw no one with them any more, but only Jesus*

The crucial new element here is the affirmation of the divinity of Jesus, the Son of Man, his prediction of his betrayal, passion and resurrection and his call for generous service, with the motivation emphatically expressed (Mk 9:8-9, 30-37; 10:43-44).

When the inversion principle is used with conscious precision,[14] as in Patrick's writings, most, if not all, of these elements appear and are practical rules of thumb for a proper interpretation of his *Confessio* and *Epistola*. In our analysis of his writings, therefore, the pairs of corresponding antiphons in each concentric passage are placed side by side, with the thematic and verbal linkages italicised to facilitate the reader.

The *Confessio* of Patrick, taken in its totality, may be considered as one grand concentric unit:

Part I	A	Prologue. Author's identification. Trust in God
Part II	B	Testimony of Patrick's sacred calling
Part III	C	Rejection and betrayal
Part IV	B'	Testimony of Patrick's mission
Part V	A'	Epilogue. Author's identification. Trust in God

The elements that make up the *Confessio* and the *Epistola* have, moreover, their own internal concentric structure. Parts I and V of the *Confessio,* for instance, form a concentric pattern, where the inversion principle is again used with precision, and whose central element is the *Apologia*:

(1-2)	A	Prologue. Author's identification
(3)	B	Statement of reasons for writing, echoing Psalm 88(89):6
(4)	C	Creed, quoting Romans 8:16-17
(5)	D	Trust in God, quoting Psalm (50)49:15
(6)	E	Confession of unworthiness
(7-8)	F	On truthfulness
(9-15)	X	Apologia
V.(54)	F'	On truthfulness
(55)	E'	Confession of unworthiness
(55-56)	D'	Trust in God, quoting Psalm 55 (54):23
(57-60)	C'	Doxology, quoting Romans 8:16-17
(61)	B'	Restatement of reasons for writing, quoting Psalm 119(118):111
(62)	A'	Epilogue. Author's identification

The beginning of Part I of the *Confessio* (C 1-8) contains ninety-six lines of text, while Part V (C 54-62), which ends the *Confessio*, also contains ninety-six lines of text. This is one indication of the perfect symmetry of the *Confessio*, and of the tight control Patrick keeps on his composition.[15] The concentric and parallel patterns of Patrick's writings, in sum, fit together like the wheels of a clock.

---

14 Bailey, *PP*, 50.

15 Howlett, *CLTBS*, 17; his plan of the concentric/chiastic structure of the *Confessio* is adapted here.

These literary patterns are common to both classical and biblical literature. I have also discovered many examples of them in early, medieval and modern Gaelic poetry. All the sacred songs composed by the poet, mystic and catechist, Tadhg Gaelach Ó Súilleabháin (1715-95), demonstrate clearly that the concentric pattern was understood and used in Penal Days in Ireland and possibly down to the Great Hunger of the mid-nineteenth century, which culminated in a second cultural disaster for the Gaelic order.[16] However, an initial flexibility coupled with a slight effort is called for, in practice, in order to adapt ourselves to these patterns, because they are different from those to which we are accustomed.

LITERATURE, A REFLEX OF GOD'S CREATIVE ACTION
These chiastic or concentric patterns show balance not only in the statement and restatement of ideas, but in the numbers of words and syllables and letters. These are arranged usually in one of two forms, either perfect symmetry or division by extreme and mean ratio, the golden section.[17]

There are, in Dr Howlett's analysis, twenty-six chapters and 4,570 words in the original Latin version of the *Confessio*. The central sentence of the entire text is *Ecce, dandus es* | ***tu*** | *ad gradum episcopatus, Look, you are to be given over to the order of the episcopate*.[18] From the first word to the pivotal *tu*, inclusive, there are 2,285 words; from the last word to the same pivotal *tu*, inclusive, there are 2,285 words. The seven-worded central element could thus be written on a horizontal line through the point at the centre of the overall structure.

In producing mathematical compositions of literary texts, it is said that writers imitate in their compositions what they believe God to have done in the creation of the world. In Wisdom 11:21, for example, 'Solomon' addressing the Creator says: 'but You have disposed all things by measure and number and weight'. And in the New Testament Jesus states in Matthew 10:30: 'but even the hairs of your head are all numbered'. This belief that literary creation was a reflection of God's creative action was common to both biblical and classical writers. There is explicit discussion in the Talmud of the counting of verses, words and letters of the text of the Hebrew Bible; Plato,

16 For an eighteenth-century Gaelic example of concentric structure cf. de Paor, *TG*, 1995, 55 ff, and the forthcoming *Fílíocht Thaidhg Ghaelaigh*.
17 In the former there are exactly as many words or syllables or letters in one part as in the other. In the latter the number in the minor part (m) relates to the number in the major part (M), as the number in the major part relates to the number in the whole (m+M): m/M = M/(m+M). To calculate the major part one could multiply a number by 0.61803, and to calculate the minor part one could multiply a number by 0.38197 (Howlett, *CLTBS*, 17).
18 Howlett, *BLSPB*, 109.

in a famous dialogue, makes Timaeus discuss in minute particulars the mathematical creation of the world.[19]

The account of the perfection of the Sabbath-rest after the Creation in Genesis 2:1-4 contains forty-six Hebrew words. The numerical value of the Greek letters in the name A△AM is $1+4+1+40=46$. As human work should reflect God's work, it took forty-six years to build the Temple in Jerusalem (Jn 2:20). So in the Greek text of John 1:3, the account of Creation by Christ, there are forty-six letters. There are also forty-six letters in the Latin text of that same passage.[20]

Patrick, in addition, makes skilful use of the less important, biblical, literary technique of significant biblical numbers such as seven, eight, twelve and forty[21] at various points in his *Confessio*, but in particular in Part II, the testimony of his sacred calling (C 16-25).

The *Epistola*, like the *Confessio*, is concentric in structure. It is composed of four concentric paragraphs with a prologue and an epilogue, while it introduces many of the themes to be developed later in the *Confessio*.

Practically every line of text in both compositions exhibits one of the commonly accepted cursus rhythms, and the possibility that excerpts from the *Confessio* could be sung or chanted, as the bardic poetry was sung and chanted in the great houses of the old Irish, Scottish and Welsh nobility, to a contrapuntal accompaniment on the harp, is currently being explored.

PATRICK'S USE OF SACRED SCRIPTURE

In the *Apologia* (C 9-15), which is almost a miniature of the whole *Confessio*, Patrick writes:

> *Sicut facile potest probari ex saliva scripturae meae,*
> *qualiter sum ego in sermonibus instructus atque eruditus,*
> As it can easily be proved from the flavour of my writing
> how 'I have been' taught and 'educated' in styles of speech (C 9:10-11).

David Howlett, in *Ex Saliva Scripturae Meae* (1989), sets out to demonstrate how Patrick draws on Sacred Scripture, not only for copious quotations, but also for 'the structure of his thought, and the manner of implying more than he seems to say'. To show the truth of this claim, Mark 1:1-15 is selected as a model, in preference to many others, for clarity of language and terseness of method and style. Howlett then systematically examines this concentric passage for balance of words and phrases. Of its many striking features, he singles out two as being particularly noteworthy: one is 'the density of allusion' to Old Testament antetypes, for which Mark is here providing the

19 Howlett, *CLTBS*, 6 f; Menken, *NLT, passim.*
20 Howlett, *BLSPB*, 22.
21 Schokel, op. cit., 84-7.

fulfilling types; the other is the extent to which Mark relies for effect not just upon words cited from the Old Testament, but upon their *context,* which he uses almost as a commentary to expand his meaning. At no point does he explicitly tell the reader what he is doing; he merely implies and expects us to infer.

Mark's arrangement of words by symmetry is then highlighted. A case in point is that in the original Greek version of this passage, the word 'Holy', in the sentence 'He will baptize you with the *Holy Spirit*' at the crux of this passage, is the 121st word from the beginning and the 121st word from the end. In addition, three of the main themes – the Way, the Kingdom, Baptism – in this excerpt are repeated in the parallel reading, Mark 10:35-11:11. The arrangement of words by extreme and mean ratio is also repeated so that the number in the short part relates to the number in the longer part as the number in the longer part relates to the number in the whole. Howlett proves this by showing where the Golden Section falls.

As we do not now possess the actual version of the Old Latin Bible which Patrick probably used, the Latin text of Mark 1:1-15, in Jerome's Vulgate, is the next best thing.

With Mark's model in mind, Howlett now proceeds to apply the same principles to Patrick's *Apologia,* and finds that 'Patrick has reproduced every feature exhibited in the original text of Mark!'[22] In *The Book of Letters of St Patrick the Bishop*, Howlett has demonstrated that what is true for the *Apologia* is true for the whole of the *Confessio.*

If we wish to sound the real depths of this great spiritual masterpiece, then, it is not enough to read it; we are advised to come to know, not only the sources, but also the context of its biblical quotations and significant biblical allusions, of which Patrick makes highly effective use in his *Confessio.*

If we accept that Patrick adopted such a biblical method, then he had an obvious precedent among the New Testament literary artists with their 'evident penchant for references to the Old in order to shape essential typological messages'.[23] 'At almost every point the evangelists, often by means of subtle hints and allusions, convey their belief that what God has accomplished in Christ was analogous to his great acts recorded in the Scriptures.'[24]

This close study will be further enriched by focusing also on how Patrick's writings were influenced by the Fathers of the Church, and by the official pronouncements of the Church in contemporary controversies. We are greatly indebted to Daniel Conneelly for his painstaking research over many years in this area, and to his editors, for enabling us to do so in *The Letters of Saint Patrick, A Study of their Theological Dimension* (1993).

22 Howlett, *ESSM,* 86-100.
23 McCone, *PPCP,* 32.
24 Lampe, 1975, 157, ibid., 2.

Finally, if we endorse the view that literature is a half-way house between the reader and the writer, it should be possible to explore in this book, even if in elementary fashion, some of the key instances of Patrick's sensitive artistic use, not only of scriptural quotation but of scriptural allusion, and his manner of implying more than he seems to say, in true biblical tradition. For those who wish to study the artistry of Patrick's writings and their close biblical affinity in great detail, Howlett's masterly exposition in *The Book of Letters of Saint Patrick the Bishop* is essential reading.

CONTEMPORARY LITERARY INFLUENCES

Nora Chadwick is careful to point out that even an elementary, fleeting examination of the literary form of Patrick's writings reveals allusions and conventions of style which were current in the Gaulish compositions of the fifth century. In his use of an open-letter form, both for his *Confessio* and his *Epistola* excommunicating Coroticus, Patrick chose the literary form most favoured by the literati of Gaul in his time. Indeed *The Works of Fastidius* suggest that this literary form may also have been in vogue in Britain in his day.[25] This correspondence was largely written with an eye to publication.

The influence of Augustine's *Confessions* on Patrick's *Confessio* has already been dealt with admirably by Peter Dronke and Thomas Finan.[26]

The tendency to refer to himself as *peccator*, a sinner, is considered by some scholars to be no more than a literary convention of the day – a mark of 'literary good breeding'. Even though the signatures of the letters signed jointly by Paulinus of Nola and his wife Therasia: *Paulinus et Therasia, peccatores,* 'Paulinus and Therasia, sinners', are advanced in support of this theory,[27] it is not entirely convincing. In Patrick's case, his *Confessio* reveals that humility, in the sense of concern for the truth before God, was one of his cardinal virtues. His extraordinary sense of his lowliness, coupled with the depth of his constant prayer, made him profoundly aware of the true relationship between himself and his Creator. When, therefore, he saw himself in the light of the All-Holy One and confessed himself to be a sinner, he meant it; it was for him a reality, not a mere cliché.

The literary clichés found in Patrick's writings, *rusticissimus*, very rustic (C 1:1), and *indoctus*, untaught (C 62:5), must also be evaluated within the literary climate of his era. We meet this literary formula, which professes ignorance and rusticity, from the pen of Gallus, the *scholasticus*, or orator, from St Martin's monastery at Tours. In the *Dialogues* of Sulpicius Severus he professes himself 'blushing' and diffident about speaking in the presence of cultured Aquitanians. Such expressions are, in reality, the mark of polish and literary good taste, an oratorical cliché, as Posthumianus makes a point of

25 Caspari, 1890, Chadwick, *ASCC,* 210f.
26 Dronke, *SPR,* 21-32; Finan, *TLSP,* 141-50.
27 Bieler, *LE,* 11, 86.
28 Chadwick, *ASCC,* 25-6.

noting: 'As you are an orator (*scholasticus*) you carefully, after the fashion of orators, begin by begging us to excuse your unskilfulness because you really excel in eloquence'.[28]

It is, of course, almost universally accepted in classical circles, that modesty and eloquence were the hallmarks of the learned Gaulish Celts. Modesty was, indeed, part of the literary polish of the panegyrists for which Gaul was justly famous.[29] It was, however, no less a convention than the spiritual self-abasement of the medieval religious with which Patrick would have been conversant from their writings as well as from his much-debated sojourn in Gaul.[30]

Given Patrick's manifest gift for oratory, it is likely that the rich and colourful British and Irish idioms found unique expression in his Latin, and that some of his phrases, which defy adequate translation and have baffled scholars from Mohrmann to Bieler and Hanson, may in fact be old Irish or British idioms wearing a Roman toga.[31]

THE AUTHENTICITY OF PATRICK'S WRITINGS

Patrick's *Confessio* and *Epistola* are preserved in eight manuscripts, of which photocopies and other reproductions are to be found in the National Library and the Royal Irish Academy, Dublin. In his *Libri Epistolarum Sancti Patricii Episcopi*, which are readily available, Bieler treats of the history of these texts, as well as problems of textual criticism among other considerations. Neither document is, of course, the original. The extant copies of the *Confessio*, for instance, derive at a number of removes from a putative archetype dated, according to Bieler, to the first third of the seventh century. Though neither the archetype nor even its exemplar was the autograph, the authenticity of these writings has never been doubted by any serious scholar. 'The two compositions, though pitched in different strains, breathe such a transparent truth and simplicity, combine such utter humility with such perfect confidence in the divine guidance, mirror such singlemindedness in the pursuit of their author's life-task, the conversion of the pagan Irish, present such an extraordinary intermixture of firmness and sensitivity, are so utterly free of any effort at hagiography, in fine, speak to us so directly, vividly, unaffectedly and sincerely across the centuries, that apart from other considerations, it is beyond human imagination for them to have emanated from the pen of a medieval forger.'[32]

Readers may find this book demanding and, due to the limits of personal ability, time and space, incomplete. It is therefore recommended to approach it with the text of Patrick's writings in one hand and a copy of the Bible in the

---

29 Chadwick, *SBH*, 190ff.
30 cf. Malaspina, *PAL*, 252ff, and 248, n.133, for another point of view.
31 Bieler, *LE*, 11, 89, 201.
32 Ó Raifeartaigh, *EP*, 6.

other for close reference. 'As the Holy Spirit spoke to Patrick so he speaks to us through and within and around his narrative in harmonies that grow more complex, with resonances that reverberate through meanings that become richer and denser every time we return to his texts.... By listening to him on his own terms we can hear him speak articulately, authoritatively, compellingly, across fifteen centuries, with a power he believed to be not his own but God's.'[33]

Finally, and most importantly, it is advisable to take the *Epistola* and the *Confessio,* in conjunction with the Sacred Scriptures, before the Lord in prayer, there to dwell on them at length, reverently and with great humility, faith and joy of spirit, in imitation of Patrick himself. In that way we too, because of our Baptism into Christ, can appropriate as our patrimony Patrick's own claim that he is 'The letter of Christ for salvation to the ends of the earth' (C 11:37).

The effort required will assuredly pay rich dividends, so let us take courage. Our deepening of this baptismal, Christo-centric, biblical spirituality is, indeed, one of Patrick's own great personal desires for all his children in the faith, for he writes:

> Would that you too would strive for greater things and perform more
>   excellent deeds.
> This will be my glory,
> because 'a wise son
> is the glory of a father' (C 47:150-3).

---

33 Howlett, *BLSPB*, 3.

B
THE HISTORICAL ST PATRICK

While not wishing to get embroiled in the debate about the possible existence of two Patricks, it seems necessary, at the outset, to draw attention to the fact that the entries concerning St Patrick in the so-called fifth-century *Annals*, on which T.F. O Rahilly relied primarily for his argument that there were 'two Patricks',[1] have been shown, some thirty years later, by Alfred P. Smyth, to have no validity.[2] And even if the existence of two or more Patricks could be argued cogently, there is no doubt whatsoever as to the identity and historicity of the Christian missionary to the pagan Irish known as St Patrick and regarded as the national apostle of Ireland.

This Patrick, author of the *Epistola* and the *Confessio*, tells us that his name is Patricius, that his father, Calpornius, the son of Potitus, a presbyter, was a deacon and decurion (C 1:4-5; E 10:86).

At the age of fifteen, he was kidnapped at his father's villa in Britain, and enslaved in Ireland. Here, as a shepherd, this nominal Christian was converted with all his heart to the true God, and prayed incessantly in snow and rain, until six years later he made good his escape.

He recounts how, in the course of that escape, he had some curious adventures but finally reached home safely; he subsequently saw in a dream one Victoricius who handed him a letter headed 'The Voice of the Irish', and at the same time heard those who were 'beside the Wood of Fochoill which is near the Western Sea' entreating him to walk once more among them. After considerable hesitation, he eventually returned to evangelise the pagan Irish.

Following a brief account of his missionary initiatives and their success, he indicates how, in the course of his 'laborious episcopate', he was slandered and betrayed by his enemies with the connivance of his 'dearest friend', and consequently censured by his ecclesiastical superiors; having been on the brink of despair thereby, he was sustained by a mystical experience and by the conviction that the outstanding success of his mission was proof that it was the work of the Holy Spirit.

---

1 O Rahilly, *TP.*
2 Smyth, *EIA,* 1972.

His *Epistola,* which was written some time prior to the *Confessio,* is, as Fr John Ryan so well describes it, 'a sharp cry of anguish and indignation which had been wrung from the saint's heart by a savage outrage'.[3] It denounces Coroticus, a nominally Christian, British chieftain whose soldiers had raided Patrick's mission-territory, slain a number of his newly-baptized Christian converts, and sold others into slavery.

THE ROMANO-BRITISH CITIZEN

Since Patrick was a Roman citizen, an awareness of the political framework of the late Roman Empire helps us to understand him.[4] This great empire comprised all the countries bordering on the Mediterranean and most of Western Europe. Its boundaries were fixed roughly by the Rhine, the Danube, the Euphrates, the Atlas Mountains and the Atlantic Ocean. Inside those boundaries the Roman citizens lived in walled towns which were joined to each other by a network of Roman roads. All who lived outside those boundaries, no matter how civilised, were described as 'barbarians', and that included the pre-Christian Irish nation. A 'barbarian' was to the average Roman what an 'unclean' and despised gentile was to the average Jew: someone to be avoided. The barbarian was, simply, 'without the walls'. In AD 406 Britain was still inside the Roman Empire, nominally, at least, in spite of an earlier revolt there against the Roman occupation.[5]

EVANGELISATION IN THE ROMAN EMPIRE

It would seem that people in the Roman towns and cities had been largely converted to Christianity through contact with other Christians and the ministry of the clergy. With the exception of the wealthy landowners and their milieu, however, the country people who were more or less cut off from city influence were still pagan.[6] Individual bishops of the calibre of Irenaeus of Lyons in the second century,[7] and Martin of Tours and Victricius, Archbishop of Rouen, in the fourth, made all-out, individual efforts to rectify this situation.[8] But, with one exception, there was seemingly no organised, concerted effort made to go out and convert pagans, beyond the confines of the Western Roman Empire, until the Benedictine Pope, Gregory the Great, initiated it, in the person of Augustine of Canterbury, in the dying years of the sixth century.

Patrick's mission to the Irish pagans was that exception.[9] This fact alone

---

3 Ryan, *SP,* 114.
4 For a full treatment cf. Hanson, *OC,* 1968.
5 Hanson, *OC,* 1968, 10ff.
6 Chadwick, *ASCC,* 9; Morris, *CS,* 351-352.
7 Hamman, *LVS.*
8 Migne, *P.G.*, V11, 444, 855-856; Chadwick, *PLG,* 112.
9 Bury, in Bieler, *LL,* 19.

gives him a unique place in the history of the Church. But this singular contribution of Patrick's has never been sufficiently emphasised, a point to which I shall return later.

THE FALL OF ROME, AD 410
In the year 410 the unspeakable happened: barbarian spears were flourished in the streets of Rome; the holy, eternal city, fell to barbarian hordes. This, for Roman citizens, was almost as catastrophic as an atomic disaster would be in our day. They were totally unprepared for it – it could never happen! But it did happen, and it was final. Consequently, the remainder of the Roman legions were recalled to the Continent and Britain was left to her own devices.

By the year 420 Britain was outside the Empire, easy prey to barbarian invasions and raids. There was virtually no defence system and a very poor administrative system. This resulted in civil war. Chaotic conditions ensued under local usurpers of power, called *tyranni* in Britain,[10] though enclaves of Roman civilisation survived the disaster. By the last quarter of the century the western part of the great Roman Empire had completely disappeared.

This was the bewildered, tottering world into which Patrick was born. Here, except for the six years of his captivity, he spent his most impressionable years, until he was called to leave it forever to become a pilgrim apostle for Christ (E 17:172; C 26:5-6).

THE CHRISTIAN RESPONSE
This was the era of the great, saintly bishops, men of the calibre of Ambrose of Milan, Paulinus of Nola, Augustine of Hippo, Germanus of Auxerre, Faustus of Riez, Sidonius Apollinaris of Auvergne and, of course, Pope Leo the Great, who stepped into the breach.[11] These men not only catered for the spiritual needs of their flocks, in times of persecution they had to care for their material needs as well. We thus have the example of Paulinus of Nola selling up his vast estates to come to the aid of the sick, the dying and the starving poor. In addition, he enthusiastically initiated a simple form of monasticism in his sphere of influence. He also devoted his phenomenal administrative skills to the organisation of the Church in Campania.[12]

It is in this category that we should see Patrick.

WHEN DID PATRICK'S PILGRIMAGE BEGIN?
There are two sets of dates given by scholars for Patrick's mission: 432-c.461 and c.457-c.492/3 At the present time it seems, according to David Dumville's book, *Saint Patrick, AD 493-1993*, that the scales are tipped in

10 Hanson, *OC,* 25.
11 Chadwick, *PLG,* 112-13.
12 Chadwick, ibid., 63-88.

favour of the second half of the fifth century as the period of his Irish mission, but the question is still open.[13]

WHERE WERE THE SIX YEARS OF PATRICK'S CAPTIVITY SPENT?

In Antrim? or Mayo? While we are not absolutely certain, the evidence in the *Confessio* favours Silva Focluti, the Wood of Fochoill, on the western shore of Killala Bay in the barony of Tirawley, Co. Mayo. Victoricius, with his innumerable letters, and *Glór na nGael,* the Voice of the Irish, calling him back to walk once more among them, are all associated in Patrick's dream with Fochoill.

This in no way precludes the possibility that he graced the Sliabh Mis area in Co. Antrim with his presence as a missionary, even for a prolonged period, towards the end of his life. Surely this is something more worthy of celebration than his enforced slavery as a youth!

WHERE WAS PATRICK TAKEN CAPTIVE?

Patrick tells us that his father, the deacon Calpornius, was also a decurion in the *vicus* or town Bannaventa Berniae; he had a country seat nearby where Patrick was taken captive (C 1; E 10).

As to the precise location of Bannaventa Berniae, there are probably as many hypotheses as there are scholars who have addressed themselves to this problem. In all this debate, however, we are only sure of one thing, that is, that Patrick was a native of Britain (C 17, 23). The Romans, who conquered that country in the first century AD, called its inhabitants Britanni.

The area that was raided by the Irish was probably close to the sea and situated somewhere on the west or south-west coast. Claims are made for Ail-Cluaide, the Rock of Clyde, or modern Dumbarton, Birdoswald on Hadrian's Wall, and the estuary of the Severn, to name but a few.[14] But the indication of the precise location was not, after all, essential to Patrick's literary purpose, which was solely to reveal the Providence of God directing all his ways towards the fulfilment of his predestined plan for Patrick's sanctification, and the conversion of Ireland.[15]

Muirchú, Patrick's seventh-century biographer, says in his introduction, with refreshing honesty, that there are many conflicting opinions in regard to Patrick's life. Nevertheless, he declares that Bannaventa Berniae is 'a place not far from the sea'. 'This place, I am informed beyond hesitation or doubt', he continues, 'is [now] Ventre'.[16] Since early hagiography is modelled on the Bible and is not, therefore, constrained by the requirements of a modern historical document, Muirchú does not feel obliged to cite his source!

---

13 Hanson, *LW,* 20-25; Howlett, *BLSPB,* 119.
14 Malaspina, *PAL,* 73-8; De Breffny, *ISP,* 13-16.
15 Nerney, *SPS,* 506; Hanson, *OC,* 121.
16 *PTBA,* 67.

The place known in the seventh century as Ventre is, possibly, the Romano-British Venta Silurum, the market town of the Silures, which in turn is identified by Welsh scholars as modern Caerwent, Gwent, Wales. Though it was not a big town it had been the tribal capital of the Silures since their hill-fort capital at Llanmelin was uprooted by the Romans c. AD 75 and its inhabitants transferred to the plain below.[17] Indeed, its situation by the Bristol Channel at the estuary of the Severn makes Caerwent a plausible suggestion for Patrick's home, since it was in a region which was exposed to raids from Ireland. This view is further reinforced by archaeological excavations which have established the remains of an impressive number of villas in the rich Severn basin, whereas the numbers found in the northern part of the country so far are relatively few.

Moreover, Patrick's father, in his capacity as a Roman official, may well have seen service – and therefore may have lived for some time with his family – in various parts of the Empire, from Dumbarton in Scotland to Bononia, now Boulogne-sur-mer, France, before coming to a more settled way of life as a deacon and the owner of an estate. Writing in 1879, Cardinal Moran, for instance, asserts that for more than a thousand years it was the uninterrupted tradition of Ireland and of Scotland that St Patrick was born – not captured, mark you – in the valley of the Clyde, where his father was a decurion.[18] Such dearly-held local traditions may not be indiscriminately discarded until scholars unearth some new seams of more precise information in this whole field of study.

PATRICK'S FAMILY

Patrick identifies himself as the son of Calpornius, a deacon, who was in turn the son of Potitus, a presbyter, as already indicated above. That both his father and grandfather were clerics should not surprise us. Clerical marriage was accepted by the Church well into the Middle Ages. Some great fifth-century bishops such as Paulinus of Nola, Germanus of Auxerre and Sidonius Apollinaris of Auvergne were already married before their ordination. On the other hand, many of them, such as Faustus of Riez, Honoratus and Hilary of Arles, and Eucherius of Lyons, were monastic celibates.[19]

Neither should it come as a surprise that Patrick's father, an official of the Church, was the owner of an estate; churchmen, especially bishops, tended to be drawn from the great territorial magnates who represented the old Roman administrative system in Gaul, and possibly in Britain as well.[20] Patrick's background was not, therefore, essentially different from that of the Gaulish

---

17 Craster, 1951, 3ff.
18 De Breffny, op. cit., 14. Moran, *ISGB*, 131-33.
19 Chadwick, *PLG, passim;* ASCC, 21.
20 Beck, 1950, 6ff.

bishops of the period who used their wealth in the service of the Church and the poor.[21]

The fact that Calpornius was a decurion (E 10) or alderman meant that he enjoyed noble status. But it entailed being saddled with the prestigious if unenviable task of raising the taxes for the imperial government in the area covered by his council. Should he have failed to procure the required amount from the citizens, he was obliged to make good the deficit out of his own pocket. One way of evading this intolerable burden was to escape into the imperial service or became a senator, both options which released them from their fiscal responsibilities; others evaded the law by moving to villas in the contryside. Yet others became ordained clergy in the Christian Church, a process which the emperors had tried to stop.

By the last quarter of the fourth century, however, it was deemed prudent to establish that if a council official wanted to be ordained he would be obliged to surrender two-thirds of his property to a relative. The latter would then automatically be obliged to take on the burden of tax collector, abandoned by the cleric. This ruling undoubtedly had the desired effect of stemming a possible unseemly rush of tax-evaders for Holy Orders.[22]

All deacons, however, were not necessarily mere tax-evaders and we do not conclude that Calpornius was one such. He may, notwithstanding, have ceased to exercise his function as a decurion and have retired to work his estate, like so many contemporary Gaulish nobility,[23] before his son was captured. Some scholars infer from Patrick's avowal of the weakness of his faith at the time of his captivity (C 1:13-16) that Calpornius and his household were not distinguished for Christian fervour!

We are indebted to the formidable achievements of archaeologists, among others, for an impressive picture of Romano-British, fourth-century villas like Chedworth in Gloucestershire. Their standards of comfort, we are assured, were not to be repeated until the nineteenth century.[24] A villa or estate like Chedworth 'was run by a whole *familia* of male and female servants'.[25] Patrick was violently captured, at his father's villa, with *tot milia*, 'so many thousands of people' (C 1), while both male and female household servants were ravaged in the fray (E 10:84; C 1:11-12). It is possible that the raiders swooped down simultaneously on both sides of the Bristol Channel for their captives. Its broad sweep and a knowledge of the tides in that area would accommodate such an attack, and this might account for so great a number taken in one raid, or, perhaps, a number of raids executed in close succession.

---

21 Chadwick, *PLG*, 113.
22 Hanson, *LW*, 22.
23 Chadwick, *PLG*, 23.
24 Goodburn, *RVC, passim;* De Breffny, op.cit., 11-12.
25 Bieler, *LE*, 11, 88.

Since his father was a decurion, a deacon, and the owner of an estate we conclude that Patrick belonged to the Romanised British nobility who had been Christians for at least three generations. He always remained proud of his Roman citizenship, which was, for him, synonymous with being a Christian. There is no indication in his writings that he ever regretted the conquest of Britain by the Roman legions or that he resented his country being reduced to a Province or being considered by the Romans as a mere backwater of the Empire.[26]

PATRICK'S EDUCATION
The P-Celtic language, which evolved into modern Welsh, was, most probably, Patrick's first language; fifth-century, spoken Latin was his second. Though the services of a private tutor, in the person of a member of the native British learned classes, cannot be ruled out, it seems reasonable to suppose that he learned his Latin at school under the Roman system of education. He had, therefore, passed through the *ludus*, or first level, and was at the second or *grammaticus* stage when his formal education was rudely interrupted by the sudden and violent swoop of his Irish captors. He may have never reached the *rhetor* or third-level stage where diligent and able students learned the arts of graceful writing, oratory and law. His high-flown style of writing, however, suggests that he developed those skills at a later date, possibly during the period of his preparation for the priesthood:

> As it can easily be proved from the flavour of my writing
> how 'I have been' taught and 'educated' in styles of speech (C 9:10-11).

PATRICK'S KNOWLEDGE OF SACRED SCRIPTURE
Apart altogether from his family links with the institutional Church, being a fifth-century catechumen or Christian brought Patrick into intimate contact with Sacred Scripture. Scholars assure us that the study of the Bible in the early Church, and up into the late Middle Ages, represented the highest branch of learning. Nor was it confined to specialists. Both the language and the content of Sacred Scripture permeated medieval thought.[27] Since a course in systematic theology did not take shape for centuries to come in the Church, Patrick's training for the priesthood expanded his initial exposure to Sacred Scripture immeasurably. But, since it would take another Patrick to appreciate his synthesis, and what seems an infused understanding of Sacred Scripture by the time he came to write his *Confessio* and *Epistola*, these documents should be approached with humble faith and reverence.

That he had, however, attained competence in both classical and biblical literary skills, need not surprise us. After all, his classical education was not

---

26 Hanson, *LW*, 5.
27 McCone, *PPCP*, 2.

interrupted until he was nearly sixteen years of age, by which time even an average student would be expected to have at least an elementary grasp of classical composition and techniques of expression. Does he, then, repudiate classical learning and style in the service of the Word, in the tradition of so many great churchmen, especially monastic churchmen, before and after his era? Since it is both possible and probable, we shall come back to this point when we come to examine his marked biblical style in some detail later.

Moreover, Patrick possibly had access to the Roman theatre which, in his day, was no mean consideration. One of its more obvious advantages, apart from its ability to provide a catharsis of his youthful emotions, was that he was not obliged to allow his studies to interfere completely with his education! Dramatic skills would prove to be of considerable assistance later, in his preaching of the Word of God and in the writing of his *Epistola* and *Confessio*.

C
IN THE LAND OF PATRICK'S
CAPTIVITY

Ireland, the land of Patrick's captivity, was outside the confines of the Roman Empire. Her sister-countries, Celtic Gaul and Britain, on the other hand, had already known Roman supremacy for centuries. In the meantime, the Irish Celts had assimilated elements of traditions that were already old when Brú na Bóinne (Newgrange) was built by their predecessors on the bend of the Boyne, about four and a half thousand years ago. These ancient traditions had become part of their great mythological sagas and rituals.

THE IRISH POLITICAL SYSTEM IN PATRICK'S TIME
Patrick must have been greatly amazed and dismayed, on setting foot on Irish soil, to find that there were no towns. He suddenly found himself in a rural setting where political and social centres were hill-forts and other such places of natural strength which could be fortified in times of danger from hostile raiders. The country had no central government but was divided into a number of *tuatha* or petty kingdoms, each of which was ruled by a *rí tuatha* or kinglet.

Some historians have estimated that there were about eighty tuatha in Ireland in Patrick's time, while others put the number at a hundred and fifty. Many of these petty kings were, whether by force or choice or ancestral custom, banded together to form a larger group under a regional or provincial king; Patrick mentions both kings and sub-kings in his writings (C 52).

Each kingdom was a self-contained unit of society which held its *filí,* or poets, and *breithiúna,* or judges, in high esteem. An earnest of the prestige which learning enjoyed in Ireland was the fact that these learned classes were the only people who might move from kingdom to kingdom with impunity. It was evident, therefore, that the great bond of unity within Ireland was its common Gaelic language, culture, beliefs, laws and educational institutions, not its politico-economic system.

The king and his people claimed descent from a common ancestor. This conviction was copper-fastened by the learned classes in the interests of group cohesion and was undergirded by the belief that fruitfulness in all its forms depended on the personal, physical and moral integrity of their sacral king. Indeed, one of the duties of the learned classes was to keep the king constantly reminded of the obligations of his office.

IRISH LANGUAGE, CULTURE AND BELIEFS

We assume that Patrick became acquainted with fellow shepherds who were Irish-born, as well as with other local people, and gradually learned to communicate with them in their Irish language (C 9:9) during his enforced captivity in the Fochoill area. Indeed, his knowledge of the Irish language and institutions was possibly a deciding factor in allowing him to undertake his mission to the pagan Irish at a much later date. The difference between his native British and its sister language, fifth-century Irish, was probably not as great as that between its modern counterparts, yet it must have seemed very strange at first.

Here at Fochoill, though he was not aware of it at the time, the hand of God was at work preparing one who had possibly grown up in or near a town, for a divine mission among a rural-based, pagan people. Here, in the heart of the country, Patrick communed with nature in all her changing moods; here he learned the loving, patient, sensitive and multi-faceted skills of a good shepherd which were required of him in every season of the year.

He might, on occasion, have heard his companions mention Cruachain Aí, the seat of Connacht kings in present-day Co. Roscommon, and faraway Teamhair na Rí (Tara), in royal Meath. Snatches of great songs and sagas associated with these places and their heroes and gods would have delighted his ear and found an echo in his Celtic heart.

The high quality of Irish artefacts in gold, silver or bronze; the Irish flair for colour and the graceful curves which found elegant expression in patterns on clothes, in decorations on weapons, jewellery and domestic utensils, and in carvings on stones, must have delighted Patrick's sensitive and artistic soul over and over again, when he later returned as a missionary. The mature Patrick was then in a better position to evaluate them.

Meantime, his pagan companions would have made him aware of pagan worship, of euhemerised gods and goddesses like Lug, Aongus Óg of Brú na Bóinne, Crom na Cruaiche, Dana, Macha, Tailte and others; of the special symbolic status given to the white horse, the boar and the stag from the animal world, as well as the sacredness of the rowan and oak trees in pre-Christian rituals; of the special place which wells and springs held in the heart and imagination of the people; how places of pre-Christian worship like Brú na Bóinne were all built over springs, with their entrances facing due east towards the rising sun; how real the world of magic was; and how the spirit-world was believed to impinge on the daily affairs of the people.

Yet he could only remain an onlooker when the people of the local *tuath* trooped off over hill and dale to the *aonach* or central gathering of the people under their king. There they celebrated the great pagan seasonal festivals: *Imbolc* (1 February), to mark the beginning of spring; *Bealtaine* (1 May), which ushered in the summer with gigantic bonfires; *Lúnasa* (1 August), associated with fields ready for harvesting, and yearly rituals atop Cruachain Aighle, to be known in centuries yet to be as Cruach Pádraig; and *Samhain* (1 November), which ushered in the New Celtic Year, when the bleak sun was low in the heavens and all the landscape was ghost-like and gaunt.

The sense of belonging and of purpose engendered in the people by those rural gatherings on hills or around springs or in sacred groves, only served, however, to heighten his consciousness of his own isolation. Nevertheless, he must have been horrified at the fear of pagan gods, ghosts and fairies in the hearts of his fellow workers, particularly at *Samhain*, when the dead, allegedly, walked abroad.

All this cultural shock, apart from his personal sense of isolation, helped to awaken Patrick to the peace and beauty of his own Christian beliefs and practices to which, up to then, he had paid only nominal attention (C 1).

On the other hand, it must have been an impressive experience for the adolescent Patrick to find that, in Ireland, a man could gain the status of a *flaith* or prince through the exercise of universal hospitality. The tradition is still enshrined in the Irish word *flaithiúlacht,* which has no counterpart in the English language. It designates lavish and princely generosity worthy of a *flaith* and finds expression in the warm Irish hospitality for which Ireland of the Welcomes is justly famous down to our own day. There is a warm glow about it, like Christ's *flaithiúlacht* at the wedding feast of Cana; or his multiplication of the loaves and fishes for a starving throng; or his compassionate intervention in the miraculous catch of fish, as he stood on the shore of the lake on that memorable Resurrection morning (Jn 2:1-11; 6:1-14; 21:1-8).

Truth, strength, integrity and fair play, known as *cothrom na Féinne,* the equity of the Fianna, Patrick was to discover, were values greatly prized even by our pre-Christian ancestors, before finding expression in an old Irish poem whose modern rendering is:

> *Glaine in ár gcroí,*   Purity in our hearts,
> *neart in ár ngéag,*   strength in our arms,
> *agus beart de réir ár mbriathar.*   and action in keeping with our word.

Yet, in spite of alliances forged through the bonds of fosterage, where the sons of kings and lesser nobility were fostered by their peers in other tribes, Patrick may have been witness to the sporadic hostilities which were endemic in Irish society as elsewhere. Many of them were cattle raids, since this pastoral and rural-based people subsisted on cattle and some crops.

The bold native daring or *laochas* in the more spectacular of these forays was enshrined in song and saga, such as the *Táin,* or cattle-raid, of Cooley. Community entertainment, a sense of belonging, as well as inspiration for further 'heroic' exploits which were not always confined to their island home, as Patrick knew to his cost, were provided in this way.

DANGEROUS ENEMIES OF THE EMPIRE

References in our indigenous literature to the exploits of the Irish on the Continent in pre-Patrician times are numerous. Roman writers of the fourth and fifth centuries are no less unanimous in their claim that the Irish formed an alliance with the Picts and Britons. They raided the rich lands of the Roman Empire and pursued the imperial legions. Ammianus Marcellinus makes mention of the Irish for the first time in the year AD 360. He clearly indicates that they were, even then, old offenders. He claims that, in conjunction with the Picts, they made repeated inroads on the territory south of the Clyde, the Roman legions being quite wearied in their pursuit: '*praeteritarum cladium congerie fessas*'. He also tells us that they attacked again in 364, and that they renewed their onslaught in the year 368. After many victories they advanced into the very heart of Britain, leaving the Roman general and the count of the maritime coast among the slain in one of the battles. He consequently does not hesitate to style the Irish 'dangerous enemies of the Empire'.

The poet Claudian also mentions the Irish among the barbarian confederates who assailed the Empire in Britain towards the close of the fourth century. 'All Ireland was astir', he writes, 'and the sea was covered with her hostile oars', '... *totam cum Scotus Iernen/Movit, et infesto spumavit remige Tethys*'. And when he subsequently commemorates the triumph of the Emperor Theodosius over the barbarians, he tells us that the distant Thule was soaked with Pictish blood, whilst 'wintry Ireland wept over her Scottish (i. Irish) slain': '*Scotorum tumulos flevit glacialis Ierne'*.

It was not until the last year of the fourth century that the brave Stilicho vanquished the Picts and Irish for the last time. Peace, however, was short-lived for, four years later, the incursions were renewed. By then the Roman legions had been recalled from the northern province, and the whole of Clydesdale became a scene of ruin and desolation. By the late fifth century the Irish were already settling in great numbers in the territory north of the Solway Firth.[1]

THE IRISH BELIEVING IN CHRIST

It took at least another century before the monks and anchorites ushered in an era of intellectual attainment, or 'the Age of Enlightenment', as Norah Chadwick puts it, which proved that the pen is mightier than the sword.[2] This age was, perhaps, already at its embryonic stage in Ireland, at least, in parts of the south and east, as well as in the Meath/North-Leinster area, where scattered Christian communities had been initiated, in part, by the Roman

---

1 Moran, *ISGB*, 129-31, note 1: Ammianus, lib. xx, 1; Chadwick, *ASCC*, 4-5; Turnoch, *TMSRL*, 107.
2 Chadwick, *SBH*, 237ff.

persecutions of Christians on mainland Europe, by the later barbarian invasions,[3] and possibly by a number of traders and slaves from Britain.

The first series of Latin loanwords which had been borrowed before the mission of Palladius in AD 431 helps to prove this theory. The religious vocabulary of this series, with the help of old indigenous words, was pressed into the service of the new Creed. Thus, *Dia*: God, *cretem*: belief, *ires*: faith, *crábud*: piety, *érlam*: patron-saint or founder, provide a skeleton-service of Christian terminology. It contains all the necessary words for an emerging community with a very simple organisation, thus, priest/deacon: *cruimther*, monk: *manach*, nun: *cailleach*, Christian: *cresen*, church: *domhnach* < *dominicum*.

But the fact that there is no trace of a word for a bishop, suggests to Binchy that the first stratum of Christian loanwords was already established in the Irish language before Palladius, the first bishop, *episcop*, was sent by Pope Celestine to 'the Irish believing in Christ' in 431.[4] *Patricius*, Patrick, was transmuted to the Q-Celtic or Irish form, *Cothriche*, in this first fifth-century phase. *Patricius* did not become *Pádraig* until there was direct communication between the Irish monasteries and those of Britain in the sixth century.[5]

Despite local traditions of pre-Patrician saints such as Ibar, Ailbe, Declan and Ciaran of Saighir in the south, as well as Secundinus, Iserninus, Auxilius in the Meath/North-Leinster area, the historical fact remains that Palladius was sent as *first* bishop in 431. Had the Irish Christian communities in those areas been developed and large enough to warrant the ministry of a resident bishop prior to that date, he undoubtedly would have been requested by those communities and 'sent', as in the case of Ulfilas[6] and others in similar circumstances.

That those saints travelled to either Britain or the Continent or, indeed, to both places, for the completion of their ecclesiastical education and ordination to the priesthood, and that, on their return, they were responsible to some non-resident bishop, either on the Continent or in Britain,[7] seems, in the ecclesiastical context of the times, a plausible tradition.

Those of them who were Irish, unlike Patrick, had the rights of citizens and the status of the membership of their *tuath* under the Brehon Laws; but, on the other hand, their mission was, unlike Patrick's, traditionally limited to their own *tuath*.

Irish society was highly stratified into royalty, nobility, brehons and craftsmen, freemen and slaves. Since many years passed before the brehons made provision in their unwritten law system for Christians in this society, Patrick found himself an outcast with no protection under these laws, either

3   Malaspina, *PAL*, 30, 48; Thomas, 'Britain, Ireland and Pre-Patrician Christianity', *CRB*, 295-305.
4   Binchy, *PB*, 165-73; Hanson, *OC*, 55-6, 153 & n.3; Malaspina, *PAL*, 48-62.
5   Chadwick, *ASCC*, 11-12; Malaspina, *PAL*, 59.
6   See, Part III, ch. 4, 141, *infra*.
7   Power, *LDM*, 25.

as a slave or as a missionary. Contending with this challenge was to call forth all Patrick's faith, courage and ingeniousness as a missionary in pagan Ireland (C 35-53).

Since, in every age, God is gently drawing all his children to himself, it seems safe to suggest that many of these pre-Christian people, like their biblical counterparts, had come very close to God. Biblical characters who did not belong to the Chosen People, like Melchizedek, the Wise Men, the Roman centurion, the woman in the region of Tyre and Sidon of whom Christ declared that he had not encountered such faith in Israel, immediately spring to mind.

Irish is an Indo-European language and Calvert Watkins established in the early 1960s that Irish syllabic verse has preserved the metrical form of Indo-European poetry,[8] while Dumézil has drawn parallels between Indian and ancient Roman and Celtic spiritualities.[9] The latter has focused, however, on the external, ritualistic aspects of those spiritualities.[10] The Indian Upanishads, written, it is estimated, between four and five thousand years ago, and the *Bhagavadgita*, written some five hundred years before the Christian era, look inward towards a supreme Godhead dwelling within. In many instances, they bear a remarkable resemblance to Sacred Scripture, Patrick's *Confessio*, some early Irish lyrics, and the writings of the great Western Christian mystics. An excerpt from the *Chandogya Upanishad*, 8.1, may help to illustrate this point:

> In the centre of the castle of Brahman, our own body,
> there is a small shrine in the form of a lotus flower,
> and within can be found a small space.
> We should find Who dwells there
> and we should want to know Him.
> 'And if anyone asks,
> "Who is He who dwells in a small shrine
> in the form of a lotus flower
> in the centre of the castle of Brahman?" ' – we can answer:
> 'The little space within the heart
> is as great as the universe. The heavens and the earth are there,
> the sun, the moon, the stars;
> fire and lightning and winds;....
> for the whole universe is in Him,
> and He dwells within our heart'[11]

---

8 *Celtica* VI, 249.

9 Dumézil, *RRA* (1966); *DW* (1970); *DK* (1973); Dillon, *CH* (1973).

10 Eastwaran, *TU*, 8-12; for a brief account of an Indian *ashram* or 'forest academy', and compare it with the account of an Irish bardic school in Bergin, *IBP*, 5ff.

11 *PC*, 120; Ó Conghaile-Ó Ríordáin, *RNU*, 14, 24, 28, 42; Maloney, *TBM*, 7

Another extract from the *Bhagavad-gita*, 6:18, reinforces it:

> When the mind of the 'Yogi' [i. one who aspires to union with God]
>   is in harmony,
> and finds rest in the Spirit within,
> all restless desires gone,
> then he is in 'Yukta',
> one in God.

It seems evident, even in the earliest Vedic hymns, that one Supreme Being is being worshipped under different aspects. 'Truth is one', one hymn proclaims, 'though the wise call it by many names'.

And, though Patrick's testimony is that the pagan Irish before their conversion 'always worshipped nothing except idols and unclean things' (cf. C 41, 59), there must have been many with heartfelt religious convictions, like God's children in India, among our pre-Christian ancestors.

It is apparent from his *Confessio*, however, that Patrick was aware of some vague form of sun-worship, though he may have in mind the then contemporary revival of sun-worship in Rome and Pope Leo the Great's sermon[12] which condemned this practice (C 60:34-37).

Such was the land to which the humble pilgrim, Patrick, came, first as a slave, and much later as a slave of Christ, in answer to a divine call to inaugurate a mission that not only changed the course of Irish history but made Ireland the burning and shining light of barbarian Europe for the best part of the next thousand years.

---

12 Cf. p. 52 *infra*.

CHAPTER ONE

TO KNOW YOU, THE ONLY TRUE GOD

And 'he poured out on us abundantly the Holy Spirit,
as the gift' and 'pledge' of immortality,
who makes believers and listeners
so that they may be 'children of God' and 'joint heirs with Christ',
whom we confess and adore,
one God in the Trinity of the Sacred Name (C 4:28-33).

PATRICK, THE NOBLEMAN'S SON AND HEIR

In the opening lines of Part I of his *Confessio* Patrick is in what would seem to be a relatively peaceful and stable enclave of Roman Britain, a free man, living in a Roman city, receiving a Roman education, spending his holidays at his father's estate in the country, with servants at his beck and call, complete with all the luxuries of a Roman villa; he is secure in his father's love, enjoys noble status, with many friends in an area where there is a large concentration of Christians; this energetic, carefree, thoughtless youth is protected by both Roman and British law and can express himself in two languages. His worldly future seems secured....

Then, suddenly, disaster strikes!

PATRICK, THE ILLEGAL ALIEN SLAVE

Patrick is now violently forced to exchange his Romano-British citizenship for captivity among an alien pagan people. He finds himself 'truly humiliated by hunger and nakedness, and that daily' (C 27:22-23), 'in forests and on the mountain' (C 16:8), deprived of his father's unconditional love and supportive presence, far from the city and his parental estate. The would-be rhetor is now a shepherd; the nobleman's son and heir, a slave; the villa is exchanged for a hut; his human rights before the law for the status of an illegal alien; and to compound matters further, bilingual though he be, he finds himself tongue-tied in the face of this strange, new, 'barbarian' language. To all intents and purposes, he is parted forever from kith and kin, for, though the Christians in fifth-century Gaul had a plan for rescuing Christian slaves from the 'barbarian Franks' (E 14:129-131), there is no evidence in Patrick's writings that any such custom obtained in regard to Christians enslaved by the Irish.

His initial anguish, resentment and loneliness must have been intolerable in the extreme. But looking back at this episode, as he writes his *Confessio* in his old age, his faith sees in it the loving hand of God at work, taking the divine initiative in his ultimate conversion and the steps that led him gradually to his knowledge of and union with the Blessed Trinity (C 36:1-7).

A PROLOGUE

In order to convey the experience of his ongoing conversion process adequately, he places the story of Patrick, the nobleman's heir from Bannaventa Berniae, and the story of Patrick, the exiled slave at the Wood of Fochoill side by side, and tells them alternately in antiphonal form. The twenty-eight-line prologue (C 1-2) which enshrines these two contrasting stories is itself concentric in pattern. There is a striking resemblance between Patrick's story and that of the return of the Prodigal Son to the infinitely compassionate Father's house (Lk 15:11-32).

In the first pair of antiphons Patrick, the sinner and son of Calpornius, whom, in his now hopeless situation, he believes he will never see again, is comforted by his heavenly Father 'as a father comforts a son':

> *I,* PATRICK, A SINNER, very rustic,
> and the least of all the faithful,
> and very contemptible in the estimation of most people,
> had as *father* a deacon named Calpornius,
> *the son* of Potitus, a priest
> who was in the town Bannaventa Berniae;
> he had an estate nearby
> where I WAS CAPTURED (C 1:1-8)
> — and [the Lord] comforted *me* as *a father* [comforts] a son (C 2:28).

The infinite loving-kindness of the all-knowing God, who takes his youth and his ignorance of the true God into consideration, is now highlighted:

> *I was then almost sixteen years of age (C 1:9),*
> *— (and he) had mercy on my youth and* IGNORANCE *(C 2:24),*
> *I* WAS *indeed ignorant* OF *the true God (C 1:10),*
> *[(and he) had mercy on my youth and* IGNORANCE*] (C 2:24),*
> — that 'I might turn with all my heart to the Lord my God' (C 2:22)

In the central part of his *Confessio,* where he tells us about his ecclesiastical trial by his elders, he reinforces this statement when he adds:

> 'I do not know, God knows'
> *if I was then fifteen years old;*
> and I did not believe in the living *God,*
> nor [had I believed in him] from my infancy,
> but remained in death and in unbelief
> until the time *I was* indeed *castigated,*
> 'and truly HUMILIATED
> by hunger and nakedness', and that daily (C 27:16-23).

There is a possibility that Patrick, like Augustine, was only a catechumen at the time of his first captivity. There is a further faint chance that there may have been a small Christian community in the Wood of Fochoill area during Patrick's term of slavery there, made up, in part, of Christian slaves from Britain, perhaps some of the thousands captured with him, as well as by local people converted by them.[1] Perhaps these were the very people whose voices he later heard calling him back to his mission among the Irish people (C 23:120-127).

HUMILITAS MEA, MY LOWLINESS

> and *I WAS TAKEN IN CAPTIVITY* to IRELAND
> with so many thousands of people, and deservedly so,
> because 'we turned away from God' (C 1:11-13),
> – who *'turned his gaze round on MY LOWLINESS'* (C 2:23).

The biblical context of Patrick's 'lowliness' is the *Magnificat,* which is quoted in full because it expresses so well the essence of the *Confessio*:

> My soul magnifies the Lord,
> and my spirit rejoices in God my Saviour,
> for he has looked with favour on the *lowliness* of his servant.
> Surely, from now on all generations will call me blessed;
> for the Mighty One has done great things for me, and holy is his name.
> His mercy is for those who fear Him from generation to generation.
> He has shown strength with his arm; he has scattered the proud in the
>   thoughts of their hearts.
> He has brought down the powerful from their thrones, *and lifted up the
>   lowly [humiles]*;
> He has filled the hungry with good things, and sent the rich away
>   empty.
> He has helped his servant Israel, in remembrance of his mercy,
> according to the promise he made to our ancestors, to Abraham and
>   his descendants forever (Lk 1:46-55).

Like Mary, Patrick rejoices in God's incessant saving power in his regard, that the Lord has turned round and gazed with favour on his 'lowliness' and emptiness. Under that compassionate, divine gaze Patrick becomes conscious of his own blindness to his personal sinfulness, of his inability to help himself, and of the divine initiative in his regard:

---

[1] Archaeological discoveries, such as the five-thousand-year-old Céide Fields, prove that this part of Ireland was a highly developed area, economically and socially.

and 'we did not keep watch over his precepts' (C 1:14),
– (but he) *kept watch over* me before I knew him
and before I was wise or could distinguish between good and evil,
and he protected me (C 2:25-27),

In the *Apologia* Patrick expresses his helplessness and the Lord's initiative,
again in a *Magnificat* context, and in touching, concrete terms:

But that 'I do *know* most surely,' that indeed
'BEFORE I WAS HUMBLED'
I was like a stone lying in 'deep mire',
and he 'who is mighty' came
and 'in his mercy' he lifted me up;
and, more than that, truly raised me aloft
and placed me on the highest wall (C 12:47-52).

He had rejected the ministry of Christ's Church, in the person of the clergy,
who pleaded with him and his companions to repent and take the first step
towards salvation:

and we did not obey our priests,
who kept warning us about our salvation (C 1:15-16),
– so that, perhaps, *I might* at last *remember my sins* (C 1:21),

The keen appreciation of the role of suffering in God's plan of salvation,
and its necessity for discipleship, is a marked feature of Patrick's 'legacy' to
his children in the faith and is now highlighted as he builds up towards the
crux of his conversion narrative. In his case, this redemptive suffering resulted
in the beginning of understanding from the Lord:

and the Lord *'poured down upon us the heat of his anger'* (C 1:17)
– And THERE *'the Lord opened my heart to an awareness of my unbelief'* (C 2:20)

Progress in Patrick's knowledge of God as Father is gradual and painful, and
the initiative always divine, as in Deuteronomy 8:5b-6:

As a man disciplines his son, the Lord your God disciplines you.
So you shall keep the commandments of the Lord your God,
by walking in his ways and by fearing him.

There, that is, 'in the land of my captivity' (C 3:6; 33:3; 61:6-7), in his interior
and exterior barren, desolate wasteland, he is gradually stripped, through pain
and anguish, of all that stands between him and his God.

THERE THE LORD OPENED MY MIND TO AN AWARENESS OF MY UNBELIEF

The way is being cleared for the Lord to enter and make him aware of his unbelief (Lk 24:45). The context of this biblical allusion is the Risen Lord's appearance to his apostles and disciples in the Upper Room in Jerusalem on Easter Sunday evening:

> *Then he opened their minds to understand the Scripture*
> and he said to them,
> 'Thus it is written,
> that the Messiah is to suffer
> and to rise from the dead on the third day,
> and that repentance and forgiveness of sins is to be proclaimed in his
>   name to all nations beginning from Jerusalem' (Lk 24:45-47).

Jesus opened Patrick's mind and heart in a similar way during his long pilgrimage of faith to understand the Scriptures at ever deeper levels, as well as the role of suffering in the life of the true disciple.[2] Was it not necessary that the Christ should suffer these things and then enter into his glory (Lk 24:26)? Was it not necessary that his chosen apostle, Patrick, should also suffer?

The consciousness of his *littleness*, of his utter helplessness among pagans at the ends of the earth, forms the crux of his account of his own conversion:

> *'and dispersed us among' many 'pagans' even 'to the ends of the earth',*
> *where now my littleness is seen to be among an alien people* (C 1:18-19).

Patrick, in his *littleness* and 'lowliness' as a slave, gradually identifies with the *kenosis* or self-emptying of *the Word* [*Logos*], who took the form of a slave for his salvation:

> Who, though he was in the form of God,
> Did not regard equality with God as something to be exploited,
> but *emptied himself taking the form of a slave* (*doulos*),
> being born in human likeness.
> And being found in human form,
> *he humbled himself and became obedient to the point of death –*
> *even death on a cross.*
> Therefore God also highly exalted him
> and gave him the name that is above every name,
> so that at the name of Jesus every knee should bend,
> in heaven and on earth and under the earth,
> and *every tongue should confess*
> *that Jesus Christ is Lord* (*Kyrios*) *to the glory of God the Father* (Ph 2:6-11).

---

2 *JBC, Lk,* 179, p.163.

By portraying Christ in his pre-existence as the Word, in his role as slave and his exaltation as Lord, Paul is underscoring the cosmic significance of God's saving deed in Christ. Though he was 'in the form of God', 'Jesus emptied himself' to the point of becoming a servant, and then, after dying an ignominious death, he was 'exalted' by God to receive the homage of all creation.

Unlike Patrick, Christ had deliberately taken the form of a slave, thus giving up the glory to which his divine nature entitled him and which had been his before the Incarnation (Jn 17:5), and which, 'normally' speaking, would have been observable in his human body, as on the occasion of the Transfiguration (Mt 17:1-8). But he voluntarily deprived himself of this glory so that it could be returned to him by the Father (Jn 8:50, 54) after his sacrifice on the Cross. As man, sharing all the weaknesses of the human condition apart from sin, Christ led a life of submission and humble obedience, being the fulfilling type of the Servant in Isaiah 52:13-53:12:

> He was despised and rejected by others;
> a man of suffering and acquainted with infirmity;
> and as one from whom others hid their faces he was despised,
> and we held him of no account (Is 53:3).

Jesus and Patrick had arrived at the same point, the One from fullness, the other from nothingness. In the night of faith and hope at Fochoill, and all through his life, Patrick learned that 'God instructs the heart by sufferings and contradictions, and not by ideas'.[3]

The Lord's coming to Patrick, initially, as he tended his pagan master's sheep, in the woods and on the mountain (C 1-2;16), would seem to have been akin to his coming to Elijah, like a gentle breeze (1 K 19:9-16). His conversion seems to have been a gradual process of coming to his senses, of being gently drawn by the Father to come to Jesus, of walking towards him, as expressed in John's Gospel (1:35-51).

A' EPILOGUE
The prologue (Part I, C 1-2) is linked by Patrick to the epilogue (Part V, C 62:1-12):

> But I beseech those who believe in
> and fear God,
> whoever has been pleased to look at
> or receive this writing,
> which PATRICK, A SINNER, untaught, to be sure, has composed IN
>   IRELAND,

---

3   de Caussade, *SADP*, 16; *JB* (1966), *PH*, 339, 341, notes.

> that no one should ever say that [it was] by MY IGNORANCE,
> if I have accomplished or demonstrated any small thing
> according to God's good pleasure;
> but let this be your conclusion and it must be most truly believed
> that it was *'the gift of God'*.
> And this is my Confession
> before I die (C 62:1-12).

In both places he refers to himself as 'Patrick, a sinner', an exile 'in Ireland', and to his 'ignorance'. These are the only two places in the entire work where Patrick mentions his name and uses the terms *'peccator'*, 'a sinner', *'ignorantia'*, 'ignorance', and the phrases *'Hiberione'*, 'to/in Ireland'. In this way he clearly shows that his *Confessio* follows a concentric pattern.

Is this mention of *ignorantia*, in both places, to be equated with Patrick's avowal that he was 'ignorant of the true God'? In his singular concern for the truth, did Patrick believe, as he penned his *Confessio* in his old age, that he was still 'ignorant of the true God'? Or was it that his horizons were changing forever as he moved further and further into the depths of the mystery of 'the gift of God'? (Jn 4:10; Ac 8:20).

In applying the *Magnificat* (Lk 1:48) to himself, Patrick affirms his *humilitas*, his lowliness in the prologue (C 2:23), thus introducing Mary the Mother of God at the opening of the *Confessio*; in affirming that the success of his mission was *donum Dei*, the gift of God (Jn 4:10; Ac 8:20), he places the woman of Samaria at the close and at the centre of his *Confessio* (C 62:10, 33:2), a point to which we shall return in the conclusion.

RENEWAL OF BAPTISMAL COVENANT
Meanwhile, under the divine action Patrick turned more and more to God in prayer:

> and many times a day I WAS PRAYING.
> More and more the love of God and fear of him came to me,
> and my *faith* was being increased, and THE SPIRIT was being moved
> (C 16:3-5).

The experience of finding God's help, when no human help was available, profoundly affected Patrick's whole life. Here, as a Christian, or, perhaps initially, as a catechumen, he was all alone, possibly deprived, for a time at least, of both the food of the Word and the food of the Eucharist, with, perhaps, not even a text of the Bible to hand. Yet, here in the silence, the loneliness and the human deprivation, in the land of his physical and spiritual captivity, Patrick in his powerlessness found his God, recalled what he had learned of him from Sacred Scripture in his youth, made or renewed his baptismal covenant with him, and gradually learned to rely on him alone (C 5, 55-56).

A profound appreciation of this great sacrament of divine adoption and Christian initiation was later to be part of Patrick's *exagalliae,* or spiritual bequest, to the Irish nation (C 14:77). It is surely significant that he refers to it no less than seven times in the *Confessio* (C 14, 40:{3},42, 50, 51); and seven more times in the *Epistola* (E 3, 7, 14, 16, 17, 19, 21).

In the era when the Penal Laws (1695-1829), were enacted against Irish Catholics, which made them outlaws in their own country, Baptism came to be designated as *Baiste urláir* because the Irish had their children baptized, by their outlawed priests, on their cabin floors, for the poor could afford no beds. This 'Christening' was the very bedrock on which their baptismal spirituality was built, the Christ of *Carraig an Aifrinn*, the Mass Rock, the One who nourished and sustained it. It is perhaps noteworthy that visitors to our shores in that era marvelled at the joy and courage of the majority of our people as they sang at their back-breaking work on weekdays and danced to the tune of the piper and the fiddler at the crossroads on Sundays after Mass.

In his experiential or mystical encounter with the Lord, Patrick became increasingly aware of his sinfulness and nothingness in the light of the glory and holiness, the beauty and goodness of a merciful, loving, and steadfast God (C 1, 2, 16, 55-56). The roots of his sinfulness were now exposed to the healing touch of God's merciful love so that a great canticle of joy and praise welled up in his heart. This praise and gratitude gradually evolved into a constant openness to God in prayer (C 16), that eventually found expression in the pastoral care of the pagan people given to him by God, and, finally, found written expression in his *Confessio*.

B TO EXALT AND CONFESS HIS WONDROUS DEEDS
Now, because of the joy of his great encounter with Christ, it became imperative for Patrick to write his *Confessio*:

> Whence moreover I cannot remain silent
> 'nor indeed is it expedient' [that I should],
> concerning such great benefits
> and the great grace,
> which the Lord has been pleased to bestow on me
> 'IN THE LAND OF MY CAPTIVITY'
> because this is what we can give in return
> after God corrects us and brings us to know him:
> 'TO EXALT AND CONFESS HIS WONDROUS DEEDS
> before every nation
> which is under every heaven' (C 3:1-11).

'The land of my captivity' is the inner and outer arena of Patrick's journey of faith, a point which we shall develop in its biblical context in the conclusion below. In praising the hand of God in his captivity with all it entailed in the way of suffering: 'after God corrects us and brings us to know him, to exalt and confess his wondrous deeds', Patrick is evoking Job 5:17-18:

> How happy is the one whom God reproves;
> Therefore do not despise the discipline of the Almighty.
> For he wounds but he binds up; he strikes but his hand heals.

B' I TESTIFY IN TRUTH AND IN EXULTATION OF HEART
Patrick reiterates his great single-mindedness of purpose in returning as a missionary to Ireland in its parallel reading in the penultimate chapter:

> Look, again and again I will briefly set out the words of my Confession.
> 'I TESTIFY' IN TRUTH AND 'IN EXULTATION OF HEART BEFORE GOD AND HIS
>   HOLY ANGELS'
> that I never had any reason
> besides the Gospel
> and his promises
> for ever returning to that pagan people
> whence before I had barely escaped (C 61:1-7).

This attitude of praise and gratitude to God, 'not only in favourable circumstances, but also in pressing needs' (C 34:13-14), what is known as the *Irish Te Deum*, is part of the *exagalliae* (C 14:77) which we, his children in the faith, have inherited from Patrick, and is one of the hallmarks of our Gaelic spirituality.

The phrases, 'In the land of my captivity' and 'that pagan people whence before I had barely escaped,' form a link between those two passages. Further verbal correspondences are, 'to exalt and confess his wondrous deeds before every nation which is under every heaven', evoking Psalm 88(89):6, and 'I testify' in truth and 'in exultation of heart before God and his holy angels', which evokes Psalm 118(119):111.

C PATRICK'S CREED, QUOTING ROMANS 8:16-17
His statement and restatement of his reasons for writing are immediately followed by his Creed or Confession of Faith and the first intimation of his marked devotion to the Blessed Trinity. 'This is not a formal Creed. Its articles are incomplete; besides a regular symbolism would be strange in the context', Bieler tells us.[4] By inserting this long Trinitarian Creed here, Patrick 'wants us to see the experience of his life and the fulfilment of his mission in the light of his belief in the Holy Trinity':[5]

---

4 *LE*, 11, 7.
5 Ibid., 97.

Because there is no other God,
nor was there ever before,
nor will there be hereafter,
besides God the Father, unbegotten,
without beginning,
from whom is all beginning,
containing all things
as we have been taught;
and his Son Jesus Christ,
whom we testify
to have always existed with the Father
before the beginning of the world,
spiritually and ineffably begotten by the Father,
before all beginning,
and through him all things have been made, visible and invisible.
He was made man,
and having conquered death, he was received into heaven by the
    Father.
'And he has given him all power above every name
in heaven,
and on earth,
and under the earth,
and every tongue should confess to him
that Jesus Christ is Lord and God',
in whom we believe,
and we look hopefully for his coming, soon to be,
'the judge of the living and the dead,
who will repay each one according to his own deeds',
AND 'HE POURED OUT ON US ABUNDANTLY THE HOLY SPIRIT
AS THE GIFT' AND 'PLEDGE' OF IMMORTALITY,
who makes believers and listeners
so that they may be 'CHILDREN OF GOD' AND 'JOINT HEIRS WITH CHRIST',
whom we confess and adore,
one God in the Trinity of the Sacred Name (C 4:1-33).

This part of the *Confessio* cannot claim to be the original work of Patrick in the way the rest of his composition is original. Since its Latin style is not in harmony with the rest of the *Confessio*, that alone makes it clear that the Creed is not Patrick's own composition. In Bieler's view, Patrick draws on a Gallican Creed which he had learned in his youth and not, as Oulton holds, on the *Commentary on the Apocalypse* by Victorinus of Pettau, martyr, c. 304, in the recension of that work made by St Jerome c. 406. Indeed, the theological expressions in this chapter can almost all be paralleled in Gallican writers and documents of the fourth and fifth centuries; emphasis on the Trinity, for example, is a marked feature of Gallican creeds and writers. Oulton concludes that the 'Gallican tradition within which Patrick stands is consistent with other facts revealed by his credal statements'; and that 'analysis of the text of the *Confessio* brings its author into touch with Gaul, Spain, Milan, and finally Pannonia'. Oulton has discovered further echoes of contemporary and slightly earlier theological expressions in his contribution – Patrick refers to the great Doctrines of Faith, in particular the Divinity of Christ, which preoccupied the Fathers of the Church in the fourth century, and which are omitted by Victorinus – which, according to Chadwick, is 'a valuable testimony to the familiarity of the writer of the Patrician documents with contemporary continental writings.... From all this it is clear', she concludes, 'that the author of the Patrician documents, although a provincial, was no isolated rustic, but was a partaker in the cultural thought of the western Europe of his own day.'[6]

Whatever its source, Patrick took this Creed and made it his own, lacing it in the process, as was his wont, with lavish quotations from, and allusions to Sacred Scripture.

His testimony to his faith in the mystery of the Trinity, which is the very kernel of our Patrician heritage, finds pithy expression in one of our best-loved prayers in honour of the Blessed Trinity from Penal Days:

> *Solas na soilse, radharc na Tríonóide,*
> *agus grásta na foighne in aghaidh na h-éagóra.*
> The Light of lights, the vision of the Trinity,
> and the grace of patience in face of injustice,

while the fervent recitation of the Creed is, to this day, considered by the Irish to be a powerful prayer of intercession.

It has been noted by Hanson that there is no explicit reference to the great controversy regarding the Pelagian heresy which convulsed the Church of the fifth century in this Creed. This claim has been refuted by Daniel Conneely, who notes that Patrick found the doctrinal and literary inspiration for the phrase *facit credentes ... ut sint,* in two tracts of Augustine, *De praedestinatione sanctorum* (n. 34), and *De dono perseverantiae* (n. 67):

> and he has poured out abundantly upon us the Holy Spirit,
> a gift and pledge of immortality,

---

6 Oulton, *CSSP*, preface and *passim*; Bieler, *CVP*, 121, 4; Oulton, op. cit., 34; 12, 15, 34, 29; Chadwick, *ASCC*, 28, 29; For an impressive examination of the influence of the Fathers of the Church, and of Hilary of Potiers in particular, on Patrick's version of the Creed, cf. Conneely, *TLSP*, 27-30; Dronke, *SPR*, 34-6.

who makes those believing and obeying
that they may be CHILDREN OF GOD AND JOINT HEIRS OF CHRIST.[7]

The Pelagians were accused by their opponents of claiming, in varying degrees, that Salvation could be achieved without divine assistance and that total reliance on God's grace merely condoned failure to develop the natural virtues.[8] Though the Pelagian heresy was not finally resolved until the Second Council of Orange in 529, Patrick's *Confessio* is, from start to finish, an implicit refutation of the tenets of Pelagianism without ever mentioning that heresy explicitly. He was called and graced, after all, not to identify and eliminate heretics, but to convert a non-Christian people to faith in Jesus Christ.

C' PATRICK'S DOXOLOGY, QUOTING ROMANS 8:16-17
Patrick opens his Doxology (C 57-60), the reflex and amplification of his Creed, by quoting the great *Hallel Psalm*, 116 (114-115):12:

> Whence moreover 'shall I return [*retribuam*] to him
> for all his bounty to me?' (C 57:1-2)

This was one of the psalms which Christ chanted with his disciples at the Last Supper on the eve of his Passion:

> *What shall I return to the Lord for all his bounty to me?*
> I will accept the cup of salvation and call on the name of the Lord,
> *I will pay my vows to the Lord* in the presence of all his people....
> O Lord, I am your servant;
> I am your servant, the child of your serving girl....
> *I will offer to you a thanksgiving sacrifice*
> and call on the name of the Lord
> in the presence of all his people,
> in the courts of the house of the Lord,
> in your midst, O Jerusalem (Ps 116 (114-115):12-14; 16-19).

This making of a return to the Lord for all his bounty to him, is, as we have indicated earlier, the overarching theme of the *Confessio*:

> But what shall I say
> or what shall I promise to my Lord?
> For I can do nothing
> unless he himself enables me;

7 Hanson, *LW*, 81; Conneely, op. cit., 112-13.
8 Duffy, *PHOW*, 48-9; Hanson, *OC*, 35ff.

but 'he tests the hearts and minds',
and 'I have eagerly desired' and 'I was ready'
that he should grant me 'to drink his cup',
just as he granted to others who loved him (C 57:3-10).

The Scriptural context of 'to drink his cup' is the encounter between the All-Holy Son of God and the Zebedee brothers, James and John, at the point when Christ was on his way to Jerusalem to die an ignominious death on the Cross. In these poignantly dramatic circumstances they asked that they might sit, one at his right and the other at his left, in his glory. But Jesus said that they did not know what they were asking, and continued:

'Are you able *to drink the cup* that I drink,
or be baptized with the baptism that I am baptized with?'
They replied, 'We are able.'
Then Jesus said to them,
'the cup that I drink you will drink,
and with the baptism with which I am baptized you will be baptized;
but to sit at my right hand or at my left is not mine to grant,
but it is for those for whom it has been prepared.'
... whoever wishes to be great among you must be your servant,
and whoever wishes to be first among you must be slave (*doulos*) of all;
For the Son of Man came not to be served but to serve,
and to give his life a ransom for many' (Mk 10:35-41, 43b-45).

This biblical extract, which reiterates the three great themes of Mark 1:1-15 – Baptism, the Way and the Kingdom – is Patrick's yardstick for his own personal commitment to *ministerium servitutis meae*, the ministry of my slavery (C 49:176). He is expressing, clearly and unequivocally, his heartfelt desire for martyrdom, 'to drink his cup', to suffer and to die for Christ. He is following in the footsteps of the great apostle, Paul, whom he evokes here, and who exhorts his Roman converts thus: 'present your bodies as a living sacrifice (*hostiam viventem*) holy and acceptable to God, which is your spiritual worship' (Rm 12:1).

PATRICK'S PRAYER FOR GOD'S OWN PEOPLE
He then prays for his Irish converts (evoking Moses in Deuteronomy 7:6), God's own people!, that he may never lose them:

Wherefore 'may it never happen to me' from my God
that I should ever lose his own 'people'
'whom he has formed' [for himself] at the ends of the earth
    (C 58:11-13).

PATRICK'S DESIRE FOR MARTYRDOM

And, finally, he prays for perseverance, asks that he may be a faithful witness to Christ to the end, and reiterates his desire for martyrdom:

> I pray God that he may give me perseverance
> and to grant that I may be a faithful witness to him
> up to the point of death for the sake of my God.
> And if I have ever imitated anything good
> for the sake of my God whom I love dearly,
> I pray him to grant to me
> that with those sojourners and captives for his name's sake
> I may shed my blood,
> even if I should lack even burial itself,
> or my corpse, in most wretched fashion, be divided limb by limb for
>   dogs
> or for savage beasts,
> or 'the birds of the air eat it up' (C 58:14-26; 59:17-25).

He may be referring here to the martyrs of the British Church, Albon, Aaron and Julius, but he could also have in mind the first set of Irish martyrs on record, those of his flock who had been put to the sword by the soldiers of Coroticus while their baptismal chrism was still shining on their foreheads (E 3:20-21). He now, in firm hope, claims for himself, in the event of suffering martyrdom, what he has already claimed in his *Epistola* for his own Irish martyrs who have gone before him: that they 'will reign with the apostles and prophets and martyrs', that they 'will capture eternal kingdoms' (E 18:181-2). 'I am firmly convinced that if this should happen to me', he declares:

> I will have gained my soul along with my body,
> because 'without any doubt we will rise again' on that day, in the
>   brightness of the sun,
> this is, 'in the glory' of Christ Jesus our Redeemer,
> as 'CHILDREN OF' THE LIVING 'GOD' AND 'JOINT HEIRS WITH CHRIST',
> and 'about to be conformed to his image'.
> since 'from him and through him and in him we are to reign'
>   (C 59:28-33).

Patrick undergirds his final paean of praise and gratitude to God with a solemn and joyful profession of faith. In both the Creed and the Doxology (C 57-60) he quotes an excerpt (in italics) from Romans 8:16-17:

> When we cry, 'Abba! Father!'

it is that very Spirit bearing witness with our spirit
that *we are children of God,*
and if children, then heirs,
heirs of God
and joint heirs with Christ
if, in fact, we suffer with him so that we may also be glorified with him.

It can scarcely be considered a mere coincidence that these are the only two places in the *Confessio* where he uses this quotation and reinforces yet again the fact that the *Confessio* follows a concentric pattern.

More importantly, it evokes the wonderful encounter between the Risen Christ and his faithful disciple, Mary Magdalen, the woman whom he missioned to be the first herald of the Resurrection to the Christian Church:

Jesus said to her,
'Do not hold on to me
because I have not yet ascended to the Father;
but *go to my brothers and say to them,*
"I am ascending to my Father and your Father, to my God and your God." '
Mary Magdalen went and announced to the disciples, 'I have seen the Lord';
and she told them that he had said these things to her (cf. Jn 20:11-18).

Christ makes clear that he is not the *End*; he is *the Way* to the Father, and that we, through his Death and Resurrection, are made children of the Father and *joint-heirs with Christ.* The saint's deep consciousness of the baptized being joint-heirs with Christ also reflects his ever-deepening experience of seeing the Lord by faith in *Pobal Dé*, the People of God, and his commitment to spreading the Good News of the New Covenant of God to these people that the Lord had entrusted to his care.

CHRIST, THE TRUE SUN

He refers to 'the sun' three times in his *Confessio*, once in his vision of Helias (Elijah) (C 20), at the centre of Part II, the testimony of his sacred calling, and twice here in the Doxology. Here, as in the vision of Helias where Jesus, 'the dawn from on high' (Lk 1:78), delivers him from Satan's control, Patrick is emphatically declaring for the second time that 'Christ Jesus our Redeemer is the true Sun':

because 'without any doubt we will rise again' on that day in the brightness of the sun,
this is [to say], 'in the glory' of Christ Jesus our Redeemer (C 59:29-30).

He now vehemently repudiates sun-worship and condemns its votaries:

> For the sun which we behold rises daily for us at God's command,
> but it will never reign, nor will its splendour endure forever;
> all wretched people who adore it will, moreover, come to a wretched
>   punishment (C 60:34-6).

And, finally, for the third time, he acknowledges that *'Christ'* is *'the true Sun'* who abides forever:

> We, however, who believe and adore the true sun, Christ
> who will never die;
> nor will he 'who does his will';
> but 'he will live forever,
> as Christ also lives forever,'
> he who reigns with God the Almighty Father,
> and with the Holy Spirit before the ages,
> and now and for ever and ever. Amen (C 60:37-44).

The danger of falling back into sun-worship in the fifth century was very real due to its revival by the Romans, and Patrick's reference to it may be based on the exhortations of Pope Leo the Great.[9] He may also be affirming his own orthodoxy on the sun-worship question for reasons which I shall suggest when we come to consider his betrayal in Part III of his *Confessio*.

D TRUST IN GOD, QUOTING PSALM 50 (49):15
Patrick now professes his total reliance upon God's help in the writing of his *Confessio*:

> For he himself has said through the Prophet [David]:
> 'CALL ON ME IN THE DAY OF YOUR TROUBLE;
> AND I WILL DELIVER YOU
> AND YOU WILL GLORIFY ME' (C 5:1-4).

He knows, and expects us to recall, the preceding verse, which reads: 'Offer to God a sacrifice of thanksgiving and pay your vows to the Most High' (Ps 50 (49):14). This is exactly what he is setting out to do in writing his *Confessio*: 'to reveal and confess, moreover, the works of God is an honourable thing' (C 5:6-7).

D' TRUST IN GOD, QUOTING PSALM 55 (54):22
This great trust in God is again expressed in its parallel reading (C 55end-56), in the face of possible murder, fraud or captivity or whatever it may be. But

---

9 Sermon XXVII, 4, Migne, *PL*.

he is not afraid because he has cast himself into the hands of the Almighty, who rules everywhere as the prophet (David) says: 'Cast your cares on the Lord, and he will sustain you' (Ps 55(54):22). With corresponding confidence, therefore, he commends his soul to his 'most faithful God' for whom he is an unworthy ambassador (E 5):

> Behold, then, 'I commend my soul to my most faithful God',
> 'for whom I am an ambassador' in my obscurity,
> but 'he is no accepter of persons',
> and, for this office, he chose even me
> 'from among his least ones' that I should be one of his ministers
>   (C 56:6-10).

Psalm 50 (49):15, 'Call on me in the day of your trouble; and I will deliver you and you will glorify me', and Psalm 55 (54):22, 'Cast your cares on the Lord, and he will sustain you', form the links between these two parallel passages.

E LORD, I AM NOT WORTHY

Though he is imperfect in many respects, he wishes his 'brethren and relatives' (Lk 2:44) to know what quality of person he is, that they may be enabled to discern the vow of his soul (C 6). This solemn vow of Patrick's soul, *votum animae meae,* the implications of which he wants his 'brethren and relatives' to grasp clearly, at the beginning of his *Confessio*, is to make a *retributio*, a return (C 3, 11, 12, 57) to God for all his goodness and mercy to him, as he now reiterates in a new biblical context. By quoting from Luke 2:44, Patrick evokes the Feast of the Passover, and Christ, at the age of twelve, in the Temple of Jerusalem. Christ is not to be found, in this instance, among the 'brothers and relatives', but in the Temple, that is, in the Jewish centre of both the Presence and the Worship of God, 'in my Father's house'.

It is also possible that Patrick has in mind another Temple scene from the public life of Christ where, having watched the rich putting their gifts into the treasury, Christ makes the comment that the poor widow with the two copper coins has put in more than all the others. He then foretells the destruction of the Temple and the turmoil to which his disciples will be exposed: 'You will be betrayed even by parents and brothers, by relatives and friends, and they will put some of you to death; you will be hated by all because of my name' (Lk 21:16-17).

He then follows this with the consoling promise: 'But not a hair of your head will perish. By your endurance you will gain your souls' (Lk 21:18-19). This is Patrick's blueprint for the following through of his divine calling; his relatives and friends must understand that, though he loves them dearly, he has been called to leave them forever for the sake of the Kingdom (C 43), in spite of the hurts and misunderstandings of which he is so keenly aware (C 46, 49).

E' AND I WAS NOT WORTHY

Certain suffering, poverty, deprivation and possible death will be his portion.
But the saint affirms in its parallel reading that this is a small price to pay
when compared with the great blessings that have accrued to him:

> But I see even 'in this present world'
> that I am exalted beyond measure by the Lord,
> and *I WAS NOT WORTHY* OF IT, NOR WAS I OF THE SORT
> THAT HE SHOULD BESTOW IT ON ME,
> because I know most certainly,
> that poverty and adversity are better for me,
> than riches and luxury.
> But 'Christ the Lord' too, was 'poor for our sakes',
> for I, wretched and unhappy,
> have no resources now, even if I wished for them (C 55:1-10).

Though Patrick – and presumably his fellow-labourers – lived in constant
danger, he was never overwhelmed by fear because he had placed himself in
the hands of God:

> 'nor do I judge myself',
> because I expect daily
> either that I be massacred, or defrauded,
> or reduced to slavery or to any sort of condition whatsoever.
> 'But I fear none of these things' because of the promises of heaven,
> because I have cast myself into the hands of almighty God,
> 'who rules everywhere' (C 55:11-17).

This placing of oneself and all life's joys and cares in the merciful hands of
a loving Father forms a very important strand in Gaelic spirituality. The late
Anthony Hamson CSSp recounted, in one of his retreat conferences, a
memorable instance of this unconditional trust in God. While studying the
Irish language at Gaeltacht na Rinne, the Irish-speaking area in Rinn, Co.
Waterford, in the mid-1930s, a violent and protracted thunderstorm struck,
which devastated the area and terrified the inhabitants. When the storm had
abated somewhat, Fr Hamson visited a frail old lady who lived all alone in an
isolated part of the parish and, to his amazement, found that she had been
serene, perfectly unperturbed by the thunder and lightning. To his
incredulous and repeated exclamation '*ní raibh eagla ort!*' 'you were not afraid!'
she responded '*ní raibh, a mhic óigh*', 'I was not, son'. '*Dé chúis?*' 'Why?' he
persisted. '*Mar cuirim mo thoil le Toil Dé agus bím sásta*', 'I unite my will to the
will of God and I am always content', was her quiet and simple reply.

Patrick's sense of unworthiness links those parallel passages.

F THE MOUTH WHICH LIES DESTROYS THE SOUL
In the presence of his God, and drawing heavily on Sacred Scripture for his claims, Patrick now declares that what he is about to tell us in his *Confessio* is the truth and nothing but the truth (C 7-8:1-14):

> I AM NOT IGNORANT OF 'THE TESTIMONY OF MY LORD',
> who testifies in the psalm:
> 'You destroy those who speak a lie.'
> And again he declares,
> 'THE MOUTH WHICH LIES DESTROYS THE SOUL.'
> And the same Lord affirms in the Gospel:
> 'The careless word which people utter
> they will have to account for it on the day of judgment.'
> Whence, moreover, I ought exceedingly
> to dread this sentence 'with fear and trembling'
> on that day when no person will be able to withdraw or hide,
> but when all of us, without exception, 'shall render an account,'
> of even the smallest sins,
> 'before the judgment-seat of the Lord Christ'.

F' I DO NOT LIE
His affirmation of the truth is expressed more forcefully in the parallel reading (C 54), which in itself follows a miniature internal concentric pattern. It would seem that Patrick is here refuting certain allegations of avarice and vainglory brought against him by his enemies:

> Look, 'I CALL ON GOD AS WITNESS UPON MY SOUL' (C 54:1)
> – 'He', moreover, *'who has promised, is faithful'* (C 54:7)

> *'THAT I DO NOT LIE'.*
> Neither, I hope, is it to provide 'an occasion of flattery'
> or a pretext 'for covetousness' that I have written to you (C 54:2-4)
> – *He never lies* (C 54:8).

> Nor that I hope for honour from any of you,
> for honour which is not yet seen, but is believed in the heart *suffices for me* (C 54:5-6).

In the face of injustice Patrick's gaze is ever fixed on the Blessed Trinity and the eternal reward of patient endurance. His emphasis on the veracity of his statements links those parallel passages.

X THE APOLOGIA

We have, up to this point, considered Patrick's six years' enforced slavery in Ireland, the beginning of his gradual conversion process, and the deepening of his faith and trust in God as a missionary bishop during that period, all of which comes to a fitting culmination in his *Apologia* (C 9-15).

This *Apologia*, which is comprised of eighty-five lines, is almost a miniature of the whole *Confessio*. It is divided into five paragraphs, which are limited by an *inclusio*: *cogitavi, I have thought about*, in the first and last clauses:

> On which account *I have* long since *thought* about writing,
> but 'until now' I hesitated. (C 9:1-2)
> – which at anytime *in* my *youth* I *never hoped for nor thought about*
>   (C 15:85).

It is addressed, primarily, to the *domini cati rhetorici*, lords, learned rhetoricians, who may have been Pelagians, self-styled masters in their own actions and omissions, and who apparently despised Patrick (cf. C 1:26; E 1:11), for his lack of professional training in rhetoric, perhaps, among other things, and therefore would not consider him qualified to write a formal *Confessio*. There is a very close correspondence between Patrick's *Apologia* and that of St Paul's in 2 Corinthians, as Nerney has cogently pointed out. We read: 'His accusers contended, at least by inference, that God has respect to persons in calling to the apostolate: he takes the wise and good, not sinners, or rude, uneducated men. Realising that this was an inversion of the right order of divine vocation and an infringement of the Catholic doctrine of grace, St Patrick answered with St Paul that God chose the weak things of the world to confound the wise and mighty; and with St Augustine that persons are not called by God because they are good, but to be good: "*non enim electi sunt quia boni fuerunt, qui boni non essent nisi electi essent,* they are not chosen indeed because of their goodness, seeing that they would not have been good unless they had been chosen" ' (In Joann., tract 86, 2.1).[10]

In this portion of his *Confessio*, therefore, Patrick challenges their prejudices, their heresy and their worldliness. Though, uniquely, without a concentric pair in the *Confessio*, the *Apologia*, like the *Confessio* as a whole, is concentrically composed, with its crux at the centre. Paragraph 1 is paired with paragraph 1' and arranged in antiphons. Paragraphs 2 and 2' are similarly arranged, building up to the crux in paragraph 3:

> Et iterum Spiritus *testatur*
> '*Et rusticationem ab Altissimo Creatam. Unde....*
> And again the Spirit testifies
> even rustic work was ordained by the Most High. Whence.... (C 11:42-3)

10 Nerney, D.S. (SJ), *IER, SPS*, III, 110.

The word *testatur*, testifies, which introduces the crux, is the 245th from the beginning, and the word *unde*, whence, which follows it, is 245th from the end, showing that Patrick, like St Mark to whom we have referred in the introduction, arranges his words by symmetry.

1,1' PATRICK'S HESITATION ABOUT WRITING HIS *CONFESSIO*
Patrick enters the arena in the first antiphon from paragraph 1:

> On which account *I have* long since *thought* about writing,
> but 'until now' I hesitated (C 9:1-2).

He balances this preamble with delicate irony in its antiphon, in paragraph 1':

i *Whence, moreover, be astonished,* therefore,
ii   *'You great and small*
iii   *who fear*
iv   *God',*
iii'   *and you,*
ii'   *lords, clever rhetoricians,*
1' *hear therefore and consider* (C 13:57-60).

With a few deft strokes he ingeniously marshalls his audience, addresses them as 'lords, clever rhetoricians', and requests them to ponder carefully what he is about to say. This antiphon is a miniature concentric passage of impressive artistry – within another internal concentric passage. It is a classical parody; and all this skill is pressed into the service of the crux, God, 'the true God' (C 1), at the centre of all creation, whether in heaven or on earth.

PSEUDO-CHRISTIANS AND PSEUDO-PROPHETS
The words *usque nunc*, 'until now', in the first antiphon, are taken from Mark 13:19-20, 'the Little Apocalypse', in which Jesus foretells 'the desolating sacrilege set up where it ought not to be', when 'false Christs and false prophets will appear'. Mark writes: 'For in those days there will be suffering, such as has not been from the beginning of the creation that God created *until now*, no, and never will be ... but for the sake of the elect, whom he chose, he has cut short those days' (Mk 13:19-20).

With this, compare the quotation from Revelation 19:5 in the second antiphon, 'you great and small who fear God'. The concentric structure of this second antiphon implies that 'the lords, clever rhetoricians', are not included among all who fear him, *great and small*. The quotation comes from the centre of a passage which contrasts the fall of the harlot, Babylon the great (Rv 18:1-24), in which the blood of prophets and saints has been found, with the preparation of the Chaste Bride for marriage to the Lamb (Rv 19:6-10). It may be inferred from these quotations that Patrick has been compelled to write at a time of tribulation, and that his critics are among the pseudo-Christians and the pseudo-prophets, those in Babylon who attack prophets and saints, while he is one of the chosen ones with the Bride.

PATRICK'S FEAR OF ADVERSE CRITICISM

The reason for this delay in writing his *Confessio* would seem to be that he felt, due to the early and violent interruption of his studies, that the level of his educational attainment did not warrant such an undertaking; the anticipated criticism of the haughty learned class, moreover, made him feel still more diffident about the project:

> For I feared lest '*I should fall under the censure of the tongue*' *of people,*
> because *I have not learned* 'just as others',
> who most thoroughly, then, *have absorbed laws* and sacred letters,
> both in equal measure (C 9:3-6).
> – Who *was it that stirred me up, a fool, from the midst of those*
> who seem to be wise and *learned in law* (C 13:61-2).

Let us note the balance of words and phrases in these pairs of antiphons; Patrick feared the censure of learned men's tongues, 'lest "I should fall under the censure of the tongue" of people', because he was not learned, unlike those who 'have absorbed laws and sacred letters, both in equal measure'. Yet, in spite of their being 'learned in law', God did not choose 'the lords, learned rhetoricians'; instead, Patrick, '*a fool*', was the one who had found favour with God.

PATRICK, THE CHOSEN FOOL

In quoting Sirach, 'lest "I should fall under the censure of the tongue" of people' (cf. Si 28:13-27), because he has not studied 'just as others' (1 Th 5:6), Patrick is alluding here to the 'blessed person' (Si 28:19), 'who has been protected from the tongue of slanderers. Those, on the contrary, who forsake the Lord, will fall into its power' (Si 28:23). The inference from the unquoted text is that Patrick is 'blessed' and 'sheltered' and that he will not abandon the Lord. In 1 Thessalonians 5:6 'the others' are not Christians.

PATRICK'S ADVERSARIES *SEEM* TO BE WISE

Patrick's rhetorical question is reiterated and further qualified in the third pair of antiphons:

> and never changed their styles of speech from infancy
> but rather were always bringing them 'towards perfection' (C 9:7-8)
> – and [seem to be] 'powerful *in speech*' and in everything (C 13:63)

where 'styles of speech' in the first balances 'powerful in speech' in the second.

In using the phrase 'towards perfection', Patrick has in mind Hebrews 7:19: 'for the law made nothing perfect', implying, in ironic undertone, that the learning of 'the others' has not brought them the perfection which, on a first reading, Patrick might seem to concede to them. Similarly the phrase, those 'powerful in speech', evokes the description of Jesus, 'who was a prophet mighty in deed and word' (Lk 24:19). But this is faint praise, for those whom Patrick describes only 'seem to be', *videntur esse*, wise and learned in law and powerful in speech and in everything.

CULTURAL ADAPTATION
What Patrick had to say had, by contrast with the clever rhetoricians, to be translated into the Gaelic language, a tongue foreign to him – as both a slave and a missionary in Ireland:

> For 'our speech and spoken language' *has been translated into an alien language*,
> as it can easily be proved from the flavour of my writing
> how 'I have been' taught and 'educated' in styles of speech
> because [Scripture] says: 'Through the tongue shall the wise man be recognised,
> also his understanding and knowledge and teaching of the truth'
> (C 9:9-13).

One of Patrick's major initiatives was to prepare the Irish soil adequately to ensure a rich harvest after he had planted the seed of the Word there. In order to do this, he learned the old Gaelic language, appraised himself of the Irish people's socio-political and economic circumstances, and 'translated' the Good News of Salvation into this 'foreign language'. Not surprisingly, his people listened more readily to the Word of God proclaimed to them in their own native Gaelic, and in the context of their own traditions in a rural society. Indeed, when our forebears came to realise that their voyages and pilgrimages to sacred places, their traditional celebrations of water and light as the sources of life at those sacred places, their belief in immortality, their love of justice, *cothrom na Féinne*, together with their valued and much vaunted *flaithiúlacht*, and their celebratory feasting, were also respectable elements of biblical tradition, it helped to make the tenets of Christianity more acceptable to them. Moreover, the prospect of heaven being an 'eternal banquet', where, as guests of the Lamb of God (cf. Rv 19:9), the Irish, in colourful wedding garments, enjoyed *nua gach bia agus sean gach dí*, fresh food and mellow drink, and witty exchange, to the accompaniment of soft, celestial, *ceol cláirsí* or harp strains, must have been particularly palatable! The Word of God fell on many ears like the *ceol sí* or 'fairy music', calling them forth to fix their minds on heavenly things, even if it met with the inevitable stubborn resistance in some quarters (C 52-53).

This cultural adaptation was an important component of Patrick's integrity as a missionary. It also explains, in part, the phenomenal success of his unique missionary endeavour and makes him a missionary 'for all seasons'.

PATRICK'S KNOWLEDGE OF THE GAELIC LANGUAGE
The scriptural quotation, 'Our speech and language', has two sources. The first is Psalm 19 (18):3-4:

> There is no speech, nor are there words;
> their voice is not heard;
> yet their voice goes out through all the earth,
> and their words to the end of the world.

This quotation is consistent with Patrick's enforced speaking of the old Gaelic language at the ends of the earth. The second is John 8:43-44:

> Why do you not understand what I say?
> It is because you cannot accept my word.
> You are from your father, the devil,
> and you choose to do your father's desires.
> He was a murderer from the beginning
> and does not stand in the truth
> because there is no truth in him.
> When he lies he speaks according to his own nature,
> for he is a liar and the father of lies.

The implication here, once again, is that his critics are not inspired by the Holy Spirit. In his quotation from Sirach 4:29:

> 'Through the tongue shall the wise man be recognised,
> also his understanding and knowledge and teaching of the truth'.
> 'Sapiens per linguam dinoscetur
> et sensus et scientia et doctrina veritatis' (C 9:12-13).

Patrick has changed *sapientia*, wisdom, to *sapiens*, the wise man, and not unconsciously, Howlett claims. 'As the quotation follows directly a clause referring to his own education, the inescapable inference is that Patrick is claiming to be *sapiens*, wise'.[11] In lines 14-20, which we shall consider later, Patrick has surrounded this quotation from Sirach with an evocation of Acts 22:3, in which St Paul, addressing a hostile mob in their own language, says: 'I am a Jew ... brought up at the feet of Gamaliel, educated strictly according to our ancestral law'. Also in lines 16-17, Sirach 25:5 is echoed:

11 Howlett, *ESSM*, 97.

How attractive is wisdom in the aged,
and understanding and counsel in the venerable,
and their boast is the fear of the Lord.

THAT WITH HUMILITY AND TRUTHFULLY I MIGHT SERVE THEM
The response to this antiphon in paragraph 1' is another concentric passage, which in its turn is divided into a number of twin antiphons expressing Patrick's wonder at the ways of God. He who calls whom he wills, has chosen himself, the fool, the outcast, in preference to the clever rhetoricians:

Who was it that stirred me up, a fool...
and inspired even me, beyond the others of this detestable world,
If I should be such [a person] – if only moreover [I were] – (C 13:62-65)
– *And I was not* worthy nor *such* [a person]. (C 15:79)

These antiphons are an echo of what he has already said in his *Epistola*: 'If I am worthy, I live for my God to teach the pagans, even if I am despised by some [people]' (E 1:10-11). Conscious of the hazards of his mission, and of the opposition from friends and foes alike to that unique mission, Patrick may have Matthew 8:8; 10:37-9 in mind in both writings. The context of Matthew 8:8 is the healing of the centurion's servant, where this gentile centurion places such a profound trust in the power of Jesus to heal at a distance: 'Lord, I am not worthy to have you come under my roof; but only speak the word and my servant will be healed' (Mt 8:8). Patrick is implying that a similar quality of faith is essential for him to carry out God's work in the teeth of opposition. The context of the second citation is Christ's sending out of his apostles like sheep in the midst of wolves (Mt 10:37-9):

Whoever loves father or mother more than me
is not worthy of me;
and whoever loves son or daughter more than me
is not worthy of me;
and whoever does not take up the cross and follow me
is not worthy of me.
Those who find their life will lose it,
and those who lose their life for my sake will find it.

With comparable trust in God, Patrick too wants to lose his life for Christ's sake, in order to find it. He tells us in his Doxology of his great desire to drink Christ's chalice, 'just as he granted to others who loved him' (C 57:10).

PATRICK'S UNDERSTANDING OF HIS MISSION
Faithful to his divine call, Patrick is acutely aware of his responsibility towards
the Irish people:

> *That* 'with awe and reverence'
> and 'without complaint' I would faithfully be of service to *that pagan people*
> to whom 'the love of Christ' *translated me* [*transtulit me*] (C 13:66-8).
> – *that* the Lord should concede this to his little servant,
> after troubles and such great difficulties,
> AFTER CAPTIVITY,
> after many years among *that pagan people* (C 15:80-83).

The call 'to that people' is balanced by Patrick's mission 'among that
people' in these pair of antiphons. When he uses the verb, *transtulit*,
translated, he is conscious here, as elsewhere in his writings, of his human
anguish when Christ pulled him up by the roots, as it were, shook off his
native soil, and transplanted him in an alien land, never again to be uprooted
(C 43:99-101; E 10:90). *Transtulit* in this statement also links it to *translata* in
'For our speech and language was translated, *translata*, into an alien tongue'
(C 9:9). Exile for Christ was not sufficent; the great Apostle of Ireland, as we
have already intimated, also carefully cultivated the Irish soil for the sowing of
the Seed.

The phrase 'with awe and reverence' (C 13:66), comes from Hebrews
12:28:

> Therefore, since we are receiving a kingdom that cannot be shaken,
> let us give thanks, by which we offer to God an acceptable worship
> *with reverence and awe.*

From this context it may be inferred that Patrick is implicitly claiming that he
is acceptable to God, that he has received 'the Gift of God' (Jn 4:10; Ac 8:20).
Elsewhere in his *Confessio* he expresses the same confident attitude of heart
and mind in regard to his relationship with God when he declares:

> *[so that] today I may confidently offer in sacrifice to him,*
> *my life as 'a living host' to Christ my Lord* (C 34:3-4).
> 'You know, God also, how I have lived among you'
> 'from my youth',
> in purity of faith and in sincerity of heart (C 48:154-156).

The phrase 'without complaint' occurs three times in 1 Thessalonians –
2;10; 3:13; 5:23 – which lists Paul's heroic efforts for his converts. The
phrase 'the love of Christ' comes from 2 Corinthians 5:14-15:

> For *the love of Christ* urges us on,
> because we are convinced that one has died for all;
> therefore all have died.
> And he died for all,
> so that those who live might live no longer for themselves
> but for him who died and was raised for them.

In this context Paul claims that 'the love of Christ' is working for his converts. Patrick is implying that he has appropriated Paul's Christian convictions and operational methods for his own mission, so that he may leave a spiritual legacy (C 14:77) to his children in the faith. Far from complaining, therefore, about the strenuous demands of his 'laborious episcopate' (C 26), and urged on by 'the love of Christ', he is astonished and full of joy that the Lord has conferred such a great privilege on 'his little servant'. 'Troubles ... great burdens ... captivity' in Patrick's life are echoes of Paul's heroic efforts for his converts and alluded to here in the phrase, 'without complaint', from 1 Thessalonians, thus linking those two antiphons.

> and *granted me* [this flock] as long as I live, if I should be worthy
>   (C 13:69),
> – That *he should grant me* such great grace (C 15:84).

Patrick praises God for granting him 'such great grace' which is the privilege of being called and graced by the Lord to serve the Irish 'with humility and truth', as befits an ambassador of Christ (C 56:5; E 5:35). Patrick's *humilitas,* lowliness (C 2:23) and *donum Dei,* the gift of God (C 62:10), the twin-pillars of the *Confessio,* are evoked in this context. In spite of his human limitations and weaknesses, he faces his task with complete trust in God, because of the gift of his Indwelling Spirit, alive and active in him, and, empowered by that same Spirit, he is willing to give up his life in the effort (cf. C 16, 20, 33). The phrase, '[he] granted me [this flock] as long as I live' links this part of the *Confessio* with the crux of Patrick's testimony of his mission, 'total commitment to duty in Ireland' (C 43-45), as well as to the central section of the whole *Confessio,* where he celebrates the blessings he received from God because of his divine call to mission (C 36:1-7).

PATRICK'S LEGACY
He again declares this overwhelming desire of serving his flock 'with humility and truth', but immediately unfolds to us one of the key motives behind this devotion to the welfare of his flock, and that is that he may 'leave behind a legacy' to his brethren and sons, as he affirms in the fourth pair of antiphons:

> that at last WITH HUMILITY and in truth *I might serve them* (C 13:70).

> — *so that* even 'after my death' *I may leave behind a legacy to my brethren
>   and children,*
> whom I have baptized in the Lord, so many thousands of people
>   (C 14:77-8).

'So many thousands of people', his 'brethren and sons' in Christ, links this part of the *Confessio* to the prologue (C 1-2), where he tells us he was taken into politico-socio-economic slavery with 'so many thousand' companions who, more than likely, were Christians or 'slaves of Christ' (E 10:90). In citing Peter 'after my death' (2 P 1:15), Patrick possibly has the full context of Peter's apostolic testimony in mind, and we are meant to take it into consideration here (2 P 1:10-15):

> Therefore, brothers and sisters, be all the more eager
> to confirm your call and election,
> for if you do this, you will never stumble.
> For in this way, entry into the eternal kingdom
> of our Lord and Saviour Jesus Christ
> will be richly provided for you.
> Therefore I intend to keep on reminding you of these things,
> though you know them already and are established in the truth that has
>   come to you.
> I think it right as long as I am in this body,
> to refresh your memory,
> since I know that my death will come soon,
> as indeed our Lord Jesus Christ has made clear to me.
> And I will make every effort that *after my departure*
> you may be able at any time to recall these things.

The *Confessio* is our means of recall....

THE LORD'S ETERNAL CONSOLATION
Patrick's singular devotion to the Trinity, which echoes his Trinitarian Creed (C 4) and Doxology (C 57-60), will be the source and strength of all his apostolic motivation to expound everywhere 'the gift of God and his eternal consolation' (C 14:73-74), fearlessly and without human respect. This is the thematic crux of this concentric passage (C 13-14:64-79), and Patrick now uses a miniature internal concentric passage, rather like grace-notes in *sean-nós*, or traditional Irish singing, to emphasise this point:

iii a   And so, 'according to the measure of the faith' of the Trinity it is my
        duty, *without fear of the censure* [*I may incur*],
   b   *to make known* 'THE GIFT OF GOD'

iv   and [his] 'eternal consolation;'
iii' a'   *without fear*
    b'   faithfully *to expound everywhere the name of God* (C 14:71-76)

This second and last internal concentric passage balances the first (C 13:57-60), and the attitude of mind and heart which it enshrines is in stark contrast with that of the *domini cati rethorici*. The phrase 'according to the measure of the faith' comes from Romans 12:3: '... I say to everyone among you ... to think with sober judgement, each *according to the measure of faith* that God has assigned'. Faith is used here to mean the spiritual gifts of the Spirit bestowed by God on the members of the Christian Community to ensure its life and growth. The crux of this internal concentric passage is 'his eternal consolation', which comes from 2 Thessalonians 2:16:

> 'Now may Our Lord Jesus Christ himself
> and God our Father,
> who loved us and through grace gave us *eternal comfort* and good hope,
> comfort your hearts and strengthen them in every good work and word
> ...'

'To make known *the gift of God*' (Jn 4:10; Ac 8:20), and 'in faithworthy fashion to expound ... the Name of God' and 'his eternal consolation' everywhere, is the essence of Patrick's whole life's endeavour. This is his *exagalliae*, his last will and testament, his spiritual legacy to the Irish people. Elsewhere in his *Confessio* he encourages his brethren and fellow 'slaves in Christ' (E 10:90) to carry on this great mission:

> Would that you too would strive for greater things and perform more
>   excellent deeds.
> This will be my glory,
> because 'a wise son
> is the glory of a father'. (C 47:150-3)

LANGUAGE AND LETTERS
Patrick now reaffirms his diffidence about writing his *Confessio*:

> But of what avail is an excuse, even when it is 'close to the truth',
> particularly [when it is attended] with obstinacy,
> seeing that now 'in' my 'old age' I seek
> what *'I did not accomplish in' my 'youth'*,
> because my sins prevented me from mastering
> what I had read through before?

But who will believe me even if I shall say what I mentioned before?
(C 10:14-20)

This statement seems ironic because, while Patrick appears to protest his ignorance, each one of the fourteen lines except the biblical quotation at the end of 1d in Part 1 of this *Apologia*, ends with a *clausula*. All fourteen lines, moreover, can be scanned according to accepted cursus rhythms as well as *clausulae*.[12]

2, 2' THE DIVINE COMPASSION
In paragraphs 2 and 2' Patrick alludes at the outset to his own human powerlessness in describing himself as 'almost wordless, the extreme rustic, a captive, a refugee, untaught'. He seems acutely aware of his 'unlearnedness,' perhaps referring to his lack of formal education in rhetoric, but we must always be careful not to take what Patrick says about himself at face value! Let us note the balance of words and phrases (italicised) in these sets of antiphons in this section of the *Apologia*:

As an adolescent, indeed, *as an almost speechless boy* (C 10:21)
— Whence I, *the genuine rustic* (C 12:44),
I WAS CAPTURED (C 10:22)
— *a refugee, untaught, doubtless* (C 12:45),

The word 'untaught' and the phrase 'the genuine rustic' link these passages backwards to the phrase 'an almost speechless boy', in the first antiphon. In the next pair of antiphons:

Before I knew what I should seek
or what to avoid (C 10:23-4).
— '*who does not know how to provide*' for the future,
but that 'I do *know* most surely,' that, indeed, 'BEFORE I WAS HUMBLED'
I was like a stone lying in '*DEEP MIRE*' (C 12:46-8).

the negative phrases, 'before I knew what I should seek' and '[I] do not know how to provide for the future', balance each other, while the positive phrase 'I do know most surely' is linked to both, as well as being a significant contrast in this context. The phrases 'before I was humbled' and 'in deep mire' are significant linkages, and they are also linked forward to:

Whence therefore I blush for shame today
and I greatly fear
to expose my unlearnedness

---

12 Howlett, ibid., 96.

because I am unable 'to unfold in speech' to those trained in concise
    expression
in the way my spirit and mind desire,
and my heart's feelings suggest (C 10:25-30)
– and *he 'who is mighty' came*
and 'in his mercy' he lifted me up [*sustulit me*],
and, more than that, truly raised me aloft
and placed me on the highest wall (C 12:49-52).

The phrase 'I cannot unfold in speech', an indication of his powerlessness, is
linked to 'He who is powerful'. The former phrase also links backwards to:
'an almost wordless boy, a captive, not yet wise [before I knew what I should
seek or what to avoid]', and forwards to 'a fool' (C 13:61).

But if, then, I had been gifted 'just as others'[13]
I truly would not have remained silent 'because of the return due' [from me to
    God] (C 11:31-2)
– And therefore *I ought to cry out* aloud
in order *'to make'* some *'return'* to the Lord also
for his great benefits here and in eternity,
[benefits] which the human mind is unable to appraise (C 12:53-6).

The phrase '*I truly would not have remained silent "because of the return due"* '
balances '*I ought to cry out* aloud in order to make some return to the Lord'.
Initially, Patrick seems to admit ignorance. In 'because I am unable to enfold
in speech ...' (C 10:28), he quotes Qoheleth 1:8: All things are wearisome;
'more than one can unfold in speech', which is synonymous with his
powerlessness. Again in 'who did not know how to provide for the future' (C
12:46), he cites Qoheleth 4:13-14:

Better is a poor but wise *youth* than an old but foolish king,
who will no longer take advice [*does not know how to provide for the future*]
One can indeed come out of *prison* (*and chains*) to reign,
even though *born poor* in the kingdom.

The context, which he does not quote, links this passage backwards to the
parallel passage, in which he is 'a boy, a captive', figuratively at least, 'in prison

---

13 Howlett suggests in ibid. that the repeated quotation, *sicut et ceteris* **(in C 11, 31)**,
    from 1 Thessalonians 5:6, draws attention to another feature of Patrick's ordering of
    his text, namely citation of the same biblical sources in paired paragraphs. Thus:

Paragraph 1	**Paragraph 1'**
Mk 13:19, 'the Little Apocalypse'	Rv 19:5
1 Th 5:6	1 Th 2:10; 3:13; 5:23
Hb 7:19	Hb 12:28

and chains', and not yet 'wise'. It also links this passage forward to the paragraph in which Patrick describes himself as 'a fool'.

But if, characteristically, Patrick is deeply conscious of his own human powerlessness, he is correspondingly aware of his gifts of nature and of grace bestowed on him by God for his own divine purposes. Therefore the specific purpose of the quotation above (Qo 4:13-14) is to point a contrast to the immediately following clauses in which he says 'what he does know most certainly':

> but that 'I do *know* most surely', that indeed 'BEFORE I WAS HUMBLED' I was like 'a stone' lying 'in deep mire' (C 12:47-48)

Here he quotes 1 Samuel 24:20: 'Now I know that you shall most certainly be king'. Saul is speaking to David who will one day be the Lord's Anointed. In the next clause, by an easy association, Patrick quotes David's Psalm 119 (118): 67:

> *Before I was humbled* I went astray,
> but now I keep your word.

And in the next clause, Psalm 69 (68):14:

> rescue me from *sinking in the mire;*
> let me be delivered from my enemies and from the deep waters.

With the phrase, *'I was like a stone',* Patrick evokes 1 Peter 2:4-8:

> Come to Him, *a living stone,*
> though rejected by mortals
> yet chosen and precious in God's sight,
> and *like living stones, let yourself be built into*
> *a spiritual house,*
> to be a holy priesthood,
> to offer spiritual sacrifices
> acceptable to God through Jesus Christ....
> For those who do not believe *'The stone that the builders rejected*
> *has become the chief cornerstone'* (Ps 118 (117):22).
> *'A stone that makes them stumble and a rock that makes them fall'*
> They stumble because they disobey the word... (1 P 2:8)

Jn 8:43-44	Jn 4:10
Lk, Ac 22:3	Lk 24:19
Paragraph 2	**Paragraph 2'**
Qo 4:13-14	Qo 1:8
1 Th 3:9	1 Th 5:6
Ps 119 (118):67	Ps 119(118):112

In the passage immediately following:

> and he 'who is mighty' came
> and 'in his mercy' lifted me up [*sustulit me*];
> and, more than that, truly raised me aloft
> and placed me on the highest wall (C 12:49-52).

he quotes the *Magnificat* from Luke 1:49-54:

> for *the Mighty One has done great things for me*....
> *His mercy* is for those who fear him....
> He has brought down the powerful from their thrones,
> and *lifted up the lowly*;....
> He has helped his servant Israel, *in remembrance of his mercy*.

In the same passage the phrase *'and placed me'* comes from 1 Kings 2:24:

> Now therefore as the Lord lives, who has established me *and placed me* on the throne of my father David,

where Solomon, *the wise,* is speaking.

Through all this subtle biblical allusion the *powerless* Patrick is claiming his baptismal birthright as an adopted son of the heavenly Father; God had compassion on his helpless son who was 'like a stone' buried in the mud and filth of the human condition. Down into this *deep mire* came God's All Holy Son. With his wounded hands, he delved into that mire and searched until he found the helpless Patrick lying like a stone in its depths; then, placing those sacred hands carefully under him, he lifted him out from that mud and filth [*sustulit me*], raised him aloft, and placed him on top of the highest wall, as Patrick, the convert, the bishop and pilgrim-apostle of Ireland.[14]

PATRICK'S RETURN TO THE LORD, ECHOING PSALM 116 (114-115)

Now, having acknowledged and appropriated God's personal gifts to him, the chorus of praise and gratitude to God again wells up in his repentant heart and, finally, here at the crux, in the sentence, '*I truly would not have remained silent because of the return due* [from me to God]'. 'I' is complemented by the sentence, 'And therefore *I ought to cry out* aloud in order "*to make*" some *return to the Lord*.' Some of the hidden meaning may be elicited, as usual, when we examine Patrick's subtle use of Sacred Scripture in this context.

In the first passage he alludes to Psalm 119 (118):112: 'I incline my heart to perform your statutes forever to the end', and in the parallel passage he

---

14 Dronke, *SRP,* 37-38, for the analogue in *Pastor Hermes* (mid-second century) on which Patrick draws.

alludes to 1 Thessalonians 3:9: 'How can we *thank God* enough for you in return *for all the joy we feel before our God* because of you?' Psalm 116 (114-115): 12-14, is also evoked:

> What shall I *return* to the Lord
>   for all his bounty to me?
> I will lift up the cup of salvation
>   and call on the name of the Lord,
> I will pay my vows to the Lord
>   in the presence of all his people.

This burning desire of Patrick, the fool for Christ, to make a *retributio*, a return to God for all his bounty to him, is his overarching aim in writing his *Confessio*, and the *Apologia* is thus linked with the beginning, middle and end of that *Confessio* (C 3, 34, 57), which helps to give it its cohesion as a work of art.

Praise of the mercy, the beauty and the greatness of God, so characteristic of the early Church, was becoming blurred, even in Augustine's and Patrick's era; Augustine, for example, inveighs against confession of sin without praise. His reason for this is the example of Christ himself: 'I confess to Thee, Father' (Mt 11:25); 'the innocent Christ could not confess sin: the object of his confession was solely praise.' Besides, such will be the heavenly Confession; in heaven all lamentation for sin will be excluded but 'the eternal Confession of such great happiness' will not be wanting.[15]

3   PATRICK, THE LETTER OF CHRIST

In paragraph 3 we have reached the central part of Patrick's *Apologia* where he presents the climax of his argument, which he substantiates with long citations from Sacred Scripture. The words which frame the quotations are also biblical. He begins:

> And if by chance it may appear to some people that I am putting myself
>   forward in this,
> with my lack of knowledge and my 'rather slow tongue',
> but even so it is written
> 'Stammering tongues will quickly learn to speak peace'
>   (C 11:33-36).

The formula 'and if ... but' is from Paul, 2 Corinthians 5:16; 'even so ... it is written' is found in Matthew 4:6; 'how much more' in Matthew 6:30; 'and again' in Matthew 19:24. The quotations are carefully ordered. The words 'rather slow tongue' echo Exodus 4:10, the excuse offered by *the lawgiver,*

---

15 Ps 44:33, Solignac, quoted in *LCA*, 10-11.

Moses to God, 'I have never been eloquent ... I am slow of speech and slow of tongue.' That does not matter to God for as *the prophet, Isaiah* says (32:4), 'Stammering tongues will swiftly learn to speak peace' (C 11:36). The verses which follow immediately, and which Patrick does not quote but doubtless expects his audience to know, are:

> A fool will no longer be called noble,
> nor a villain said to be honorable
> For fools speak folly,
> And their minds plot iniquity...
> to practise ungodliness, to utter error
> concerning the Lord (Is 32:5-6a).

Patrick increases the tension with 'how much more':

> How much more ought we to seek [to speak], we who are, he affirms,
> 'A letter of Christ for salvation to the ends of the earth'.
> And though not an eloquent one, yet valid and very compelling,
> 'written in your hearts
> not with ink but by the Spirit of the living God' (C 11:37-41).

and then he makes a very bold alteration. At 2 Corinthians 3:2, *the apostle, Paul* wrote 'you yourselves are our letter', and at Acts 13:47 *the evangelist, Luke* wrote 'so that you may bring salvation to the ends of the earth', quoting the prophet Isaiah: 'that my salvation may reach to the end of the earth' (Is 49:6).

Patrick shows that he knows very well he has changed Paul's meaning by placing 'we who are' before 'he affirms'. His claim now is 'I am the letter of Christ' but by using the third person (he affirms), he attributes the claim to St Paul. He repeats Paul's words 'and if ... but' and returns to the quotation from 2 Corinthians 3:3: 'written in your hearts not with ink but by the Spirit of the living God'. 'The Spirit of the Living God', the supreme Gift of the Father and the Son (Ac 8:20) acting in him, and through him, and with him, is the *fons et origo*, the fountain and source, of the great 'Hallel Psalm' of Patrick's whole life, his missionary endeavour in pagan Ireland (C 33-34).

THE SPIRIT TESTIFIES: EVEN RUSTIC WORK WAS ORDAINED BY THE MOST HIGH
But Patrick is keenly aware that his mission to the pagan Irish was derided by a faction of the British Church on personal grounds, but also, possibly, because Ireland was outside the confines of the Empire and its inhabitants were considered to be only semi-civilised: 'For them it is a disgrace that we are Irish' (E 16:165). Patrick, who had a foot in both camps, now delivers his master-stroke in response to this unenlightened and unchristian attitude; if, up to his day, he seems to be saying, the Word of God has largely been preached in the

towns and cities of the Roman Empire, the time is ripe for bringing the Word of God to people living in rural areas even outside the Roman Empire:

> Et iterum Spiritus testatur
> 'et rusticationem ab Altissimo Creatam'.
> And again the Spirit testifies
> 'even rustic work was ordained by the Most High' (C 11:42-43).

This allusion to Sirach 7:15 has been regarded by some of Patrick's readers as being 'remote in its application' in this context, that, 'not without a certain pathos [Patrick] invokes it to justify his lack of sophistication'.[16] Even Bieler suggests that Patrick 'apparently mistakes *rusticatio*, living in the country, for *rusticitas*, rusticity or the manners of country people'.[17]

To this Howlett responds with: 'One should not assume that Patrick mistook anything. He has said already that *he, the letter of Christ, is still valid and very powerful. Patrick's concern is less with rustic style than with his life and work, hard work among a rural people* – far removed from walled Roman cities – his mission at the end of the earth in pagan, rural Ireland. Here he, *primus rusticus, the extreme rustic, the most remote countryman*, knows without a shadow of doubt what God in his mercy has done.'[18]

We have noted already that the crux of the whole *Confessio* is: *ecce dandus es tu ad gradum episcopatus*, Look, you are to be raised to the order of the episcopate (C 32:11). This is the statement which validates Patrick's ecclesiastical mission. Here at the crux of his *Apologia*: *Et rusticationem ab Altissimo creatam*, the implication may be that his mission to Irish pagans who are based in rural areas, and not in cities, is none the less, the gift of God, the work of the Holy Spirit (Jn 4:10; Ac 8:20). In taking on his opponents and citing Sirach at the crux of his *Apologia*, Patrick is possibly conscious of, and expects his readers to be aware of a whole constellation of quotations from and allusions to biblical Wisdom literature and the Lord's promise of the gift of wisdom in Luke: 21:12a, 13-15, 17-19:

> They will arrest you and persecute you;
> this will give you an opportunity to testify.
> So make up your minds
> not to prepare your defence in advance;
> for *I will give you words and a wisdom*
> *that none of your opponents will be able to withstand or contradict.*
> You will be hated by all because of my name.

---

16 Hanson, *LW*, 83.
17 Bieler, *LE*, 11, 129; Malaspina, 280-81, n. 75.
18 Howlett, *ESSM*, 99.

But not a hair of your head will perish.
By your endurance you will gain your soul,

Wisdom has to be *revealed*, he is telling his critics; one cannot attain wisdom through human study or discernment. Wisdom is God's gift. It empowers humans to acknowledge God's work in creation and especially in redemption (Ws 7:15-21; Rm 1:20). And he undoubtedly prayed Solomon's prayer for Wisdom (Ws 9:1-18), part of which is sung in the Psalter, Week 3, Saturday:

O God of my ancestors and Lord of mercy,
who have made all things by your word,...
give me the wisdom that sits by your throne,
and do not reject me from among your servants,
For *I am your slave,* the son of your serving girl,
a man who is weak and short-lived,
with little understanding of judgment and laws;
for even one who is perfect among human beings
will be regarded as nothing without the wisdom
that comes from you....
Send her forth from the holy heavens,
and from the throne of your glory send her,
that she may labour at my side,
and that I may learn what is pleasing to you.
(Ws 9:1, 4-6, 10).

Paraphrasing a passage from Wisdom, Paul asks rhetorically in Romans 11:34-36:

For who has known the mind of the Lord?
Or who has been his counsellor?
Or who has given a gift to him,
to receive a gift in return?
For from him, and through him and to him
are all things.
To him be the glory forever. Amen (cf. Ws 9:13).

All through his *Confessio*, but more specifically in his *Apologia*, Patrick is conscious that wisdom is sent down by God from above. And like Paul he identifies Christ with wisdom. Like wisdom, Christ has come down to us as gift. Patrick identifies his own mission with that of Christ who has revealed God to us, and whose mission is to restore all to God.[19]

---

19 Getty, *PAP*, 27-32.

Is Patrick also implying here that worldly standards of achievement are his critics' criteria for the sacred calling to the priesthood and the episcopacy? Are they meant to recall, at this juncture, that such standards, especially immersion in the classics to the detriment of Christian values found in Sacred Scripture and Tradition, were in Patrick's own day being repudiated by serious Christians scholars and churchmen everywhere? The same stance was taken by the great Benedictine Pope, Gregory the Great (590-604) as is evident from his oft-quoted sharp letter to Bishop Desiderius of Vienne.[20]

Let one example from one of Patrick's contemporaries, Paulinus of Nola, with whose writings he may have been familiar, suffice here; up to his Baptism, Paulinus of Nola (+430) had been 'an ambitious narrative poet and man of letters, a lover of the classics, with a delicate and genuine gift of poetry'.[21] His principal correspondent on literary matters was his old tutor and friend, Ausonius, the professor of Bordeaux. After his baptism the literary output of Paulinus gradually lessened and his correspondence makes it clear that the touching appeals of his old master, now over eighty years of age, could never succeed in winning him back to the beloved classical world of Bordeaux.

The letter in which Paulinus declares his intention to turn his back on the world of his own day, and simultaneously renounce the world of classical thought and classical tradition, is all the more impressive because of the love which it breathes for the beauty and value of all that the writer is giving up. The solemn farewell which the monk of Nola bids to the studies of his youth and the great world reveals alike the force of the new ascetic ideal, and the entralling influence of pagan culture.[22] The following is an extract from that much quoted letter, written in the form of a poem to Ausonius (emphases are mine):

> Why, my father, do you bid the Muses which I have disowned return
>   to my affection?
> *Hearts vowed to Christ are closed to the muses and cannot receive Apollo.*
> There was a time when I could join with you,
> not with the same gifts, but with like eagerness,
> in invoking the divine Muses, and deaf Phoebus in his cave at Delphi,
> and in calling upon groves and mountains to bestow
> the favour of eloquence, the gift of the gods.
> *Now another power impels my soul,*
> *a mightier God imposes new ideals upon me....*
> *He forbids me to fill my time with idle ploys,*
> *whether business or pleasure,*
> *or with the literature of myth and legend,*

---

20 Epist. X1, 54, Migne, *PL*, LXXV, 117 C.
21 Chadwick, *PLG*, 65.
22 Dill, in Chadwick, *PLG*, 66.

> *that I may obey his precepts*
> *and that I may have the vision of his light,*
> *which is obscured by the casuistries of the sophists,*
> *and the eloquence of the orators,*
> *and the vain imaginings of the seers,*
> *who fill our hearts with fictions and illusions....* [23]

The place of the liberal arts was recognised, not repudiated, however, though only as an instrument for the exact understanding of the Holy Word. Patrick, who, like Paulinus,[24] belonged to the territorial magnates' class, had sold his nobility for the benefit of others (E 10:85-9); he was:

> a slave in Christ for that remote pagan people
> because of the unspeakable glory 'of eternal life'
> in Christ Jesus our Lord. (E 10:90-92)
> I pray him to grant to me
> that with those sojourners and captives for his name's sake
> I may shed my blood.... (C 59:19-21)

PATRICK, THE SUBTLE AND SOPHISTICATED WRITER

Every word of Patrick's *Apologia* is in its correct place. This scriptural quotation (Si 7:6) forms the central line of this eighty-five-line passage, forty-three lines from the beginning and forty-three lines from the end. There are 2,724 letters, of which the central fall exactly at the centre of *et iterem Spiritus testatur*, and again the Spirit testifies.

Howlett demonstrates how each paragraph is carefully ordered so that what is most important in each section is emphasised in a subtle and sophisticated manner. We may therefore reasonably conclude that, though not a trained rhetorician, Patrick is showh by the perfection of this composition to be the intellectual peer of 'the lords, clever rhetoricians', while its Christian content and commitment might suggest that he is a spiritual giant by comparison, a Gulliver among the Lilliputians!

Howlett sums up his study by remarking that Patrick, while seeming to protest his ignorance, produces *clausulae* and *cursus* rhythms, and balances his words, ideas and biblical sources. By a discriminating use of scriptural quotation he seems to concede some praise to his critics while actually attacking them. There is evidence, more than once, in the *Apologia* that Patrick knows how to build towards a rhetorical climax. In the central paragraph 3 he applies to himself, simultaneously, the words of Moses, Isaiah, Paul, Luke and Sirach, claims as his own the authority of lawgiver, prophet, apostle and evangelist, and uses the unquoted context of his quotations to attack his critics.

---

23 Chadwick, ibid., *(Carmen X,* line 20ff) 66-7.
24 Migne, *PL,* LXXXIX, 355 A; Rand, *FMA,* 26.

If the stupendous claims Patrick makes for himself have gone largely unnoticed, that is because modern readers have paid more attention to what is said than to *what is meant*. The proof of what is meant lies partly in the utter consistency with which Patrick leaves the sting of his remarks in the context of what he cites.

Howlett, in his examination of the manuscript of the Lindisfarne Gospels (698), as well as the Books of Durrow, Kells and Armagh, suggests that the scribes' use of illuminated letters, coloured initials surrounded by dots, double initials and smaller initials, show signs of order, though the system is not quite perfect. He demonstrates, by the use of capitals and other devices, how close these ancient markings are to his own concentric division of the text of Mark 1:1-15.[25] If this is so, are we to conclude that in Ireland, up until about a hundred and fifty years ago during the Great Hunger (1845-51), when the manuscript tradition more or less died out, the scribes were conscious of this order of things? And, if indeed they were, then it goes a long way in explaining to us the perfection — allowing for minor scribal mistakes — with which they transmitted Patrick's *Confessio* to posterity. This they did because they were probably aware that here, not only is every word in its right position but, in places, as we have seen, the syllables, even the letters are in significant positions in this text! This ensured that no one could tamper with Patrick's text without the fraud being exposed. It would also seem that the concentric structure of the *Confessio* is the missing link in all the scholarly efforts in this field, made with such dedication and single-mindedness of purpose by Tarlach Ó Raifeartaigh and other scholars, as regards the positioning of the text.[26]

I am convinced that scholars will come to appreciate, sooner or later, that David Howlett has, in his rediscovery of the *Confessio's* inner concentric structure and biblical style, 'split the atom', as far as Patrician studies in this century are concerned, and that his contribution has superseded all that has preceded it.

---

25 Howlett, *ESSM*, 99-100.
26 *MTPC*, 67-71; Bieler, *LL*, 62.

CHAPTER TWO

PATRICK'S TESTIMONY
OF HIS SACRED CALLING

The Lord testifies, it is not you who speak
but the Spirit of your Father speaking in you (C 20:95- 6)

Patrick's testimony of his vocation in Part II of his *Confessio* opens with one of
the most familiar scenes from the whole of his life, that of the young
shepherd-slave at prayer 'in the woods and on the mountain' (C 16:8) during
the six demanding years of his first captivity:

> But after I had come to Ireland,
> I was herding flocks daily,
> and many times a day I WAS PRAYING (C 16:1-3).

CALLED BY THE SPIRIT
In this section of his *Confessio*, Patrick's primary concern is to testify
that the Holy Spirit is the source of his divine vocation to be the
Apostle of Ireland. He is, like Moses on Mount Nebo, an ageing, toil-
worn bishop taking a backward, contemplative look at the long and
perilous *tóchar* or pathway which he has trod, both as a slave and as a
rural missionary, in Ireland. Since he presents his reminiscences of that
journey in a contemporary literary form with which modern readers are
not very familiar, let us begin by looking at an outline of its concentric
pattern:

(16-18)	1	Arrival in Ireland. Dreams of return to Britain
(19)	2	twenty-eight-day journey and near-starvation
(19end)	3	God's Providence. Provision of food
(20)	4	Vision of Helias (Elijah)
(21-22)	3'	God's Providence. Provision of food
(22end)	2'	twenty-eight-day journey and near-starvation
(23-25)	1'	Arrival in Britain. Visions of return to Ireland

In paragraph 1, Patrick describes his sojourn in Ireland as a slave-
shepherd, as well as a pair of dreams he had there which indicated his
imminent escape to Britain. He tells us in paragraph 1' of his arrival in Britain
and his visions regarding his return to Ireland.

In paragraphs 2 and 2' he puts in perspective his arrival in Britain, his twenty-eight-day journey and near-starvation, as well as his second captivity many years later.

In paragraphs 3 and 3' he recounts God's Providence in supplying, it will be suggested, food, shelter and dry weather 'every day' on those two traumatic occasions. This section of the *Confessio* culminates in his seventh awesome dream, his vision of Helias (Elijah) in paragraph 4.

The story of Patrick's escape from the Wood of Fochoill in the north-west, which included his hazardous journey to find the ship, is paralleled with that of his encounter with the ship's crew, three hundred kilometres distant, in order to highlight, at the crux, *the divine source of that escape*. The two stories unfold in antiphonal form, rather like the interlocking spurs of some of the countryside which he traversed. Thematic and verbal correspondences between each pair of antiphons are again italicised as they build up to that crux.

> More and more the love *of God* and fear of him came to me (C16:4)
> – because of *the fear of God*,
> but rather I hoped to come by them to the faith of Jesus Christ
> because they were pagans,
> and thus *I* got my way with them,
> and *we set sail* at once (C 18:47-50).

'The faith of Jesus Christ' is what Patrick is longing to share with those 'pagans' ignorant of the true God. At the time of his capture, Patrick confessed that he did not know the true God, that he did not keep his commandments, and that he had ignored the ministry of his priests. Now, having been brought close to God by suffering, he is gaining *hokmâ*, a wise heart (Ps 89 (90):12), which is the gift of filial fear of the Lord. This is a reverential fear before the majesty and holiness of God, so poignantly present in the soul of Christ during the Agony of Gethsemane. There is a close affinity between this gift of filial fear and the first beatitude of poverty of spirit, which gradually renders Patrick increasingly docile to the influence of the Holy Spirit. 'Blessed are the poor in spirit', those who are utterly detached from everything, who desire no riches save the Trinity. This in turn is the root of Patrick's true humility which undergirds his whole *Confessio,* where he repeatedly acknowledges his defects and his lowliness, *humilitas mea*, while his constant gratitude to God for the gift of his Holy Spirit to him, *donum Dei*, is, as has been said already, the leitmotif running from end to end of his *Confessio*.

Patrick's increasing awareness of the Presence of God becomes more and more apparent in this part of his *Confessio*. In treating of his conversion we have already noted how forced solitude, hardship and the evident lack of all human hope had driven him to seek divine aid. His power was in his empty hands at this crucial time. Deprived, in one fell stroke, of all that was nearest and dearest to him, he gradually became aware of the action of the Holy Spirit working within him, leading him into a life of prayer and to appropriate Christian responses in the details of daily living. He eventually came to find such peace and strength in prayer that he rose before dawn to commune with God, and such was his fervour that he was in no way affected by the inclemency of the outdoor, winter weather:

> and my *faith* was being increased, and THE SPIRIT was being moved,
> so that in one day I would say as many as a hundred PRAYERS,
> and at night nearly the same,
> even while I was staying in woods and on the mountain;
> and before daybreak I was roused up to PRAYER
> in snow, in frost, in rain;
> and I felt no ill-effects from it,
> nor was there any sluggishness in me,
> as I see now, because the spirit was fervent in me then.
> And there one night in a dream (C 16:5-14)
> – 'Come, because we are receiving you *on faith*,
> make friends with us in whatever way you wish.,
> and on that day, accordingly, I refused 'to suck their breasts'
>   (C 18:43-45).

In this second pair of antiphons, Patrick's 'faith' in God, which 'was being increased', contrasts starkly with the pagan sailors' lack of faith in God. Their declaration of 'receiving' Patrick 'on faith' had no Christian connotations; it merely meant that they were prepared to accept his word as his bond. We shall return to consider Patrick's encounter with those sailors shortly.

The beginning of his spiritual life finds expression in 'the Spirit was being stirred up', and his progress is marked by 'the Spirit was being fervent in me then'. He gradually yielded himself to the promptings of this Spirit, in solitude, hard work, night vigils, fasting, and disregard for personal comfort. The gifts of the Spirit were then poured out on Patrick. Eventually, the Spirit glowed within him as he glowed in the Heart of Christ himself, the One who, according to the Scriptures, was incessantly 'led by the Spirit' (Mt 4:1).

Did his fellow shepherd-slaves begin to notice how changed he had become over the years? Did their questions give him an opportunity to share his Christian beliefs with them? Did they, being Irish, fit him with the telling sobriquet 'holy youth'? Did he make converts to the true faith among them? This youthful, Christian ministry to his peers seems almost certain.

But his faith was soon put to the test by the pagan sailors. Though he had the wherewithal to ship with them, the captain initially refused to take him on board the 'ship' which 'the voice' had indicated was 'ready' for him. Patrick, characteristically, began to pray and the Lord immediately intervened, for, suddenly, the captain changed his mind. Perhaps the sailors in the meantime had reminded him of the commercial usefulness of Patrick's trilingualism, and his ability to handle Irish wolfhounds. His courage, youth and intelligence were added considerations.

His assurance that he could pay his way may simply have meant that he had enough food in the form of apples and oatcakes – probably provided by his host who had given him the use of *a hut* – to supply his needs on the journey.[1]

Divine intervention and mystical experiences follow the classical pattern in Patrick's pilgrimage of faith to God, in that they are preceded and followed by trials in order to purify and strengthen that faith more and more. The arresting quality of the saint's Christian presence is already evident in this situation because, though he repudiated their pagan pact of friendship, the sucking of their breasts, they accepted him on his own Christian terms and the ship set sail at once (C 18:45-50).

1   Dreams concerning Patrick's return to Britain
This escape had already been suddenly and unexpectedly heralded by the first in a series of eight dreams, seven of which are concerned with this section of the *Confessio*. These 'dreams' seem to have taken three main forms: that of a locution, where 'a voice' is heard; 'a divine answer' to intercessory prayer, *responsum divinum*; 'a vision of the night', *visus noctis*, while in some instances the dream is a combination of both vision and locution.

In this first recorded dream Patrick seems to have been asleep, when 'a voice', or a locution, told him that he was soon to return to his own country. In the case of this first very important message the word *responsum* is not used, and Noel Dermot O'Donoghue suggests that there is probably a distinction to be made between 'locutions which come as an answer or response to prayer, and the sudden, unexpected and totally receptive experience described in this first dream'. This division between 'the divine monologue', or better, 'the other-world monologue', and 'the divine partnership in the dialogue of prayer', runs all through Patrick's accounts of his visionary experiences.[2]

> And there one night in a dream
> *I heard* a voice saying to me,
> 'It is well that you are fasting, soon *you will go* to your own country.'
> And again after a short time
> I heard the answer saying to me,

---

1   Ó Raifeartaigh, *EP,* 30.
2   O'Donoghue, *AS,* 12.

> 'Look, your ship is ready'
> And it *was not nearby,*
> but was at a distance of perhaps two hundred miles;
> and I had never been there,
> nor did I know anybody there;
> *and then later I took to flight,*
> *and I abandoned the person with whom I had stayed for six years,*
> *and I came in the power of God*
> *who was directing my way unto my good,*
> *and I was fearing nothing until I reached that ship* (C 17:15-28).

Aware that the supernatural quality of this dream is sometimes queried, it may be useful to focus for a moment on what the great doctor of mystical theology, St John of the Cross, has to say on the subject of the *other world monologue*. In his spiritual classic, *The Ascent of Mount Carmel*, he treats of various kinds of locutions.[3] Patrick's particular locution would seem to correspond to what the theologian designates as 'an interior, substantial locution because what the *voice* says impresses its significance substantially upon the soul' of Patrick. 'For example', he continues, 'if Our Lord should say formally to the soul: "Be good", it would immediately be substantially good; or if he should say: "Love me", it would at once have and experience within itself the substance of the love of God; or if he should say to a soul in great fear: "Do not fear", it would without delay feel ample fortitude and tranquillity.'[4]

He draws on biblical evidence to substantiate these statements: 'For as the Wise Man declares, God's word and utterance is full of power [Qo 8:4], and thus it produces substantially in the soul what is said. David meant this when he stated: "Behold he will give his voice the voice of power" (Ps 67:34). God did this to Abraham, for when he said: "Walk in my presence and be perfect" [Gn 17:1], Abraham immediately became perfect and always proceeded with reverence for God. We observe this power of God's Word in the Gospel; with a mere expression he healed the sick, and raised the dead.'[5]

John affirms the value and importance of these 'substantial locutions': 'In this fashion he bestows substantial locutions upon certain souls. These locutions are important and valuable because of the life, virtue, and incomparable blessings they impart to the soul. A locution of this sort does more good for a person than a whole lifetime of deeds.'[6]

The one who receives 'substantial locutions,' he attests, has no cause for fear: 'It [the soul] need not fear any deceit, because neither the intellect nor

---

3   St John of the Cross, *AMC*, 202-10.
4   Ibid., 210.
5   Ibid.
6   Ibid.

the devil can intervene in this communication. The devil is incapable of passively producing the substantial effect of his locution upon the soul, unless, as it may happen, the soul has surrendered itself to him by a voluntary pact.... In comparison with God's locutions and their effect, those of the devil and their effect are nothing. God affirms this through Jeremiah: "What has the chaff to do with the wheat? Are not my words perhaps like fire and the hammer that breaks rocks?" (Jr 23:28-29).'[7]

He discloses some of the spiritual advantages of 'substantial locutions': 'Consequently these substantial locutions are a great aid to union with God. And the more interior and substantial they are, the more advantageous they are for the soul. Happy the soul to whom God speaks these substantial words. Speak, Lord, for your servant is listening' (1 K 3:10).[8]

Having received what seems to be his first mystical grace, in the form of that 'other-world monologue' or 'substantial locution', it would seem from the context that Patrick, on awaking, recalled this first locution, and, consequently, prayed for enlightenment as to how he was to go about complying with its promise to reach his own country. The second *locution* or 'divine answer' followed 'after a short time':

> And again after a short time
> I heard the answer saying to me,
> 'Look, your ship is ready.' (C 17:17-19)

The scriptural context of '*the divine answer*', which he uses several times in relation to his eight dreams, is the dialogue between Elijah and God in prayer, cited by Paul in Romans 11:2-5:

> God has not rejected his people whom he foreknew.
> Do you not know what the scripture says of Elijah, how he pleads with
>   God against Israel?
> 'Lord, they have killed your prophets,
> they have demolished your altars;
> I alone am left,
> and they are seeking my life.'
> But what is *the divine reply* to him?
> 'I have kept for myself seven thousand who have not bowed the knee
>   to Baal.'
> So too at the present time there is a remnant, chosen by grace.

This subtle allusion to Elijah in prayer is noteworthy because of the importance Patrick gives to prayer in this section of the *Confessio*, apart

---

7   Ibid., 211.
8   Ibid.

altogether from the prominent role this prophet plays in his great *peirasmos* or test, *the vision of Elijah* (C 20), at the crux of this chapter. As he contemplates God's plan for him in his old age, and, in particular, his escape from slavery, he is undoubtedly conscious of, and expects us to notice, the many close parallels between the vicissitudes of his own life and of Elijah's, not least, this prophet's mysterious and meteoric movements from one end of the country to the other, under the inspiration of God's Holy Spirit.

The driving force behind all Elijah's movements, as well as Patrick's, is obedience to the Will of God. This presupposed an openness to the Voice of the Spirit in prayer, which eventually led them to the holy mountain of God:

> O send out your light and your truth;
> let them lead me; let them bring me to your holy hill
> and to your dwelling place (Ps 42(43):3).

Here, in these two *locutions*, then, we have Patrick at the foothills of mystical experience and he will climb this 'holy mountain'[9] – symbolised perhaps, by his seventh-century 'biographers' as Cruach Phádraig – right to the summit (C 29:9). It is from this vantage point that he will gaze, retrospectively, like Moses on Mount Nebo (Dt 34), over *Tóchar Phádraig*, or the perilous road he has travelled in his journey in faith (C 62). But as yet the development of his life's drama has only begun.

In his impressive analysis of 'St Patrick's Way to Sanctity' Fr Nivard Kinsella notes that: 'The indication of the port where the ship was waiting and his later success throughout the whole adventure, rule out the possibility of self-deception or imagination. One of the signs that such [locutions] come from God is the certainty they leave. The words sink into the soul, so that even years afterwards they are remembered with accuracy and exactitude. The certainty accompanying these locutions is such that they cannot be confused with ordinary dreams.' 'This certainty was definitely present in the case we are discussing', he continues, 'since it inspired Patrick to undertake a journey', which probably took him from the north-west of the country to the south or south-east, 'risking capture and even death in order to follow out its command.'[10] This certainty is now highlighted by Patrick in another miniature internal concentric passage. Here he responds to the captain's refusal to take him on board by turning with complete confidence to God in prayer:

> *I heard* a voice saying to me (C 17:15)
> – And when *I heard* these things I left them,
> in order to return to the little hut where I was staying,
> and on the way back I began TO PRAY (C 18:34-36)

9   Ibid., 66-7; Ex 14:20; 1 K 19:4-8; Mk 9:2-8.
10 Kinsella, *SPWS, IER*, 1961, 153.

Next we learn that Patrick was a guest (*hospitabam*) in 'a little hut', which suggests that the owner was possibly a Christian who made no distinction between slave and freeman, in accordance with the teaching of Christ, since traditional hospitality was not usually extended to runaway slaves under the pre-Christian dispensation in Ireland. We have already indicated that there were scattered Christian communities in the south and south-east before Patrick's time.

Ó Raifeartaigh suggests that there is not necessarily any contradiction between Patrick's spending a night in *a little hut* and finding, 'on that day that I arrived', a ship ready to sail, since in those days of the lunar calendar, the evening before was counted as part of the following day, just as, in our day, the vigil forms part of the liturgical festival. The Vigil of Easter is a case in point.

IT IS WELL THAT YOU ARE FASTING
This journey by land, which may have taken the best part of a week, was followed by a three-day journey by sea in the company of pagan traders and, according to some manuscripts, their cargo of hounds (*canes*).

> 'It is well that you are fasting, soon *you will go* to your own country'
>   (C 17:16).
> – 'By no means will you *try to go* with us' (C 18:33).

It is noteworthy, in passing, that the first *other-world monologue* that Patrick 'heard' was: 'It is well that you are fasting'. He has already told us how, prior to this first mystical experience, his 'faith was being increased, and the Spirit was being moved', so that he prayed almost constantly, day and night. He also tells us, when referring to this period, that he was 'really humiliated by hunger and nakedness, and that daily' (C 27:22-23). It would seem from the context then, that Patrick was 'led by the Spirit', for his own divine purposes, to accept this humiliation and to unite his enforced fast, as well as further deliberate curtailments of his meagre fare, with that of Christ's in the desert (Mt 4:1-11). If he was not aware, at the time of his captivity, of the strong, biblically-based tradition of fasting in the early Church, we may take it for granted that he was abundantly so by the time he came to write his *Confessio*.

The importance of authentic fasting in our lives is an integral part of Patrick's spiritual legacy to the Irish, and has been practised by all our great saints down through the ages. Though advantageous to health and general well-being, this kind of fasting was primarily focused on God, and was motivated by a desire for conversion of heart. This resulted in the opening up of the penitent's heart to the spiritual and temporal needs of the neighbour, and true fasting was thus linked with almsgiving and prayer:

> Is not this the fast that I choose:

> to loose the bonds of injustice, to undo the thongs of the yoke,
> to let the oppressed go free, and to break every yoke?
> Is it not to share your bread with the hungry, and bring the homeless
>   poor into your house;
> when you see the naked to cover him, and not to hide yourself from
>   your own kin?...
> Then you shall call and the Lord will answer; You shall cry for help,
>   and he will say, here I am (Is 58:6-7,9).

The prophet Daniel, with whose captivity in Babylon Patrick readily identified – 'in the land of my captivity' (C 3) – fasted in 'sackcloth and ashes' and 'made confession' of his personal sins 'and the sins of my people Israel', as he prayed to God to grant him 'wisdom' to understand 'a vision' he had already seen (Dn 9:1-23).

Then the *Didache*, an early manual outlining Christian belief and practice, recommended that Christians 'fast for those who persecute you'. The words of Jesus to his disciples were to *pray* for their persecutors. The wording of the *Didache*'s counsel, however, is an indication that the faithful were finding the exercise of Christian charity so difficult in the early Church, at a time of persecution, that Christian leaders became convinced that prayer had to be combined with *fasting* to bring about forgiveness and reconciliation (Mt 5:23; Mk 9:29). Moreover, the concern of the *Didache* with the question of fasting is regarded by scholars as 'further confirmation of how closely linked the early Church considered fasting and prayer'.[11]

In Patrick's case, authentic fasting and prayer won for him the grace to forgive his captors their grave injustice towards him, and opened his heart to receive God's graciousness. He must also have had ample opportunities to exercise the corporal and spiritual works of mercy and forgiveness among his pagan companions, which probably earned him the sobriquet 'holy boy'. This motif of *prayer and fasting* underpins this whole section of his *Confessio*.

I CAME IN THE POWER OF GOD

> 'It is well that you are fasting, soon *you will go* to your own country'
>   (C 17:16).
> – 'By no means will you try *to go* with us' (C 18:33).

When the captain had angrily refused to take him on board, Patrick began to pray on his way back to *the little hut*. Because he had become sensitive to the voice of God in prayer, he was equally sensitive to the Lord speaking to him through the circumstances of his daily life, which in this instance, was the initial refusal of the ship's crew to take him on board.

---

11 Neilsen, *FPA,* 10,

Here Patrick's faith is again being tested and strengthened because the *other world monologue* in the first antiphon seems to be contradicted in the second one. His holiness, after all, is to be measured more by the twelve fruits of the Spirit (Ga 5:22-25), and the living out of Christ's new commandment of love (Jn 13:12-17), than by his *visions and locutions*. Being a man of faith, his immediate response is to turn with complete trust to God in prayer about the problem, and he is not disappointed:

> And again after a short time (C 17:17)
> — *and before I had finished* MY PRAYER (C 18:37)

The third pair of antiphons emphasises that it is the depth of faith rather than the amount of time spent in prayer, that 'pierces the heart of God', to quote a dear and prayerful nun now long since gone home to God. To his astonishment, before he had time to settle down to serious prayer, the Lord intervened. We shall see, presently, how the equivalent of this statement links this part with its parallel, paragraph 1' (C 24:138; C 25:148), in order to emphasise the importance of prayer.

We have now reached the crux of this concentric passage where the 'divine answer' came to Patrick, this time through the lips of a pagan:

> I heard the answer saying to me (C 17:18),
> — *I heard one of them,*
> *shouting out vigorously after me,*
> 'Come quickly because these people are calling you.'
> And I returned immediately to them,
> and they began to say to me (C 18:38-42)

The sentence, 'I heard the answer saying to me', becomes concrete reality in the sentence, 'I heard one of them and he was shouting out vigorously behind me':

> 'Look, your ship is ready' (C 17:19)
> — *and I was fearing nothing until I reached that ship* (C 17:28).

His own words catch some of the stunned surprise, joy and challenge at this turn of events:

> and *it was not nearby*,
> but was at a distance of perhaps two hundred miles;
> and I had never been there,
> nor did I know anybody there (C 17:20-23)
> — and on that day on which I arrived the ship had set out from its
>   anchorage,

> and I said that I had *the wherewithal to take passage with them*;
> and the captain was not pleased,
> and he answered sharply with indignation (C 18:29-32),

These antiphons are linked by the cause of fear – that the ship was not near – and Patrick's lack of fear. *'There'* must have been some sea-port in the south or south-east coast, perhaps Waterford or Wexford, about three hundred kilometres away from the Wood of Fochoill in the north-west. Patrick was twenty-two, vigorous, healthy, inured to hardship. Without a moment's hesitation he took to his heels with complete trust in God:

> *and then later I took to flight* (C 17:24)
> – [God] *who was directing my way unto good* (C 17:27)

The *flight* is linked to the *route* in this case. A fugitive slave, he very likely chose zig-zag paths to avoid human haunts, for he was an illegal alien and had no rights under Irish law. But he was not alone:

> *and I abandoned the person with whom I had stayed for six years* (C 17:25),
> – *and I came in the power of God* (C 17:26)

Here, at the crux of the greater concentric passage, his escape is linked to 'the power of God', the source of his escape. Patrick, at the end of his six years' 'novitiate' in the school of prayer and fasting at Fochoill, was learning to rely completely on God and to be continually led by his Spirit, like Moses and Elijah, in the Old Testament, like Christ in the New.

1' Arrival in Britain. Visions concerning Patrick's return to Ireland

In this parallel paragraph (C 23-25), Patrick tells us of his arrival in his native Britain, of his two visions concerning his divine vocation to be Apostle of Ireland, and of the Holy Spirit praying within him.

PATRICK'S STORMY, THREE-DAY VOYAGE BACK TO BRITAIN

Patrick succeeded in being accepted on board the ship that carried him away on a three-day voyage from Ireland back to his native land. The essential importance of a three-day journey, in Professor Powell's view, lies in its conformity to a Pauline type in a general scheme of signs and revelations, and the 'ship' is stressed to identify Patrick's companions as a 'ship's company'.[12] Paul was involved in a shipwreck which he thought, initially, would be 'with danger and much heavy loss, not only of the cargo and the ship, but also of our lives' (Ac 27:10). He was later assured, however, by 'an angel of God' that 'God has granted safety to all those who are sailing with

---

12 Powell, *TI, AB,* 1969, 399.

you' (Ac 27:24-26), with the loss, however, of the ship and the cargo (Ac 27:41). Paul's ship initially set out for Italy but was forced by the storm to land in Malta.

The original destination of Patrick's shipmates was probably the Bristol Channel. We assume that they were deflected from their course, like Paul's crew members, by a storm, or even by pirates, and were obliged to make a forced landing on the west coast of Britain. In Roman times a ship could, with a fair wind, cover about 125 miles in twenty-four hours. Bieler remarks that the term Patrick uses for having made land, *terram cepimus* (C 19:51), carries a suggestion of effort.[13] Moreover, Patrick tells us elsewhere that he had only barely, *vix*, managed to escape from Ireland (C 61:7).

Unlike Paul, however, Patrick does not seem to have been involved in any shipwreck; what he did have was a ship and a ship's company, providentially saved, by his intercession, from death and starvation, with only a possible loss of part of the cargo of *canes*, possibly Irish wolfhounds (C 19:70). If this seems fanciful, it must be remembered that not only is the account in Acts a singularly striking piece of writing, it is also the only scriptural account of a voyage, apart from the Book of Jonah.

The significance of Patrick's three-day voyage in the context of Jonah's three-day sojourn in the belly of the fish (Jon 1:17), did not escape the notice of Muirchú, his seventh-century 'biographer'. In his distress Jonah began praying to the Lord his God from the belly of the fish saying:

> ... As my life was ebbing away, I remembered the Lord;
> and my prayer came to you, in your holy temple;
> Those who worship vain idols forsake their true loyalty.
> But I with the voice of *thanksgiving* will *sacrifice* to you;
> *what I have vowed I will pay*; deliverance belongs to the Lord! (Jon 2:7-9).

'Then the Lord spoke to the fish and it spewed Jonah out upon the dry land' (Jon 2:11). We conclude that, like Jonah, Patrick and the crew members reached land by divine intervention, in answer to his fervent prayer.

WITH MY PEOPLE WHO RECEIVED ME AS A SON
The warmth that existed between Patrick and his kith and kin glows like a welcoming turf fire in the hearth. 'After a few years' spent as a slave at Fochoill he was now back with his own people who received him 'as a son' and requested him, in view of all the great tribulations which he had endured, never again to depart from them (C 23).

'As a son' might suggest that Patrick's father and mother were then dead, or that, because of the disaster that had befallen them six years previously, they had moved to another part of the country. At any rate, if this was the

---

13 I1 (i), Bieler, *PTA*, 69.

case, he obviously had very close bonds with his extended family. This warmth, sensitivity and loving kindness stood him in good stead in all his apostolic endeavours in the years that lay ahead. More importantly, perhaps, 'as a son' also links this part of the *Confessio* backwards to his identification of himself as 'the son of Calpornius, the son of Potitus', and to his account of his conversion in the *Prologue*, where he assures us that God the Father 'consoled me as a father consoles a son' (C 1-2).

That he had remained faithful to the guidance of the Holy Spirit and thus increased the intensity of his spiritual life is evident from a number of mystical experiences which he now relates.

THE VOICE OF THE IRISH

His own native land was to be the privileged location of his unique missionary calling to be the apostle of pagan Ireland; there, 'in a vision of the night', he saw a man named Victoricius, coming as if from Ireland with countless letters, one of which he handed to Patrick. While reading the beginning of that letter containing the 'Voice of the Irish', he kept imagining hearing at that same moment the voice of those men who lived beside the Wood of Fochoill 'near the western Sea'. They were shouting 'as if from one mouth': 'We request you, holy boy, that you come and walk once more among us'. He was so overwhelmed that he could not continue reading. Thanks be to God, he adds, that after many years the Lord answered their request (C 23).

The scriptural context of 'I saw in a vision of the night' is Daniel's apocalyptic vision of the four beasts, which is a vision of the passing of pagan kingdoms to make way for the kingdom of God. God, 'the Ancient One', will then give the Messiah, the Word made Flesh, a universal and 'everlasting dominion':

> As I watched *in the night visions*,
> I saw one like a human being coming with the clouds of heaven.
> And he came to the Ancient One
> and was presented before him.
> To him was given dominion and glory and kingship,
> that all peoples, nations, and languages should serve him.
> His dominion is an everlasting dominion that shall not pass away,
> and his kingship is one that shall never be destroyed (Dn 7:13-14)

Whether or not Patrick was conscious of the nuanced connection between his vision of Victoricius and that of Daniel, at the time when all this first happened, is debatable. But by the time he came to write his *Confessio*, this great Confessor of the faith was in no doubt as to its implications and its message of hope, both for himself and for his children in the faith, and for all those who, through their ministry, would be brought into the kingdom of God.

There is also a very close affinity between Patrick's vision and call to Ireland and Paul's vision and call to go from Asia to the Macedonians in Europe. And Paul, being a Jewish rabbi before his conversion, undoubtedly recalled Daniel's vision with all its nuances of meaning on that occasion: 'During the night Paul had a vision: there stood a man of Macedonia pleading with him and saying, "Come over to Macedonia and help us" ' (Ac 16:9).

Since the vision came to Patrick 'at night', he was probably asleep at the time, so that what we have here is possibly another supernatural dream. On the other hand Patrick may have been in a state of profound recollection — *ar rinnfheitheamh*, waiting at the needlepoint of his whole being, as it were, for the divine action — when this vision occurred. In dealing with spiritual visions of this kind (those which exclude the bodily senses), John of the Cross distinguishes 'two kinds relating to the intellect: those of corporal substances, and those of separate or incorporeal substances'. 'The corporal visions', he writes, 'deal with the material things of heaven and earth. The soul, even while in the body, can see these objects by means of a certain supernatural light derived from God, which bestows the power of seeing all heavenly and earthly objects that are absent. We read of such a vision in Revelation 21:9-26, where John describes the excellence of the heavenly Jerusalem which he beheld as it descended from heaven'.[14]

Patrick's *vision* — like those of Daniel and Paul already cited — would seem to fall into this category of spiritual, corporeal visions since he saw a figure, Victoricius, as well as hearing '*the voice* of the Irish'. He seems to have been initially overwhelmed by this profound, spiritual experience of *vision* and *locution* combined, 'And "I was" truly "cut to the heart" and I could not read further' (C 23:128-9). It may be inferred, however, that, unlike Paul's immediate response (Ac 16:10-40), Patrick's response was deferred for many years:

> thanks be to God,
> that after very many years the Lord has given them
> according to their cry (C 23:131-3).

VICTORICIUS
Apart from his father, Calpornius, and his grandfather, Potitus, the letter-bearer of this dream, Victoricius, is the only other person whom Patrick mentions by name in the whole of the *Confessio*. Who was this individual? Was he the saintly Victricius, fervent disciple of Martin of Tours, and apostle of the rural poor of Normandy before becoming archbishop of Rouen and metropolitan of the British bishops?[15] Could Patrick have heard of his visit to

---

14 St John of the Cross, op.cit.,189.
15 Thomas, 1981, in Malaspina, *PAL*, 55.

Britain in the last decade of the fourth century, in response to letters of invitation from the British bishops, to resolve ecclesiastical disputes?

Could Patrick also have been aware of the efforts then made by Victricius to promote monasticism in Britain and to convince the Christian, aristocratic city-dwellers of their influence on, and their Christian obligations to spread the Gospel among the rural pagan poor?[16] Was the memory of this working subconsciously in Patrick's mind in his last few years in Ireland among the pagan poor? We can only surmise, but if Patrick had heard of Victricius – which in view of his close family ties with the institutional Church is likely – then he was left with the seed of an idea which would later bear a rich harvest.

Since we have no solid ground here to come to any firm conclusion, let us return to the intricacies of Patrick's text, that we may hear the Spirit speaking to us.

WE REQUEST YOU, HOLY BOY

Paragraph 1' (C 23-25) contains two closely interwoven concentric passages; the first highlights at its crux Patrick's divine call mediated through *Glór na nGael,* the Voice of the Irish; the second, Christ and the Holy Spirit praying within Patrick.

The request of his Christian family that he remain with them in Britain, and the request of the pagan Irish to come once more among them, are juxtaposed, and thus held in tension, in the first pair of antiphons in the first concentric passage:

> And once again, after a few years I was in the Britains
> with my people,
> who received me as a son,
> and in faith *besought me* (C 23:110-113)
> – *We request you*, holy boy, (C 23:126)

In the next pair of antiphons the memory of Patrick's 'many hardships' which he had endured during his period of slavery are recalled by his people in an effort to keep him in Britain, and balanced by Patrick against his experience of being 'truly cut to the heart' by the unique divine call to return to Ireland to convert the pagan Irish:

> *that* now, at least, after all the many hardships which I had endured,
> *I should not ever depart from them* (C 23:114-115)
> – *'that you come and walk once more among us.'*
> And 'I was' truly 'cut to the heart' (C 23:127-8)

---

16 Ibid., 67-69. Cf. p. 134 *infra.*

These two antiphons are linked by the mutually contradictory requests of his family and the Irish that 'I should not ever depart from them' and 'come and walk once more among us'.

I WAS TRULY CUT TO THE HEART
The biblical context of 'cut to the heart', and what decided Patrick's choice, is the response of the Jews and Gentiles to Peter's preaching in Jerusalem on the first Pentecost, and is an indication of what Patrick's call will involve:

> Now when they heard this, *they were cut to the heart*
> and said to Peter and the other apostles,
> 'Brothers, what should we do?'
> Peter said to them,
> 'Repent,
> and be baptized every one of you
> in the name of Jesus Christ so that your sins may be forgiven;
> and you will receive the gift of the Holy Spirit.
> For the promise is for you, for your children, and for all who are far
>   away,
> every one whom the Lord our God calls to him' (Ac 2:37-39).

In addition, Patrick, through the subtle arrangement of his text, is possibly alluding to the great archetypal figures of the Old and New Testament, men like Moses and Elijah, Christ himself, Peter and Paul, whose divine call brought *great hardships* in its train, but who were sustained in all their distress by the almighty hand of God; one example attributed to Moses from many in Sacred Scripture will suffice:

> From there you will seek the Lord your God, and you will find him
> if you will search after him with all your heart and soul.
> In your *distress* when all these things have happened to you
> in time to come, you will return to the Lord your God and heed him.
> Because the Lord your God is a merciful God,
> he will neither abandon you nor destroy you;
> he will not forget the covenant with your ancestors that he swore to
>   them (Dt 4:29-30).

Patrick has already told us in the *Apologia* how he too has been cared for by the Lord:

> *that* 'with awe and reverence'
> and 'without complaint' I would faithfully be of service to *that pagan people*
> to whom 'the love of Christ' *translated me* [*transtulit me*] (C 13:66-8)

> — *And I was not* worthy nor *such* [a person]
> *that* the Lord should concede this to his little servant,
> that after troubles and such great difficulties,
> after captivity,
> after many years among *that pagan people*,
> that *he should grant me* such great grace,
> which at any time *in* my *youth, I never hoped for nor thought about.*
>   (C 15:79-85).

COME AND WALK AMONG US

The contradictory requests are sustained in the following antiphons, thus creating a tension and a contrast between his people's request to him not to *leave*, and his vision of Victoricius, bearer of the request of the pagan Irish to *come* and walk further among them.

> *I should not ever depart from them.*
> And there indeed 'I saw in a vision of the night' a man coming as if
>   from Ireland,
> whose name [was] Victoricius,
> with countless letters,
> and he gave me one of them (C 23:115-119),
> — '*that you come and walk once more among us*' (C 23:127).

This tension between the domestic demands of family and friends and the demands of Patrick's sacred ministry is sustained throughout his *Confessio* until it climaxes in his declaration that, as bishop, he is 'bound by the Spirit' never to leave Ireland again because of the demands of his mission (C 43:93). This pain of total exile for Christ blossomed into the *glasmartra* or 'green martyrdom' of Patrick's children in the faith, who, as missionaries, deliberately left Ireland forever, from the sixth century down to comparatively recent times.

The next pair of antiphons is linked by the words 'I read' and the sentence 'I could not read further', while they sandwich the crux of this miniature concentric passage, which is 'the Voice of the Irish':

> *and I read the beginning of the letter containing the 'Voice of the Irish'*
>   (C 23:120)
> — *and I could read no further* (C 23:129)

We have now reached the thematic crux of this whole section: the unanimous voice of the men beside the Wood of Fochoill is synonymous with *Glór na nGael* calling Patrick back to evangelise pagan Ireland:

and as I was reading the beginning of the letter aloud
I imagined I heard, at that moment, the voice of those very people
    who lived beside the Wood of Fochoill,
which is near the Western Sea,
and thus they cried out 'as if from one mouth' (C 23:121-125)

No one can come to Me unless the Father draw him (Jn 6:44)
This missionary dream, in which Patrick 'was truly "cut to the heart" ', evokes
his own life's story up to then (C 1-2). The great trial of his captivity, which
stripped him of every human prop, and whereby he became conscious of his
'lowliness', was the occasion of his great awakening to the reality of his
spiritual patrimony as a child of God:

> ... 'before I was humbled'
> I was like a stone lying in 'deep mire',
> and he 'who is mighty' came
> and 'in his mercy' lifted me up;
> and, more than that, truly raised me aloft
> and placed me on the highest wall (C 12:47-52).

Now he is being made aware, through 'the Voice of the Irish' — which is, in
reality, the Spirit of the Father speaking through Victoricius — that the love
and mercy which God the Father had shown towards him, as an individual,
he is now showing towards this pagan race by calling them to conversion.
God's eternal plan for the pagan Irish, and Patrick's role in that divine plan,
are beginning to unfold: he is being called by the Father to be the apostle of
Ireland (cf. Jn 6:44). Now, as an old bishop writing his *Confessio,* he thanks
God that this mission is being fulfilled.

Patrick experiences Christ praying within him
We are next introduced to what would seem to be one of Patrick's early
ecstatic experiences:

> *And thus I have learned by experience* [*et sic expertus sum*],
> thanks be to God,
> that after very many years the Lord has given them
> according to their cry.
> And on another night, 'I do not know, God knows',
> whether within me or beside me (C 23-24:130-135),
> — *And thus I have learned by experience* [*et sic expertus sum*],
> and recalled to mind, as the apostle says,
> 'the spirit helps the weaknesses of our prayer
> for we do not know what to pray for as we ought,

but the spirit himself intercedes for us with unspeakable groanings' (C 25:149-153).

The sentence 'And thus I have learned by experience' forms the linkage between this pair of antiphons, in which the two mystical experiences of the prayer of Christ and the prayer of the Spirit in Patrick are introduced. In this way, Patrick 'retains the very primitive christology where the risen Christ and the Spirit are almost identified. This is the theology preserved also in two high crosses where we see a dove descending on the head of the corpse of Jesus in the tomb. It was the Spirit who anointed Jesus, that made him the Christ, and raised him from the dead, and it is this Spirit and this Christ who dwell within us.'[17]

But this sentence also links these two antiphons backwards to the parallel passage, *'we request you, holy boy'* (C 23:126), the divine call to mission mediated through Victoricius. The words of that dream, as well as the earlier dreams regarding his escape, have been proven in fulfilment, 'and thus I have learned by experience'. And Patrick, in his retrospective appraisal of God's hand in the details of his life and mission, attributes the fulfilment to the Lord: 'Thanks be to God, that after many years the Lord has given them according to their cry'. Thus, this significant sentence fuses this triad of mystical experiences – the prayer of the Father through the Voice of the Irish, the prayer of Christ, and the prayer of the Spirit of the Father and the Son – into intrinsic unity. Though they are separate in their time sequence, they mingle like the waters of three sister-rivers to form one great river of prayer at their confluence.

The scriptural context of 'I do not know, God knows' is 2 Corinthians 12:2-4, where St Paul is speaking of *ecstasy,* which in Sacred Scripture is often referred to as *sleep*:

> I know a person in Christ...
> who was caught up to the third heaven
> – whether in the body
> or out of the body *I do not know*;
> *God knows* –
> was caught up into Paradise
> and heard things that are not to be told,
> that no mortal is permitted to repeat.

Since there is a marked resemblance between Paul's and Patrick's interior locutions it seems likely that, in this instance, Patrick was in fact awakened from an ecstatic state of prayer. In this mystical experience he is brought beyond what he knows:

---

17 de Bháldraithe, *Hallel,* v.19, 1994, no.2, 1980.

in most learned words I heard those whom
I could not understand (C 24:136-37).
— '[things] which cannot be expressed in words.'
And again: 'the Lord our advocate intercedes for us' (C 25:154-55).

THE SPIRIT HELPS US IN OUR WEAKNESS

This second pair of antiphons is held in tension by the phrases 'in most learned words' and 'things which cannot be expressed in words'. The scriptural context of the latter phrase is Paul's letter to the Romans, where he claims that human weakness is sustained by the Spirit's intercession and by the knowledge of God's loving purpose (Rm 8:26-30):

> Likewise the Spirit helps us in our weakness;
> for we do not know how to pray as we ought,
> but that very Spirit intercedes *with sighs too deep for words.*
> And God who searches the heart
> knows what is in the mind of the Spirit,
> because the Spirit intercedes for the saints according to the mind of
>   God (Rm 8:26 -27).

St Paul's claim is further authenticated in the second scriptural quotation from St John, 'My little children, I am writing these things to you so that you may not sin. But if anyone does sin *we have an advocate with the Father, Jesus Christ the righteous'* (1 Jn 2:1).

The Irish called again, indubitably, but this time in words which he could not understand. However, the truth of Paul's statement is corroborated because 'the words were very likely impressed directly on his understanding', Nivard Kinsella suggests, 'since even though he did not understand them, he recognised at once their import'.[18]

> *except that at the end of* THE PRAYER *one spoke out thus* (C 24:138).
> *— but at the end of the* PRAYER *he declared that he was the* SPIRIT
>   (C 25:148).

The phrase 'at the end of the prayer', links this third set of antiphons which affirms that the Spirit is speaking in Patrick.

We have already noted how prayer and fasting undergird this whole section of the *Confessio*. (The captain refuses to take him on board.... Patrick, undaunted, begins to pray.... God intervenes in his favour 'and before I could finish my prayer' (C 18:37), the captain changes his mind and Patrick eventually reaches Britain.) At this point he has already had two mystical experiences in which the Lord has asked him to return to convert his captors.

---

18 Kinsella, *SSPC, IER,* 1959,163.

In the first of these he 'was truly cut to the heart' by the action of the Holy Spirit, like those who were gathered in Jerusalem on the first Pentecost. In the second he experienced Christ himself praying within him. He has not been able to understand what the Irish were saying during this particular time of mystical prayer, 'except that at the very end of the prayer one [of them] spoke out thus':

> 'He who has laid down his own life for you
> he it is who is speaking in you';
> and I was thus awakened rejoicing greatly.
> [et sic expergefactus sum gaudibundus] (C 24:139-41).
> — who he might be who WAS PRAYING in me (C 25:147).

The immediate effect of this experience was that Patrick woke up full of the Spirit of Joy, the sure sign of the Presence of God, that same Spirit who pervades and illuminates his entire *Confessio*.

He has just been overwhelmed by the *vision* of Victoricius and 'the Voice of the Irish' calling him back as a missionary to 'the land of my captivity'. Now he hears the Voice of Christ himself unmistakably calling him to this unique mission, the primary focus of which was to be pagans outside the confines of the Roman Empire, assuring him that he would be with him, that his Spirit would speak through him, as he assured the disciples at the Last Supper (Jn 14:25; 15:26-27) and after the Resurrection (Mt 28:19-20). This 'experience of Christ praying in him', this complete openness to his indwelling Spirit at work in him as a member of the Mystical Body of Christ, is the foundation on which his whole spiritual life is built and the cause of his complete trust in the Lord in all that pertains to himself and to his divine mission.

PATRICK'S VISION OF THE HOLY SPIRIT PRAYING WITHIN HIM
We have now reached the crux of one of the most mysterious experiences in the whole history of hagiography: Patrick's vision of the Holy Spirit praying within him. This time he is at prayer and suddenly becomes conscious of another praying within him. He writes:

> And again I saw him PRAYING within myself
> and I was, as it were inside my body,
> and I heard [him] over me, this is [to say], 'over the interior person',
> and there HE WAS PRAYING earnestly with groans,
> and amidst these things 'I was astonished and I kept wondering and thinking' (C 25:142-46).

Here Patrick was drawn into the centre of his being and from that vantage point he saw his own 'interior man' over whom someone else was praying, whom Patrick both *heard* and *saw*, as if inside his own body, without leaving his own body. He was astonished and wondered and thought with himself who it could be that prayed in him. Howlett notes how 'the layers of seeing and relating are wonderfully presented, Patrick seeing within himself the Spirit who is overseeing his interior man, the Spirit both praying over the interior man and informing Patrick who He is, so that he may relay this to us without'.[19]

St John of the Cross would probably classify this third vision as being a supernatural, spiritual, *incorporeal vision*, as opposed to Patrick's inner, corporeal vision of Victoricius. 'The visions of incorporeal substances', the mystical theologian tells us, 'cannot be seen by means of the light derived from God, but by another higher light, the light of glory.... If God should desire the soul to see these substances essentially (as they are in themselves), it would immediately depart from the body and be loosed from this mortal life.'[20] He substantiates this statement with examples from Sacred Scripture: 'God, when asked to show His essence, proclaimed to Moses, *No man will see Me and be able to remain alive* [Ex 33:20]. When the children of Israel thought they were going to see God, or that they had seen him or some angel, they were afraid of dying. We read of this in Exodus where they fearfully exclaimed: *May God not openly communicate himself to us, lest we die* [Ex 20:19]. In the Book of Judges we read too that Manoah, Samson's father, thinking that he and his wife had seen in its essence the angel that had appeared to them as a most handsome man, declared to his wife: *We shall die because we have seen the Lord* [Jg 13:22]'.[21]

These 'incorporeal visions' only occur in rare cases and 'in a transient way', John of the Cross continues. 'In such an instance, through a dispensation of the natural law, God preserves the nature and life of the individual, abstracts the spirit entirely, and by His own power supplies the natural functions of the soul toward the body.'[22] The saint then recounts three such visions drawn from Sacred Scripture. He points out that Paul (2 Co 12:2,4) 'was transported above the ways of natural life through the intervention of God'. Also, when God, as is believed, revealed his essence to Moses, he declared that he would place Moses in the cleft of the rock and protect him from death at the passing of the divine glory by covering him with his right hand. This 'passing' indicates both God's transient manifestation of himself and the concomitant preservation, with his right hand, of the natural life of Moses (Ex 33:220).[23]

19 Howlett, *BLSPB*, 114.
20 St John of the Cross, op.cit., 189, 2.
21 Ibid., 189.
22 Ibid., 189-190.
23 Ibid., 190.

Finally, the saint affirms that 'Such substantial visions as those of St Paul, Moses, and Elijah (when he covered his face at the whistling of the gentle breeze of God [3 K 19:13]), even though transitory, occur rarely or hardly ever, and to only a few. For God imparts this kind of vision only to those who are very strong in the spirit of the Church and God's law, as were these three.'[24]

In the light of this great theologian's insight, it seems fitting that the early Irish Christians consistently compared Patrick to Paul and Moses. In our own day Eoin Mac Néill has said of him that 'No one man has ever left so strong and permanent an impression of his personality on a people, with the single and eminent exception of Moses'.[25] Is it any exaggeration to suggest then, in passing, that Patrick, the lawgiver, prophet, evangelist and apostle (cf. C 11:34-41) is worthy of being ranked among the Fathers and Doctors of the Church?

I HAVE LEARNED BY EXPERIENCE
Though the saint longed to bring the Irish pagans whom he encountered – the pagan sailors are a case in point (C 18:45-48) – to the feet of Christ, it did not occur to him that he would be the one chosen by God for such a work (C 15:79-85); hence he may have tended to discount this first vision. God, therefore, followed it by a second mystical experience which more or less confirmed the first and in which Patrick also unmistakably heard the voice of Christ. This in turn was followed by Patrick's experience of the Spirit praying within him, which was all he required as complete confirmation of the two earlier visions.[26]

Patrick had now come into intimate relationship with each of the Three Persons of The Blessed Trinity in an experiential way – 'I have learned by experience' – beyond the capacity of words to express adequately. I can think of no more fitting commentary than Paul's address to the Corinthians, which I apply to Patrick at this point on his spiritual pilgrimage: 'That no eye has seen, nor ear heard, nor the heart of man conceived, what God has prepared for those who love him' – these things God has revealed to Patrick through the Spirit ... no one comprehends what is truly God's except the Spirit of God. Now Patrick has received ... the Spirit that is from God, so that he might understand the gifts bestowed on him by God. And he speaks of these things in words not taught by human wisdom, but taught by the Spirit, interpreting spiritual things to those who are spiritual ... He has the mind of Christ (1 Co 2:9-16).

---

24 Ibid., 190.
25 Shaw, *RSP*, 3.
26 Kinsella, op. cit., 1959, 165.

2 Twenty-eight-day journey and near-starvation

We now come to consider Patrick's twenty-eight-day trek with his companions on their arrival in Britain, and their near-starvation, in paragraph 2:

> And after three days we reached land,
> and for twenty-eight days we travelled through deserted country
>   (C 19:51-2).

Having cast anchor, they began their journey through a land devastated by civil war and famine in the wake of the Roman withdrawal. Their original aim was, possibly, to sell their cargo of Irish wolfhounds to the wealthy villa owners of the Severn valley. Their provisions soon dwindled and, eventually, they were faced with the stark reality of imminent death from starvation. This awful prospect inspired the pagan captain 'on the next day', that is, on the twenty-ninth day, to challenge Patrick, the Christian. Obviously, Patrick had already been sharing the Good News of Salvation with these pagans. Their conversation is cast in the form of a concentric passage with its antiphons alternating like interlocking spurs in their desolate surroundings:

> *And food failed them* (C 19:53)
> – *'so that today he may send food to you* until you have sufficient
>   on your way' (C 19:64)

Though there were no human grounds for hope, Patrick assured his companions that God had abundant supplies everywhere. Having already 'learned by experience' in prayer and inner visions, Patrick's trust in God is unbounded and he urges the captain to turn with complete confidence to the true God:

> and *'hunger overcame them'* (C 19:54).
> – *'because for him there was abundance everywhere'* (C 19:65)

> And on the next day the captain began to say to me,
> 'How is this, Christian?
> *You say your God is great and all-powerful?*
> Why then can you not PRAY for us?' (C 19:55-8)
> – But *I said* to them with confidence, (C 19:61)
> 'Be converted 'in faith' with all your' heart to the Lord *my God* (C 19:62)
> – *because nothing is impossible to him'* (C 19:65)

These three pairs of antiphons are held in tension by the contrasting words and phrases, *hunger* and *abundance*, *you* and *I*, *say* and *said*, *your God* and *my God*, *is great and all-powerful*, and by the sentence: *because nothing is impossible to him*, around the crux:

> because we are in danger of starving,
> that it is indeed doubtful if we will ever see a human being again
>   (C 19:59-60)

2' Twenty-eight-day journey and near-starvation

In paragraph 2' Patrick recapitulates the long journey and intimates how his prayer for food was answered on their twenty-ninth night on British soil (C 19:51-55, 67-69; 22:109). In the event of coming into contact with people, they were always assured of food because of traditional hospitality:

> As I have indicated above,
> we travelled through deserted country *'for eight and twenty days'*,
> and on the [29th] night on which we encountered people *we had indeed no food left* (C 22:107-109).

These are the only places in the *Confessio* in which Patrick uses the phrase about the twenty-eight-day journey, thus linking paragraphs 2 and 2'.

It seems implicit that, though food appears to have been very scarce indeed, as many of 'their hounds had "fainted away" and were left behind "half-alive by the wayside" ' (C 19:71-72), God had supplied Patrick and his companions with 'food' and, possibly, 'fire' and dryness *'every day'*, as happened during his second captivity (C 22:104-105), up to and including the twenty-eighth day.

3   God's providence. Provision of food

Patrick then tells us, in paragraph 3, how, on the twenty-ninth night, a herd of domestic pigs *(porci)* appeared on the road before their eyes (C 19:67), which meant that human habitation was not far distant. The pigs were possibly being driven to a wood nearby to feed on mast, fallen from oak or beech, and, as Ó Raiftearaigh suggests, 'the owner of the pigs may well have felt discretion to be the better part of valour in face of a band of starving strangers!'[27] 'People *(daoine, homines)*', in this context, are of course understood to be ordinary citizens, whether Christian or pagan. They were not brigands. They were possibly the owners of the pigs and the swineherds; the latter could not, on their own, dispose of their master's property with impunity. The barter of pigs for hounds was, of course, a practical option on this occasion.

This paragraph exhibits an internal concentric passage in which the story of the pigs and that of the sailors' find of wild honey and their sacrifice of it to their pagan gods, are related in alternating antiphons:

> and with the help of God it so came to pass. (C 19:66)

---

27 Ó Raifeartaigh, op. cit., 31.

> *— Thanks be to God,*
> I tasted none of it. (C 19:79-80)

Here Patrick is thanking God both for the provision of food and for the grace of not being party to pagan worship, by refusing to taste the wild or forest honey which the sailors had offered in sacrifice to their pagan deities. In Leviticus 2:11b-12, moreover, it is stated that honey was not acceptable as a sacrifice to the true God:

> You must not turn any leaven or *honey* into smoke as an offering by fire to the Lord.
> You may bring them to the Lord as an offering of choice products,
> but they shall not be offered on the altar for a pleasing odour.

This is Patrick's second and significant denial of pagan practices; his first was when he refused to enter into the sailors' pagan pact of friendship before boarding their ship. The provision of food in the form of pork and wild honey, as well as the pagan sacrifice, are related in the following two sets of antiphons: without delay they killed many of the pigs:

> Look, *a herd of pigs appeared on the road before our eyes* (C 19:67),
> *— they even found* 'wild honey' (C 19:76),
>
> *and they killed many of them* (C 19:68),
> — and *'offered a part to me'*,
> and one of them said, '*It is a* [pagan] *sacrifice*' (C 19:77-8).
>
> and there *they remained for two nights and were well fed*,
> and their hounds received their fill,[28]
> because many of them had 'fainted away',
> and were left behind 'half-alive by the wayside' (C 19:69-72),
> — and from that day they had food in abundance (C 19:75);

By quoting Luke 10:30 in this context, Patrick is possibly evoking the plight of the traveller who fell among robbers on his journey from Jerusalem to Jerico, and of God's fatherly care for him in the person of an outcast and despised Samaritan. Like this traveller, Patrick's companions may have been partially robbed of their food supply by hungry wayfarers during their journey through this barren part of the country; and now the God of surprises provided for both animals and humans by sending people, *homines* (C22:109), and a flock of pigs their way on the road.

---

28 *canes* (hounds) according to some MSS.

The crux of this paragraph is:

> *and after this they rendered the highest thanks to God,*
> *and I became honourable in their eyes* (C 19:73-74)

Patrick's miraculous provision of food, and his refusal to be party to their pagan practices, had been a moment of grace for those pagans. They now united with him in an act of gratitude to the true God, and he became a hero in their eyes.

Patrick's terrifying vision of Helias, which we shall consider shortly, followed that very night on the heels of his exaltation by the pagan sailors.

3' Patrick's second captivity. God's Providence. Provision of food

In paragraph 3' Patrick tells us of his second captivity which took place many years later, possibly when he was a missionary in Ireland. This account is closely linked to his escape from Ireland back to Britain and, like its parallel paragraph, is concentric in structure:

> And again many years later I WAS CAPTURED.
> And *on that first* night I stayed with them
> I heard moreover *'a divine answer'* saying to me (C 21:97-99)
> – until, *on the tenth day,* we encountered people (C 22:106)

Again, because of traditional hospitality, their worries were over as soon as they encountered other people.

> 'For *two months* you will be with them' (C 21:100)
> – *On the sixtieth night thereafter*
> 'the Lord delivered me out of their hands'.
> He even provided us on the journey with food
> and fire and dry weather every day (C 21-22:102-105),

The phrases *'for two months'* and *'on the sixtieth night'*, indicate the divine promise, and the fulfilment of that promise. Meantime, the Creator provided for all their needs of warmth, food and dry weather *every day* as he had provided the Israelites with manna (Ex 16:13-27), and Elijah with food and drink (1 K 19:4-8) in the desert.

The scriptural context of 'the Lord freed me from their hands' (Gn 37:21) is the conspiracy of the eleven jealous sons of Israel to kill their brother, Joseph, the shepherd and dreamer (Gn 37:21-22):

> But when Reuben heard it, *he delivered him out of their hands*, saying, 'Let us not take his life.'

> Reuben said to them, 'Shed no blood; throw him into this pit here in
>   the wilderness,
> but lay no hand on him',
> *that he might rescue him out of their hands* and restore him to his father.

Joseph's deliverance from the pit by foreign traders, his subsequent sojourn
in Egypt, his eventual reconciliation with his brothers, reunion with his father
and return to his own country, are then recounted. During all these
vicissitudes, temptations and sufferings, 'the Lord was with Joseph ... and
caused all that he did to prosper in his hands' (Gn 39:2-3). By this subtle
allusion, Patrick may be identifying his own plight with that of Joseph's. Are
we to infer, then, that Patrick's shipmates were planning to enslave or even
kill him before he made good his escape? It seems possible.

The principal point he wishes to emphasise, however, is that the same Lord
who was with Joseph was also with him in his joys and adversities, and provided
for him daily, until he too was eventually reunited with his family, in the first
instance, and escaped from captivity in the second, and caused his mission to
prosper.

The crux of this internal concentric passage, '*Quod "ita factum est"* ', *which
was what came to pass* (C 21:101; cf. Gn 1:7, 11, 24, 30), reiterates these
statements. '*Et adiuvante Deo "ita factum est"*, ' *And with the help of God 'it so
came to pass'* (C 19:66), links Patrick's safe escape from Ireland back to
Britain, in paragraph 3, to his second captivity here in 3'. His intention here
is to underscore God's miraculous provision of food, and his later deliverance
by the Lord out of the hands of his captors on both occasions.

In their scriptural contexts these two antiphons evoke God's creation and
his provision of food for his people in Genesis (cf. Gn 1:7, 11, 24, 30).
During these two distressing occasions the Lord has made the same provision
every day (C 22:105) for Patrick and his companions.

MANNA AND 'THE FOOD OF ANGELS' IN THE DESERT

This journey through a deserted countryside suggests the powerfully evocative
Exodus of Moses and the Jews from Egypt, their forty years in the desert, the
manna in the desert and the Covenant on Mount Sinai (Ex 14:20). It recalls
the despair of Elijah who, on his forty days' journey to Mount Horeb, was
strengthened by 'the food of angels' (1 K 19:4-8). Christ's forty days' fast in
the wilderness, to where 'He was led up by the Spirit ... to be tempted by the
devil' (Mt 4:1-11), is also evoked. All these biblical events are full of
significance for Patrick.

ON THE SIXTIETH NIGHT THE LORD FREED ME FROM THEIR HANDS

The time element in these two episodes is noteworthy. In the first instance
the journey by land took twenty-eight days (C 19:51-55); they met people on

the twenty-ninth night (C 19:51-55; 22:109); they spent the twenty-ninth and thirtieth nights in this wasteland (C 19:69). As they had reached land after a three-day period, they had possibly spent only two nights at sea. This adds up to thirty-two nights in all since they had left Ireland. Let us allow twenty-eight days and nights for the return journey to their ship, during which time they may have purchased such goods as wine, oil and salt, commodities which were unavailable in Ireland. Thirty-two and twenty-eight add up to sixty nights. Is Patrick telling us, in his usual subtle and elegant way, that on the sixtieth night he made good his escape from the sailors, as he was to do many years later at the end of his second captivity (C 21:97-103), thus forging another link between those two episodes? Again, it seems a distinct possibility.

4 The vision of Helias (Elijah)

But as Patrick was still only a novice in the spiritual life, the danger of vainglory due to this miracle may have been lurking in the background. Or perhaps the whole trauma of the past six years up to this point had suddenly come to a head.... At all events, on that very night, at this 'wasteland', of his 'first miracle', Patrick endured his great *pierasmos* or test (C 20). He now experienced, for the first time, the full brunt of his human weakness and his total dependence on God.

In his recounting of this great test, Patrick takes us to the crux of this whole chapter, the purpose of which, as we have already said, is to testify that he has been called to his mission by the Holy Spirit. He has chosen to highlight this crux artistically in three ways. He has first arranged three dreams before this seventh and most important dream, in this section of the *Confessio*, and three visions after it:

1   It is well that you are fasting, soon you will go to your own country
2   Your ship is ready....
3   For two months you will be with them....
4   Vision of Helias (Elijah)
3'   Prayer of the Spirit
2'   Prayer of Jesus Christ
1'   *Victoricius* – The Voice of the Irish

Those before the crux are the two divine messages about his immediate return to his own country (C.17:i, ii) and the divine message which said: 'For two months will you be with them' (C 21:100). The three that follow concern the voice of the Irish, or *Glór na nGael,* calling him back to pagan Ireland, the reiteration of this call and his personal encounter with Christ praying within him, together with his vision of the Spirit praying within him (C 23-25).

He next places his seven *references to the Holy Spirit* in such a way that there are also three before the crux (C 16; 25:i-ii) and three after it (C 20; 24:i-ii). Finally, we recall that he has also disposed his thirteen references to prayer before and after and in this crux, in exactly the same proportions.

The saint begins his account of this spiritual experience by telling us how, on the night following the miraculous provision of food for the starving sailors, he was asleep:

> *Now on the same night, when I was sleeping* (C 20:81),
> – as he affirms in the Gospel, '*On that day*',
> the Lord testifies: *It is not you who 'speak*
> *but the* SPIRIT *of your Father speaking in you'* (C 20:94-96).

For Patrick 'it was night' (Jn 13:30), 'and the power of darkness' (Lk 22:53), the night when the Lord allowed him to be tried by the Evil One, as he allowed his Son to be tempted in the desert. But when Patrick has been 'sifted like wheat' (Lk 22:31), he too, like Peter, will strengthen his brothers (Lk 22:32).

The scriptural context of the second antiphon is the instruction Jesus gave to the twelve apostles before sending them out to *proclaim the good news: 'The kingdom of heaven has come near'* (Mt 10:7):

> See, I am sending you out like sheep in the midst of wolves....
> Beware of them for they will hand you over to councils
> and flog you in their synagogues;
> and you will be dragged before governors and kings before me, as a
>   testimony to them and the Gentiles.
> When they hand you over
> *do not worry about how you are to speak or what you are to say;*
> *for what you are to say will be given you at the time;*
> *for it is not you who speak but the Spirit of your Father speaking through you....*
> and you will be hated by all because of my name.
> But the one who endures to the end will be saved....
> A disciple is not above the teacher, nor the slave above the master....
> If they have called the master of the house Beelzebub,
> how much more will they malign those of his household
> (Mt 10:7,16a,17-20, 22, 24, 25b).

Though Patrick had endured great physical and emotional trauma up to now, he had also experienced 'the consolations of God' when he was first converted; he had been given the gift of prayer; the Spirit was fervent in him then; he had been, moreover, blessed with divine interventions in his difficulties, as well as visions, locutions and divine answers, interspersed with trials to strengthen his faith and to encourage and prepare him to follow his divine call to be the apostle of Ireland. The Jesus he had come to know was, by and large, a personal, trustworthy friend, a Jesus of comfort and consolations, representing God's fatherly care for him as an individual, assuaging his adolescent anxieties, seeing to it that he eventually reached home safely after many exciting, if traumatic adventures, with the performance of a miracle for good measure. He had, as it were, come through the first spring, summer and autumn of the spiritual life. But he must now endure the winter before he can experience a second spring.

The hour has come when, as a mature man, he must take on the responsibility of a divine mission to others. He has been called and graced to teach and minister to his flock in the name of Jesus Christ. In order to be prepared adequately for this mission, he has first to come to know the Jesus who was concerned for others – the Jesus who confronted social and political corruption, exposed injustice, sat at table with tax gatherers and sinners, disturbed 'the peace' of power and privilege, and paid for it with his life – and willingly accept the consequences of that encounter, daily.

By placing those two antiphons side by side in this biblical context, Patrick is affirming that he came to realise that the spiritual experience of this night opened his heart to the reality and implications of his divine call, of his absolute dependence on God's indwelling Spirit to overcome the powers of darkness, withstand opposition, and spread the Good News of salvation. He must fix his eyes on his crucified Master, that he may gradually come to be identified with him:

> *Satan vigorously put me to the test,*
> in a way I shall remember 'as long as I shall be in this body'
>   (C 20:82-83).
> *– and I believe that I was sustained by Christ my Lord,*
> *and that his SPIRIT was even then crying out on my behalf,*
> and I trust that it will be so 'on the day of' my 'pressing need' (C
>   20:91-93).

When he was asleep, Satan tried him vigorously. The experience has in its onset a nightmare quality. Indeed, what is described is the archetypal nightmare of oppression, suffocation and annihilating power.[29] Patrick had no doubt but that this annihilating power was Satan who had come to him as a temptation or test, 'which I shall remember as long as I shall be in this body'. O'Donoghue affirms that for Patrick, 'as for the writers of the New Testament, as well as for Christian consciousness up to Patrick's time and long after, indeed until comparatively modern times, Satan was seen as a mighty annihilating or destroying force whose naked presence was utterly

---

29 O'Donoghue, op. cit., 13.
30 Ibid., 13.

terrifying to the human spirit. This contact brought a kind of living annihilation that was named the *peirasmos* or test; by comparison with this, all other human ills including poverty, imprisonment, death and even torture, however terrible and fearful, were challenges to faith and trust in God. But the "test" brought the total undoing or lived annihilation, the total absence of God and all the messengers of goodness and mercy.'[30]

Paul's kindred experience, recounted in 2 Corinthians 12, comes immediately to mind. Significantly, the context of Paul's affliction is that, fourteen years previously, he 'was caught up into Paradise and heard things that are not to be told, that no mortal is permitted to repeat' (2 Co 12:4). Patrick, too, had had similar mystical experiences, of which this dark one is, significantly, for him as for Paul, pivotal. The latter, conscious of the dark danger of pride and self-glorification, continues:

> Therefore, to keep me from being too elated,
> a thorn was given to me in the flesh, a messenger of Satan to torment me.
> Three times I appealed to the Lord about this, that it would leave me,
> but he said to me, 'My grace is sufficient for you,
> for my power is made perfect in weakness.'
> So I will boast all the more gladly of my weaknesses,
> so that the power of Christ may dwell in me.
> Therefore I am content with weaknesses,
> insults,
> hardships,
> persecutions
> and calamities for the sake of Christ;
> for whenever I am weak, then I am strong (2 Co 12:7b-10).

As I have already suggested, the *Confessio* is a retrospective appraisal of Patrick's whole life, seen from the last *ula* or halting stone on his life's pilgrimage; consequently, when he speaks of 'the day of my pressing need' here, Patrick may have specifically in mind the day of his rejection and betrayal, when he would have fallen into the sin of despair had not the Lord come mightily to his help in his affliction (C 26:3-8). This part of the *Confessio* is thus linked artistically with the central section and crux of the whole *Confessio*.

There is a terrifying poignancy about Patrick's attempt to convey his utter powerlessness in his horrific encounter with the Evil One, before Christ snatched him from his control:

> *and he fell upon me like a huge rock,*
> *and I had no power over my limbs* (C 20:84-85).
> *— and immediately freed me of all oppressiveness* (C 20:90)

This vision is the centre of a convergence of texts from both the Old and New Testaments, in which the prophet Elijah has a leading role. In his old age, as he writes, Patrick was still full of wonder at how he was so fittingly inspired on that momentous occasion to call on Elijah, the herald of Christ, the man all-powerful in his prayer, the one who opens the pathway along which Christ comes (Jm 5:17; Lk 1:17):

> But whence did it occur to my ignorant spirit to call upon *Elijah?*
> (C 20:86)
> *– and while I was shouting 'Elijah, Elijah'* with all my might (C 20:88)

And, as he, the man of prayer, was shouting *'Elijah! Elijah'* with all his might, the Risen, glorified Christ came to rescue him:

> And meanwhile I *saw the sun rise into the heavens,* (C 20:87)
> *– lo, the splendour of his sun [helios] fell on me* (C 20:89)

These antiphons around the crux are linked together by 'I saw the sun rise into the heavens' and 'the splendour of his sun [*helios*] fell on me'. This was obviously an intense religious experience, the exact nature of which is uncertain. The aura of unnatural brilliance is associated with mystical experience in several parts of Sacred Scripture, as, for example, in the accounts of the Transfiguration in the Synoptic Gospels (Mt 17; Mk 9; Lk 9) and in Exodus 34:29-35 and Acts 9:3.

THE SUN OF RIGHTEOUSNESS SHALL RISE

We are reminded in this vision of Christ, 'the true sun' of the *Doxology* (C 60:37), which we have already considered. Patrick seems to have Malachi 4:2-6 specifically in mind at this point:

> But for you who revere my name *the sun of righteousness shall rise,*
> *with healing in its wings....*
> you shall tread down the wicked for they will be ashes under the soles
>   of your feet,
> on the day when I act, says the Lord of hosts....
> Lo, *I will send you the prophet Elijah* before the great and terrible day of
>   the Lord comes.
> He will turn the hearts of parents to their children
> and the hearts of children to their parents
> so that I will not come and strike the land with a ban of utter
>   destruction.

---

31 Conneely, quoted in *TLSP*, 125-6.

Bieler points out that a certain fusion of *Helias* (vocative, *Helia*) and *helios* was common in Christian art and literature in Patrick's time, and he continues: 'The sun that dispelled Patrick's nightmare was, of course, understood by him as ... the Messianic *Sol Justitiae* (Ml 4:2). Here again we have the very interesting parallelism of a Christian tradition conceiving of Christ, the Creator of the sun, as the Sun of our Salvation, *Sol Salutis*, opposed to the pagan and Imperial sun-god, *Sol Invictus*.'[31]

THE TRANSFIGURATION ON MOUNT TABOR
Christ in his glory and the invocation of Elijah recall the Transfiguration of Christ on Mount Tabor, recounted in three of the four Gospels. Christ climbed this mountain with three of his disciples, Peter, James and John, to be alone with them in prayer. When they reached the summit he was transfigured before them. His garments became dazzling white such as no one on earth could bleach them:

> And there appeared to them Elijah with Moses,
> who were talking to Jesus....
> Then a cloud overshadowed them,
> and from the cloud there came a voice,
> 'This is my Son, the Beloved; listen to Him!'
> Suddenly, when they looked around, they saw no one
> with them any more, but only Jesus (Mk 9:2-8).

The Transfiguration is not only the revelation of Christ's glory but also a preparation for facing Christ's Cross. The Law and the Prophets, represented by Moses and Elijah, were now fulfilled in the Person of Jesus Christ; John the Baptist, the 'second Elijah', had come 'clothed with camel's hair, and had a leather belt around his waist' just like Elijah (2 K 1:8; Mk 1:6). Therefore:

> the time is fulfilled, and the kingdom of God has come near;
> repent and believe in the good news (Mk 1:15)
> And just as Moses lifted up the serpent in the wilderness,
> so must the Son of man be lifted up,
> that whoever believes in him may have eternal life (Jn 3:14-15).

MY GOD, MY GOD, WHY HAVE YOU FORSAKEN ME?
Matthew brings all these events to their climax in his account of the Crucifixion scene (Mt 27:45-51), which is powerfully evoked in this paragraph:

> From noon on until three in the afternoon darkness came over the whole
> land.

and about three o'clock Jesus cried out with a loud voice,
'Eli, Eli, lama sabachthani?'
that is, 'my God, my God, why have you forsaken me?' (Ps 22(21):1).
When some of the bystanders heard it, they said,
'This man is calling for Elijah....
Wait, let us see whether Elijah will come to save him.'
Then Jesus cried out again with a loud voice and breathed his last.
At that moment the curtain of the temple was torn in two
from top to bottom,
the earth shook
and the rocks were split.

Patrick's vision involves word-play on *Helias*, 'Elijah', *Eli*, 'my God' and *helios* 'sun',[32] and it seems to be implied that Patrick had a real experience here of the dark desolation of Christ on the Cross when he cried out: 'My God, my God, why have you forsaken me?'

Did the Son of Man, as he writhed in agony on the Cross, experience this *peirasmos*, this terror of living annihilation, of being cut off for ever from the One in whom we live, and move, and have our being? The anguished cry of him who is like us in all things except sin, suggests that it was so. Patrick, who would seem to have shared this anguish of Christ on the Cross, now experienced the power and glory of his Resurrection.

Prepare the way of the Lord
The terror of this great *peirasmos* on his steep, upward climb towards a true knowledge of the 'true God' (C 1) remained vividly with Patrick in his old age, perhaps over fifty years after the event. Here he learned experientially the reality of his own powerlessness, but also the power of the Spirit, the Source and Fount of all holiness, *Tobar na naofachta go léir*, as it is so richly and beautifully expressed in the Irish language.[33]

The parallel between Elijah's experience of the gentle breeze, and his own experience of the rising sun, in his night of tribulation, must have struck Patrick very forcibly. He would bring people to the feet of Christ, not by spectacular miracles like that of Elijah's on Mount Carmel (I K 18:20-40), or his own more modest provision of pork for his ship's crew, but rather by the gentle, persuasive example of a profound union with God in prayer, and a sincere and modest effort at authentic Christian living. He must have been aware, too, of the significance of the link between Elijah and John the Baptist (Mk 1:6), the great model for all who, like Patrick himself, are called to prepare the way for the One who will baptize with the Holy Spirit (Mk 1:8).

---

32 Howlett, op. cit., 105.
33 Eucharistic Prayer 2.

As he prayed the great *Benedictus* canticle, which was to become so dear to the hearts of the Irish people, he undoubtedly visualised the Baptist's father, Zechariah, holding his newly-born son in his arms, foretelling how the child would prepare a way for the Lord, 'the Dawn from on high', who will forgive the sins of the people:

> By the tender mercy of our God,
> *the dawn from on high has broken upon us*
> to give light to those who sit in darkness
> and in the shadow of death,
> to guide our feet into the way of peace (Lk 1:78-79).

Here, it would seem, Patrick was being brought to realise that he had to be prepared to suffer and to die with Christ in his capacity as Apostle of pagan Ireland in order to bring the light of the Resurrection 'to those who sit in darkness and in the shadow of death' (Lk 1:79).

His initial experience of conversion during his first captivity was intensified and immeasurably deepened in this second experience of conversion, where he became more closely identified with the crucified Christ in the school of suffering:

> 'Oh, how foolish you are and how slow of heart to believe all that the
>   prophets have declared!
> Was it not necessary that the Christ should suffer these things and then
>   enter into his glory?'
> Then beginning with Moses and all the prophets,
> he interpreted to them the things about himself in all the scriptures
>   (Lk 24:25-27).

'Was it not necessary that the *Christ* should suffer these things and then enter his glory?' Was it not necessary that *Patrick* should also suffer these things? This is the quality of faith in the crucified Christ and in the Triune God that sustained Patrick in all the trials and tribulations which his response to his divine call to mission as Apostle of pagan Ireland entailed (C 14:71-78).

By the careful ordering of his text, Patrick, once again, highlights the nerve centre of his thesis, his magnificent act of living faith in his divine call by the Holy Spirit, the Spirit of Jesus, to the evangelisation of the Irish pagan nation. Thus the 155 lines of Part II divide by extreme mean and ratio at 96 and 59. The last line of the crucial paragraph 4 is line 96:

> [The Lord testifies, it is not you who speak]
> *'but the SPIRIT of your Father is speaking through you'* (C 20:96).[34]

The same verb, *testatur*, introduces the central quotation of the *Apologia*, where Patrick defends his mission among the rural-dwelling pagan Irish:

> again the SPIRIT testifies [testatur]
> 'even rustic work was ordained by the Most High' (C 11:42-43).

---

34 Howlett, op.cit., 106.

CHAPTER THREE

PATRICK'S TESTIMONY OF HIS MISSION TO THE IRISH

There [in Ireland] I wish 'to wait hopefully for the promise' of him
who assuredly never deceives (C 38-39:14-18).
God knows *I greatly desired it [i. to visit friends in Britain and Gaul]*;
But 'I am bound by the Spirit',
who 'protests' to me that if I do this,
he will pronounce me guilty;
and I am afraid of losing the labour which I have begun,
and not I,
but Christ the Lord
who has commanded me
to come to stay with them for the rest of my life,
'if the Lord wills it',
and he will keep watch over me 'from every evil way',
so that I do not 'sin in his sight' (C 43:93-103).

In Part IV of his *Confessio*, the testimony of his mission to pagan Ireland, Patrick outlines the five main features of his missionary endeavour: apostolic missionary journeys; proclamation of the Good News through the medium of the Irish language, and the consequent 'baptism' of Irish culture; administration of the sacraments of Baptism, Confirmation, and celebration of the Eucharist (cf. C 49:169); ordinations to the priesthood; and the affirmation, if not the initiation, of the order of consecrated virgins and of proto-monasticism (C 41-2:49).

This section of the *Confessio* gives symmetrical balance and fullness of meaning to the testimony of his vocation in Part II. It revolves around the saint's total commitment to his mission in Ireland:

(37end-53)	G'	Testimony of his mission to the Irish
(37)	1	There [in Ireland] I desire to spend it [my life] up to the point of death (quoting 2 Co 12:15)
(37end)	2	If the Lord should concede to me. Echo of Romans 1:14
(38)	3	What God has given to Patrick
(38-40)	4	Baptisms, ordinations and confirmations in remote places
(41-42)	5	Monks and virgins of Christ
(43)	6	Influence of the Holy Spirit
(44-45)	7	Total commitment to the Irish mission
(46)	6'	Influence of the Holy Spirit

(47-49)	5'	Christian brethren and virgins of Christ
(49end-51)	4'	Baptisms, ordinations, and confirmation in remote places
(52-53)	3'	What Patrick has given
(53)	2'	Echo of Romans 15:24
(53end)	1'	That I may spend myself for your souls (echoing 2 Co 12:15)

1, 1' That I may spend myself

Nerney has already cogently argued the close parallel between Paul and Patrick in the way each of them presents his defence or testimony of the execution of his mission in the face of a similar set of accusations.[1] Because of the power of the Lord's indwelling Spirit, Patrick has already resisted all those who tried to impede his mission. Now, echoing his great exemplar, St Paul (2 Co 12:15), in both antiphons, he tells us that it is there in Ireland that he wishes to spend his life until he dies if the Lord would grant it to him:

> And there [in Ireland] 'I choose to spend' it [my life] 'until I die' (C 37:1)
> – that 'I may spend' myself 'for your souls' (C 53:218)

2, 2' If it is the Lord's will

He acknowledges his continuing dependence on the power of the Lord, and his complete and unwavering trust in the Lord to complete that mission:

> If the Lord should grant [that] to me (C 38:2)
> – The Lord is mighty to grant me afterwards (C 53:217)

3   God's gifts to Patrick

He characteristically acknowledges God's gifts to him, echoing Romans 1:14:

> BECAUSE 'I AM' VERY MUCH GOD'S 'DEBTOR',
> WHO HAS GRANTED TO ME SUCH GREAT GRACE (C 38:3-4),
> – I do not regret it
> nor is it enough for me
> that 'I still spend and shall spend more' (C 53:214-6).

3'   What Patrick has given back to God

Since Patrick was a refugee, *profuga* (C 12:45; E 1:4), without protection from the Brehon Laws even as a missionary – because he did not belong to any native Irish *tuath* or petty kingdom – he reveals that he, in turn, was a bestower of gifts. In order to gain access to their territories and their people, he was obliged to pay the kings sums of money. He tells us how he was also

---

1 Nerney, *SPS, IER,* 1949, 499ff.

compelled to pay the kings' sons (C 52:196-8). One explanation for this expenditure may be that those young men accompanied him and his fellow missionaries, in order to give them safe conduct through their territories. In the event of their sons becoming priests or monks, Patrick had, in all likelihood, to give generous compensation to their royal fathers as well.

But this was no guarantee of immunity from harm for, in spite of the fees, the kings laid hands on Patrick and his companions and on that day they eagerly wished to kill him, but his time had not yet come. They robbed them of all their possessions and put Patrick in irons. But on the fourteenth day the Lord delivered him from their power, and the missionaries' belongings were returned to them because of God and the intervention of their dear friends (C 52:199-206).

Patrick reminds his accusers about the amount he has paid to those who administer justice in all those districts to which he has come frequently. He thinks he has distributed among them not less than the price of fifteen men (C 53:207-212). It can scarcely be considered a coincidence, in this context, that in the Book of Judges, fifteen men are said to have judged Israel. The implication here may be that Patrick redeemed his own captive clergy, laity and slaves from pagan masters or captors. He tells us in his *Epistola* how the Church in fifth-century Gaul did as much for Christians captured by the pagan Franks and other nations (E 14:129-132). Echoing Romans 15:24, he affirms that the intention behind all this expenditure was the welfare of his converts:

> so that 'you might enjoy' me,
> and that 'I might' always 'enjoy you' in God (C 53:212-13).

In addition, he probably had to expend extra sums for the services of the indigenous learned classes. Once they had been converted they helped him and his companions to translate the Word of God into the Irish language, to become *au fait* with the laws and traditions of the land, and to devise ways, means and methods of providing a Christian form of the native system of education for the clergy, the laity and the emerging proto-monastics.

Provision had also to be made for churches, hospices for the sick and indigent, and modest educational establishments. We know from contemporary records that the great Gaulish, fifth-century bishops were engaged in similar ventures on the Continent in the wake of barbarian destruction.[2] Archaeological findings, both in Ireland on and the Continent, have revealed, moreover, that many Christian churches were built on former pagan sites of worship — the cathedral of Chartres is a case in point. It seems reasonable, therefore, to speculate that those sites were originally yielded up for Christian worship by the Christianised druids and learned classes who

---

2 Chadwick, *PLG*, 112-133. For *aosdána*, cf. Bergin, *IBP*, 3-22.

owned extensive lands. But Patrick's expenditure does not cause him any regret, nor is it enough for him that he spends and will overspend further (C 53:214-16) to accomplish his mission.

Should it surprise us that this new method of tackling an unfamiliar culture, much of which was unnecessary and unheard of within the confines of the Roman Empire, alarmed Patrick's friends and supplied grist to the mill of his enemies?

4   Baptisms, ordinations and confirmations in remote places

Patrick's actual missionary labours in remote rural areas in Ireland are emphasised by means of an internal concentric passage. He considers himself to be greatly indebted to the Lord for being instrumental in the rebirth of so many people to God in the waters of Baptism, and that they are afterwards brought to the highest perfection by confirmation in the faith:

> that *a multitude* through me *should be reborn* to God
> and afterwards be confirmed [in the faith] (C 38:5-6),
> – and exhort a needy and desiring *people* (C 40:30),
>
> that *a multitude* through me *should be reborn* to God (C 38:5)
> – and everywhere there should be *clergy to baptize* (C 40:29)

'Should be reborn' and 'to baptize' refer to the sacrament of Christian initiation and divine adoption, so dear to Patrick's heart that he mentions it fourteen times in his writings (C 14:78; 40:29, 34, 40; 42:66; 50:178; 51:190; E 3:24; 7:55; 14:131; 16:63; 17:174; 19:193; 21:218).

Being a contemporary of St Leo the Great (440-461), it is at least possible that he was conversant with that great Pope's famous sermon on the Nativity (Sermon 1 Nativ, 1-3), which is now familiar to so many people because it forms part of the Office of Readings for Christmas Day. Let me quote an extract from it here, which always evokes for me a few of the main characteristics of Patrick's legacy to us, especially in the Penal era, as it found expression in the poetry of Tadhg Gaelach Ó Súilleabháin (1715-95). These elements are conversion, ongoing repentance, praise and gratitude to the Triune God, consciousness of the Indwelling Trinity and of being members of the Mystical Body (*Pobal Dé*), a profound appreciation of the sacrament of divine adoption and devotion to the Passion of Christ: 'My beloved, let us offer thanksgiving to God the Father, through his Son, in the Holy Spirit. In the great mercy with which he loved us, he had pity on us, and "in giving life to Christ, he gave life to us too, when we were dead through sin", so that in him we might be a new creation, a new work of his hands.... O Christian, be aware of your nobility – it is God's own nature that you share; do not then, by an ignoble life, fall back into your former baseness. Think of the Head, think of the Body of which you are a member.

Recall that you have been rescued from the power of darkness, and have been transferred to the light of God, the kingdom of God. Through the sacrament of baptism you have been made a temple of the Holy Spirit; do not by evil deeds, drive so great an Indweller away from you, submitting yourself once more to the slavery of the devil. For you were bought at the price of Christ's blood.'

Patrick now continues by expanding this missionary theme while drawing profusely on related quotations from Sacred Scripture:

> as the Lord affirms in the Gospel,
> He admonishes and teaches, saying,
> 'Go therefore and teach all pagans now,
> baptizing them in the name of the Father and the Son and the Holy Spirit,
> teaching them to observe everything that I have commanded you;
> and behold, I am with you all days,
> to the end of time.'
> And again he says, 'Go therefore into the entire world,
> and proclaim the Gospel to every creature.
> The one who believes and is baptized will be saved,
> but the one who does not believe will be condemned.'
> And again, 'Proclaim this Gospel of the Kingdom throughout the
>   whole world,
> as testimony to all pagans,
> and then the end will come.'
> And similarly the Lord announces beforehand through the prophet, he
>   affirms,
> 'And in the last days it will be, the Lord declares,
> that I will pour out from my Spirit over all flesh,
> and your sons and your daughters will prophesy,
> and your youths will see visions,
> and your elders shall dream dreams;
> and assuredly over my slaves
> and over my handmaids in those days,
> I will pour out from my Spirit and they will prophesy.'
> And in Hosea he says, 'Those who were not "my people"
> I will call "my people",'
> and 'her who has not obtained mercy as her who has obtained mercy',
> and in the very place where it was said to them, "you [are] not my people",
> there they will be called children of the living God' (C 40:31-57).

One of his greatest concerns, however, is the selection, training and ordination of clergy:

> and that *clergy* everywhere should be ordained for them (C 38:7)
> – and everywhere there should be *clergy to baptize* (C 40:29)

for these new converts:

> for a people *coming* recently *to belief* (C 38:8)
> — just as we believe that *believers will come* from all parts of the world
> For that reason, therefore, it is indeed our duty to fish well and
>   diligently (C 39-40:21-22)

whom God has chosen at the ends of the earth:

> whom *the Lord* has 'taken up from the ends of the earth' (C 38:9)
> — as *the Lord* admonishes in advance and teaches, saying,
> 'Come after me and I will make you fishers of people' (C 40:23-4)

These conversions had been foretold by the prophets:

> just as he had, in times past, *promised through his prophets* (C 38:10)
> — and again he says through the prophets (C 40:25).

He quotes the prophet Jeremiah (16:19 and 16:16):

> 'To you will the pagans come from the ends of the earth, and say:
> "Our ancestors established idols as worthless things,
> and there is no benefit in them"';
> And again: 'I have placed you as a light for the pagans,
> so that you may bring salvation to the ends of the earth' (C 38:11-15)
> — 'Look, I am sending fishers and many hunters, says God', and so forth.
> Whence, moreover, it was especially fitting to spread our nets,
> so that 'a copious multitude and throng' should be taken for God
>   (C 40:26-8)

And there, at the ends of the then known world, Patrick wishes to live out his *glasmartra* (green martyrdom) in reverse, serving his people in joyful hope for the sake of the kingdom, as he says emphatically at the crux of this concentric pattern:

> and there I wish 'to wait in hope for the promise' of him,
> Who assuredly never deceives.
> Just as he guaranteed in the Gospel,
> 'They will come from the east and the west,
> and they will recline with Abraham and Isaac and Jacob' (C 39:16-20)

4'   Baptisms, ordinations, and confirmations in remote places

In paragraph 4' Patrick declares that he 'should act with *caution* in all things' on account of his hope of everlastingness. Acting thus, his enemies would not, on any legal charge of unfaithfulness, capture him or the ministry of his slavery. Nor would he give a place even in the least degree 'to defame or detract' (C 49:173-7). He immediately goes on to refer to baptisms and confirmations in remote parts of Ireland:

> Perhaps moreover when I baptized so many thousands of people
> (C 50:178)
> — or to confirm the people in the faith (C 51:192)

But, in addition, he is now refuting claims of avarice and unworthy motives. His tactics in this situation, and his strategy in regard to Coroticus in the *Epistola*, are similar. This fearless and direct confrontation gives us an insight into his strong and fiery 'Pauline' temperament. He points out that when he 'baptized so many thousands of people', he did not expect from any of them as much as half a scruple.[3] He challenges his accusers, as Samuel challenged all Israel (1 S 12:3-5), to testify against him in the matter of defrauding them, and he will repay them. He, likewise, ordained clergy everywhere free of charge (C 50:182):

> Or when the Lord ordained clergy everywhere (C 50:181)
> — or ordain clergy. (C 51:191)

Then the clergy too are challenged. If he even asked the price of his shoe in return for his services, he asks them to tell him to his face and he will give more back to them. He goes on to say, echoing 2 Corinthians 12:15:

> I 'have spent' for you that they 'might receive' me,
> and both among you and wherever I journeyed for your sake
> in many perils (C 51:185-6).

He seems to have accepted the belief, then current, that the end of the world would come about when the Gospel had been preached to the furthest limits of the earth: '*even to the remotest regions*' (C 51:187), which, in his cosmic consciousness, was the west coast of Ireland. This does not mean an end to the physical world, but the waning of the old pagan order before the new era of Christianity. He rejoices, therefore, that in spite of many dangers, he has gone for their sakes even to the farthest districts beyond which there lives nobody and where nobody has ever come to baptize or ordain clergy or to confirm the people. He rejoices that the people who once enslaved him are emerging as a nation under the Lordship of Christ.

---

3   [i.e.1/576th of a unit], Howlett; *screpall* (a small silver coin), [1/48th of an ounce, Kelly, Fergus, *GEIL* 114].

> With the Lord's grace,
> with loving care and most willingly,
> I have done everything for your salvation (C 51:193-5)

He did not know that, due largely to his unique missionary initiative, Ireland was being prepared for its role in coming centuries to be the burning and shining light of barbarian Europe and the saviour of civilisation.

5   Monks and virgins of Christ

From the prologue to the epilogue of his *Confessio*, Patrick never ceases to wonder and rejoice at the conversion of his pagan Irish. He pauses now to dwell more specifically on this point, with Luke 1:17 in mind:

> Whence moreover in Ireland those who never had a knowledge of God,
> up to now they always worshipped nothing except idols and 'unclean
>   things',
> have recently 'been made a people of the Lord',
> and they are called children of God (C 41:58-61).

For Patrick, the scriptural context of what is happening in Ireland is the Angel's message to Zechariah concerning John the Baptist, who was to be a second Elijah preparing the way for the Lord:

> He will be filled with the Holy Spirit.
> He will turn many of the people of Israel to the Lord their God.
> With the Spirit and power of Elijah he will go before Him,
> to turn the hearts of parents to their children,
> and the disobedient to the wisdom of the righteous,
> *to make ready a people prepared for the Lord* (Lk 1:15c-17).

The testimony of his mission is thus linked with the crux of the testimony of his vocation, the vision of Helias (C 20), where Patrick, in his extremity, invoked Elijah, and where the Lord snatched him from the clutches of Satan.

Great though his joy and wonder are at the conversion of pagans, the concrete proof of the success of his mission among them, as well as its crowning glory, is – he assures us – that:

> The sons and daughters of the petty Irish kings
> are seen to be monks and virgins of Christ (C 42:62-3).

In extolling the glory of consecration to a life of virginity, Patrick is highlighting what had been one of the hallmarks of the Christian Church from the beginning (Mt 19:10-12; 1 Co 7). 'But this is possible only on the basis of a special vocation and in virtue of a special gift of the Spirit. For in such a life baptismal consecration develops into a *radical* response in the following of Christ through the acceptance of the evangelical counsels, the first and most essential of which is the sacred bond of chastity for the sake of the Kingdom of Heaven. This special way of "following Christ", at the origin of which is always the initiative of the Father, has an essential Christological and pneumatological meaning: it expresses in a particularly vivid way the Trinitarian nature of the Christian life and it anticipates in a certain way that eschatological fulfilment towards which the whole Church is tending.'[4]

There were officially three 'orders' of women: widows, virgins and deaconesses. Over the centuries the order of widows disappeared, as did that of the deaconesses. The virgins' total donation of themselves to God was known as the 'white' martyrdom in the early Church, in comparison with the 'red' martyrdom of the years of persecution. From that latter time, the order of virgins gradually became incorporated into religious life.

The Apostolic Tradition 12 of Hippolytus (c. AD 215), says hands are not to be imposed on a virgin; her *propositum*, that is, her 'decision' or 'intention' alone, makes her a virgin of Christ. The Fathers of the Church, Gregory of Nyssa, John Chrysostom and Ambrose of Milan, have spoken of the *propositum* of remaining chaste for the sake of the kingdom in glowing terms. Indeed, Marcellina, Ambrose's sister, had received the veil of consecrated virginity at the hands of Pope Liberius, presumably in the year 353/4. Ambrose's treatise on virginity, *De Virginitate*, did not appear for another twenty-five years, in c. 378, which would coincide with the silver jubilee of his sister's 'taking of the veil' as a virgin of Christ.

In Patrick's time there was no question of taking a vow. The 'following of Christ' had known long centuries of fervour, of ardent rigour, of creativity, long before the formula of the three vows was imposed. This formula was not generalised, and only became so gradually in the West at the turn of the twelfth century.

'It is the duty of the consecrated life', Pope John Paul II writes in *Vita consecrata*, 'to show that the Incarnate son of God is *the eschatological goal towards which all things tend*, the splendour before which every other light pales, and the infinite beauty which alone can fully satisfy the human heart'.[5]

PULCHERRIMA, A BLESSED IRISHWOMAN

It is well for us to bear all this in mind in order to appreciate a personal and touching encounter between Patrick and one of his converts whom he describes as *'una benedicta Scotta'*, a blessed Irishwoman.[6] With an economy of words appropriate to a great artist, but which lose some of their force in translation, Patrick presents her to us:

---

4 *VC*, n. 14, 20-24.
5 Ibid., n. 16, 25.

> and there was even one blessed Irishwoman, of noble birth,
> most beautiful as a grown woman,
> whom I baptized (C 42:64-6).

This beautiful young woman, let us call her Pulcherrima, returned to him after a few days to confide to him that she had received an answer from a messenger of God who advised her that she should be a virgin of Christ and that she should draw close to God. 'Thanks be to God', exclaims Patrick,

> six days later she most laudably, most ardently laid hold of that
> [way of life],
> because all virgins of God do this even now (C 42:72-4).

May I say here in passing that, two centuries later, Tíreachán, in his *Memoirs*, may have had this scene in mind for his skilful creation of what must be one of the most sensitive and evocative vignettes in Christian literature, the portrayal of the Baptism, by Patrick, of Eithne and Fidelma, daughters of King Laoire of Tara, at the Well of Clebach, beside Ráth Cruachan, in present-day Co. Roscommon. Shortly afterwards they too heard and followed the call to the consecrated life.[7]

Patrick immediately conveys to us the price that had to be paid in fifth-century Ireland by those close followers of the Virgin Christ, the Lamb of God, when their own parents rejected their choice:

> but they even suffer persecutions
> and false reproaches from their own parents,
> and, nevertheless, their number ever increases (C 42:75-77).

He goes on to say that he cannot reckon the number from those of his own race who have been born in Ireland and who consecrate themselves to God as virgins of Christ apart from 'widows and married persons who live a life of continence'.

De genere nostro, translated by Hanson as 'those of our race', refers, according to him, to those of British extraction who have settled in Ireland, of whom there must have been a considerable number. They undoubtedly constituted part of 'the Irish who believe in Christ' – mentioned by Prosper of Aquitaine – to whom Pope Celestine had sent Palladius *as first bishop* in 431. Howlett, however, translates *de genere nostro* as 'from our begetting', which simply means those whom Patrick had baptized into Christ.

---

6 The Irish were known as the *Scotti* up to the tenth century, and Scotland derives her name from the Irish or *Scotti* who settled there in the early centuries of the Christian era.

7 Bieler, *PTBA*, n. 26, 143-5.

Widows refers to women who had lost their first husbands and had made a decision not to remarry – a course which, though not obligatory, was highly recommended in the Church from the beginning. The Fathers of the Church, including St Ambrose in his treatise *Exhortation to Widows* (*De Viduis*) in 377/378,[8] reiterated this recommendation.

'People living a life of continence' probably refers to married couples who, like Paulinus of Nola and his wife, Theresia, after becoming monastics, lived together as brother and sister like Mary and Joseph at Nazareth.[9] Paulinus and Theresia lived in this way within a proto-monastic setting in Campania. A minority of married couples, outside the cloister, have been called to this mysterious way of life – this vocation within a vocation – in all ages of the Church.

Though the sufferings of the consecrated virgins from noble rank were great, the keenest suffering of all, was reserved for those women who lived in slavery. All the time they had to endure terror and threats. But, Patrick concludes:

> the Lord has given grace to many of his own handmaids,
> because even if they are forbidden, they nevertheless continue steadfast
> in their imitation of him [*tamen fortiter imitantur*] (C 42:83-4).

The 'imitation' or following of Christ, in this context, 'means a determination to live a life of peculiar strictness, for the sake of Christ'.[10] Herren suggests that whatever the 'official' role of the virgins was in the Church – which, as we have already suggested, is to be the 'sign' of the Church, the Bride of Christ (Rv 19:7-9; 21:2; Ga 4:26) – their spiritual role was to suffer and to be seen to suffer. The tears of virgins were the seed of Christians. Not only did suffering strengthen the faith of virgins themselves (after all, their suffering is their only reward), it also won sympathy among the Christian populace at large and united it against the offending persecutors.[11]

Herren also suggests that, in recounting the sufferings of the virgins, Patrick seemed to be conversant with the martyrologies popular in his day. And, not satisfied with describing the sufferings of his women 'martyrs', he must also depict them as beautiful and noble as well![12] In so doing Patrick was in tune with the culture of the Irish people to whom he ministered. In the 'Triads of Ireland' which have come down to us from pre-Christian times, the three glories of a gathering were: a beautiful woman, a good horse, and a swift hound![13]

---

8 Migne, *PL,* 16, 233-62.
9 Jerome, Ep. 58 $ 6; Hanson, *LW*, 111.
10 Hanson, ibid., 111.
11 Herren, *MM*, 84.
12 Ibid., 84; cf. *G'6*.
13 Triad 88, *Treching Breth Féne.* Kelly, op. cit., 69.

Under the early Irish legal system, too, women enjoyed certain privileges. There were, for example, factors which might confer independent legal capacity on a woman; in addition to 'the woman who turns back the streams of war' and 'the hostage ruler', the list refers to other women of special status or skill: 'the female wright (*banshaer*), the woman-physician of the *tuath* (*banliaig túaithe*), the woman revered by the *tuath* (*airmitnech túaithe*)'. But, in the centuries that followed Patrick's time, when the rights of Christians began to find their place in that Brehon Law system, pride of place among women seems to have been given to *'the woman who is abundant in miracles,* i. the *bandeorad Dé,* i. the female virgin, i. the female hermit',[14] presumably regardless of whether she was originally a slave or a freewoman.

Under the same law system, the rights of an outsider (*peregrinus*) were very restricted unless he was a *'deorad Dé'*, literally 'an outsider or exile, or pilgrim of God, i. a hermit', in which case he had special status and privileges, according to a text on distraint.[15]

There were, moreover, three churchmen whose evidence could not be overturned, even by a king; they were: a *suí* or learned person, 'a bishop', and a *deorad Dé* or hermit. In the seventh and eighth centuries, the latter was especially revered for his ability to perform miracles and was obliged to act as enforcing surety (*naidm*) in cases where a contract had been bound by the Gospel of Christ or by the heavenly host.[16]

Bearing this tradition in mind, one can appreciate why the Irish people, in every generation, prayed for vocations in the family, and considered it a great privilege to be called on by God to give a son or daughter to the priesthood or the religious life.

It seems reasonable to conclude, then, from the evidence of his own writings, that Patrick had a deep appreciation of a simple form of the religious life, which we shall term 'proto-monasticism', in which celibacy, prayer and involvement with the local Christian community were the principal components; that he actively promoted this way of life among his converts in Ireland, both male and female, and that this was one of the aims closest to his heart.

PATRICK'S MODEL OF CHURCH

Though there is no clear evidence that Patrick was a monk himself, it is the opinion of some scholars that it may be inferred from his profound sympathy for a broadly defined version of monasticism or 'proto-monasticism', that he had undergone 'an intense monastic experience of some duration before beginning his apostolate in Ireland and that he may, like Victricius of Rouen,

---

14 Ibid., 77.
15 ibid., 77.
16 *Eriu* [1955], 66.7, in ibid., 41.

have seriously considered the role of religious in his mission to the Irish people'.[17]

Since, on the other hand, there is no reference to either monastic buildings or to religious superiors such as abbots and abbesses in his writings, it is possible that Patrick's model of Church was more like the Church portrayed in the Apostolic Tradition, rather than that rigid type of monastic tradition which originated with Anthony and Pachomius a century or so later. The former model of Church, which is closely akin to the Church depicted in the Acts of the Apostles, is a Church that included married people, virgins, widows, presbyters and catechumens. The local Church was the *primary* community; consequently there was a regime of morning and evening prayer in common, which *all* were asked to attend, if possible. Other hours of prayer took place at home. The whole local Christian community was expected to gather for the Sunday Eucharist. Christian marriage was a charism within that community, and virginity another (1 Co 7:7). The latter term applies to both men and women who imitated the celibacy of the Lord himself. They lived at home, for the most part, and were expected to be particularly active in works of charity, since they had no family commitments. It is noteworthy that there is no indication of 'flight from the world' in this early model. For St Basil the Great (c. AD 330-379), in his treatise *Concerning Baptism,* it is the *baptized* and not merely 'the monks and virgins of Christ' who are 'separated from the world'.[18]

Conversely, single-sex religious communities had developed about a century before Patrick's time, under the influence of the monastic movement. It was possibly at that stage that the male virgin, *monachus,* came to be distinguished from the female virgin, *monacha.*[19] Since Patrick himself favoured this monastic terminology, it is possible to speculate that before his death, at least, a simple form of monasticism, perhaps in the form of double monasteries, had begun to evolve. We shall return to this point presently, when we come to consider briefly the monastic ideal that was to flower in the Church in Ireland in the sixth century.

The only clear and unambiguous evidence we have regarding the organisation of the Patrician Church is that Patrick ordained clerics to baptize (C 38; 40; 50; 51); that he and, presumably, his clergy, made apostolic journeys; that they proclaimed the Gospel in an innovative manner that was adapted to the dictates of Irish culture; that they administered the Sacraments; and that vocations to the priesthood and the religious life were fostered and cherished. Though Patrick does not say in his writings that he ordained bishops, it seems reasonable to suppose that he did so as circumstances warranted it. Indeed, his establishment of Christian

17 Herren, op. cit., 77.
18 De Bháldraithe, *RLR,* v. 32, Sept/Oct 1993, 261-262.
19 Herren, op. cit., 81.

communities under bishops and his constant journeys to make new converts and establish new Christian communities may not be what his elders in Britain visualised when he was consecrated bishop. In all fairness to them, his innovative approach to a mission, for which they were responsible, may have alarmed them. They were fully entitled and duty-bound to question it. They, for their part, seem to have functioned in more stable communities. At all events, it may have been part of the cause of his rejection, which we will consider in the next chapter.

5' Christian brethren and virgins of Christ

In the parallel reading, paragraph 5', Patrick tells his brothers and fellow slaves who have believed in him that he has given them this account in order to strengthen and confirm their faith (C 47). He is probably alluding to the unquoted part of this quotation from Paul and it is likely that he expected his hearers to recall it here:

> Christ ... is powerful in you.
> For he was crucified in weakness, but lives by the power of God....
> Examine yourselves to see whether you are living in the Faith....
> Do you not realise that Jesus Christ is in you? (2 Co 13:3-5).

With this great reality undoubtedly in mind, he now expresses the wish that they too would strive for greater things and do better than he has done. We are immediately reminded of his great exemplar's Trinitarian Canticle in the Letter to the Ephesians:

> I bow my knees before the Father of our Lord Jesus Christ,
> from whom every family in heaven and on earth takes its name.
> I pray that, *according to the riches of his glory*,
> he may grant that you may be strengthened in your inner being with
>   power through his Spirit,
> and that Christ may dwell in your hearts through faith,
> as you are being rooted and grounded in love.
> I pray that you may have the power to comprehend, with all the saints,
> what is the breadth and length
> and height and depth,
> and to know the love of Christ that surpasses knowledge,
> so that you may be filled with all the fullness of God.
> *Now to him who by the power at work within us*
> *is able to accomplish abundantly*
> *far more than all we can ask or imagine,*
> *to him be glory in the Church and in Christ Jesus*
> to all generations forever and ever. Amen (Ep 3:14-20).

'This will be my glory', Patrick continues,

> because 'a wise son
> is the glory of a father' (C 47:152-3).

Who are these 'brethren and fellow slaves' whom Patrick addresses? Since the audience envisaged by Patrick varies throughout the *Confessio,* it is difficult to conjecture. It may be a network of fellow clerics, anchorites, monks and virgins of Christ, widows, and some married people who live like brother and sister, together with the laity, married and single, who are in the majority; in a word, they probably correspond to *Pobal Dé,* the whole Christian community, in all its charismatic giftedness.

PATRICK'S FAREWELL

Now, in what resembles a poignant farewell, Patrick looks back once more over the long, weary road that has brought him to this point, and with characteristic honesty and frankness, recalls some of its salient landmarks to his fellow labourers, as to old and cherished friends:

> You know, God also, how I have lived among you
> 'from my youth'
> in purity of faith and in sincerity of heart (C 48:154-6)

The background to all this is Paul's farewell, pastoral testimony to his friends at Miletus (Ac 20:18-38), from which Patrick quotes here, and the nuances of which he expects us to recall. He reiterates, as did Paul on that occasion, his abiding concern for the unbelievers among whom he lives:

> Even these pagans among whom I dwell
> I have kept and I will keep my word to them.
> God knows 'I have not taken advantage of any' of them (C 48:157-9).

Patrick possibly has in mind the persecution stirred up against Paul and Barnabas by the Jews of Paul's native city, Antioch, who were jealous of their success in preaching the Word of God there (Ac 1 3:50), when he writes:

> nor do I think of [doing so], on account of God and his Church,
> lest 'I should stir up persecution' against them and all of us (C 48:160-1)

But, most of all, Patrick dreads the thought of being a stumbling-block, being conscious, no doubt, of the Lord's warning that 'If any of you put a stumbling-block before any of these little ones who believe in me it would be better for you if a great millstone were fastened around your neck and you were drowned in the depths of the sea' (Mt 18:6), which immediately precedes the verse he is about to quote:

> and lest the name of the Lord should be blasphemed through me,
> because it is written, 'Woe to the person
> through whom the name of the Lord is blasphemed' (C 48:163-4).

GIFTS ON THE ALTAR

When Patrick says 'For even if I am unlearned in all things' (2 Co 11:6), he is assuming that we are familiar with the remainder of that Pauline statement, which is: 'I may be untrained in speech but not in knowledge'. I take that to mean that he is not lacking in the gift of Wisdom. Under the influence of the Spirit of Wisdom, therefore, he has tried to be vigilant, even in his engagements with devout Christians:

> I have, nevertheless, tried in some measure to save myself
> even also from the Christian brethren
> and from the virgins of Christ and devout women,
> who of their own accord kept giving me little gifts,
> and who kept casting some of their own ornaments on the altar,
> and I kept returning them again to them,
> and they in turn were annoyed with me because I kept doing this
> (C 49:165-172).

Consequently, he has deemed it prudent to return their gifts, even though they have been offended because of his persistence in this matter. But he was sensitive to the hurt he had caused them because he feels obliged to explain that he had been constrained to do so because of the hope of eternal life.

The mention of the *altar* here is the only reference to anything directly to do with the celebration of the Eucharist in Patrick's writings. This makes sense only when we remember that in the fifth century, as well as in the early Church, the initiation of converts to Christianity took the form of a single comprehensive ceremony, which included Baptism, Confirmation and the Eucharist, and which was usually held at Easter and Pentecost. When, therefore, Patrick mentions the first two stages, the third stage, the Eucharistic celebration, is always understood.

6   New Christians with whom Christ commanded Patrick to stay in Ireland, echo of Psalm 119 (118):60

Patrick has just bidden a tender farewell to his 'brethren and fellow-slaves' (C 47:147) who have shared with him the burden and heat of the day. Now we have also come to Patrick's farewell and final missionary testimony to his close family and friends. Its context is still Paul's farewell and pastoral testimony to his friends, which he made in person, at Miletus (Ac 20:18-38). But Patrick's farewell, unlike Paul's, is made on paper only, for he is already parted from many of them, and he will never see their faces again. Some of the human anguish that his 'exile for Christ' causes him, comes through here, for he fears that if he visits family and friends, he may lose the fruits of his labours among the pagan Irish (C 43:85-86). We sense, too, the warmth of his character, in his longing to be among his relatives in Britain, and to visit Gaul. He *was* certainly *prepared* to set out at once:

> and 'I was' most willingly 'prepared'
> [to make that journey]
> in order to see to my homeland and family
> and not only that
> But even [to travel] as far as the Gauls to visit the brethren
>   (C 43:87-90),

The scriptural context of 'I was prepared' is Psalm 119 (118):59-60:

> When I think of your ways, I turn my feet to your decrees;
> I hurry and do not delay to keep your commandments.

The deciding factor is always God's holy will. The saint once again reiterates his longing to see them all, and his reasons for staying away:

> and 'that I might see the face' of the saints *of my Lord* (C 43:91).
> *– if the Lord* wills it,
> and he will keep watch over me 'from every evil way',
> so that I do not 'sin in his sight' (C 43:101-3).

Here, Patrick reiterates his primary values, adherence to God by obedience to his will, and trust in the grace and mercy of the Lord for the grace to avoid sin.

> God knows *I* greatly desired it (C 43:92)
> *– and not I* (C 43:98)
>
> But '*I am bound by the Spirit*' (C 43:93)
> *– but Christ the Lord* (C 43:98).
> *Who 'protests' to me that* if I do this (C 43:94),
> *– who has commanded me* (C 43:99)
> *he will pronounce me guilty* (C 43:95),
> *– to come to stay with them for the rest of my life* (C 43:100)

He is affirming up to this point that he has a great longing to visit Britain and Gaul, but that he is bound by the Spirit, who testifies to him that he would be found guilty of sin should he leave his flock. Furthermore, Christ the Lord has commanded him that he must remain with them for the rest of his life. He trusts in God for the grace to obey him in this and in all things.

The crux of the matter is his fear of his work being undermined should he leave Ireland. Is he afraid that if he left he might not be allowed to return?

and I am afraid of losing the labour which I have begun (C 43:96).

When Patrick speaks of staying lest he lose the fruit of his labours, he is, in Herren's view, referring to the virgins of Christ – who, in a country which was still relatively pagan, had to be protected – and not to his entire flock. He consequently feels strongly obliged by the Spirit to remain permanently in Ireland for their sakes. 'This vivid concern of Patrick's', Herren concludes, 'sets him squarely within the religious *mentalité* of fifth-century western Europe. Because the celibate state is regarded as the highest state available to Christians, the loss of this state is regarded as particularly lamentable.'[20]

While it might be argued that this *mentalité* is further substantiated in his *Epistola* (E 12), I cannot agree with Herren that Patrick's 'sole reason' for staying in Ireland was the protection of the virgins of Christ. However great his reverence for and appreciation of their unique and minority calling, it seems to me that it is abundantly evident, from both his *Confessio* (38-40) and his *Epistola* (1; 3; 15-19), that Patrick's major concern as bishop, was always, of necessity, for *Pobal Dé*, the one and undivided People of God, of whom the laity are always in the majority in every age.

THE CHRISTIANS IN GAUL

Patrick, as we have already noted, would otherwise go to Gaul 'to visit the brethren and that I might see the face of the holy men of my Lord' (C 43:90-1). He expresses no similar wish to see Christians of any rank in Britain, apart from his own unnamed relatives. Nor does he ever refer to the sanctity or piety of any British cleric, quite the contrary! (C 26; 29; 32; E 7). The expression 'saints/holy men of my Lord' (in Gaul) seems to indicate that these men possess a special holiness which is different from that of ordinary Christians. Though this phrase does not prove them to be monks, it does show them to be Christians with whom Patrick can identify himself. Indeed, the Christians of Gaul are the only national group of Christians who are depicted positively in Patrick's writings. In the *Epistola* they are praised for their charity in ransoming captives (E 14:129-132), in contrast to the indifference of the British Christians (E 12; 14:132).

Patrick evidently looked to them and not to the Church in Britain for Christian inspiration, for, in imitation of the Church in Gaul, he sent 'a holy presbyter' to the soldiers of Coroticus for the same purpose (E 3:22-23), and

---

20 Ibid., 82.

distributed among those who administered justice not less than the price of fifteen men (C 53:211), possibly for the ransom of captive laity or even clerics.

In view of this, it seems natural to suppose, Herren points out, that the advocacy of religious celibacy was also done in imitation of that nation of Christians whom Patrick most admired and whom he longed to see in his hour of need. In contrast – Herren continues – Patrick's image of the non-celibate clerical members of his own family seemed to be rather negative:

> I ... had as *father* the deacon, Calpornius,
> *the son* of Potitus, a priest,...
> *I was then almost sixteen years of age,*
> *I was indeed ignorant of the true God,*
> ... 'we turned away from God',
> and '*we did not keep watch over his* precepts,
> and *we did not obey our priests*
> *who kept warning us about our salvation* (C 1).

It would appear, from this text that, though Patrick was the son of a deacon and the grandson of a priest, neither of them helped him to grow in the faith. His later conviction about the value of celibacy for men and women in religious life was clearly not derived from his home environment; nor is there anything in his writings to connect this value of celibacy for the sake of the kingdom with Christianity in Britain, except the phrase 'some of my elders' (C 26:1), which need not refer to monks. We have noted already that 'elder' (senior) and 'bishop' were two terms used for the same office in the early Church.[21]

THE PROTO-MONASTIC IDEAL

It would seem, then, that Patrick gradually became convinced that the 'proto-monastic' ideal, which was a simple form of monasticism, akin to the Syrian rather than the Egyptian monastic model,[22] was the antidote to clerical laxity, and that clerics who were also monks had a deeper commitment to the Faith. Though that is debatable, it could be argued that a celibate clergy would be more viable in the Irish missionary situation, where resources were scarce, living conditions probably rather primitive, and where, initially at least, they had to move frequently from place to place.

---

21 Ibid., 82, n. 36, 85. *Elder* and *bishop* (Tt 1:5-7) are two terms for the same office in the Church (*NRSV, NT*, 312, n. 1:5, 7). *The laying on of hands* (Tm 5:22) is not an empty gesture but expresses the donation and reception of a gift; e.g. Jesus blesses children (Mk 10:16); he heals with a touch (Mk 6:5); the Spirit is given to the baptized (Ac 8:17; 19:6); believers are set aside for special tasks in the Church (Ac 6:6; 13:3). Ibid., 303, n. 14.

22 Brock, *TLE,* Ch. 8; *TAI,* 107-17.

Besides, some of the nobility, among them the sons of petty kings, had sold their nobility for that of the democratic status of monks for the sake of Christ and his Gospel (C 41:62-63). Patrick himself had sold his noble status in order to come to Ireland as a missionary (E 10:87-89). This, too, brings Patrick's Church into harmony with the Church in Gaul where, already in the late fourth and early fifth centuries, the monastic movement represented a new element in Gaulish society, essentially popular and democratic.

This movement was fuelled in no small way, it would appear, by St Athanasius, the hero of the Egyptian peasants, who initiated a popular movement among the Copts. The renunciation of wealth and the world by men like Sulpicius Severus and Paulinus of Nola testifies to the strength of these new ideals. The attitude was undoubtedly Christian and inspired by the Gospel; but it was strengthened by the very force which was making Christianity strong – a widespread growth of self-conscious democracy.[23]

This is not to say that there were no married clergy among Patrick's followers, nor are we to conclude that they, as a class, were lax; but in Ireland, as in Gaul, a struggle between conservative elements and the new ascetic ideal must have caused considerable tension, and all the more so in a country like Ireland, whose native structures were conservative and hierarchical. In the matter of Church organisation, did Palladius, like Pope Celestine, who, initially at least, viewed monasticism with distrust,[24] oppose monasticism in Ireland?

We have already noticed the animosity towards Patrick in the charges, which in the interests of the Church he was obliged to refute. Were some of those charges made by pre-Patrician clergy and Christian laity? Were some of the learned rhetoricians whom Patrick addresses in his *Apologia* (C 9-15) among their number?

All that we can postulate here, pending further research in this area, is that it seems likely that the connection between mission and monasticism came to Patrick largely through the Church in Gaul. Bearing this in mind and adding to it the many Gallican influences perceived in his writings and to which we have already alluded, it seems permissible to conjecture that part, if not all, of his own religious formation for the priesthood was received in that country, possibly in a monastic setting. This does not preclude a stay – even a protracted stay – in a monastery or monasteries in Britain, possibly Glastonbury and Whithorn, before and after his ordination.[25]

During Patrick's period of priestly formation, the *Life of St Martin of Tours*, with its account of his simple form of monasticism, was circulating widely. Moreover, the monastic mission of Victricius among the poor of Normandy was already documented in two letters of Paulinus of Nola.[26] We have noted

23 Chadwick, *PLG*, 111.
24 Migne, *PL*, Vol. L, col. 430.
25 Hanson, *OC*, 53, 158.
26 Ep. 18, 37; Migne, *PL*, XX, 443-58.

in passing when considering the testimony of Patrick's sacred calling, how, as archbishop of Rouen, Victricius had made a prolonged journey to Britain at the request of the British bishops around 396, possibly as their metropolitan.[27] The object of the visit was to strengthen the orthodox faith which was menaced by the Arian heresy. Among his proposals to the Church in Britain was the development of monasticism with a view to converting the poor country people.[28] Patrick, even as a youth, would undoubtedly have been aware of Victricius' initiative through his family involvement with the institutional Church; it may be of some significance, in this context, that in one manuscript of the *Confessio* the name of the letter-bearer in his 'dream' (C 23) is Victoricius, and in another less perfect copy, Victricius.[29] We may only conjecture, for want of firm evidence, that Victricius of Rouen may well have been the subconscious inspiration behind the Victoricius of this 'dream' (C 23:117), calling him back to mission in pagan Ireland.

Now, in his capacity as missionary bishop among country people in Ireland, Patrick was undoubtedly aware that, though he might baptize *tot milia hominum* (so many thousand people), he could still fail to create a Christian society that would stand the test of time. With the example of Martin and Victricius for guidance and inspiration, he was in a position to grasp 'the essential connection between the monastic and the missionary ideals'.[30] The Patrician Church then was, in some areas at least, organised, it is tentatively suggested, along simple monastic lines. These home-based groupings possibly formed the nuclei of some of the future sixth-century monasteries.

We assume that these monks and virgins of Christ, together with their lay associates, funded Patrick's nascent Church from whatever resources were at their command and that they put their gifts and skills at its disposal. In this way, manuscripts of Sacred Scripture probably came to be copied, sacred vessels were designed and crafted, altar linen and vestments were provided, trees were cut down to use in the construction of a modest *domhnach* or church, apart from the usual corporal and spiritual works of mercy to which they undoubtedly attended. 'This Patrician pattern was to become the model of all future Irish missionary activity in the middle ages.'[31]

But this pattern did not preclude the Patrician Church being initially organised as a diocesan Church with Patrick's primatial See at Armagh.[32] It was not until the advent of the great monastic centres in the following century that the monastic Church seems to have superseded the fifth century *domhnach* in some areas. The role of the bishop was subordinate to the role of

27 Thomas, *Christianity*, 55, in Malaspina, 1984, 69, n. 20.
28 Ibid., 67-9, n. 22. Cf. 90-91 *supra*.
29 Bieler, *LE*, 1, 19.
30 Herren, op. cit., 84.
31 Herren, ibid., 84.
32 de Paor, *TAA, HS,* V111, 96.

the abbot only in the administration of temporalities within those monastic centres, including Armagh.

6' Former willingness to go to Ireland, echo of Psalm 119 (118):60

In the counterpart of this section of the *Confessio,* paragraph 6', Patrick gives vent once more to one of his many outbursts of praise and gratitude to God for his steadfast mercy and love in spite of his own faltering responses:

> *Whence moreover, I ought to give* unceasing *thanks to God* (C 46:125),
> – Now I understand *what I ought* [*to have understood*] *earlier* (C 46:146),
>
> *Whence moreover I ought to give* unceasing *thanks* [*gratias*] *to God*
>   (C 46:125),
> – and I myself was slow to recognise *the grace* [*gratiam*] which was then
>   in me (C 46:145).

The scriptural context of the second antiphon is the first pastoral letter to Timothy 4:14, in which the recipient is being encouraged to exercise his God-given gift of ordination in the service of the people of God: 'Do not neglect the gift [*gratiam*] that is in you, which was given to you through prophesy by the laying on of hands (i. ordination) by the council of elders (Greek: by the presbytery)'.

Patrick was not, initially, conscious of the full enabling power of his ordination, and so he hesitated to implement his call to the pagans in Ireland, because of his own felt shortcomings:

> Who has often pardoned *my lack of wisdom,*
> *and my negligence,*
> and who, on more than one occasion
> refrained from growing vehemently angry with me,
> who had been chosen as his helper;
> and yet was slow to act in accordance with what I had been shown,
> and as 'the Spirit was suggesting to me';
> the Lord 'has shown mercy' to me 'thousands and thousands of times'
>   (C 46:126-133)
> – because of *my rusticity* (C 46:144)

Patrick extols the Lord's patience with him when he was reluctant to follow the inspirations of his Holy Spirit and is conscious of God's pity shown him on countless occasions.

The scriptural context of God's boundless mercy is Revelation 5:6f, concerning the Lamb who was slain and whose blood ransomed for God saints from every tribe and people and nation:

> You have made them to be a kingdom and priests serving our God, and
>   they will reign on earth.
> Then I looked, and I heard the voice of many angels surounding the
>   throne and the living creatures and the elders;
> they numbered myriads of myriads and *thousands of thousands,* singing
>   with full voice,
> 'Worthy is *the Lamb that was slaughtered*
> to receive power and wealth and wisdom and might
> and honour and glory and blessing!' (Rv 5:10-12)

By referring to this text of Scripture in the context of his sinfulness, Patrick
is aware that he has been purchased at a great price – the blood of the Lamb
that was slain. We have now reached the crux of this concentric section:

> *because he saw in me that 'I was ready'* [*paratus eram*] (C 46:134)
> *– but that I did not know* [*nesciebam*] *what to do in these circumstances,*
> what I should do about my own position,
> because many were trying to hinder my embassy.
> They were even talking among themselves behind my back
> and saying, 'Why does this man throw himself into danger
> among enemies who do not know God?'
> Not out of malice,
> but it did not seem wise to them,
> – as I myself testify (C 46:135-144).

He tells how difficult it was for him to make up his own mind about
coming to Ireland on the mission; how many tried to prevent that embassy
for Christ; they would even talk to each other behind his back about the
danger and foolishness of such a venture among enemies and pagans. It was
not malicious on their part, he notes; they merely felt that the task which
Patrick was setting himself was inappropriate and unwise; besides, his
proposed task was unprecedented since there were no organised missions to
convert pagans, in the western part of the Roman Empire at least, until
Gregory the Great initiated them when he sent Augustine to Canterbury in
the closing years of the sixth century, well over a hundred years after Patrick's
time.

7. Total commitment to the mission in Ireland
Patrick has finally reached the penultimate *ula* or halting stone on his
missionary pilgrimage, his total commitment to his mission in Ireland. This is
the crux of his defence of his mission to the Irish.
    He begins by reassuring himself that this *glasmartra* [green martyrdom] in
reverse is what God wants of him: 'I hope moreover [*spero autem*] that I ought

[*debueram*] to do this' (C 44:104). This echoes the beginning of the preceding paragraph 6: 'Whence moreover [*unde autem*] even if I wished to leave them' (C 43:85), as well as the beginning of paragraph 6': 'Whence moreover [*unde autem*], I ought to give unceasing thanks to God' (C 46:125).

He then testifies that he knows he has not lived a perfect life like others, and, like Peter, whom he quotes here, he does not trust himself 'for as long as I am in this body of death' (2 P 1:13), because of the temptations of the Evil One who endeavours daily to turn him from the faith:

> *because he is strong who strives daily to turn me away from the faith*
>   (C 44:107)
> — 'and up to now', with God's grace, 'I have kept the Faith'.
> Let who will, moreover, laugh and insult,
> I shall not be silent, nor do I conceal the signs and wonders,
> which have been shown to me by the Lord
> many years before they came to pass,
> since he knows all things even 'before the ages began' (C 44:119-24).

But in spite of the machinations of Satan he has, with God's help, kept the faith. He has also been shown many signs and wonders, even before they came to pass:

> *and from the chastity of an enfeigned religion which I have proposed to keep*
>   (C 44:108)
> — *there grew in me the love of God and fear of him* (C 44:118)

Though Satan tries to lead him down heretical paths, the temptation has only strengthened him, and his love and filial fear of God, which is true religion, has increased (cf. C 16):

> *to the end of my life for Christ my Lord* (C 44:109)
> — from the time I came to know him *'from my youth'* (C 44:117)

Though he has known Christ since his youth, he must be vigilant to the end of his days, in order to win salvation:

> *to the end of my life for Christ my Lord* (C 44:109)
> — but I confess *to my Lord*,
> and 'I do not blush for shame' in his presence,
> 'because I do not lie' (C 44:114-16),

Though he confesses and does not lie when he acknowledges that the love and filial fear of the Lord has increased in his heart over the years, he never forgets the power of temptation:

> But the 'hostile flesh' always dragging towards death (C 44:110),
> – and 'I know in part' wherein I have not lived a perfect life
> 'just as the others' also believing (C 44:112-13).

Patrick experiences a constant moral struggle. Human weakness is always dragging him towards sin and spiritual death. The scriptural context of 'I know in part' is Paul's lyric chapter, 1 Corinthians 13, where he affirms that the great gift of the Spirit is not tongues or even prophecy, which Patrick has been given, but *caritas*, 'love'. This 'love' is not love in an ordinary or general sense, but the love for others which is known within the Church, inspired ultimately by the love of God in Christ for us through the Holy Spirit. In the evening of life Patrick knows that he will be judged on this *caritas*, 'love':

> For *we know only in part*,
> and we prophesy *only in part*;
> but when the complete comes,
> the partial will come to an end....
> For now we see in a mirror dimly,
> but then we will see face to face.
> Now *I know only in part*;
> then I will know fully, even as I have been fully known.
> And now abide
> faith, hope, and love,
> these three;
> and the greatest of these is love (1 Co 13:9-10, 12-13).

The scriptural context of 'just as others' is 1 Thessalonians 5, where Paul reminds them that 'the day of the Lord will come like a thief in the night' (5:2b).

The crux of this concentric passage is the seeming attractiveness of temptation: that is, towards allurements to do that which is forbidden (C 44:111), and, implicitly, the need to watch and pray in preparation for the Lord's coming:

> So then let us not fall asleep *as others do*,
> but let us keep awake and be sober....
> put on the breastplate of faith and love, and for a helmet,
>   the hope of salvation.
> For God has destined us not for wrath but for obtaining
>   salvation
> through our Lord Jesus Christ,
> who died for us,

so that whether we are awake or asleep we may live with him.
Therefore encourage one another
and build up each other, as indeed you are doing (1 Th 5:6, 8b-11).

The twenty-one lines divide by extreme mean and ratio at 13 and 8, and the 134 words divide by extreme mean and ratio at 83 and 51, at the last two words of the eighth line (111) at the crux of the concentric passage. The 1,305 words of Part IV divide by extreme mean and ratio at 807 and 498, in the sentence, 'The Lord has shown mercy to me [*in milia milium*] thousands and thousands of times' (C 46:133).[32] Patrick, by this subtle textual arrangement, is thus affirming the Lord's infinite mercy and compassion for human frailty. This is the sure foundation of his unfailing joy and boundless trust in God, which are important elements of his spiritual legacy to his children in the faith.

---

32 Howlett, *BLSPB*, 107.

CHAPTER FOUR

PATRICK'S TESTIMONY
OF HIS REJECTION AND BETRAYAL

Whence therefore I give unwearied thanks to my God,
Who has kept me faithful 'in the day of my trial',
so that today I may confidently offer in sacrifice to him
my life as 'a living host' to Christ my Lord,
who 'has saved me from all my troubles'....
Behold, we are witnesses that the Gospel has been proclaimed
to the limit beyond which nobody dwells (C 34:1-5, 29-30).

In his testimony of his rejection and betrayal in Part III (C 26-37) Patrick places the Cross of Christ at the centre of his *Confessio*. This section, which reaches its culmination in his elevation to the episcopate (C 32:11), is concerned with the saint's dealings with his ecclesiastical superiors and antagonists, his rejection by them, and his betrayal by his 'dearest friend' (C 32:13-16).

Before we focus our attention on the text of this central section it may help to make a résumé of Patrick's career up to this, as best we can from the paucity of information available to us, in an effort to try to identify what caused him such terrible suffering.

In his testimony of his vocation (C 16-25), to begin with, Patrick tells us nothing about the circumstances of his actual decision to respond to it. It would seem, however, that, even from a practical point of view, the first step on the road to the priesthood in any age would involve consultation with, and acceptance by a bishop and his consultants and advisors. We may infer that Patrick went through such a procedure, and entered on a course of ecclesiastical studies, since he tells us that he was ordained a deacon: 'a word which I had confessed before I was a deacon' (C 27:11). The inference from his passing reference to 'the altar' (C 49:170) is that he had been ordained a priest, while he expressly tells us in his *Epistola* that he is 'a bishop ... established in Ireland' at the time of writing (E 1:1).

Already, in the fourth century, rules had been drawn up by Pope Siricius (384-399), pertaining to the ordination of deacons and priests. It was recommended by him that a deacon be at least thirty years of age before being ordained to the diaconate, which meant that a candidate for the priesthood had to be older still.

Where and how Patrick prepared for the diaconate and holy orders are still matters for speculation. We assume that he adapted himself to the prevailing system that obtained in the fifth-century Church. Seminaries, as we know them today, did not exist until after the Council of Trent. It can, however, be inferred from his own *Epistola* that a suitable candidate was apprenticed to an ordained priest and was thus gradually introduced to prayer, study and the practical demands of the priesthood from the very beginning: 'a holy presbyter whom I taught from his infancy' (E 3:22-3).

We have, in the last chapter, briefly considered some of the close links between the Church in Gaul and the Church in Britain in the fourth and fifth centuries. Those links, together with some of the Gallic influences on Patrick's writings, and his great desire to travel,

> even [to travel] as far as the Gauls to visit the brethren
> and 'that I might see the face' of the saints *of my Lord* (C 43:90-91),

give reasonable, though not conclusive, grounds for suggesting that part, if not all, of his priestly formation took place in that country, and that a substantial part of his time there was spent within a monastic setting. Let us now consider some of the challenges that arose for Patrick because of his particular call from God within the framework of that fifth-century Church.

PATRICK, THE FOREIGN MISSIONARY

In order to appreciate Patrick's plight in his capacity as first recorded foreign missionary bishop to pagans outside the western part of the Roman Empire, it is important to bear in mind that in the early history of the Church, bishops were only '*sent*', whether by the Pope or by other bishops, *at the request of a Christian community*. A case in point is Ulfilas, a Cappadocian, born into a Christian family c. 311, who was captured with his parents by raiding Goths and taken beyond the Danube. He was later commissioned by the Christians among them to go as part of an embassy to Constantinople to request a bishop. There, in 341, Eusebius of Nicomedia consecrated him as missionary bishop and 'sent' him back to his own Gothic community, that is, 'sent' him back invested with the ecclesiastical authority of a bishop within that community.

Likewise, in Patrick's own day, 'Palladius was sent' by Pope Celestine 'as first bishop to the Irish believing in Christ' in 431, possibly as a follow-up to the 429 anti-Pelagian mission of Germanus, bishop of Auxerre, to Britain. Palladius's mandate was not the conversion of pagans. In the first place, he could not have plunged into a preaching campaign among a people of whose language he was, almost certainly, totally ignorant. His priorities were, probably, the ordination of deacons, priests and a few bishops for the maintenance of the already established and scattered Christian communities, as well as the identification and elimination of any Pelagian heretics in their midst. That Pelagianism had already affected the scattered Irish Christian communities is a distinct possibility. Pelagius's *Commentaries on the Epistles of St Paul*, written in Rome before the sack of that city by Alaric in 410, were preserved in the schools of Ireland. This may, in part, account for a letter of the year 640 to a number of Irish abbots and others, in which John, the Pope Elect, warned them to beware of Pelagianism spreading *again* among them.[1]

Almost two centuries later Pope Gregory the Great sent his fellow-Benedictine monk, Augustine, and his companions, under obedience and in fear and trembling, 'to make angels of the Angles' in the spring of 595. But the would-be apostle of the Angles lost heart in the south of France and returned to Rome. He was sent back and arrived at the month of the Thames at Easter 597. These missionaries had to prove that they were capable of establishing a viable mission *before* Augustine was brought back to Arles in southern France to be consecrated bishop of Canterbury by Vergilius, the former Abbot of Lérins, in 597.[2]

And what then of Patrick, whose unique call in the Church of his day was to organise and implement a mission geared specifically towards pagans *outside* the Roman Empire? It is to be clearly inferred from his own writings that he had been accepted by the relevant ecclesiastical superiors and ordained for this mission (E 1:1; C 27, 32, 49), which was without precedent, in the western part of the Empire at least, its nearest parallel being Paul's mission to the Gentiles in the early Church. But even Paul's mission, like that of Victricius in Normandy, and that of Martin of Tours, was *within* the confines or on the borders of the Empire.

Towards the climax of his *Confessio* Patrick writes: 'I was not present nor was I in Britain' when his candidature for the episcopacy was being considered by an *assembly* of British bishops (C 32:6-7). Where was he, then, at that time? If we keep Patrick's mission firmly in the context of early Church history, it seems almost axiomatic to conclude that he had already been in Ireland for a considerable time establishing his viable mission among pagans before his consecration as bishop.

The saint's own faith was not, initially, equal to this task, for he admits that he did not realise at once the grace that was in him then, so that he hesitated for a long time before embarking on this mission (C 46:145-6). But he eventually responded to the call of the Spirit and set sail for Ireland as a priest with, possibly, a few helpers. He followed the call of the Spirit against the advice of dear friends and some friendly bishops who feared for his safety (C 46:137-40). Though this mission did not meet with the unanimous approval of his ecclesiastical superiors at the time (C 37:2), it is clear that it was sanctioned by a quorum, otherwise he could not have been missioned and financed by the British Church to whom he was responsible (C 26). On the question of finance, incidentally, he tells us in his *Epistola* that he sold his nobility for the good of others, meaning the pagan Irish (E 10:87-90). This statement may imply, among other things, that he sold his father's estate and

---

1 Ó Raifeartaigh, *EP*, 18; Kenney, *SEHI*, 161-3.
2 Bede, *HE*, (ed. Plummer), i, 23-ii, 3.

used the proceeds to help finance his mission. At any rate, it may be clearly inferred from his *Confessio* that he, like St Paul, was self-supporting and that his particular mission involved a considerable outlay of money or its equivalent (C 48-53).

SABHALL PÁDRAIG

Though Patrick gives no indication as to where in Ireland he began his missionary activity, Muirchú, his seventh-century biographer, tells us that the place was Sabhall [Saul], near Downpatrick, Co. Down.[3] Since the northern half of Ireland had not yet been converted to Christianity at this time, at least to any great extent, there are good grounds for accepting the Sabhall tradition. It can be tentatively concluded that here, in the Leath-Chathail [Lecale] district, Patrick established, with no small difficulty, a flourishing mission among the pagan Irish who had once enslaved him (E 10; C 1; 61).

When a bishop was needed to ordain clergy for the growing numbers of converts, Patrick and his Christian community – according to my conjectural reconstruction of the scene – requested his ecclesiastical superiors in the British Church to send one to Ireland. He tells us categorically that he did not ask to be made a bishop himself (C 32:8). In the event, Patrick was the one chosen by the Council of Bishops and their consultants, though he may not have been a unanimous choice at this particular Assembly (cf. C 13; 46). He returned to Britain, possibly from Ireland, for his episcopal ordination, was duly consecrated bishop, presumably according to the rules laid down at the Council of Arles in 314,[4] and thereafter resumed his mission in Ireland.

THE TRIBUNAL OF INQUIRY

The years rolled by and, at this point in his pilgrimage Patrick, in his capacity as bishop, had already been conducting a very difficult mission in Ireland (C 26:2) for many years. It then became apparent that very serious charges had been made by his enemies against his character and his method of conducting his mission. Consequently, it would seem that a decision had been taken by an ecclesiastical tribunal of inquiry held in Britain, to send a delegation to Ireland to censure Patrick and, perhaps, even deprive him of his episcopal office.

Following Ó Raifeartaigh's lead here, let us, for clarity's sake, call this convocation of elders which accepted him for the episcopacy, the *Assembly,* and that of the mid-mission, the *Tribunal*.[5] We have now arrived at the most significant *ula* or halting-stone in Patrick's whole pilgrimage. Let us look, then, at an abstract of this concentric section which will serve as a guide in our consideration of this, the most painful event in Patrick's whole life:

---

3   Bieler, 1, 11 (10), (3-6), *PTA*, 79.
4   Chadwick, *ASCC* 68, cf. Introduction, *supra.*
5   Ó Raifeartaigh, op. cit., 70.

(26-7) H   Rejection by elders[6]
(28)   L   Blessings which resulted from his abduction
(29)   M   The divine answer; [*pupillam*] apple of eye
(30)   N   Thanksgiving to God
(31)   O   I say boldly
(32)   P   Elevation to the episcopate
(33)   O'   Again I say boldly
(34)   N'   Thanksgiving to God
(35)   M'   The divine answer; [*pupillum*] poor little pupil
(36)   L'   Blessings which resulted from loss of homeland and parents
(37)   H' Refusal to defer to elders.

H PATRICK'S REJECTION BY THE ELDERS
Patrick significantly juxtaposes the story of his rejection and betrayal with that of his captivity (C 1-2) at this strategic point in his *Confessio*. The two stories are told simultaneously in antiphonal form:

> and when *I was tried* [*temptatus sum*] by a number of my elders who came
> and cast up my sins as a charge against my laborious episcopate,
>   (C 26:1-2)
> — 'and [*I was*] truly HUMILIATED [*humiliatus sum*]
> by hunger and nakedness, and that daily' (C 27:22-3).

The first antiphon refers to Patrick's rejection and betrayal on this occasion; the second to his first captivity and sojourn in Fochoill where his daily humiliation by hunger and nakedness led to his conversion. Likewise, his painful and humiliating rejection was instrumental in bringing him to an ever-deeper knowledge of 'the true God', culminating in mystical union with the Blessed Trinity (C 29:9-11). Moreover, the memory of God's mercy to him in Fochoill helped him at this time to show mercy and forgiveness to his enemies. By evoking Paul (2 Co 11:27): 'in toil and hardship, through many a sleepless night, hungry and thirsty, often without food, cold and naked' (C 27:22-3), Patrick is identifying with the great Apostle of the Gentiles, as he has already done elsewhere in his *Confessio* (C 11:38-41).

---

6 Elders (*seniores*): the *episcopi* or supervisors who are not yet bishops seem, in some scripture passages (Tt 1:5,7; Ac 20:17,28), to be identical with elders. By the time of Ignatius of Antioch (c.107), an assembly ruled by a single bishop, *episcopos*, set over a number of priests, *presbyteroi*, had evolved. This transformation must have involved an intermediate stage when a single *episcopos* in each community was given the same powers over that community which had previously been exercised over several communities by the apostles or their representatives like Timothy or Titus. Cf. *The Jerusalem Bible*, NT 369, note 6; McKenzie, J.L., *Dictionary of the Bible*, 225-7.

The first antiphon suggests that an episcopal delegation was dispatched to Ireland, either to summon Patrick to stand in person before the Tribunal, or officially to hand over to him the document containing the verdict of repudiation already given at the Tribunal in his absence. Either way, their arrival seems to have been completely unexpected by him since, in all probability, he had been totally unaware of the plot against him.

It may be inferred from these statements that allegations, probably in the form of a document or letter (cf. C 29:3-4), had been drawn up by Patrick's enemies with the connivance of his 'dearest friend' (C 32), and handed over to the British bishops. In any case, allegations made against him are liberally sprinkled throughout his *Confessio*.

The first charge was spiritual unfitness for his task: 'they cast up my sins as a charge against my laborious episcopate' (C 26:2). They further alleged that his perceived cultural ineptitude disqualified him for his mission (C 1; 9; 12; 46; 49). They treated him as a contemptible and despicable figure (C 1; 13; E 1), and repudiated him (C 29; E 11; 12). They reproached him with arrogance and presumption (C 10; 11). They challenged his disinterestedness as displayed by his refusal to accept gifts, even to the point of scandalising the faithful (C 49), the gratuitous exercise of his ministry (C 50), his generosity to kings and to the faithful in all parts (C 52-3).

At variance with these allegations, they charged him with cheating the pagans (C 48), as well as with long-sighted covetousness and ambition (C 54-55). His motives for coming to Ireland in the first place were questioned (C 54; 61; E 10), and his very orthodoxy was weighed in the scales and found wanting.[7]

Nerney further suggests that such a charge could help to explain the presence of a 'Credo or profession of faith' early in the *Confessio* (C 4); his protestation that 'up to now, with God's grace, I have kept the faith' (C 44:119); that his 'faith was approved by God and men' (C 30:6); his appeal to his brethren and fellow servants to testify that he had lived from his youth 'in purity of faith and sincerity of heart' (C 48:154-6); 'the measure of my faith in the Trinity' (C 14:71); and other references to the faith of the Gospel: 'the faith increased in me, the faith of Jesus Christ' (C 16; 28; 34; 60; 61).[8]

The origins of some of these charges may, possibly, be traced back to a predictably bitter reaction from a faction in the British Church, to certain unfavourable statements made in their regard by Patrick, in his *Epistola* to the soldiers of Coroticus, which was written some time prior to his *Confessio*.

In this *Epistola* he affirms that he has been called by God to preach the Gospel (E 6:40-5). He consequently requests his fellow-bishops (E 6:49-50) to excommunicate Coroticus and his fellow-murderers, until the said criminals repent and do penance for their crimes:

---

7 Nerney, *SPS*, 504-5.
8 Ibid., 505.

> that it not be permissible to flatter such people,
> 'to take food' or drink with them,
> nor ought one be obliged to accept their alms
> until, with tears poured out to God, they perform penance rigorously
>   enough
> and liberate the slaves of God and the baptized handmaids *of Christ*,
> for whom he died and was crucified (E 7:51-6).

The obvious implication seems to be that some members of the British clergy continued to engage in such unworthy practices, even after the murder of Patrick's Irish converts. Since Coroticus was a prince, the members of the clergy most likely to be considered eligible to share his table would be those of the landed gentry stock.

Patrick then launches into a blistering attack on ill-gotten gain, which would apply equally to the *modus operandi* of Coroticus and his associates, as well as to those British Christians, be they lay or clerical, who sat at table with them and accepted their alms – or was it their bribes?

> 'The most High is not pleased with the offerings of unjust people.'
> He who offers sacrifice from the property of the poor
> [is] like one who makes a victim of a son before his father's eyes....
>   (E 8:57-9)
> Avarice [is] a deadly crime.... (E 9:70)

This public, forthright and fearless confrontation on Patrick's part was not calculated to ingratiate him with that section of the British clergy and laity who turned a blind eye to the criminal behaviour of Coroticus and his minions, and we are not surprised when he further reveals in this *Epistola* how he was repudiated, hated and despised by his own British people whom he so dearly loved.

It must immediately be said, however, that this was not their only reason for rejecting him, since jealousy was also a factor:

> Even if my own people do not recognise me,
> 'a prophet has no honour in his own country'... (E 11:93-4)
> jealousy is shown to me.
> *What shall I do, Lord?*
> *I am greatly despised...* (E 12:107-9)

It is possible, as has already been suggested, that Patrick's innovative approach and his use of the Irish language and culture to further his mission to the pagan Irish may also have alarmed his ecclesiastical superiors, to whom he was responsible. Not being skilled in the art of diplomacy, necessary discussions regarding the pros and cons of certain initiatives between Patrick and his ecclesiastical superiors may not have taken place.

At all events, so grave were the charges made against him, that the bishops were left with no option but to convene a tribunal or ecclesiastical court of inquiry. We know from his statement that his 'dearest friend' (C 32:1) threw in his lot with his enemies by betraying his confidence *coram cunctis*, 'in the sight of all good and bad' (C 32:14). This court found against Patrick.

It is impossible to exaggerate the anguish Patrick endured on this occasion. The only other part of his writings that can be compared with this chapter is his horrific testing by Satan (C 20), the terror of which was still a vivid memory almost half a century after the event. So excruciating was this episcopal inquisition for him, and so soul-shattering were the allegations made, that he was stunned by the verdict to a point verging on despair:

> and when *I was tried* [*temptatus sum*] by a number of my elders who came
> and cast up my sins as a charge against my laborious episcopate, (C 26:1-2)
> – and [*I was*] truly HUMILIATED [*humiliatus sum*]
> 'by hunger and nakedness', and that daily. (C 27:22-3)
> On that day, assuredly, 'I was vigorously *overwhelmed* [*impulsus sum*],
> to the point of falling' here and for eternity,
> but the Lord spared the sojourner and exile
> because of his own kindly name,
> and he came powerfully to my support in this crushing under heel [*in hac conculcatione*],
> so that in disgrace and in shame [*obprobrium*] I did not come out badly (C 26:3-8)
> – until *I was* indeed *castigated* [*castigatus sum*] (C 27:21)

Here, as elsewhere, his intense feelings could find appropriate expression only in a biblical framework; in this instance the great Hallel Psalm 119 (118) – which is one of gratitude to God for deliverance from distress and death – met his needs adequately. It is significant that this is one of the Psalms which was chanted by Christ himself at the Last Supper before he entered into his Agony in the Garden and his bitter Passion and Death on Calvary. Patrick's own Agony had now begun.

This Psalm opens and closes with: 'O give thanks to the Lord, for he is good; his steadfast love endures forever' (v. 1). God's eternal love is the very foundation on which this magnificent Psalm is built. Patrick was undoubtedly familiar with the whole of it and found in it potent expression of God's goodness to him in this, the greatest trial of his whole life:

Out of my distress I called on the Lord, the Lord answered me
and set me in a broad place (v.5).
The Lord is on my side to help me; I shall look in triumph
on those who hate me (v.7).
It is better to take refuge in the Lord than to put
confidence in princes (v. 9).

His profound faith and trust in God were not without reward, for God came to comfort and sustain him — as he had already done during his first captivity (C 1-2) — in what he describes as 'a crushing under heel' (C 26:7). He who never exaggerates conveys the depths of his humiliation in these circumstances with dignity and restrained understatement: 'in collapse and in shame I did not come out badly' (C 26:8). 'Shame' is the one word he stresses to express his feelings on this occasion. A profound awareness of the horrors of sin in the sight of the All-Holy God, and the memory of the power of Satan (C 20), fill his heart with a mature, Christian concern for the salvation of his enemies:

I pray *God* that 'it may not be reckoned to them as sin' (C 26:9).
— and I did not believe in the living God,
nor [had I believed in him] from my infancy,
but I remained in death and in unbelief (C 27:18-20).

His judgement is also tempered by the memory of his own youthful sinfulness and ignorance of 'the true God' (C 1:10,13-15; 27:13-20). His next response is, therefore, to pray, as St Timothy had done in similar circumstances, for the perpetrators of this crime, which he judges to be, objectively, a grave sin: 'At my first defence no one came to my support, but all deserted me', Timothy tells us. He then prays for his enemies in words which Patrick makes his own here: 'I ask God that it may not be counted against them' (2 Tm 4:16).

After thirty years 'they invented an occasion [*occasionem*] against me'
   (C 26:10)
— *if I was then fifteen years old* (C 27:17)

The phrases *after the lapse of thirty years* and *fifteen years old* link the occasion on which he confessed the sin of his adolescence to his *anamchara* or soulfriend some thirty years earlier before his ordination to the diaconate, and the Tribunal of Inquiry when that confession was brought against him. If Patrick had reached the required age of thirty before being made deacon in accordance with the fourth-century ruling already mentioned above, we may now conclude that he was at least sixty at the time of the Tribunal.

By judicious use of a scriptural quotation: 'We shall not find any *ground for complaint* against this Daniel unless we find it in connection with the law of his God',

> non inveniemus Daniheli huic aliquam *occasionem* nisi forte in lege Dei sui (Dn 6:5),
>
> After thirty years 'they invented an occasion [*occasionem*] against me' (C 26:10),

Patrick now places this episcopal enquiry in a comparable biblical context. By so doing, the obvious parallel between his own helpless plight in the face of his enemies, 'in the land of my captivity' (2 Ch 6:37; C 3; 33; 61), and that of Daniel 'the stranger', 'exile', and captive in Babylon in *his* dilemma (Dn 6:13) becomes apparent. For, as has been already said, Patrick knows and expects us to know, the context of this biblical quotation: the Persian king, Darius, has elected three presidents, one of whom is Daniel, and a large number of satraps or envoys to administer his kingdom. Daniel, because of his personal integrity, soon achieves such distinction in his office that the king plans to set him over the whole kingdom. This provokes jealousy among his companions and spurs them to plot Daniel's downfall.

It seems possible that in his discreet use of this quotation, Patrick is implying that jealousy was the motivation behind the plot and the complaints against himself. We have already seen how Patrick refers to 'the enemy' showing 'his jealousy through the tyranny of Coroticus', and how, by implication, a faction in the British Church, presumably in high places, was in league with him to some extent (E 6-8; 13). Furthermore, Daniel's enemies cannot destroy him because he is faithful, unless they 'find a complaint against him in connection with the Law of his God' (Dn 6:5). Is Patrick extending the parallel here between himself and Daniel when he tells us that the only 'ground for complaint against himself' which his own enemies could find, was also 'in connection with the law of his God?' In other words, the inferred allegations of avarice, ambition and perhaps simony (C 48-53) had been proved to be groundless.

As a pretext for proceeding against him they found – 'after thirty years'! – a confession of a sin against the Law of God which he had made to his 'dearest friend' before he was ordained a deacon:

> *a word* [*verbum*] *which I had confessed before I was made a deacon.* (C 27:11)
> – *what I had done* [*gesseram*] *in my boyhood on one day*
> more precisely in one hour,
> because I had not yet gained self-control.
> 'I do not know, God knows' (C 27:13-16)

Patrick was then an adolescent, barely fifteen years of age. The nature of his sin has been the subject of much conjecture among scholars. We know that in the early Church three sins were deemed extremely serious: adultery, murder and idolatry. There are, it seems to me, indications in the *Confessio* that the sin of which Patrick accused himself was that of idolatry.

To begin with, the Silures who inhabited Venta Silurum, present-day Caerwent — and possibly, as we have already indicated, Patrick's home town — had, like their Gaulish and Irish counterparts, their pre-Christian, Celtic festivals. Patrick and his companions, in the flush of youthful exuberance, may have gone off to one of them and taken an active part in pagan sun-worship, perhaps in the form of offering wild honey to pagan gods. His pagan Irish companions had offered wild honey to their earth-god, when, in answer to Patrick's fervent prayer, the Lord had providentially sent a herd of pigs their way one memorable morning to allay their hunger (C 19:76-80).

Another possibility is, of course, that he could equally have taken part in pagan Roman sun-worship which, in the fifth century, was making something of a come-back, to such an extent that Pope Leo the Great (461) thought fit to warn the Church against it in a famous sermon. It all happened, whatever it was, 'in one hour' (C 27:14), and it was then over and done with. But it came up again to trouble Patrick's delicate conscience just before his ordination to the diaconate, when he repented of it, confided it to his friend and was forgiven by God.

In the context of his unique vocation to concentrate on the conversion of pagans, one can see why he would, at this point, be acutely aware of his youthful denial of Christ. We have already noted his emphatic triple repudiation of pagan practices: the sucking of the sailors' nipples, which symbolised a Celtic pact of friendship (C 18:45-8), the wild honey which his pagan ship's crew had offered in sacrifice (C 19:76-80), and, finally, the worship of the sun in his *Doxology* (C 60:34-40).

There is, moreover, a triple affirmation of Christ as the 'true Sun' in the *Confessio*: once in the vision of Helias (C 20:89-91), and twice in the *Doxology* (C 59:29-30; 60:37). Is Patrick conscious here of the parallel between his own and Peter's denial of Christ during his Passion (Mt 26:69-75), Peter's humble threefold confession of faith and love after the Resurrection, and his designation by the Lord as Head of the Church (Jn 21:15-19)?

Now, as a bishop, Patrick's main focus was on pagans, *gentes*. He preached the Good News to them through the medium of their own language and culture, and in his Christian compassion, highlighted the plight of the slaves (C 1; 18; 34; 37-38; 40; 48; E 1; 10; 14). This approach to mission, almost unique in the Church at that time, may have been a cause of misunderstanding both in Britain and among certain factions in the Church in Ireland, and was latched on to, as a pretext for punishing him, by his jealous enemies. His orthodoxy in that age of 'heretics' had, perhaps, become suspect, and the sin of his youth was used to reinforce this allegation.

Whatever the nature of the sin, it was not the real issue; there was a hidden agenda. If we accept the biblical parallel between Daniel and Patrick, on the other hand, the real cause of his rejection by a substantial number – but not all – of the elders would seem to have been one of jealousy and, perhaps, misunderstanding.

At the crux of this concentric passage Patrick explains that, because his conscience was troubled by the remembrance of that sin as he prepared for the diaconate, he confessed it to his 'dearest friend':

> In the anxiety of my troubled mind I disclosed to my dearest friend
> (C 27:12)

This 'dearest friend', some thirty years later, committed the unspeakable crime of revealing the penitent's soul-secret. Patrick highlights his 'shame' and the anguish which he endured because of his trusted friend's betrayal, by artistically emphasising the words *obprobrium* [shame] and *amicissimo meo,* my dearest friend, through the use of extreme and mean ratio at this point in his *Confessio.*[9]

H' REFUSAL TO DEFER TO ELDERS

Patrick now judiciously balances his rejection by the elders with a flashback to his circumstances prior to setting out for the first time as a missionary priest (?) to Ireland (C 37 H'). In this instance, he is among genuine friends, both lay and clerical, as he organises himself for that mission. This journey he undertakes, he assures us, under the guidance of the Holy Spirit. He embarks, however, in spite of much well-meant opposition from those friends, because they doubt his capacity for such an undertaking and are, therefore, concerned for his welfare. But, strengthened by the Spirit, he refuses to defer to them:

> And many gifts were offered to me with weeping and tears,
> and I offended [the donors],
> and also against [my] wish *a certain number of* MY ELDERS,
> but, with God as my pilot, in no way did I consent nor acquiesce.
> It was not my grace but God who conquers in me,
> and I stood firm against them all,
> so that I might come to the Irish pagans to proclaim the Gospel,
> and to endure insults from *unbelievers,*
> 'so that I might hear the *shame of my* EXILE',
> and [endure] many persecutions *'even unto chains',*
> and so that I might surrender my freeborn status for the benefit of
>   others;
> and if should be worthy *I am 'prepared',*

---

9 Howlett, *BLSPB,* 107.

[to give up] 'even *my life*'
unhesitatingly and 'most gladly' *for his name* (C 37:1-14).

Are the *'certain number of MY ELDERS'*, the friendly ecclesiastical superiors
who opposed him in this instance (cf. C 46), among the same 'elders' who
later tried him and cast his sins against him (C 26:1-2)? Is this proof that even
his friends among the elders were forced to agree in conscience to the setting
up of this inquiry because of the gravity of the allegations made against him
by a jealous clique? It seems possible.

His categorical statement 'so that I might come to the Irish pagans to
proclaim the Gospel' contradicts the assertion of some scholars that he came
among Christians in Ireland. He refers once again to the 'shame' and
sufferings he had to endure as a missionary, and he reiterates his desire 'to
drink the chalice' of suffering as his Master did and to give up his life as a
martyr for his name. It is significant that he never asks for more visions or
locutions; his only desire is to be made conformable to his suffering Saviour.

The italicised words and phrases correspond to related words and phrases
in the concentric pair, H (26-27). These are the only two places in the
Confessio where Patrick uses the words 'shame, exile' and the phrase 'my
elders'.[10]

L. BLESSINGS WHICH RESULTED FROM HIS ABDUCTION
Patrick's coming to Ireland was very much against his own will:

On the other hand I did not set out for Ireland of my own accord
'until the time' I had nearly *'perished.'*
But this was rather to my advantage,
since because of this I have been freed from fault by the Lord,
and *'he has fitted me'* so that today I may be
what was once far beyond me,
that I may be concerned
or rather be labouring for the salvation of others,
whereas *at that time* I was not thinking even about myself (C 28:1-9).

Here, at the heart of his *Confessio*, Patrick now reiterates all that he has already
said about God's merciful Providence in his regard. 'The time I had nearly
perished' refers to the period before his coming as a slave when, he tells us,
he did not know 'the true God' (C 1:10). This first captivity and the struggle
which it involved was the source of many blessings for, in the process, Patrick
was purified, strengthened, and fitted for his mission by the Lord himself.

---

10 Howlett, ibid., 108.

L' BLESSINGS WHICH RESULTED FROM LOSS OF HOMELAND AND PARENTS

In its parallel reading (C 36:1-7), Patrick emphatically claims, yet again, that God's Providence has directed all things for the best towards his ultimate goal for him, which is his vocation to be the Apostle of pagan Ireland. It begins with a question: 'Whence did this wisdom come to me?' (Mt 13:54), whose context is Jesus teaching in the synagogue in his own country, and his rejection by his own people:

> 'prophets are not without honour except in their own country and in their own house.'
> And he did not do many deeds of power there, because of their unbelief (Mt 13:57-8).

Is this an oblique reference to 'the elders' – his own household – who have rejected him as Christ was rejected before him?

> *Whence did this wisdom [come] to me,*
> *which was not in me,*
> *who knew neither 'the number of my days',*
> nor did I have any discernment about God?
> *Whence [was given] to me afterwards the gift so great, so salutary,*
> to know or to love God wholeheartedly,
> but at the loss of country and kindred? (C 36:1-7)

Here we are back again to *donum Dei,* one of the twin pillars on which the whole *Confessio* hinges, 'the gift of knowing and loving God', compared with which, even the cost of leaving country, relatives and friends for the sake of the Gospel and God's promises seems very small indeed to Patrick. The reference to this cost – this *glasmartra* or 'green martyrdom' in reverse – links this part of the *Confessio* artistically and meaningfully with Patrick's total commitment to his mission in Ireland. This latter point is the penultimate *ula* or halting stone of Patrick's pilgrimage, for here, not only had he left country, family and friends for the sake of the Gospel, he had left them 'forever,' bound in the Spirit *never* to return (C 44-5). This example of our father in the faith was to be the inspiration of the great missionary exodus from Ireland to countries all over the globe down to our own day.

These two parallel, complementary chapters (C 28; 36) are connected to each other by thematic and verbal correspondences. Thus, 'until I had nearly perished' (C 28:1), a quotation from Psalm 18 (17):38, evokes a quotation from Psalm 38(39):5, 'who knew neither the number of days' (C 36:3). Likewise, And 'he has fitted me, so that today I may be, what once was far beyond me' (C 28:5-6) recalls 'From where did this wisdom come to me, which was not in me?' (C 36:1-2), while 'that I may be concerned, or rather be labouring for the salvation of others' (C 28:7-8) is complemented by: 'whence afterwards was given to me the gift so great, so salutary' (C 36:5).

M THE DIVINE ANSWER; (*PUPILLAM*) PUPIL OF EYE

As he gradually edges nearer the very heart of his *Confessio,* Patrick refers once again to that terrible day when he was reproved by the envoys sent by the Tribunal (C 29). 'On that night', Patrick continues,

> I saw *in a vision of the night*
> what had been written against my face without honour
> and meanwhile I heard the *'divine answer'* saying to me,
> *'We have seen with disapproval* the face of the designated man
> with his name stripped naked',
> and he did not say, 'You have seen with disapproval',
> but *'We have seen with disapproval'*
> as if he had joined me to himself,
> just as he has said, *'He who touches you*
> [*is*] *as he who touches the pupil of my eye'* (C 29:3-11)

This 'vision of the night' (Dn 7:13) is Patrick's last explicitly recorded 'dream-vision'. He was undoubtedly aware that the biblical context of this 'vision' is that of the son of man depicted in Daniel 7:13-14, and that this Old Testament image provides the backdrop for Paul's and other early Christian writers' interpretation of the saving work of Christ:

> As I watched in the *night visions,*
> I saw one like a son of man coming with the clouds of heaven.
> And he came to the Ancient One
> and was presented before him.
> To him was given dominion and glory and kingship,
> that all people and nations and languages should serve him.
> His dominion is an everlasting dominion that shall not pass away,
> and his kingship is one that shall never be destroyed.

Christ, the fulfilling type of Daniel's 'son of man', is commissioned to restore all to God, as Paul says (1 Co 15:24-5):

> Then comes the end,
> when he hands over the kingdom to God the Father,
> after he has destroyed every ruler and every authority and power.
> For he must reign until he has put all his enemies under his feet.

Perhaps what Patrick saw was simply a literal 're-view' of what had already happened to him 'on that day' when the envoys handed him the legal document of repudiation, with all that it entailed in the way of suffering and shock. Now, 'on that night', he saw this document again in 'a vision', but this time the Lord revealed to him that the Triune God had seen with disapproval what had befallen him because of the treachery of his 'dearest friend', and those who had slandered the chosen one and divested him of his good reputation. This is God's assurance to Patrick that he is innocent in his sight. This interpretation seems more in keeping with the scriptural context in which Daniel's wily enemies drew up a document and tricked an unsuspecting king into signing it, their hidden purpose being to use this legal weapon to destroy Daniel (Dn 6:6-9). Now, in the scriptural context of this vision, Patrick is assured of the victory through Christ over his enemies. In any case, what is of real importance for Patrick is 'the divine answer', which is possibly unique in Christian hagiography:

> and amidst these things I heard *'the divine answer'* saying to me...
> 'We have seen with disapproval'...
> and he did not say, 'You have seen with disapproval'
> but, 'We have seen with disapproval'
> as if he had joined me to himself
> [*quasi sibi me iunxisset*] (C 29:5-11).

Patrick makes the stupendous claim that the Triune God has joined him to himself as closely as to the pupil of his eye. He has at last reached the pinnacle of the holy mountain of contemplation, stripped, in the process, of everything, even his good name.[11] And it is from this vantage point that he looks back on the pilgrim's path over which he has travelled, which is really Christ's way of the Cross, and gives praise to the Blessed Trinity, '[You] who have appeared to me with such divinity' (C 34:8).

Once again Patrick measures the content of this vision objectively against the Word of God, and concludes that when the Lord said 'We have seen with disapproval the face of the designated man with his name stripped naked', it is the equivalent of the scriptural quotation: 'He who touches you is as he who touches *pupillam*, the pupil of my eye' (C 29). For Patrick, this meant the ineffable realisation of how closely God had united him to himself, a union and a joy that even he himself feels powerless to convey in mere words.

M' THE DIVINE ANSWER; (*PUPILLUM*) A POOR LITTLE PUPIL
This 'divine answer' (C 29 M) reminds Patrick of similar 'divine answers' which he now recalls for us in the parallel reading (C 35 M'). He starts by saying that it would be tedious to give a detailed account of all his labours in whole or in part; yet he wants to tell us briefly,

---

11 John of the Cross, *AMC* and *DNS, passim.*

> how the most holy God has often freed [me] from slavery
> and from *twelve perils whereby my soul was endangered,*
> besides numerous treacheries
> and *'things which I am unable to express in words',*

about which he supplies no details for fear of boring his readers. 'But I have God as my authority', he continues,

> 'who knows all things even before they come to pass' (Dn 13:43),
> that me, *pupillum,* a poor little pupil,
> an ordinary person, [his] *'divine answer'* would frequently warn
>   (C 35:8-10).

We may tentatively conclude from this that the pattern of Patrick's visions and locutions continued, at least sporadically, all through his 'laborious episcopate' (C 26), and not just up to this point of rejection and betrayal, as is commonly believed. His clever word-play and elegant linkage of *pupillam* (C 29:11 M) with its contrasting parallel, *pupillum* (C 35:9 M'), evokes *Anaw,* Christ, the helpless One, who put all his trust in God alone. Patrick, 'the poor little pupil [*pupillum*]' who identifies with Christ, is, as it were, the pupil [*pupillam*] of (the Lord's) eye.

These two chapters (C 29; 35) are linked together by phrases and scriptural quotations common to both. The 'divine answer' is from Romans 11:4, where Paul is affirming that Israel's rejection is not final. As in Isaiah's time (1 K 19:19, 20, 29-34), there is 'a remnant' of the faithful. Paul – and in this context, Patrick – is no more alone than Isaiah was. 'He who touches you [is] as he who touches the pupil of my eye' is from Zechariah 2:8, indicating special favour and affection, while 'that me a poor little pupil' is a word-play on the same scriptural quotation. Here, yet again, Patrick, by a careful balance of word and phrase, highlights *pupillam, pupillum* and *responsum divinum,*[12] thus emphasising Patrick's special favour, akin to that of Isaiah and Paul, in the sight of God.

N. GRATITUDE TO GOD

His immediate response to 'the divine answer' (C 29:5) is, predictably, one of praise and gratitude to God who has carried him as a father carries his child all along the pilgrim's path he has travelled. In the light of the Tribunal which found against him, his praise is all the more intense. Having now realised that his mission could have been impeded at the beginning, rather than towards the end of his 'laborious episcopate' (C 26:2), he is specifically grateful that he was enabled to execute his 'task which I had learned from Christ my Lord'

---

12 Howlett, op.cit., 108.

(C 30:4). He rejoices that he felt within himself a not insignificant God-given power, and that 'his faith was approved before God and men' (C 30:6).

The biblical context of 'from him "I felt within myself" no little *power*' is the cure of the woman who touched the fringe of Christ's clothes, in Luke 8:45-8:

> Then Jesus asked,
> 'Who touched me?'
> When all denied it, Peter said,
> 'Master, the crowds surround you and press in on you.'
> But Jesus said,
> *'Someone touched me;*
> for I noticed that *power had gone out from me.'*
> When the woman saw that she could not remain hidden,
> she came trembling; and falling down before him,
> she declared in the presence of all the people
> why she had touched him,
> and how she had been immediately healed.
> He said to her,
> 'Daughter, your *faith* has made you well; go in peace' (Lk 8:45-8).

It is implicit in this biblical context that, like this sick woman in Luke, Patrick too has touched, by faith, the hem of Christ's garment, and power has gone forth from the Saviour to him to sustain him in all his ways.

N' Gratitude to God

The nearer Patrick approaches the culmination of the whole *Confessio*, the greater and the more extended becomes his song of praise and gratitude to God, as is evident in the parallel reading (C 34) to which I shall return at the end of this chapter.

O I say boldly

Having at length reached the last two contrasting parallels of this concentric passage – which Patrick links to each other by contrasting word-play: *Audenter dico; dico audenter rursus,* 'boldly I say; I say boldly again', in (C 31) and (C 33) – he courageously proclaims his innocence and testifies, as he has already done (C 7-8; 54), to the truth of all that he has said in his *Confessio*:

> Whence therefore *I say boldly*
> *that my conscience does not reprove me*
> here and in the future.
> 'God is my witness'
> 'that I have not lied'
> in the speeches which I have recounted to you (C 31).

O' AGAIN I SAY BOLDLY
This part of the *Confessio* is linked backwards to the exposition (C 3), and forward to the resolution (C 43-45) with the evocation of 'the land of my captivity' (C 33:3), which is the inner and outer arena of Patrick's pilgrimage, of his life's great Hallel Psalm of Praise, a point to which I shall return later. Here he vigorously sought him and there he found his God. 'He kept me from all iniquities ... on account of his indwelling Spirit' (C 33:6) links this central part of the *Confessio* back to the crux of the testimony of his vocation, the vision of Elijah, where the dying Christ, crying out in agony *'My God, my God, why hast Thou forsaken me?'* (C 20), is evoked:

> and I believe that I was sustained by Christ my Lord,
> and his SPIRIT was even then crying out on my behalf,
> and I trust that it will be so 'on the day of' my pressing need [*in die pressaurae*]
> as he affirms in the Gospel, 'On that day,'
> the Lord testifies, *It is not you who speak*
> but the Spirit of your Father is speaking in you (C 20:91-6).

Patrick's *day of tribulation,* his Crucifixion, has come, but he is not alone....

P   ELEVATION TO THE EPISCOPATE
We have now arrived with Patrick at the pivotal point of his whole *Confessio* (C 32), the point where he grieves for his 'dearest friend' and where there is exhibited an internal concentric passage where the Assembly, at which he was elected bishop, and the Tribunal, which came mid-way or towards the end of his 'laborious episcopate', are placed side by side:

> But I grieve the more for my dearest friend,
> because we merited to hear such a response from this man
> to whom I had entrusted my very soul.
> And I have learned from some of the brethren
> *before that defence,*
> at which I was not present,
> nor was I in the Britains (C 32:1-7)

I have already tentatively suggested that Patrick may have been in pagan Ireland for a considerable time as a Christian missionary; the ministry of a bishop was required; a request was made to Patrick's ecclesiastical superiors in Britain, to whom he was responsible. He had been told by 'certain brethren', who were presumably priests or bishops, that his 'dearest friend' would make a very strong case for Patrick's candidacy for the Irish bishopric in his absence. Consequently, it may be inferred that he was happy in his conscience that Patrick was a suitable person for this office, and that he did it with complete freedom of choice. The inference here is that his 'dearest friend' had the power to advocate or prevent Patrick's nomination, so that he was, by that time, probably a bishop or a monastic superior or, at least, one of their consultants. Patrick was not present at that Assembly, nor was he in Britain, so we assume that he was still in Ireland looking after his flock.

> nor did it *arise from me,* (C 32:8)
> – he should put *me* to shame even publicly
> over something which before he had conceded [to me] joyfully
> and of his own accord,
> and the Lord 'who is greater than all'? (C 32:15-17)

In the first of these two antiphons Patrick now testifies that he did not ask to be made bishop. In the second antiphon he is referring to the Tribunal. Patrick had, at this stage, borne the burden of episcopal office for a long time when his 'dearest friend' barbed the attack made on him by divulging his confession of the sin of his youth, to his disparagement and confusion (C 27:5-7); he thus defamed Patrick publicly, before friends and enemies alike – *coram cunctis* – at this mid-mission Tribunal, in a matter that previously, at the Assembly, had had his free and hearty approval. This friend had, seemingly, been party to an ignominious document: 'what had been written against my face without honour' (C 29:4). We may assume that the letter or document was for Patrick's superiors; and it is certain that the writer aimed at thwarting his mission (C 30:3), as already noted. Indeed, the context seems to suggest that he now pleaded that Patrick was unworthy of being bishop and, therefore, that he should be deposed from office.

> that, *in my absence, he would also plead for me* (C 32:9)
> – But whence did it occur *to him* afterwards
> that in the sight of everyone, good and bad (C 32:13-14)

Patrick's anguish, shame and bewilderment are sustained here. This transparently honest man cannot come to grips with the treachery of a person who could at one time plead, in complete freedom, that he should be elected bishop, and afterwards shame him before friends and enemies alike:

> that, *in my absence, he would also plead for me* (C 32:9)
> – *of which I was not worthy* (C 32:12)

Because of his profound union with God, Patrick sees the divine call to the episcopacy through the eyes of the Lord, and consequently he can say with all his characteristic truthfulness and honesty that he was unworthy of that divine call. But he also affirms that, not only had his 'most intimate friend' conceded gladly that he should be a bishop, but 'the Lord who is greater than all' (C 32:17). God had turned his gaze round on his *humilitas*, his lowliness (C 2:23), his unworthiness (C 15:79; 55:3), and, for his own wise purposes, had chosen to bestow his gracious gift on him, and thus had empowered him to fulfil this office worthily, 'because of his indwelling Spirit who has worked in me up to this day' (C 33:7-8).

It seems reasonable to conclude that Patrick was then summoned back to Britain from Ireland after that defence or Assembly at which he had been elected bishop. On arrival, it would seem from the context that he was met by his 'dearest friend'. It is to that occasion that Patrick is possibly referring when he writes:

> He himself had even *said* to me *from his own mouth* (C 32:10)
> — 'Ecce dandus es tu ad gradum episcopatus'
> 'Look, you are to be granted the order of the episcopate' (C 32:11)

This central statement is tantamount to saying that Patrick had been legally elected to episcopal office by the Assembly, though he was probably not a unanimous choice (C 13; 46), and that he was now being congratulated as bishop-elect. This all-important statement is the heart of the matter, the pivotal point of the entire *Confessio*, for it was the seal of divine approval placed on his divine calling by the voice of the Church. All that had gone before built up towards it; all that followed flowed from it. This very fact gives the lie to speculation by some scholars 'that there was something odd or irregular about Patrick's consecration'.[13] Had that been so, this would surely have been used by his enemies against Patrick in their effort to destroy him. Indeed his 'dearest friend', now turned traitor, was in the ideal position to know and make known such an allegation at the mid-mission Tribunal, since he had been a member of the Assembly at which Patrick had been elected to the episcopacy, and since, ironically, he had been one of the staunch advocates of his candidacy at that time. But he declined to do so, for the only real cause which they could find for proceeding against Patrick, which was a much weaker one, was the sin of his youth (C 26:11).

In our résumé of this crucial part of his *Confessio*, it is clear that this betrayal of his confidence by his *anamchara* was central in both Patrick's spiritual and temporal pilgrimage, as well as being the occasion of his greatest suffering and of his conformity to Christ:

> On that day, assuredly, '*I was* vigorously *overwhelmed*
> to the point of falling' here and for eternity (C 26:3-4)

---

13 Powell, *TI*, 404.

For behind this immediate betrayal was the implicit betrayal both of his divine calling and of his divine mission to the pagan Irish. It is an earnest of Patrick's Christian stature that his first concern on this occasion was for the spiritual welfare of his 'dearest friend' and his enemies alike:

> But I grieve the more for my dearest friend,
> because we merited to hear such a response from this man
> to whom I had entrusted my very soul (C 32:1-3)

Patrick is referring here to the seal of Confession to an *anamchara* which had been broken by his 'dearest friend'. Conscious of the objective gravity of this sin as well as the complicity of the others involved, Patrick intercedes for them before God:

> I pray *God* that 'it may not be reckoned to them as sin' (C 26:9).

Patrick does not say 'I grieve the more for my dearest friend turned traitor'; no, nothing has changed, he still is his 'dearest friend', perhaps dearer than ever because he has been forgiven. One cannot but compare Patrick's forgiveness and pastoral concern with Christ's loving and compassionate attitude towards Peter and the rest of his own Apostles after the Resurrection. He never once rebukes them for either denying or abandoning him during his Passion and Death on the Cross.

Here, then, at the heart of his *Confessio*, Patrick presents us with a triptych, the central panel of which depicts Patrick's conformity to the Crucified Christ. Rays of divine light are emanating from this central panel to incorporate the two subsidiary side-panels.

The left panel represents his youthful ignorance of 'the true God,' his captivity and conversion. The memory of his utter helplessness and God's mercy to him then, when he consoled him 'as a *father* [comforts] a son' (C 2:28), was engraved indelibly in his heart and soul:

> But that 'I do *know* most surely', that indeed 'BEFORE I WAS HUMBLED'
> I was like a stone lying in 'deep mire,'
> and he 'who is mighty' came
> and 'in his mercy' lifted me up
> and, more than that, truly raised me aloft
> and placed me on the highest wall (C 12:47-52).
> And '*we did not keep watch over* his precepts'
> And *we did not obey our priests,*
> *who kept warning* us *about our salvation* (C 1:14-16),
> – and *kept watch over* me before I knew him
> and before I was wise or could distinguish between good and evil,
> and he protected me (C 2:25-7).

His experience of ongoing conversion, of turning back resolutely towards 'the true God' and his mystical experiences, were for Patrick what the experience of the Transfiguration of Jesus on the Mount was for the three disciples; it was for him, as for them, a little Easter, a foretaste of the Resurrection, and part of his preparation for his mission among the Irish, and for the Crucifixion experience of the central panel of our triptych. In placing a flashback to his conversion, and to the circumstances that led to it, side by side with his account of his rejection by the elders, his possible purpose is to light up his picture with the glow of God's patient love and mercy for the sinner, and the forgiveness of sin won for us on Calvary. In this way he is implicitly stating that, though his enemies are objectively guilty of serious sin, God, whose steadfast love for them is unchanged in spite of their conduct, is turning his gaze round on them with infinite love and compassion; that he is keeping watch over them, even though they have denied him; that he is waiting for an opportunity to touch the hardness of their hearts that they may remember their sins, so that they may turn with their whole heart to the Lord their God, and find him, as he had found him, in the land of their spiritual captivity (C 1-2; 33).

In the right-hand panel he depicts a Resurrection scene, in which Patrick identifies with the Risen Jesus who showed his glorious wounds to his disciples in the upper room on Easter Sunday evening. With his eyes ever fixed on Jesus, he is enabled to forgive his enemies, and his 'dearest friend' in particular, in the name of the Crucified and Risen Lord. Patrick must have contemplated long and lovingly, all through his life, Christ's Last Supper with his disciples....

> I give you a new commandment, that you love one another.
> Just as I have loved you, you also should love one another.
> By this everyone will know that you are my disciples,
> if you have love for one another (Jn 13:34-5).
> I am the vine,
> you are the branches.
> Those who abide in me and I in them,
> bear much fruit,
> because apart from me you can do nothing (15:5).

Both his *Epistola* and *Confessio* testify that, in the circumstances of his daily life, Patrick met with constant opposition, jealousy and treachery, such as Christ had experienced before him. This meant that he was being perpetually challenged to exercise Christlike forgiveness, by the power of his indwelling Spirit (C 33:7-8), and so it was on the day of his tribulation (C 20:93; 34:14).

> Happy indeed the man whom God corrects!
> Then do not refuse this lesson from the Lord.

For he who wounds is he who soothes the sore,
and the hand that hurts is the hand that heals (Jb 5:17-18).

Professor Eoin Mac Néill (1867-1945), the distinguished historian and Patrician scholar, was so impressed by the depth and quality of Patrick's Christian forgiveness, his students tell us, that he made constant reference to it in his lectures on Patrick. He maintained, moreover, that it was this unique dimension of Christianity that ensured the rapid growth of the Christian Church against all the odds in the early centuries of the Christian era.

In his rejection and betrayal Patrick, the toil-worn bishop, shares in the dignity and composure of that Master, whom he so faithfully served, as he stood before Annas and Caiaphas, Herod and Pilate, the Innocent Victim of their jealousy, greed and insecurity, and for whom he prayed on the Cross. His *Confessio* is, in part, a cry of the heart to be reconciled with his enemies 'before I die' (C 62), possibly with Matthew 5:23-4 in mind:

So when you are offering your gift at the altar,
if you remember that your brother or sister has something against you,
leave your gift there before the altar;
and go first to be reconciled with your brother or sister,
and then come and offer your gift.

In the chapter on 'Justice and Reconciliation' in *Reconciliation in Religion and Society*, Terry Anderson, the American journalist held hostage in the Lebanon, is quoted as telling a Derry audience: 'It is the victim who must make the first approach towards his oppressor, signal his willingness to forgive the man who has tortured him, if either is to [experience] ... the freedom and the peace that come from reconciliation'. The author, Gerry O'Hanlon, no more than Patrick, does not, however, advocate peace at any price, but explains that the cost of forgiveness refers, in the first instance, 'to the willingness of the injured party to absorb the offence to the relationship by his or her own suffering'. He later treats the cost which the injuring party needs to face also.[14] Were this sort of Patrician spirituality to percolate through every aspect of culture and society, like the two downcast disciples on their Easter pilgrimage to Emmaus, we might have to stop referring in the past tense to our hopes for permanent peace in our own hearts, in our country, and in the world at large. Christian reconcilation with God and neighbour, therefore, is at the very heart of our Patrician heritage.

Looking at Part III as a unit, *Satis dico*, 'I say enough' (C 33:1), following hard on Patrick's betrayal (C 32), is a perfect *caesura,* after which the pain and

---

14 Hurley (ed.), *RRS*; Una O Higgins-O Malley, critique, *Furrow*, November 1994, 661-2. cf. also *Reconcilation, Essays in honour of Michael Hurley,* for a comprehensive study of this all-important subject.

suffering of the saint's Calvary changes to the joy and triumph of the Resurrection. *Sed tamen*, 'but nevertheless', is the turning-point which introduces the crucial element in the lower half of this concentric passage, which is not in the upper part:

> '*I say*' enough.
> *But nevertheless* // I must not hide 'THE GIFT OF GOD'
> which has been lavished on us 'IN THE LAND OF MY CAPTIVITY',
> because then I earnestly sought him,
> and there I found him,
> and he kept me from all iniquities – this is my I belief,
> 'because of his indwelling Spirit'
> who 'has worked' in me until this day,
> 'Boldly' again [am I speaking].
> But, God knows, if a human being had said this to me,
> I would perhaps have remained silent about 'the charity of Christ'
> (C 33 O').

Patrick, it seems, is asserting here that he is speaking out of his own personal experience and not from the testimony of others: *Et sic expertus sum*, 'And thus I have learned by experience', he has already stated when recounting his mystical experiences (C 23:130; 25:149; 29:1-10).

Gratitude to God for this pouring out of the Spirit, the gift of God, on Patrick and on the Church 'in the land of my captivity' is the culminating point, the very essence of his *Confessio*:

> AND 'HE POURED OUT ON US ABUNDANTLY THE HOLY SPIRIT
> AS THE GIFT' AND 'PLEDGE' OF IMMORTALITY,
> who makes believers and listeners
> so that they may be 'CHILDREN OF GOD' AND 'JOINT HEIRS WITH CHRIST',
> (C 4:28-31)

> 'And so, according to the measure of the faith' of the Trinity it is my duty,
> *without fear of the censure* [*I may incur*],
> *to make known* 'THE GIFT OF GOD'
> and [his] 'eternal consolation' (C 14:71-4)

> Whence [was given] afterwards to me the gift so great, so salutary,
> to know or to love God wholeheartedly,
> but at the loss of country and kindred? (C 36:5-7)
> It was 'THE GIFT OF GOD' (C 62:10)

Patrick's response to this divine outpouring is his own great, personal *Exsultet*, which must be among the finest subjective affirmations of gratitude to God in

Christian literature. Here he pauses, as it were, and looks back, from this penultimate halting stone, over the whole precarious road he has travelled; here, like Jeremiah of old, he considers which path has stood him in good stead long ago ... this path he is determined to continue, for this is the one that has brought peace to his soul (Jr 6:16). This, as suggested earlier, is the apex of a great triangle of praise to the Blessed Trinity, beginning with his reason for writing his *Confessio* (C 3), and sustained through his Credo (C 4) on the one side, to be balanced by his magnificent *Doxology* (C 57-60) on the other:

> *Whence therefore I give unwearied thanks to my God,*
> *who kept me faithful 'in the day of my trial',*
> so *that* today *I may confidently offer in sacrifice to him,*
> *my life as 'a living host' to Christ my Lord*
> *who 'has saved me from all my troubles',*
> so that I also may say, 'Who am I, Lord',
> or 'What is my calling?'
> [You] who have appeared to me with such divinity,
> so that today 'among pagans'
> 'I may' steadfastly 'exalt
> and glorify your name'
> wherever I may be;
> and that not only in favourable circumstances,
> but also in pressing need [*in pressuris*] (cf. C 20:93),
> so that 'whatever may happen to me,
> be it good or bad',
> *I ought to accept with equanimity,*
> *and always give thanks to God*
> *who has shown me*
> that I should always believe in him without any hesitation,
> and who must have heard me,
> so that I unknowing and 'in the final days'
> may dare to undertake this work so holy and so wondrous,
> so that I to some degree may imitate those
> whom the Lord long ago had foretold
> would proclaim his Gospel,
> 'as a testimony to all pagans' before 'the end of the world'.
> So we have seen it, and so it 'has been fulfilled'.
> Behold, we are witnesses that the Gospel has been proclaimed
> to the limit beyond which nobody dwells (C 34:1-30).

The context of the quotation 'before the end of the world' (C 34:27), from Acts 2:17, is the first Pentecost in Jerusalem. Peter addresses the crowds gathered 'from every nation under heaven' and quotes the prophet Joel:

> *in the final days* it will be, God declares,
> that I will pour out my Spirit upon all flesh,
> and your sons and your daughters shall prophesy,
> and your young men shall see visions,
> and your old men shall dream dreams.

Patrick firmly believes that those last days have come and he praises God who has chosen him to be the one to preach his name at the confines of the then known world, to a people from whom once before he had barely escaped (C 61:7).

CHAPTER FIVE

ST PATRICK'S EPISTOLA EXCOMMUNICATING COROTICUS

Far from the love of God is the betrayer of Christians
into the hands of Scots and Picts.
'Rapacious wolves' have swallowed up the flock of the Lord,
which was indeed growing excellently in Ireland with the
greatest loving care (E 12:112-15).

INTRODUCTION

Patrick's *Epistola*,[1] which predates his *Confessio*, was written after the soldiers of a British ruler named Coroticus had raided the Irish coast and had conducted a cruel massacre of Patrick's newly-baptized Christians.

A considerable amount of readers' energy has been expended in an effort to establish the identity of Coroticus, the enemy of Patrick's Irish mission. It would seem that this undertaking was primarily motivated by the conviction that an approximate date for Patrick's mission could be determined if the floruit of this British tyrant[2] were established.

In the event, the process became complicated and obscured by the unfortunate fact that there were two British princes of the name Ceretic (latinised Coroticus by the Romans during the fifth century), one of whom held sway in Wales, the other in present-day Scotland. Both men originated in Scotland.

CERETIC (COROTICUS) OF WALES

Cunedda, the father of the Welsh Ceretic,[3] with his eight sons, migrated from the territory of the Votadini – which extended southward from the Firth of Forth – settled in North Wales and expelled the Irish, or *Scotti*, from that region so that they never returned. Cardiganshire took its name from Cunedda's fifth son, Ceretic, or Coroticus. Professor Chadwick has put forward cogent reasons for placing Ceretic, son of Cunedda, on the throne about AD 460, while Sir John Lloyd would put him much later: 'his position in the pedigree is compatible with a date not far removed from AD 500'.[4]

---

1 In modern usage, a distinction is often made between the terms 'letter' and 'epistle'. The letter is, so to speak, a slice of life, while the epistle is a product of literary art. (*NRSV*, 206, *NT*). Since it can be shown that Patrick's *Epistola* has considerable merit as an art form, the Latin form, *Epistola* [Epistle], has been retained.
2 Tyrant: a native British ruler.
3 Cunneda, Modern Welsh of Cunedag; Ceretic, Old-Welsh for Coroticus.
4 In Binchy, *PB*, 106; Hanson, *OC*, 21-2.

Ceretic Guletic (Coroticus) of Ail-Cluaide

The second prince of this name is mentioned in two, if not three, documents whose sources may go back to the fifth century. *Muirchú's Life of Patrick* includes the heading, *De Conflictu sancti Patricii adversum Coirtech regem Aloo*, 'Of St Patrick's conflict with Coroticus king of Aloo', that is, king of Ail-Cluaide, the Rock of Clyde, or modern Dumbarton, in Scotland.[5]

Old Welsh genealogies also mention a Ceretic Guletic (i.e. Ceretic Imperator or Generalissimo), who ruled over what was later known as 'the kingdom of Strathclyde'. We assume that the king of Ail-Cluaide and Ceretic Guletic are one and the same person, and that his stronghold was at Ail Cluaide.[6]

Pending further research, the weight of the evidence so far would seem to warrant that the credit for this dubious historical achievement be, tentatively, given to Ceretic Guletic of Ail-Cluaide rather than to Ceretic of Cardigan. At all events, it is clear from his *Epistola* that Patrick's mission was well established and flourishing at the time that Coroticus and his soldiers struck it a devastating blow.

The Irish proto-martyrs

Where, it is often asked, did this massacre take place? Which part of Ireland can lay claim to the fifth-century Irish martyrs? Though we cannot say for certain, Ulster would seem to be the most promising contender. Since the primary focus of Patrick's mission was on pagans, to begin with, it is likely that he initiated that mission in Ulster which, as far as we know, had not yet been touched by Christianity, at least, to any great extent. The traditional belief that the place where Patrick landed and initiated his mission to the pagan Irish was Sabhall [Saul], in the Leath Chathail [Lecale] district of present-day Co. Down, has never been seriously challenged.

---

5   The table of contents of *Muirchú's Life of Patrick* which is displaced, contains a number of headings to which nothing in the narrative corresponds. Binchy, *PB*, 108.

6   Moran, *ISGB*, 127 ff. The genealogy is Pedigree V in MS Harl 38, 59. The genealogists further place Riderch Hen, son of Tutwal (The *'Rodercus filius Tothail'* of Adamnán's *Vita Columbae* (1, 15) as fifth in descent from him (Hanson, *OC*, 22-3). By allowing the usual span of thirty years to a generation, this would place Coroticus of Ail-Cluaide between about AD 430 and about 470 or 480. It would seem, then, that the dates for both these rulers can be reconciled with the theory put forward by some scholars that Patrick's mission took place in the second half of the fifth century (c. 557-593).

    With which Coroticus, then, was the *Epistola* concerned? On this question scholars are divided. Arguments advanced by O Rahilly (*TP*, 38 f) against the Stratclyde king on his alleged ignorance of Latin, to the effect that he and his followers would not have been able to understand the terms of the *Epistola* which Patrick ordered to be read in their presence, have been demolished by Binchy (*PB*, 107-8). The latter points out that Chadwick's research into the early history of the British kingdoms in Southern Scotland tends to demonstrate that they were established under the auspices of the

Since it could be argued, moreover, that Patrick had spent part of his life in preparation for his ordination as a priest, living a simple form of monasticism before coming to Ireland, it is tempting to speculate that he may have spent some time at the monastery of Candida Casa (Whithorn or Whitherne, the White House, in southern Scotland), deepening his spiritual life and gaining pastoral experience for his mission.

Ninnian, founder of Candida Casa, is reputed as having already been engaged in a comparable mission to the southern, pagan Picts at the beginning of the fifth century, inspired, possibly, by Victricius, Archbishop of Rouen.[7] The journey by sea between Candida Casa and Sabhall would be considered a short one, even in Patrick's day, and the hazards of the tides of Strangford Lough would possibly have been known at Candida Casa, so that Patrick would have come prepared. If we accept that the enemy was based in the Strathclyde area of Scotland, then adjacent Ulster would be the most likely target for an attack.

---

imperial authorities as bulwarks against the 'barbarians', and the names of Cunedda's immediate ancestors suggest that their rulers had at least been partly romanised (Chadwick, *Early Scotland,* 150.) If, then, Coroticus of Ail-Cluaide wished to communicate with rulers in the romanised part of Britain, Latin would be the obvious channel. Nor would Patrick have denied that the king of Dumbarton was a Roman citizen, as is alleged by O Rahilly; on the contrary; Coroticus was a nominal Christian, and Binchy affirms that, to Patrick's mind, all Christians were *cives sanctorum Romanorum,* 'citizens of the holy Romans' (E 2). It was the unholy alliance of Coroticus with the pagan *Scotti* and the *apostates and Picts,* Binchy is rightly careful to stress, that made Patrick refuse to call him and his subjects by this proud title (E 2).

Furthermore, how did Muirchú or the *later scribe,* Ferdomhnach of Armagh, know about Ceretic Guletic of Dumbarton – who elsewhere survives only as a name in Old Welsh genealogies – Binchy asks, unless there was a written or oral tradition linking him with Patrick? That corroboration from external and independent sources inclined Binchy to believe that the identification was at least as old as Muirchú's day (*PB* 108).

Binchy then advances another argument in favour of this identification; Patrick, he points out, denounces Coroticus for having allied himself with the *Scotti* and the apostates and Picts (E 2), to whom he had sold the Irish Christians captured after his recent raid. While it is comparatively easy to account for close relations between the Dumbarton Coroticus and his neighbours the Picts and the *Scotti* – since the last term could also be used to denote the Irish settlers in Scotland – he maintains that a similar alliance between the ruler of Cardigan and these distant peoples seems rather less likely (ibid., 108-9).

7   cf. Testimony of his mission to the Irish, p.134 *supra,* re the visit of *Victricius* to Britain. Moran, op. cit., 129-31, 135f.

PATRICK'S FIRST *EPISTOLA*

Patrick's first practical response to this attack, in any case, was to dispatch an *Epistola* of remonstrance, through a priest-envoy, to the court of Coroticus, to condemn the raid made on his mission-field. It is an earnest of the disdain in which Patrick and his mission were held that this emissary had only met with scorn and contempt (E 3:25). That first *Epistola* is no longer extant.

When Patrick dispatched his first *Epistola* to the court of Coroticus, he tells us that the bearer was 'a holy presbyter' whom he had 'taught from his infancy' (E 3:24). Since Pope Siricius (+399) had recommended that a man be at least thirty years of age before receiving the diaconate, prior to ordination to the priesthood, this may imply that Patrick had, at the time of writing, already worked in Ireland for at least a quarter of a century or more.

PATRICK'S SECOND *EPISTOLA*

In his second open *Epistola* Patrick once more states his case, points out the crime committed by Coroticus and his associates against fellow Christians, declares them 'estranged' from him and from Christ, *a me alieni sunt et a Christo Deo meo* (E 5:33-4), for whom he is an ambassador (E 5:35; C 46:147; 56:5), until they repent. He then demands the release of the captives.

He also rebukes those Christians, among whom was a faction of faint-hearted, British clerics, who, in spite of this scandal, sat at table with, flattered, and took alms from Coroticus, thus becoming accomplices in crime. In the process, he firmly and unequivocally requests those British bishops who had the authority to do so, to excommunicate Coroticus and his minions until they had repented of their crimes and freed the slaves of God and the baptized handmaids of Christ (E 6-7).

Since this *Epistola* is both a formal excommunication order administered in the name of the Church, as well as an ostracisation of Coroticus,[8] the diction is somewhat different from that of the *Confessio*, being more vehement and at the same time slightly more elaborate, as befits both the occasion and the group of people addressed, namely Coroticus and his collaborators, and, by extension, the whole Christian Church in Britain, of which these were at least nominal members.[9]

In the beginning Patrick says that this *Epistola* is to be sent to the 'soldiers' of Coroticus (E 2:13), but later the writer unmistakably defends himself against contempt on the part of some factions of the Church in Britain who may have been tainted with Pelagianism, and who are too anxious to keep on good terms with the tyrant (E 10-13); towards the end of the document Coroticus is addressed by name in the singular, though in association with his collaborators (E 19; 21).

---

8   Hertling, *CPEC, passim*; McCue, 161-96; Smothers, *BSP*, 79-88.
9   Bieler, *LL,* 37; Conneely, *TLSP*, 126-7, 179-82.

Structure, content and biblical context of second *Epistola*

This relatively short *Epistola* opens with a prologue and ends with an epilogue, which are integrated into the four paragraphs in which Patrick has arranged it, each of whose boundaries are established by an internal concentric pattern: I (1-5), II (6-9), III (10-16), IV (17-21).

Paragraph I

PROLOGUE: A SOJOURNER AND A REFUGEE FOR THE LOVE OF GOD
The prologue of the *Epistola* is closely akin to that of the *Confessio* (C 1-2):

> I, Patrick, a sinner, manifestly untaught, *established in Ireland,* profess that I am a bishop.
> I most certainly believe that 'I have received' *from God* 'that which I am'.
> And therefore I live in the midst of barbarian pagans,
> a sojourner and a refugee for the love of God.
> He is my witness that this is so.
> Not that I chose to utter anything in so harsh and unpleasant a manner,
> but I am compelled by the zeal for God; and the truth of Christ roused [me] up
> *for love of* [*my*] *nearest neighbours and children,*
> for whom 'I have given up' country and parents and 'my life up to the point of death.'
> If I am worthy I live for my *God to teach* the pagans
> even if I am despised by some [people] (E 1:1-11).

Indeed, the only ostensible difference between the two prologues is that, whereas he declares himself 'to be a bishop' in the *Epistola*, he confesses himself to be 'the least of all the faithful' in the *Confessio*. On the other hand, one wonders into which category one would put a bishop, enduring 'a laborious episcopate' (C 26:2), 'a sojourner and a refugee for the love of God' (E 1; 17; C 26; 37; 59), 'living among barbarian pagans' (E 1; 10; 14; C 18; 37-38; 40; 48), 'in constant danger of persecution and death itself' in their midst (C 14; 35; 51), and yet betrayed by his 'dearest friend', disowned, reviled, and despised by a faction of his own pseudo-Christian fellow countrymen (E 1; 12; C 1; 26; 29; 32), who should have been his support – into which category, if not among the *anawim*, the helpless and often despised ones, 'the least of all the faithful' who have learned to place all their trust in

God alone?[10] This prologue, as we shall demonstrate later, is balanced by a contrasting epilogue (E 21:216-22).

DIVINE CALL TO IRISH MISSION

The prologue to the *Epistola* incorporates the 'untaught' Patrick's affirmation of his God-given episcopal authority 'to teach'. He amplifies this statement in its antiphon with a reference to his fruitful evangelisation of the Irish people:

> I, Patrick, a sinner, manifestly untaught, *established in Ireland*,
> profess that I am a bishop,
> I believe most certainly that 'I have received' *from God* that 'which I am'.
> And therefore I live in the midst of barbarian pagans,
> a sojourner [*proselitus*] and a refugee [*profuga*] for the love of God.
> He is my witness that this is so (E 1:1-5).
> — [the mission] which in these last times he has
> most excellently [and] kindly *planted in Ireland*
> and it has been established [*taught*] *with God's favour* (E 5:38-9).

The close and subtle links, by word and phrase, between the twin statements are noteworthy: the 'untaught' Patrick has been chosen by God to come 'to Ireland' to convert pagans to Christianity. He has 'received from God' the authority of a bishop 'to teach' in his name, and his mission 'in Ireland' has received the seal of 'divine favour'.

The scriptural context of Patrick's affirmation of his divine call 'to teach', at the opening of his *Epistola,* is, characteristically, an evocation of St Paul (1 Co 15:10): 'But by the grace of God I am what I am, and his grace towards me has not been in vain.'

Patrick's sense of his own 'lowliness' (C 2:23), as a creature in a true relationship with his Creator, and his total dependence on God's gift of the Spirit (C 62:10), which are the twin pillars of the *Confessio*, are already present here in his *Epistola* (E 5:39).

AN AMBASSADOR OF CHRIST

Patrick affirms that he has been impelled by a God-given zeal and a concern for the truth of Christ to undertake this mission, and in its antiphon he affirms the claim of being Christ's ambassador:

> but I am compelled by the *zeal of God; and the truth of Christ* roused [me]
>   up (E 1:7).
> — *'for whom I am an ambassador'.* [*'pro quo legationem fungor'*]
> Parricide, fratricide, 'rapacious wolves devouring the people of the Lord
>   as a meal of bread'.

---

10 Schillebeeckx, *MMR*, 38ff.

Just as [Scripture] declares, 'The unjust have utterly destroyed your
Law, O Lord' (E 5:35-7).

When he speaks of being an ambassador in the second antiphon, a motif
which he will reiterate twice in his *Confessio* (C 46:137; 56:5), he has
Ephesians 6:20 in mind. Towards the end of that great Epistle, Paul exhorts
his Christian converts to 'pray in the Spirit at all times in every prayer and
supplication' (Ep 6:18). He then requests their prayers for himself,

> so that when I speak, a message may be given to me
> to make known with boldness the mystery of the Gospel
> for which I am an ambassador in chains (Ep 6:19-20a).

The biblical context for the 'zeal of God' is Christ's cleansing of the temple:

> The Passover of the Jews was near, and Jesus went up to Jerusalem.
> In the temple he found people selling cattle, sheep, and doves,
> and the money changers seated at their tables.
> Making a whip of cords,
> he drove all of them out of the temple,
> both the sheep and the cattle.
> He also poured out the coins of the money changers
> and overturned their tables.
> He told those who were selling the doves,
> 'Take these things out of here!
> Stop making my Father's house a marketplace!'
> His disciples remembered that it was written,
> *'Zeal for your house will consume me'* (Jn 2:13-17).

When the Jews asked Christ for a sign for doing that, his answer was,
'"Destroy this temple and in three days I will raise it up"... he was speaking
of the temple of his body' (Jn 2:19b). After the Resurrection 'his disciples
remembered that he had said this and they believed the scripture and the
word that Jesus had spoken' (Jn 2:22).

The 'truth of Christ' – in the first statement – with which Patrick in turn
was consumed to the point of death, is closely linked to the performance of
'an embassy for Christ' in the second; the one is the concrete expression of
the other. The 'truth of Christ' is also subtly linked by Patrick with 'zeal for
Christ', who is 'the way, the truth, and the life' (Jn 14:6).

Coroticus and his minions are, for Patrick, the 'rapacious wolves' of Paul's
prophecy in his farewell speech to his friends at Miletus: 'I know that after I have
gone, "savage wolves" will come in among you, not sparing the flock' (Ac 20:29).

MISSION TO THE BARBARIAN, PAGAN IRISH

Patrick's mission is among the pagan Irish for whom he has put his very life at risk. They are, geographically, his nearest neighbours, and also his children, because he has begotten them in the waters of Baptism. The stark contrast between Patrick's beloved 'nearest neighbours and children' and Coroticus and his accomplices — who, until they repent of their crimes, are declared by Patrick to be 'estranged', that is, excommunicated from him and from Christ and his Church by their own free choice — is laconically evoked by one deft stroke in the second antiphon:

> *for love of* [my] *nearest neighbours and chldren,*
>   for whom 'I have given up' country and parents and 'my life up to the
>   point of death' (E 1:8-9).
> — [that] they are *estranged from me* (E 5:33).

Paul requests the Philippians to welcome his messenger, Epaphroditus, with all joy 'because he had come close to death for the work of Christ' (Ph 2:30); Patrick possibly had this in mind in this section, though he, who was so conscious of his dependence on God's grace, could be also be mindful of Christ's warning to Peter, who had declared:

> 'Lord, why can I not follow you now?
> I will lay down my life for you.'
> Jesus answered,
> 'Will you lay down your life for me?
> Very truly, I tell you,
> before the cock crows you will have denied me three times' (Jn 13:37).

I LIVE FOR MY GOD

Patrick's all-consuming concern is to live for God, 'the true God' (C 1:10), to whom he consistently refers as *Deus meus*, my God (C 2; 19; 58; 59). His characteristic sense of 'lowliness' (C 2:23) finds appropriate expression in 'if I am worthy', with which he prefaces this statement:

> If I am worthy I live for my God *to teach* the pagans,
> even if I am despised by some [people] (E 1:10-11)
> — Wherefore let every *God*-fearing person learn. (E 5:32)

The 'fear of God' (Si 2:7-17), alluded to in this antiphon, is not, for Patrick, a servile fear; it is rather the complete trust of a little child in a loving Father, as exemplified in various parts of his *Confessio* (C 16:4; 44:118).

THE DESPISED TEACHER OF PAGANS

Patrick's love of God finds concrete expression in his mission among
barbarian pagans in Ireland, even though he is despised as 'untaught', possibly
by the *'domini cati rethorici'* (the lords, learned rhetoricians), whom he
addresses with impressive competence in the *Apologia* of his *Confessio* (C 9-15):

> If I am worthy I live for my God *to teach* the pagans,
> even if I am despised by some [people] (E 1:10-11).
> – [*I dispatched an epistle* with a holy presbyter]
> whom *I taught* from his infancy, with clerics,
> so that they might return something to us from the booty
> or from the baptized captives whom they captured:
> they only jeered about them (E 3:23-5).

One of the biblical contexts of 'teaching', and the one that Patrick probably
had in mind here and which he had made his own, is *Jesus, the Teacher* in the
Temple at Jerusalem during the festival of Tabernacles:

> Then Jesus answered them,
> *'My teaching* is not mine but his who sent me.
> Anyone who resolves to do the will of God
> will know whether the *teaching* is from God or
> whether I am speaking on my own.
> Those who speak on their own seek their own glory;
> but the one who seeks the glory of him who sent him
> is true and there is nothing false in him' (Jn 7:16-18).

It is indeed ironic that the 'untaught' Patrick – possibly in the sense that
he is not a professional rhetor (C 9-11) – has been the one chosen by God,
in preference to those rhetoricians, 'to teach gentiles', that 'he has taught a
holy presbyter' from his infancy [*quem ego ex infantia docui*], and that 'God's
law ... had been taught' in Ireland.

> With my own hand I have written and composed *these words* (E 2:12).
> – *I dispatched an epistle with* a holy *presbyter* (E 3:22).

'These words', in the first antiphon, refer to Patrick's second *Epistola* which
we are considering here. 'An epistle', in the second antiphon, refers to his
first *Epistola* to Coroticus which, as we have already said, is no longer extant.
This second *Epistola* is a formal, public excommunication order in the name
of the Church to be formally handed over to Coroticus and his soldiers:

to be given and handed over, *dispatched to the soldiers of Coroticus* (E 2:13)
– *I dispatched an epistle* with a holy presbyter (E 3:22)

CHRISTIAN FELLOW-CITIZENS
The pseudo-Christians, Coroticus and his accomplices, who by their crimes
have excommunicated themselves from the Church, are numbered neither
among Patrick's fellow Irish Christians, nor those within the Roman Empire:

> I do not say to *my fellow citizens*, [*nor*] *to fellow citizens of the holy Romans*
> (E 2:14)
> – on the day following that on which *the newly baptized* in white clothing
> were anointed with chrism (E 3:20).

By linking 'fellow citizens' with 'newly baptized', Patrick is asserting that his
fellow citizens are not only the Christians who happen to be Roman citizens,
but also his 'newly baptized' converts whom he has anointed with chrism, his
children in the faith among the pagan Irish.

FELLOW-CITIZENS OF DEMONS
In forceful, emotive language, Patrick addresses Coroticus and his soldiers as
'fellow citizens of demons', 'blood-stained people', because they have
murdered countless numbers of his innocent Christian converts:

> but to fellow citizens of demons *because of their evil works* (E 2:15).
> – *Blood-stained people who are weltering in the blood of innocent Christians*
> 'whom I have begotten' for God, a countless number, and confirmed
> 'in Christ' (E 2:18-19).

A LIVING DEATH
At the heart of this concentric paragraph Patrick underscores their horrendous,
sinful behaviour, which places them on a par with pagans and apostates:

> *By hostile behaviour they live in death,*
> *allies of the Scots and Picts and apostates* (E 2:16-17).

Paragraph II

PATRICK'S DIVINE INHERITANCE
Patrick opens this second paragraph as he does the first, with a profession of
his God-given authority to proclaim the Gospel. This statement is amplified
in its antiphon:

I make no false claim.
I have a part
with those whom he has called to [*him*]
and predestined to proclaim the Gospel
amidst no *small* persecutions
'*to the ends of the earth*' (E 6:42-5).
— *whom 'he has' recently 'acquired at the ends of the earth' through the exhortation of our littleness* (E 9:78).

The first scriptural allusion in this section is to Romans 20:28-30, which deals with 'life in the Spirit' and 'prayer in the Spirit', so characteristic of Patrick:

In all things God works for good for those who love God,
who are called according to his purpose.
For those whom he foreknew
he also *predestined* to be conformable to the image of his Son
in order that he might be the firstborn within a large family.
And those whom he predestined he also called,
and those whom he called he also justified,
and those whom he justified he also glorified (Rm 8:28-30).

The motifs of suffering the proclamation of the Word of God as far as the remotest boundaries of the earth, which in the cosmological consciousness of the time, was Ireland, and the sense of his *parvitas*, 'littleness', so characteristic of Patrick, is repeated in the *Confessio* (C 1:19).

THE TYRANNY OF COROTICUS
Patrick continues to proclaim the Gospel:

even if the enemy shows his jealousy through the tyranny of Coroticus,
who has reverence for neither *God* nor his priests (E 6:46-7).
— How much more *guilty is he* [i. Coroticus]
who has stained his own hands in the blood of the children *of God*
    (E 9:76-7).

Patrick's skilful, laconic linkage of the complementarity of the 'reverence for God' and 'the children of God' is noteworthy. It is also clear here that there were courageous clergy who, like Patrick himself, challenged the criminal behaviour of Coroticus, though they too were ignored: 'Coroticus has no reverence for ... his priests'. Later, in his *Confessio,* where he tells of his own conversion to 'the true God', Patrick humbly confesses that he too, together with his fellow captives, ignored those priests who kept admonishing them about their salvation. But in spite of that, he recounts how God took pity on him, and kept watch over him before he knew him, and consoled him as a father consoles a son (C 1-2). At the time of writing his *Epistola*, he was probably very conscious of this great personal experience of God's mercy and was, therefore, holding out great hopes for the conversion of Coroticus and his henchmen. He takes up the motif of 'the jealousy of his enemies', which is linked again with the tyranny of Coroticus, in paragraph III (E 12:107-15).

REPENT, DO PENANCE

In this, the most hard-hitting part of the *Epistola,* Patrick focuses on the faction of the British clergy who implicitly condone the atrocities carried out by Coroticus and his criminals; he requests them to excommunicate Coroticus:

> whom he has chosen *and to whom he has granted the highest divine sublime power*
> that *'those whom they may bind on earth are bound also in the heavens.'*
> Whence therefore I beseech most of all, [you] 'holy and HUMBLE OF HEART,'
> that it be not permissible to flatter such men,
> 'to take food' or drink with them,
> nor ought one be obliged to accept their alms
> until, with tears poured out to God, they perform penance rigorously enough (E 6-7:48-54)
> — 'He who hates his own brother *is' ascribed* 'a murderer'
> or, *'Whoever does not love his brother remains in death'* (E 9:74-5).

Patrick begins by reminding the clergy of the sublime dignity of their calling to the priesthood and the episcopacy. He then pleads earnestly with them, exhorting them to humility and fidelity towards their God, even in times of persecution, like the three youths in the fiery furnace, in the time of Daniel and the Babylonian captivity. He does this by alluding to the *Prayer of Azariah*, part of which is a long hymn of praise and gratitude to God who saved them 'from the power of death' (v. 66), sung by the youths in the furnace while the flames danced around them:

> Bless the Lord, *you who are holy and humble in heart;*
> sing praise to him and highly exalt him forever (v. 65).

He is also encouraging those faint-hearted clergy to trust in the power and the mercy of God by alluding to this prayer; for Patrick knows, and expects those clergy to recall, that God, 'whose mercy endures forever' (v. 67), rewarded the fidelity of his faithful followers in time of great stress, when he 'delivered' them 'from the midst of the burning, fiery furnace' (v. 66).

He then earnestly requests them not to court the favour of such people, nor to take food or drink with them, nor even to accept their alms — possibly in favour of the Church and the poor — until they make reparation to God in hardships, through penance, with shedding of tears.

The context of the quotation from Matthew: '...Those whom they may bind on earth are bound also in heaven' (Mt 16:19; 18:18; E 6:49) is Peter's confession of faith in the Messiah at Caesarea Philippi: 'You are the Messiah, the Son of the living God'.

Those chosen men who have likewise professed faith in Jesus Christ, and who have, like Peter, received the power of binding and loosing, have now betrayed him by their collaboration with Coroticus, when it was their duty to excommunicate him and his fellow-murderers. By deft linkage, the condoning clerics are, moreover, put in the one category with Coroticus and his soldiers, the homicides who are cut off from Christ, until they repent and do penance because of their crimes. But, far from excommunicating those criminals at Patrick's forceful request, the behaviour of those very churchmen seemed to condone rather than condemn their criminal action (E 6-7:48-54).

Though this severe, public *correptio* and excommunication order on Patrick's part was clearly his duty, as shepherd of his flock, his confrontational approach was not calculated to win him favour or make him popular in the Church in Britain! It seems possible and, indeed, probable, that Patrick's later rejection and betrayal in the *Confessio* (C 26-37) was, in part, instigated by this stinging *correptio* and excommunication order, which must have been a grave public embarrassment for the Church in Britain.

FREE THE SLAVES OF GOD

Having already urged repentance and penance, Patrick now asks for the release of his baptized Christians:

> and liberate the slaves of God and the baptized handmaids *of Christ* (E 7:55)
> — A murderer cannot be with *Christ* (E 9:73)

These twin antiphons underscore the truth that 'the handmaids of Christ' are the direct antithesis of 'a murderer [who] cannot be with Christ', who, therefore, has, by his crime, excommunicated himself from Christ and his Mystical Body, the Church, until he repents.

GREED

Patrick now furnishes evidence from Sacred Scripture for his claims against the baneful sin of greed which has led to the murder of God's children, and he uses a powerful biblical simile — directed, it would seem, at the churchmen who offer the Holy, Eucharistic Sacrifice — to bolster his claim:

> for whom he died and was crucified,
> 'the Most High is not pleased with the gifts of unjust people.'
> 'He who offers sacrifice from the property of the poor
> [is] like one who makes a victim of a son before his father's eyes.'
>   (E7-8:56-9)
> — 'You *shall* not *kill*.' (E 9, 72)

Those who share in the spoils of unjust people are, in this context, accomplices in the crimes of greed and murder. They crucify again the Son of God and make a mockery of him, in the sight of his heavenly Father.

WHAT DOES IT PROFIT...?
He continues to inveigh against greed in ever-stronger language as he comes nearer the crux of this second paragraph:

> 'The riches,' [Scripture] affirms, 'which he gathered unjustly, will be
>   vomited from his belly' (E 8:60)
> — And therefore, *'Woe to those who fill themselves with what is not their own'*;
> or, 'What does it profit a person should he gain the whole world,
>   and suffer the loss of his own soul?'
> It is tedious to set forth or make known from single cases,
> to gather from the whole Law testimonials against such greed.
> Avarice [is] a deadly crime.
> 'You shall not covet your neighbour's possessions' (E 8-9:65-71).

THE WAGES OF SIN....
He spells out clearly and unequivocally, that the wages of sin are death and damnation:

> The angel of death drags him away (E 8:61)
> — *'unquenchable fire', moreover, 'devours him'* (E 8:64)

ETERNAL DEATH
The crux of this concentric passage, which is the thematic centre of the entire paragraph, is the eternal punishment that awaits the unrepentant, avaricious person:

> *'with the fury of dragons he will be mutilated'*.
> *'The serpents' tongue shall slay him'* (E 8, 62-3).

Paragraph III

Paragraph III, which is very closely twinned with Paragraph I, reiterates Patrick's claim to being called by God to the Irish mission. This repeated testimony of his vocation to go outside the confines of the Roman Empire to bring the Gospel to the pagan Irish was probably partially evoked by taunts from his enemies as to his motives for going to Ireland as a missionary in the first instance. This same motif is developed at some length in his testimony of his mission in the *Confessio* (C 37-53; 61).

A SLAVE IN CHRIST
Patrick once more evokes Paul's farewell speech at Miletus here: 'And now as *a captive to the Spirit*, I am on my way to Jerusalem not knowing what will happen to me' (Ac 20:22; C 43). His leaving of his kindred for ever in obedience to the voice of the Lord is seen by Patrick in the light of Abraham's call to depart from Haran for the land of Canaan, never to return:

> Now the Lord said to Abraham,
> 'Go from your country and your kindred and your father's house
> to the land that I will show you.
> I will make of you a great nation,
> and will bless you and make your name great so that you will be a
>   blessing....
> In you all the families of the earth shall be blessed (Gn 12:1-3; cf. C 3).

Now, as Patrick looks back over the long, weary road he has travelled since the period of his enforced slavery by the Irish, to the period of his slavery for Christ in their midst (C 49:176), he refutes the claims of his enemies that his decision was the outcome of mere personal desire as opposed to being divinely inspired.

A DESPISED MISSION
He also finds it necessary to establish his identity as the son of a Roman decurion, possibly in the face of taunts from his enemies that he was a mere slave, because of his enforced slavery in Ireland. He affirms, however, that he is indeed a slave because he has deliberately, and without shame or regret, sold his noble rank to become *a slave in Christ* in the service of Irish pagans:

> Was it that *I came to Ireland* without God's [inspiration] or 'according
>   to the flesh'?
> Who compelled me?
> I am 'bound by the Spirit' not to see any 'of my kindred'.
> Could it be by myself alone that I exercise a pious act of mercy

> towards that pagan people
> who once took me captive
> and wreaked havoc on the slaves and handmaids of my father's house?
> I was freeborn 'according to the flesh';
> I am born of a decurion father.
> But I have, in fact, sold my noble rank,
> I do not blush nor does it cause me regret,
> for the benefit of others.
> In short I am a slave in Christ for that remote pagan people
> because of the unspeakable glory 'of eternal life
> in Christ Jesus our Lord'.
> Even if my own people do not recognise me,
> 'a prophet has no honour in his own country' (E 10-11:79-94).
> – For them it is a disgrace that we are *Irish*
> Just as [Scripture] declares, 'Have you not one *God?'*
> 'Why has each one of you abandoned his own neighbour?'
>   (E 16:165-7)

These two antiphons are linked by the phrase 'to Ireland without God', and the words 'Irish' and 'God'. This is the only place in all of his writings where Patrick identifies with the Irish. Bieler draws attention to what he calls this 'subtle personal trait in Patrick's writings'.[11] As a follower of Christ he had gladly and unreservedly sacrificed family and homeland for the benefit of those who had previously enslaved him. How intimately he felt bound up with his Irish converts is manifest in his exclamation: 'for them it is a disgrace that we are *Irish*'.

Yet he never refers to the Irish as *'these'* people, or to Ireland as *'this'* country; where he does not use the proper names *Hiberio* and *Hiberiones*, it is always *'those'* and *'there'*, although he is writing in Ireland. Patrick, the man, remained a Roman; he had become one of the Irish as an apostle of Christ.[12]

DIVINE ADOPTION

Patrick responds to this repudiation of the Irish people by emphasising the inestimable dignity of divine adoption, which is conferred on God's baptized people regardless of era, race or culture, and which makes them 'sons of God and joint heirs with Christ'. Patrick implies that his enemies seem not to be aware of this Christian dignity:

> *Perhaps we are not 'from the one sheepfold'* (E 11:95)
> *– Perchance they do not believe that we have received 'one baptism'* (E 16:163).

---

11 Bieler, *LL*, 79.
12 Ibid., 80

ONE GOD AS FATHER

Patrick is painfully aware that his enemies are acting out of jealousy towards him and that they are unmindful of the values of Christ and his Gospel in behaving towards him and his converts as if they were not baptized children of the one Father:

> nor *'do we have one God as Father';*
> just as [Scripture] declares, 'He who is not with me is against me,
> and he who does not gather with me scatters.'
> It does not come together:
> 'One destroys;
> another builds.'
> 'I do not seek the things which are mine.'
> Not by my grace,
> but God 'who has put this eagerness into my heart'
> so that I should be one 'of the hunters or fishers'
> whom God foretold once before 'for the last days.'
> Jealousy is shown me (E 11-12:96-107).
> — *or that we* have *'one God as Father'* (E 16:164).

These two antiphons are linked by the phrases 'one God as Father'. Here Patrick reiterates once again the dignity of divine adoption.

COROTICUS, BETRAYER OF CHRIST AND CHRISTIANS

We have now reached the first of four internal concentric passages which function rather like the grace-notes in *sean-nós*. In this miniature concentric passage Patrick pauses, as it were, to convey an anguish of soul that verges on despair, which swells to a poignant crescendo at the crux:

> *What shall I do, Lord?* (E 12:108).
> — *what can I do for you?* (E 16:159).

> *I am greatly despised* (E 12:109).
> — *I am not worthy to come to the aid of either God or humans* (E 16:160).

> *Look, around me are your sheep torn to pieces and looted*
> and that by the aforesaid wretched little thieves, at the behest of
> the hostile-minded Coroticus (E 12:110-11)....
> — *'The injustice of the unjust has prevailed over us'* (E 16:161).

The heart of the matter is:

> *Far from the love of God is the betrayer of Christians* (E 12:112).
> — *'we have been made', as it were, 'remote outsiders'* (E 16:162).

The Scriptural context of 'outsiders' is Psalm 69 (68):(8) 9, 'I have become *a stranger* to my kindred, *an alien* to my mother's children.' Patrick has the whole of this Psalm, which echoes Christ's dereliction on the Cross, in mind. It is the only adequate means at his disposal for conveying to his readers the anguish of his own plight, and that of his Irish Christian community:

> Save me, O God! For the waters have come up to my neck.
> I sink in deep mire where there is no foothold (vv. 1-2).
> More in number than the hairs of my head are those who hate me
>   without cause;
> Many are those who would destroy me, my enemies who accuse me
>   falsely (v. 4).
> It is zeal for your house that has consumed me;
> the insults of those who insult you have fallen upon me (v. 9).
> [With your faithful help] rescue me from sinking into the mire;
> Let me be delivered from my enemies and from the deep waters
>   (v. 14).
> Insults have broken my heart, so that I am in despair.
> I looked for pity but there was none;
> and for comforters, but I found none.
> They gave me poison for food,
> and for my thirst they gave me vinegar to drink (vv. 20-21).

It might be said that this psalm of human distress and trust in God alone undergirds and expresses the essence of the *Epistola* and, indeed, Patrick's whole pilgrimage of faith, just as the *Confessio* is like a joyful orchestration of the great Hallel Psalm 116 (114-115), where he confidently offers a sacrifice to him, 'my soul as a living host to Christ my Lord' (C 34:3-4).

In trying to grapple with his plight, Patrick sums it up in the words of his great exemplar, St Paul, in his Letter to the Ephesians (4:5-6): 'Perchance they do not believe that we have received one baptism, or that we have "one God as Father" ' (E 16:163-4).

NUMBERLESS CHRISTIANS MASSACRED OR REDUCED TO SLAVERY
The cause of Patrick's profound anguish is the massacre of countless Christians, both laity and virgins of Christ, while the remainder are sold as slaves into the hands of Scots and Picts. He is probably referring here to the Southern Picts who inhabited Scotland south of the Grampian mountains, and among whom Ninnian of Candida Casa is recorded as having made converts early in the fifth century.[13] They are now involved in the slave traffic with Coroticus. The Scots *(Scotti)*, were an Irish colony who had settled in south-western Scotland and were still largely pagan in Patrick's time, though

some among them may have been converted by Ninnian. A number of those converts seem to have reverted to paganism.

Patrick's horror is conveyed in colourful, concrete imagery in this internal concentric passage within another internal concentric passage, whose crux, 'I cannot count their number', conveys the extent of the disaster:

> *Far from the love of God is the betrayer of Christians* (E 12:112).
> – *Christians are reduced to slavery* (E 15:154).

> [Christians betrayed] *into the hands* of Scots and Picts
> 'Rapacious wolves' have swallowed up the flock of the Lord,
> which was indeed growing excellently in Ireland with the greatest loving care (E 12:113-15).
> – Particularly among the most degraded, most vile apostates and *Picts*. Therefore I shall cry aloud in sadness and grief (E 15-16:155-6).

> *Both sons and daughters of the petty Irish kings*
> [*were*] *monks and virgins of Christ* (E 12:116-17).
> – O most beautiful and *most beloved brethren and children 'whom I have begotten in Christ'* (E 16:157).

At the crux Patrick lingers on the vast number, both of those who were slain, and of those who were sold into slavery:

> *I cannot count* [*their number*] (E 12:118).
> – *I cannot count them* (E 16:158).

THE CHURCH GRIEVES FOR HER SLAVES AND MARTYRS

In this third internal concentric passage Patrick orchestrates some of the motifs he has already introduced, such as 'injustice, accomplices in crime, martyrs and slaves who have been deported to far-off places where sin gravely and shamelessly abounds'. He brings this orchestration to a climax by calling on all Christians, but more particularly the clergy, who are called in a special way to be 'the holy ones' (E 13:121), to grieve with the Church for her suffering members instead of feasting with murderers:

> *Wherefore, 'may 'the injustice done to the righteous not please you',*
> *even 'as far as the lowest depths it will not please,'*

> Which of the saints would not be horrified to make merry
> or to enjoy a feast with such people? (E 12:119-22)

---

13 Hanson, *OC*, 60ff; Moran, *op. cit.,* 136-7.

– of *the children of God* (E 15:143)
– *her own sons and daughters* (E 15:149)

whom the sword has stricken with dire harshness (E 15:144)
– *whom so far the sword has not yet killed,*
but who are banished and deported to distant lands
where 'sin' openly, gravely, shamelessly 'abounds;'
there citizens are put up for sale; (E 15:150-53)

for it is written, 'Weep with those who weep' (E 15:145)
– *Therefore* the Church *'bewails and laments'* (E 15:148)

The crux is:

and again, *'If one member grieves*
all members should grieve together with it' (E 15:146-7)

The Church crying and bewailing her innocent martyrs murdered by
Coroticus and his brutal soldiery evokes the massacre of the Holy Innocents
by Herod, with whom Coroticus is implicitly compared (Mt 2:18). Yet there
is hope, for 'where sin abounded grace did more abound' (Rm 5:20).

THE GREED OF COROTICUS AND HIS ACCOMPLICES
Patrick repeatedly identifies avarice as the root cause of the evil:

They have filled their houses with the spoils of *deceased* Christians.
They live by plunder (E 13:123-4).
– *about the deceased* [ones] (E 15:142)

Because of this rapaciousness they have not baulked at murdering innocent
Christians before plundering them. The word 'deceased' links the two related
statements.

A GIFT OF POISON
Not satisfied with personal crime, Patrick's enemies implicate others by
sharing their spoils with family and friends:

They *do not know*, wretched people, that they offer poison, a deadly
food to their own friends and children (E 13:125).
– I do not know 'what I shall say'
or 'what' more 'I shall speak' (E 15:140-1).

DAMNATION FOR BOTH INSTIGATOR AND COLLABORATOR

Patrick now introduces his fourth and final internal concentric passage in this part of his *Epistola* to stress that evil men are, as it were, handing over the members of Christ into a brothel. The culmination of this miniature concentric passage is that the collaborators, as well as the instigators, of such deeds will merit eternal punishment:

> Just as Eve did not understand that she truly *handed over* death to her own husband (E 13:126)
> — *you are handing over,* as it were, 'the members of Christ' into a brothel.
> What hope in God have you,
> or anyone who concurs with you,
> or who converses with you in words of flattery?
> God will judge (E 14:133-7).

> *So are all who do evil* (E 13:127);
> — For it is written, *'Not only those who commit evil deeds* (E 14:138),

The crux of this internal concentric passage is:

> *'they work death'* as an eternal punishment (E 13:128)
> — *'but also those who agree with them are to be condemned'* (E 14:139)

CHRISTIANS OF ROMAN GAUL CONTRASTED WITH BRITISH CHRISTIANS

After a careful and measured build-up, Patrick has now, at the crux, reached the pith and marrow of this entire paragraph, which is the contrast between the attitude of the Christians of Gaul and those of Britain in this situation; whereas the Gauls ransom Christians, the British kill them and sell them to pagans:

> This is the custom *of the Christian Roman Gauls:*
> they dispatch holy, competent people *to the Franks and other* pagans
> with so many thousands of solidi *to redeem baptized captives;* (E 14:129-31)
> — *you* [i. Coroticus] rather kill and *sell them to a remote pagan people*
> ignorant of God (E 14:132)

Paragraph IV

With the crux of Paragraph III, 'the martyrdom and sale of Christians to remote gentiles ignorant of God', in mind, Patrick opens Paragraph IV thus:

> Therefore I grieve for you,
> I grieve, my dearest ones (E 17:168-9)

Then looking back over the road he has travelled, the sun suddenly comes up from behind the dark and lowering clouds, as it were, and his heart fills to overflowing with the Spirit of joy as he triumphantly exclaims:

> but then again I rejoice within myself.
> 'I have not laboured' for nothing,
> or my pilgrimage has not been 'in vain' (E 17:170-72),

for, in spite of the horrendous deed that has been perpetrated, the blood of martyrs is the seed ground of a harvest of saints. Patrick finds appropriate expression for his joy in Paul's words: 'It is by your holding fast to the word of life that I can boast on the day of Christ that I did not run in vain or labour in vain' (Ph 2:16).

Saints and Martyrs

He then apostrophises his martyred Christians, with a grief that is now tempered with rejoicing, and appeals to Coroticus and his men to free the baptized Christians whom they have captured so that they may deserve to live for God and be made sane here and in eternity:

> And there happened a crime, so horrendous and unspeakable!
> thanks be to God, as *baptized* faithful people
> you have departed from this world to paradise
> I can see you clearly,
> you have begun to journey where 'there shall be no night'
>   'nor lamentation nor death anymore',
> 'but you shall leap like calves loosened from chains,
> and you shall tread down the wicked underfoot,
> and they shall be ashes under your feet' (E 17:174-180).
> – and that they may release *the baptized* captive women whom they
>   previously seized,
> so that they may thus deserve to live for God
> and be made whole
> *here and for eternity.*
> Peace to the Father and to the Son and to the Holy Spirit. Amen.
>   (E 21:218-21).

The link between 'baptized faithful men' and 'baptized captive women' in these two antiphons is noteworthy. The men were certainly martyred. Were the women saved from the sword of red martyrdom in large numbers to endure a worse form of martyrdom as captive slaves among Picts, Scots and apostates? The context suggests that this was so.

MARTYRS CROWNED WITH GLORY

Patrick continues with the apostrophe of his martyrs who will reign with the apostles and prophets and martyrs, as those prophets and apostles have foretold in Sacred Scripture:

> You therefore shall reign with *the apostles and the prophets and* the martyrs;
> you shall gain everlasting kingdoms. (E 18:181-2).
> — '(*The words are not mine*)
> but God's and the *apostles and prophets*,'
> which I have set forth in Latin,
> who of course have never lied.
> 'He who believes shall be saved,
> but he who does not believe shall be damned.
> God has spoken.'
> I earnestly request that whatever servant of God shall volunteer,
> to be bearer of this letter,
> that on no account it be stolen,
> or hidden by anyone,
> but rather that it be read before all the people,
> even in the presence of Coroticus himself.
> May God inspire them, at some time or another 'to return to their
>   senses before God',
> so that they may repent [however] late of such a heinous deed,
> the murder of the brethren of the Lord (E 20:203-17).

The twin antiphons are here linked by the phrase 'apostles and prophets'.

GOD'S OWN TESTIMONY

By means of a double reiteration, Patrick is laying particular emphasis on the fact that what he is saying is on God's warranty and not his own:

> As he himself [God] testifies (E 18:183),
> — 'I' [*Patrick*] '*bear witness before God* and his angels' that it shall be so *just
>   as he intimated to my unlearnedness* (E 20:201),
>
> [*Scripture*] *affirms* (E 18:184),
> — *The words are not mine* [i.e. not Patrick's, but God's] (E 20:202).

The two sets of antiphons are linked by the sentences 'He himself testifies' and '[Scripture] affirms.' In the penultimate chapter of his *Confessio,* Patrick will again 'testify, before God and his holy angels', not about the rewards of martyrs, but that he had no other motive other than the Gospel and its promises for returning to a people who had once before enslaved him (C 61).

THE FELLOWSHIP OF APOSTLES AND PROPHETS

With his gaze still fixed on the glorious martyrs, Patrick continues, drawing heavily on Sacred Scripture to celebrate their victory over sin and death:

> 'They shall come from the east and from the west
> and recline [at table] with Abraham and Isaac and Jacob in the kingdom of
>   heaven' (E 18:185-6).
> — 'But the just shall feast in great confidence' with Christ.
> 'They shall judge nations, and 'Lord it over' wicked kings
> For ever and ever. Amen (E 19:198-200).

The linkage here between 'with Abraham and Isaac and Jacob', Christ's ante-types, and 'with Christ', the fulfilling type, is noteworthy. 'The just shall feast' is a subtle warning to those whom Patrick, perhaps ironically, designates as 'the holy and lowly of heart' (E 7:50), but who collaborate with Coroticus, by sharing his table.

'They will judge nations and they will lord it over wicked kings' is not without a touch of Patrick's Celtic wit, for it is an unequivocal reminder to Coroticus and his henchmen of their future fate if they persist on their evil course. The mere thought of being 'lorded over' for all eternity by 'barbarian' Irish would, as Patrick knew well, be a particularly galling prospect for the sneering, bloodstained, rapacious war-lord, Coroticus, and his retainers!

> Perchance they do not believe that we have received 'one baptism' or we have 'one
>   God as Father'.
> For them it is a disgrace that we are Irish (E 16:162-5).

THE POOL OF ETERNAL FIRE

Patrick next contrasts the reward of the wicked with that of the glorious martyrs. The two antiphons are manifestly linked by the synonyms 'lying perjurers' and 'fraudulent sinners':

> 'Outside [are] dogs and sorcerers and murderers,'
> and 'their portion [is] with lying perjurers in the pool of eternal fire'
>   (E 18:187-8).
> — 'Like a cloud of smoke, which is indeed dispersed by the wind,'
> so shall fraudulent 'sinners perish from the face of the Lord'
>   (E 19:196-7).

REBELS AGAINST CHRIST

And finally, here at the crux of this entire paragraph, Patrick, using rhetorical questions, focuses on Coroticus and his fellow evil-doers who will pay the penalty of their deeds in the company of 'fraudulent sinners':

Not without just cause the apostle declares, *'Where the righteous shall
scarcely be saved,
where will the sinner and the impious transgressor of the Law find himself?'*
(E 18:189-90)
— *Whence, then, Coroticus with his accursed henchmen,
rebels against Christ, where will they find themselves,*
they who distribute baptized maidens as prizes
and that for a wretched temporal kingdom
which may indeed pass away in a moment? (E 19:191-5)

The linkages between the two antiphons, 'the sinner' and 'impious
transgressor of the Law', and 'Coroticus with his accursed henchmen'
highlight the heart of the matter, that is, that they are 'rebels against Christ'
and have thus excommunicated themselves from the Christian community.

EPILOGUE

In the epilogue (E 21:209-22) which, as I have already indicated, forms an
integral part of Paragraph IV, Patrick implores some willing, trustworthy
servant of God to volunteer to be his envoy to the court of Coroticus so as to
ensure that the *Epistola* be read before the 'tyrant' and all the people, and not
suppressed. Patrick, moreover, appears to assume that his *Epistola* will be read
out several times to several different audiences and, probably, that it will be
translated.[14]

This epilogue, unlike that of his *Confessio,* stands in contrast to, but is
balanced by, the prologue. Here Patrick, 'the sinner' of the prologue, is, in
the epilogue, 'asking sinners to repent'. The unlearned exile for Christ is
asking a powerful, nominal Christian to release Christian captives. The
insignificant bishop, the least of all the faithful, is challenging influential
pseudo-Christians to repent, that they may deserve to live a Christian life.
Patrick, whom those angry criminals despise and hold in the greatest
contempt, prays, that there may be 'peace in the name of the Triune God', a
peace which they can never know, until they have 'repented' of their crimes
and 'restored the captives'.

Indeed, Patrick sums up his whole *Epistola* in his heartfelt prayer that God
may inspire Coroticus, his soldiers and his accomplices, lay and clerical:

to repent ... release the baptized captive women ... live to God ... and
that there may be peace to the Father, and to the Son, and to the
Holy Spirit. Amen;
[*ut ... paeniteant ... (ut) liberent ... ut mereantur Deo vivere .... Pax Patri et
Filio et Spiritui Sancto, Amen*] (E 21, 216-22)

---

14 Hanson, *LW*, 75.

Themes in the *Epistola*

The concentric and parallel patterns which determine the limits of the four paragraphs of his *Epistola* comprise only part of Patrick's comprehensive ordering of his thought and prose. He also linked Paragraph I to Paragraph III, and Paragraph II to Paragraph IV with a series of parallels.[15] There are ten main themes in Paragraph I which are paralleled in Paragraph III in exactly the same order, while the four themes of Paragraph II are paralleled in Paragraph IV.

The upper-case letters A to M correspond to the ten themes of Paragraph I, while A' to M' correspond to those of Paragraph III. The four themes, N O P R, of Paragraph II have their matching counterparts, N' O' P' R' in Paragraph IV. When placed side by side these themes yield a greater fullness of meaning. Let us designate the combined themes of paragraphs I and III as AA' to MM', and those of Paragraphs II and IV as NN' to RR'.

AA' PATRICK'S DIVINE CALL AND MISSION

Theme AA' explores seven aspects of Patrick's divine call to mission. The links between the pairs of themes are italicised:

1. **A bishop in Ireland**
   I, Patrick ... *established in Ireland,* profess that I am a bishop (E 1:1)
   — Was it that *I came to Ireland* without God or 'according to the flesh'? (E 10:79)

2. **Bound by the Spirit, the Gift of God**
   'I have received' *from God* 'that which I am' (E 1:2)
   — Who compelled me?
   I am 'bound by the Spirit' not to see any 'of my kindred' (E 10:80-81).

3. **A sojourner and a refugee**
   I live in the midst of barbarian pagans
   a sojourner and a refugee for the love of God (E 1:3-4)
   — I exercise a pious act of mercy towards that *pagan people*
   who once took me captive (E 10:82-83)

4. **An exile for Christ**
   for whom 'I have given up' country and parents and 'my life up to the point of death' (E 1:9).
   — and wreaked havoc upon the slaves and handmaids of my father's house (E 10:84)

---

15 Howlett, op. cit., 41.

5.   *I live for my God*
If I am worthy I live for my *God to teach* the pagans (E 1:10).
– I was freeborn 'according to the flesh';
I am born of a decurion father.
But I have, in fact, sold my noble rank
for the benefit of others (E 10:85-8)

6.   *To teach pagans*
If I am worthy I live for my *God to teach* the pagans (E 1:10)
– I am a slave in Christ for that remote pagan people (E 10:90)

7.   *Even if I am despised by my own people*
even if I am despised by some [people] (E 1:11).
– Even if my own people do not recognise me (E 11:93).

BB'   Coroticus, the betrayer of Christ and Christians
With my own hand I have written and composed these words
to be ... *dispatched to the soldiers [of Coroticus]* (E 2:12-13)
– Your sheep are torn to pieces around me and looted
...by the aforesaid wretched little thieves, at the behest of... Coroticus...
Far from the love of God is the betrayer of Christians
into the hands of Scots and Picts (E 12:110-13)

CC'   Rapacious wolves have devoured the flock of the Lord
By hostile behaviour they live in death,
allies of the Scots and Picts and apostates. (E 2:16-17)
– *into the hands* of Scots and *Picts*
'Rapacious wolves' have swallowed up the flock of the Lord
which was indeed growing excellently in Ireland
with the greatest loving care (E 13:113-15).

DD'   Red and white martyrdom
Blood-stained people who are weltering in the blood of innocent Christians,
     (E 2:18)
– *Both sons and daughters of the petty Irish kings*
[*were*] *monks and virgins of Christ* (E 12:116-17)

Monks and virgins of Christ, who are called to imitate the virginity of Christ
himself (Rv 14:4), and are the *living sign of the Church, the Bride of Christ* (Rv
19:7-9; 21:2), were the crowning glory of Patrick's mission because they were
a concrete, living proof that the faith had taken deep root. By linking them
here with the innocent martyred Christians, he is possibly wishing us to
remember that 'the white martyrdom' of consecrated virginity for the sake of

the Kingdom is as heroic and as precious in the eyes of God as 'the red martyrdom' of shedding one's blood for the faith. An additional interpretation, in this context, may be that the virgins of Christ, so prized by Patrick, were among those who were martyred by Coroticus.

Virgins of Christ lived in their own homes in the early Church, and many of them, including Agatha and Lucy, were martyred for the faith during the persecutions of the Church, thus earning a double crown. When the Age of the Martyrs was replaced by the Monastic Age in the fourth and fifth centuries, some of the virgins joined monasteries and lived in community or in hermitages, while others continued to live in their own homes. This is the only reference in the whole of the *Epistola* to the minority in the Church of Christ, known as 'monks and virgins of Christ'. This sole reference links the *Epistola* with the same motif in the *Confessio* (C 41-2; 49). Patrick refers to them in both places as proof of a thriving Christian Church.

His great concern and duty as shepherd, however, is for the 'whole flock', the vast majority of whom, then as now, consisted of the laity, who through matrimony, are the living, concrete sign of the union of Christ with his Church (Ep 5:22-30), and many of whom certainly earned the crown of martyrdom in this massacre.

EE'   A COUNTLESS NUMBER WHOM I HAVE BEGOTTEN IN CHRIST
Patrick here tries to convey the enormous scale of the disaster which befell his beloved neophytes:

> 'whom I have begotten' for God, a countless number, and confirmed in Christ (E 2:19)
> – *I cannot count [their number]* (E 12:118)
> – *whom I have begotten in Christ,*
> *I cannot count them* (E 16:157-8).

FF'   MARTYRED NEOPHYTES AND WHITE SLAVES
> ... *the newly baptized* ... were anointed with chrism ... they were cruelly slaughtered
> and slain with the sword (E 3:20-21).
> – I do not know *'what I shall say'*
> *about the deceased [ones]*
> *of the children of God*
> *whom the sword has stricken with dire harshness* (E 15:142-44).

GG'   THE CHURCH MOURNS FOR HER CAPTIVES AND MARTYRS
Patrick is so distraught that he does not know whom to lament the more – the slain, the captives or the perpetrators of the crime:

G1   Therefore I do not know what I should lament more (E 4:26)
G'1   Therefore I shall cry aloud in sadness and grief (E 16:156).

G2a   those who have been slain, (E 4:27)
G'2a   [those] whom so far the sword has not yet killed (E 15:150),

G2b   Those whom the devil has gravely ensnared (E 4:28).
G'2b   Where 'sin' openly, gravely, shamelessly abounds (E 15:152)

G 3   Wherefore let every God-fearing person learn
       that they are estranged from me
       and from Christ my God
       'for whom I am an ambassador'.
       Parricide, fratricide, 'rapacious wolves devouring
       the people of the Lord as a meal of bread' (E 5:32-6)
G'3   – Therefore the Church 'bewails and laments
       her own sons' and daughters (E 15:148-49).

HH'   **THE INJUSTICE OF UNJUST MEN HAS PREVAILED OVER US**
       Just as [Scripture] declares: The unjust have utterly destroyed Your
          Law, O Lord (E 5:37),
       – The injustice of the unjust has prevailed over us (E 16:161).

LL'   **PATRICK'S IRISH MISSION REJECTED AND DESTROYED**
       ... 'The unjust have utterly destroyed your Law, O Lord,'
       which in these last times he had most excellently [and] kindly planted
          in Ireland (E 5:37-38)
       – For them it is a disgrace that we are Irish (E 16:165)

MM'   **PATRICK'S MISSION FAVOURED BY GOD, REJECTED BY THE CHURCH IN
          BRITAIN**
In the final theme Patrick implies that the hallmark of the divine origin of his
mission was the manner in which it had gone from strength to strength under
God's favour and blessing:

       And it [i. the mission] had been established [taught] with God's favour (E
          5:39).
       – Just as [Scripture] declares: Have you not one God?
       Why has each one of you abandoned his own neighbour? (E 16:166-7)

Yet, Patrick is, by implication, reiterating that his mission had for its
foundation the Cross of Christ in the form of the hatred and contempt in
which he and his Irish converts were held by a faction of his own countrymen

who had abandoned him to become accomplices in crime against his converts.

These parallels are not only clear; they extend to the letters M and M', as the internal concentric and parallel elements of both paragraphs I and III extend to the letters m and m'. Howlett points out many other links between paragraphs I and III, moreover, which do not occur in parallel order.[16]

II and IV
There are four themes – N, O, P, R – in Paragraph II, which are paralleled in Paragraph IV. The linking words and phrases are also italicised here for the sake of clarity.

NN'   ETERNAL REWARD AND PUNISHMENT
In this theme Patrick claims that he has been called by God to share with the apostles in proclaiming the Gospel to the furthest limits of the earth. The tyranny of Coroticus is reiterated and its consequences form a stark contrast in the parallel theme; the two antiphons are linked by the words 'part' and 'portion':

> I have *a part*
> *with those whom he has called to* [*him*]. (E 6:41-2)
> – 'their *portion* [*is*] *with lying perjurers in the pool of eternal fire*'
>   (E 18:188).

OO'   REBELS AGAINST CHRIST
In theme OO' this appeal is addressed primarily to a faction of the British clergy who feast with, flatter and take alms from Coroticus:

> Whence therefore I beseech most of all, [you] holy and HUMBLE OF
>   HEART (E 7:50),
> – *Whence, then, Coroticus with his accursed henchmen*
> *rebels against Christ, where will they find themselves*.... (E 19:191-2)

PP'   EXCOMMUNICATE COROTICUS. REPENT, DO PENANCE
Patrick repeats his poignant appeal to a faction of the British clergy who condone, by their actions and omissions, the crimes of Coroticus. He calls all of them to repentance, and appeals for an envoy to carry this *Epistola* to Coroticus in person:

> Whence therefore *I* beseech most of all, [you] holy and lowly in heart
> that it be not permissible to flatter such people;
> 'to take food' or drink with them,

---

16 Ibid., 42.

nor ought one be obliged to accept their alms
until, with tears poured out to God, they perform penance rigorously
    enough (E 7:50-54),
– I earnestly request that whatever servant of God shall volunteer
that it [this *Epistola*] be read before all the people
even in the presence of Coroticus himself.
May God inspire them, at some time or another, to return to their
    senses before God,
so that they may repent [however] late of such a heinous deed,
the murder of the brethren of the Lord (E 21:209-17)

RR' RELEASE THE CAPTIVE CHRISTIAN WOMEN

Characteristically, Patrick reserves his final clarion call for the liberation of women in theme RR':

> And *liberate* the slaves of God and the baptized handmaids *of Christ*
>   (E 7:55)
> – and that they may release *the baptized* captive women whom they
>   captured before (E 21:218).

Patrick, the Apostle of Ireland and 'a man for all seasons', is the first person to call for the abolition of slavery and for the liberation of women. That call will not be made again until the seventeenth century.

Finally, Howlett has arranged the text of this *Epistola per cola et commata,* i. 'by clause and sense', as Patrick had done. That leaves us with thirty-nine lines in Paragraph I, thirty-nine in Paragraph II, eighty-nine in Paragraph III, and fifty-five in Paragraph IV, exactly two hundred and twenty-two in the entire composition. We can be certain the number of lines is correct, Howlett points out, if we compare the thirty-sixth line of Paragraph I, 'savage wolves devouring the folk of the Lord', with the thirty-sixth line of Paragraph III, 'savage wolves have swallowed up the flock of the Lord', and with lines 132-3, thirty-sixth from the end of Paragraph III: 'you rather kill and sell them to a remote pagan people ignorant of God; you are handing over, as it were, 'the members of Christ' into a brothel [*lupanar*, literally 'house of she-wolves'], the members of Christ'.[17]

Patrick further links Paragraphs I and II and Paragraphs III and IV, the clearest indications of this being that Paragraphs I and II both begin similarly with a profession of authority: 'I ... profess myself to be a bishop' (E 1) and 'I have a part with those whom he has called to him and predestined to proclaim the Gospel' (E 6:41-2). Both end similarly with accounts of his evangelisation: 'Your Law ... which in these last times He has propagated in Ireland most excellently, kindly, and it has been built up [also 'instructed,

---

17 Ibid., 44.

taught'] with God favouring it' (E 5:38-9), and '[the sons] whom he recently acquired in the ends of the earth through the exhortation of our littleness' (E 9:78). Also the word 'righteous' occurs in Paragraph III f (E 12:119) and 'the righteous man' in Paragraph IV f (E 18:189). These are only a few of the many indications of the integrity of Patrick's style.

The most important indication of 'the textual integrity of Patrick's *Epistola*', however, and the one that confirms all the others is the counting of words and their disposition at arithmetically fixed intervals.[18] This is shown in his division of words by symmetry and by extreme and mean ratio in this text.

Though Howlett has made what seems like an exhaustive analysis of the art of Patrick's *Epistola*, he claims that it merely scratches the surface! It merely suggests what may lie in the depths of this remarkable letter.[19]

---

18 Ibid., 43.
19 Ibid., 46.

CONCLUSION

And 'I know in part' wherein I have not lived a perfect life,
'just as the others' also believing.
But I confess to my Lord,
and 'I do not blush for shame' in his presence,
'because I do not lie',
from the time I came to know him 'from my youth',
there grew in me the love of God and fear of him,
'and up to now', with God's grace, 'I have kept the faith' (C 44:112-19).

PATRICK THE PILGRIM

The symbol of journey or pilgrimage has always spoken to the human heart. In the Irish tradition there is a group of stories in which the journey is the main interest, and W.F. Thrall stresses that the voyages of hermits and missionaries are the most probable sources for these Irish *immrama* or voyages.[1]

As with all journey-stories, Patrick's begins in a particular time and place, that is, with his captivity in the early fifth century. It takes him to distant places, first to Ireland as a slave, then back again to his own country, possibly to the Continent, and finally to Ireland as a missionary to pagans. In the process he encounters and overcomes dangers, and, with great determination, reaches new horizons. In keeping with the classical journey-stories, Patrick conveys more than the outer events; he explores the mystery of life itself, its relationships, its paths to self-knowledge and wisdom, its purpose and meaning, its final goal.

Through all life's vicissitudes Patrick has his eyes constantly fixed on Jesus, who journeyed with his disciples through the Holy Land preaching and proclaiming the Good News of the Kingdom of God. The journey of Patrick's discipleship was a journey of conversion, of openness to the healing power of Jesus. His captivity was the point of departure for his outer pilgrimage, his conversion the starting-point of his spiritual adventure. It involved a break with life up to that point; it was a prerequisite for entering the kingdom: 'the time is fulfilled, the kingdom of God is at hand; repent, and believe in the Gospel' (Mk 1:15). It presupposed above all that Patrick decided to set out on a new path: 'sell all that you own and distribute the money to the poor, and you will have treasure in heaven; then come, follow me' (Lk 18:22). Without this second dimension the break with his former life would lack the focus that a fixed horizon provides and would ultimately be deprived of meaning.

---

1   Thrall, *MAS*, 276-83; Dillon, *EIL*, 124ff.

This second element of his conversion was not something that was attained once and for all. It entailed development, even a painful one, that was not without uncertainties, doubts and temptations to turn back on the less-travelled road (C 46). It involved a journey into contemplation and discernment. The memory of his own weakness filled Patrick with a great compassion for those who rejected and betrayed him (C 26-37).

MARY, THE MOTHER OF GOD, *MUIRE MÁTHAIR DÉ*

It has already been mentioned in passing that the twin pillars of Patrick's *Confessio* are *humilitas mea*, my lowliness (Lk 1:48), and *donum Dei*, the gift of God (Jn 4:10; Ac 8:20). Patrick has placed the first pillar, *humilitas mea* (C 2:23), at the opening of his *Confessio,* and the second, *donum Dei,* at the close (C 62:10). His confession of his 'lowliness' at the outset, however, is not a denial of his God-given gifts, nor is it an avowal of ineptitude or lack of courage in the face of life's challenges; it is, rather, an early indication of his profound insight into his true position as creature in relation to his Creator, and is repeated in its *Magnificat* context, at two other points in the *Confessio* (C 12:49-50; 19:63).

Our Lady – bearing in her womb her Divine Son as she travels in deep contemplation over the hill country to her cousin Elizabeth, listening for the voice of the Lord, (Lk 1:48) – is thus brought delicately and unobtrusively into our company at the beginning of Patrick's pilgrimage to seek 'the true God' and see him face-to-face at journey's end. He is evoking, in this incarnational context, the whole life of Christ, from his conception in the womb, through all his further life of action, completed finally in his death and resurrection and his enthronement as Lord and sender of the Paraclete. It is prolonged everlastingly in his uninterrupted sending of the Holy Spirit.[2]

As soon as Elizabeth hears Mary's greeting, the Baptist in her womb, Christ's herald, leaps for joy, and Elizabeth, whose name, significantly, means 'house of God', is filled with the Holy Spirit (Lk 1:40-41). Joy and the outpouring of the Holy Spirit are the two signs of the advent of the Messianic era. When Patrick is called to usher in the Christian era in pagan Ireland, he too is filled with the same Spirit of Joy (C 24-5). Patrick, in this incarnational context, is undoubtedly conscious of the sanctity and sacredness of the family as the primary unit of all God's people, as well as of the Christian community. In this domestic situation family ties and family responsibilities are seen to be held sacred. Thus, a young, expectant mother, totally open to the prompting of the Holy Spirit, comes in haste, surmounting all difficulties, to care for her older pregnant cousin and keep her company as a watching-woman for three months.

---

2   Schillebeeckx, *CSEG*, 25ff. for a deep understanding of the mystery of the earthly adoration of God the Father by God the Son Incarnate, so fundamental to an understanding of Patrick's spirituality.

Elizabeth praises Mary for her faith, which recalls another very important Messianic theme of the Old Testament underscored by Isaiah, who received his call of faith immediately before his oracle concerning Emmanuel (Is 7:14). Likewise, Patrick's openness to the Spirit (E 10:81; C 43:93), his profound faith in the Blessed Trinity, and his equally profound knowledge of Sacred Scripture, form the corner-stone of his whole life's endeavour (C 4, 14, 29).

In Luke's account of the Visitation, Mary, the virgin daughter of Sion, the dwelling-place of Yahweh, and the perfect eschatological personification of Israel, is presented as the new ark of the Covenant. There is a marked literary dependence on 2 Samuel 6:9-15, which tells the story of the bringing of the ark to Jerusalem by David. As David and his people rejoiced in the presence of the ark (2 S 6:12-15), so did Elizabeth and her unborn child rejoice in the presence of Mary. As David leapt for joy before the ark (2 S 6:14), so did John in his mother's womb (Lk 1:44). The cry of David, 'How can the ark of the Lord come into my care?' (2 S 6:9), is echoed by that of Elizabeth, 'And why has this happened to me, that the mother of my Lord should come to me?' (Lk 1:43), which is probably a paraphrase of David's words. As the ark remained for three months in the house of Obed-edom (2 S 6:11), so did Mary remain for three months in the house of Zachary (Lk 1:56).[3]

With the Council of Ephesus of 431 possibly in mind, Patrick thus puts Mary the Mother of God in prominent relief at the very beginning of his *Confessio*, as that superb artist, Luke, has done in the Incarnation scene in his Gospel. The fifth-century Irish poet, Sedulius, is similarly inspired when he writes in his *Easter Hymn*:

> Hail holy mother who brought forth the king
> Who rules the heavens and the earth.
> He is God who rules forever, who encloses all in His power.
> Your blessed womb had the joy of motherhood with the honour of
>   virginity.
> You alone of all women pleased Christ the Lord.
> There was none like you before you.
> There will be none like you after you.[4]

Patrick may also have been influenced by the Advent liturgy which was introduced by the Church between 420 and 430 to counteract Pelagianism. His anti-Arianism affirmations of Christ's divinity and of our total reliance upon God are equally subtle and all-pervasive in his writings. That his children in the faith were conscious of this is manifested in a succinct triad in the Irish language which enshrines the principal tenets of his teaching:

---

3   *NCE*, 14, 721.
4   Flanagan, *IPM*, 12.

Íosa Chríost, Mac Dé;	Jesus Christ, the Son of God;
Muire Máthair Dé;	Mary, the Mother of God;
le congnamh Dé.	With the help of God.

THE SAMARITAN WOMAN

The second pillar is *donum Dei,* the gift of God (Jn 4:10; Ac 8:20), mentioned in the very last chapter (C 62:10), as well as in other key places throughout the *Confessio* (C 4:29; 14:73; 33:2; 36:5). Through means of this scriptural allusion Patrick brings us face to face with another woman, this time the alien Samaritan woman who encounters Christ at the well of Samaria. Patrick must have learned many of his apostolic coping skills, especially in his mature and reverent dealings with women, from his contemplation of this touching and humorous scene with its dramatic, 'apostolic' irony. In his *Epistola,* in the context of the massacre of his Irish Christian community at the instigation of Coroticus, Patrick declares:

> 'The injustice of the unjust has prevailed over us',
> 'we have been made', as it were, 'remote outsiders'.
> Perchance they do not believe that we have received 'one baptism'
> or that we have 'one God as father'.
> For them it is a disgrace that we are *Irish*.
> Just as [Scripture] declares: 'Have you not one *God?*'
> 'Why has each one of you abandoned his own neighbour?'
>   (E 16:161-7)

A pseudo-Christian faction in the British Church, according to Patrick's testimony, despised the Irish Christians, including himself, possibly because they were 'barbarians' in the sense that they were outside the confines of the Roman Empire: 'for them it is a disgrace that we are *Irish*' (E 16:165). Likewise, the Samaritans, of whom this nameless Samaritan woman is a symbol, were despised by the Jews for their infidelity to the Mosaic covenant. Their infidelity was symbolised by their acceptance, after the return of the remnants of the northern tribes from Assyrian captivity, of the worship of the false gods of five foreign tribes from Babylon, Cuthah, Avva, Hamath and Sepharvaim (cf. 2 K 17:13-34), which they mixed with their worship of Yahweh. The Samaritan woman's 'five husbands' represent these five pagan tribes (Jn 4:18). Since Samaria's Yahwehism was, therefore, tainted by false worship, even the 'husband' she now has (a reference to her relationship with the God of the Covenant) was not really her husband (v. 18) in the full integrity of the covenantal relationship.

But 'Jesus goes to Samaria, the land of the hated "other", to confront and to heal the ancient divisions and to integrate into the New Covenant not those who were merely ignorant of, but those who had been unfaithful to, the Old

Covenant. No one is excluded, no one may be excluded, from the universalist reign of the Saviour of the world.'[5] He addresses the Samaritan woman with reverence:

> ... If you knew the gift *(ten dorean)* of God
> and who it is that is saying to you, 'Give me a drink,'
> you would have asked him, and he would have given you living water
> (Jn 4:10)

The phrase *ten dorean*, 'the gift', is found in John 4:10 and in Acts 8:20, in which latter 'Samaritan' context it means the gift of the Holy Spirit. The Samaritan woman is so transfigured by this one encounter with the All-Holy Christ, so profoundly aware of the power of his Spirit within her, that she — and not Jesus' Jewish disciples, in this instance — becomes the first 'Christian' apostle of the despised and 'unclean' Samaritans, by bringing her own community to the feet of Christ (Jn 4:28-30, 39-43).

Similarly, it may be inferred, perhaps, that, at one level, this woman is an archetypal image of the despised and rejected Patrick himself, whom Christ has called to conversion and to turning the hearts of a despised 'barbarian' nation to Christianity (C 1-2, 61; E 1, 6). At another level she is an archetypal image of the 'barbarian' pagan Irish rural dwellers who have responded to the call of Christ to personal conversion and Christian mission:

> AND 'HE POURED OUT ON US ABUNDANTLY THE HOLY SPIRIT,
> AS THE GIFT' AND 'PLEDGE' OF IMMORTALITY,
> who makes believers and listeners
> so that they may be 'CHILDREN OF GOD' AND 'JOINT HEIRS WITH CHRIST'
> (C 4:28-31)

These two women of faith: the Virgin-Mother of the Redeemer and her reflex, the repentant Samaritan outcast, embody the *anawim* of Sacred Scripture to whom the Messiah will be sent (Is 61; Ps 34), that is, the lowly, powerless ones, the universal representatives of the despised and the excluded 'others' throughout history, who place all their confidence in God alone.[6] And these two dauntless women, as well as the Irish Christian women who identified with them, accompany Patrick all through the *Confessio* and 'keep the great vigils', to quote Patrick Pearse, both at the beginning and at the end of his journey of faith. They are the faithful disciples who keep all Christ's words, and the events of his life, pondering them in their hearts as they go

---

5   Schneider, *TRT*, ch. 7, 186.
6   Schillebeeckx, *MMR*, 40ff.

about their day's work. And Patrick, in his own humble faith in *Anaw*,[7] the gentle and humble Christ (Mt 11:29), in his prayerfulness, and unremitting hard work, shared with them as equal partners, identifies with and is thoroughly at home with them. His respect, reverence and concern for the Irish women, whom he so graciously served in the course of his mission, and who actively participated in that mission, is remarkable. Is it surprising that he was such an inspiration for them and that he won from them such admiration, gratitude and generosity (C 41-2,49; E 12)? His Christian conviction as to the fundamental dignity and equality of all peoples (E 11:95-6; 16:163-7), his concern for oppressed people and, more specifically, for the *cumal*, or female slave, who was persecuted by her own parents on becoming a virgin of Christ, has an arresting quality about it in an era when the degradation of the slave was more or less taken for granted (C 42-3). While this heartfelt, Christlike sensitivity stemmed, in no small measure, from his own personal experience as a *mug* or male slave — '*Mugonius*' (the Slave), was one of his Hibernico-Latin titles! — it had its roots in the first instance in his reverence for their dignity as members of the Mystical Body of Christ through Baptism; we have noted how he refers to this great sacrament seven times in both his *Confessio* and his *Epistola*. It is reinforced in his impassioned plea to Coroticus to free the captive women whom, as he puts it, they have sold to a remote Gentile people ignorant of God, as if they were handing over the members of Christ to a brothel or a 'house of she-wolves' (E 14, 19, 21).

These twin pillars, *humilitas mea* and *donum Dei* frame Patrick's profound devotion to the Blessed Trinity; his fasting and unremitting contemplative dialogue with God in prayer; his discipleship of Christ; his divine vocation and mission; his joy and sense of unworthiness in the face of such a call and mission, all of which are permeated with, and undergirded by his impressive knowledge, love and use of Sacred Scripture.

THE ARENA OF PATRICK'S PILGRIMAGE

Ireland, 'the land of my captivity', *terra captivitatis meae* (C 3, 33, cf. 61), is simultaneously the arena of both Patrick's outer and inner pilgrimage. This biblical allusion is taken from 2 Chronicles 6:37. Its context is the prayer of Solomon at the dedication of the Temple in the presence of a massed choir of singers and musicians, as well as a representation of all the people of Israel:

> If they sin against you...
> and you are angry with them, and give them to an enemy,
> so that they are carried away captive...
> if they repent with all their heart and soul
> in the land of their capivity
> *of their captivity*...

---

7 Ibid., 41.

and pray towards their land...
and the house that I have built for your name,
then hear ... their prayer...
and forgive your people who have sinned against you. (2 Ch 6:36-9)

Here the chronicler is addressing the Jews of the post-exilic period and here the returned exiles are being reminded of God's steadfast love and mercy towards them during their time of lonely exile in Babylon, and of the centrality of the Temple – the place of God's Presence – and of Temple worship in their lives.

Patrick sees in the circumstances of his own captivity (C 1-2, 16, 61), a replica of the Jewish experience of exile, especially that of the prophet Daniel, and, at the outset, he declares:

I cannot remain silent
'nor indeed is it expedient' [that I should],
concerning such great benefits
and the great grace
which the Lord has been pleased to bestow on me
'IN THE LAND OF MY CAPTIVITY' (C 3:1-6).

At the turning-point just past the centre of his *Confessio,* where he has described his experience of rejection and betrayal (C 32), he cries out:

satis dico [*I say* enough],
Nevertheless I must not hide 'THE GIFT OF GOD' (Jn 4:10; Ac 8:20)
which has been lavished on us 'IN THE LAND OF MY CAPTIVITY;'
because then I earnestly sought him,
and *there* I found him,
and he kept me from all iniquities – this is my belief –
'because of his indwelling Spirit',
who 'has worked' in me until this day (C 33:1-8).

Deprived, like the Jews of old, of family, homeland, Temple and all human rights, Patrick gradually became a true adorer of the Father, with a worship not dependent on locality but flowing from the Spirit of Truth (cf. Jn 4:23-4) like Christ himself.

Unlike the Jews of old, however, Patrick never returned to his native land once he had been made bishop. Now, like those strangers and captives for Christ's sake (cf. C 59:20), he was 'bound by the Spirit' (C 43:93; E 10:81), never again to leave the land of his new-found captivity, because:

... *I am afraid of losing the labour which I have begun,*
and not I,
but Christ the Lord

Who has commanded me
to come to stay with them for the rest of my life,
'if the Lord wills it'
and he will keep watch over me from 'every evil way',
so that I do not 'sin in his sight' (C 43:96-103).

This belief in the power of God's Spirit within him is at the very heart of all that Patrick is and does. The essential question about him is not 'What is the great driving force in his life?' but *'Who is the great driving force, the great motivator* behind all that he is and all that he does?' (C 25, 33). But this stage in his journey towards God, this complete openness to the voice of the Lord, this abandonment to the Divine Will and Providence, was only reached after many trials and tribulations, unremitting prayer and fasting... (C 16-17). He had also to experience, in his own personal circumstances, the Spy Wednesday, Holy Thursday and Good Friday betrayals of the founder of Christianity, whom he was to serve 'not only in favourable circumstances, but also in pressing need' (C 34:13-14). 'To make known the gift of God and his eternal consolation without fear' (C 14:74-5), to offer 'my soul as a living sacrifice, *hostiam viventem,* to Christ my Lord' (cf. C 34:4), and 'to drink his cup' (C 57:9) are salient features of the life of this heroic priest and bishop, and they underpin Patrick's legacy or *exagalliae* to us, his children in the faith.

PATRICK'S TWELVE PERILS

The motif of suffering in Patrick's writings encapsulates his 'twelve perils' whereby his soul's salvation was endangered (C 35:3). It is significant that he refers to these twelve experiences in the context of his mystical experiences, thus binding them together inseparably.

The first peril was the sin he committed in his boyhood before coming to Ireland, which he confessed to his dearest friend prior to his ordination to the diaconate, and which is closely related to his eighth 'dream' or mystical experience:

> a word which I had confessed before I was a deacon.
> In the anxiety of my troubled mind I disclosed to my dearest friend
> what I had done in my boyhood in one day (C 27:5-11).

The second was the kidnapping and enslavement related in C 1-2, which followed a year after the sin he had committed and which in turn was followed by his conversion and intimacy with the Lord in prayer (C 16-17, 33). The third was the danger of his escape to a place three hundred kilometres distant, where he had never been and where he knew no one, but during which:

> *I came in the power of God*
> *Who was directing my way unto good,*
> *and I was fearless nothing until I reached that ship* (C 17:26-28)

The fourth was the perilous involvement with his fellow-travellers, who first refused him passage on the ship, and then tried to involve him in a pagan ceremony of promising fidelity by sucking their nipples:

> And on that day, accordingly, I refused 'to suck their breasts'
> because of *the fear of God,*
> but rather I hoped to come by them to the faith of Jesus Christ
> as they were pagans,
> and thus I got my way with them,
> and *we set sail* at once (C 18:45-50).

The fifth peril was his near-starvation in the company of the same men; on this occasion he almost ate wild honey which had been offered in pagan sacrifice (C 19:76-80). The sixth was the night on which Satan vigorously put him to the test, and when Christ revealed his presence to him in the splendour of his sun (C 20:81-92).

The seventh was another captivity of sixty days' duration many years later but:

> *on the sixtieth night thereafter*
> 'the Lord delivered me out of their hands' (C 21:102-3).

The eighth was the daily temptation by Satan at the crux of the account of his mission to Ireland, 'because he is strong who strives daily to turn me away from the faith' (C 44:107).

The ninth was the objection of some elders and well-meaning friends to his proposed mission to Irish pagans; they asked: 'why does this man throw himself into danger among enemies who do not know God?' (C 46:139-40).

The imprisonment of fourteen days' duration and confiscation of goods (C 52:204) was the tenth.

The eleventh was the martyrdom and enslavement of Patrick's new converts related in the *Epistola,* when 'the injustice of the unjust has prevailed over us' (E 16:161). That provoked Patrick's excommunication of Coroticus, which may have led in turn to the ecclesiastical trial of Patrick by British ecclesiastical elders.

The revelation of the first of Patrick's perils, the sin committed in boyhood, was the occasion for the twelfth, when Patrick saw 'in a vision of the night what had been written against my face without honour' (C 29:3-4).

His account of those twelve perils, from which God rescued him, is very closely related to his account of the visions which we have already considered and in which God revealed to him his divine purpose and himself.[8]

SPIRAL MOVEMENT OF THE *CONFESSIO*

We have noted how the *Confessio* and its component parts are concentric. The crucial statement in each concentric passage is thus engraved, as it were, around each *ula* or halting stone on Patrick's pilgrim path. These are the vantage points from which we review both his geographical and his interior spiritual journeys.

Perhaps we might compare the dynamic movement of the *Confessio* to a spiral which curves continually as it winds around its central axis, while continually changing plane, as in a spiral staircase or the thread of a screw. The spiral symbol is suggested because it combines the ideas of movement or continuity, with that of a static, central point. It further suggests the fluidity of the movement from one level of meaning to the other, as we move down into the hidden depths of the mystery, as well as the artistic harmony between all the elements, in Patrick's *Confessio*.

This symbol is, moreover, deeply embedded in our Irish culture. The spirals on the stones at Brú na Bóinne (Newgrange), for instance, are either centripetal, descending in anti-clockwise motion (as water goes down a drain), or centrifugal, ascending in clockwise motion, symbolising the expanding, creative force of fire (hence, the sun moves in a clockwise motion, the opposite of the movement of water). These two movements can be combined to demonstrate the two poles of energy, contemplation and apostolic action in Patrick's *Confessio*. Like the founder of Christianity, Patrick, drawn by the Holy Spirit, descended into the depths of his being, where he remains *ar rinnfheitheamh*, waiting at the needle-point, so that he might hear what the Lord God would speak to him. This 'God-towardness' of Patrick's, as the late Professor Thomas Marsh expressed it in *The Triune God*, 'is a basic and essential feature of the human being, of being human. There is in the human being a basic orientation which continually directs it to seek to relate to and exist in relationship with a transcendent Absolute God. When this orientation, this drive, is given expression, there is prayer.... God discloses God, reveals God to humans... initially and progressively in the history of Israel and then finally and fully in the event of Jesus Christ.'[9]

It may be inferred from Patrick's writings that he was in intimate contact with the Word of God, and, according to Daniel Conneely in *The Letters of Saint Patrick*, with the writings of the Fathers of the Church, and Church documents.

His faith in the Trinity thus issued centrifugally in his humble,

---

8   Howlett, *BLSP*, 111.
9   Marsh, *TTG*, 28.

compassionate and fearless efforts to make known the gift of God and his eternal consolation, in order that after his death he might leave behind 'a legacy' to his fellow labourers and to his children in the faith (C 12).

A triple spiral is also found on stones at Brú na Bóinne, which includes the third force, the play of attraction and repulsion between opposites.[10] This suggests the difficulty of maintaining a right balance between contemplation and apostolic action. It also represents the struggle in Patrick's life, particularly at the rejection and betrayal point at the centre of his *Confessio*, and his heroic effort, in the power of the Spirit, to be reconciled with his enemies.

ARCHETYPAL IMAGERY IN THE *CONFESSIO*

His life as a slave as well as his missionary life in rural Ireland, *ministerium servitutis meae*, the ministry of my slavery (C 49:176), brought Patrick into constant contact with people close to the soil and profoundly sensitive to the world of the spirit. All this experience strongly coloured his literary output and gave it a freshness and a uniqueness rarely equalled among classical writers. Let us note, in this context, his choice of the powerful, primeval, archetypal imagery of the elements, so akin to biblical imagery: the sun (C 60); hail, rain, snow and ice; images drawn from nature such as the mountain, the wood (C 16); stone, mud, wall (C 12); rock (C 20); all of which have an enduring quality like the *Confessio* itself, perhaps in some ways, too, symbolic of the ruggedness and tenacity of the confessor in action!

PATRICK, THE GOOD SHEPHERD

For here, we are always conscious of this uniquely indomitable, energetic character, now lost in contemplation in the woods and on the mountain, now alert and active during the lambing season, now skilfully shearing sheep, now rounding them up with his sheep-dogs as he calls out to fellow-shepherds, now attending to the wounded ones or to those that have gone astray.... Then, as a missionary, travelling with his companions and the sons of Irish kings, from one petty kingdom to another, speaking to the people in their own language, about their traditional beliefs, their rural, socio-economic and political interests, their hopes, their fears, proclaiming the Word of God to them in fluent, colourful Gaelic, illustrating his teaching from their own culture and their native landscape as Christ did before him to his Chosen People in the Holy Land, being constantly in tune with Christ in his Mysteries from one end of the Church's Year of Grace to the other, administering the sacraments, celebrating the Eucharist at holy wells or wherever the people traditionally gathered, thus laying the foundations of small, tight-knit Christian communities, taking part in their celebrations, so dear to Irish

---

10 Brennan, *BVV*, 30ff.

hearts, as Christ participated in the Wedding Feast of Cana and the Feast of Tabernacles, in constant danger from enemies, plots, outlaws, hunger, cold, exhaustion, yet, somehow, enjoying the challenge every step of the way.

The scents and colours, the variegated shapes, the light and shade, the calm and the storm, the orchestra of sounds alternating with long silences, associated with mountain, forest and wild-life, as season follows season in its yearly cycle – all are evoked here in this rural setting.

These 'rustic' experiences must have touched the sensitive soul of this young city-dweller profoundly, and should, perhaps, alert us to some of the nuances of meaning in his varied and subtle references to 'rusticity' (C 1, 11, 12, 46).

The lure of lonely, secluded places was later to find an echo in the hearts of many of his children in the faith, the anchorites and others, who have left us such an exquisitely delicate heritage of nature lyrics.[11] The difference was that Patrick the slave had no choice in the matter, whereas Patrick the missionary did not have the option to withdraw, except for brief periods for prayer and relaxation, like the One in the Gospels for whom he was an ambassador (E 5; C 46, 56). It is surely significant that he only found time in his old age, and possibly in his retirement, to write this superb document. Some time prior to that he had been coerced by circumstances into writing his impassioned *Epistolae* to Coroticus.

IMAGERY FROM DOMESTIC LIFE IN THE *CONFESSIO*
His imagery from domestic life: villa, servants, pirates; hut, sheep, shepherd; cold, hunger, nakedness; ship, sailors, wolfhounds; deserted country, pigs, wild honey; food, fair weather, firing; homeland, people, hospitality; family, gifts, friendship ... are not without human and divine significance and, in their context, suggest a warm-hearted, practical, dynamic contemplative who toiled resolutely and relentlessly on Irish soil solely in the interests of his flock.

Patrick presents us, also, with the great antithetical themes: human helplessness, the love of God; human misery without God, the beatitude effected by the Presence of God in a person, so basic to any understanding of the world or the human condition. Like all great works of art, it is a universal and timeless statement of the human condition and of God's dealing with his creation.

In view, therefore, of its concentric structure and dramatic spiral movement; its unity, symmetry, measure and harmony; the saint's significant use of biblical quotation and allusion; its universality and timelessness as a statement of the human condition, it seems tenable to maintain that the *Confessio* of St Patrick can indeed bear comparison with a classical or biblical

---

11 Carney, *EIP*, 4.

work of art, and that scholars may be obliged to make a reappraisal of both Patrick's literary aim and acumen at the dawn of Irish letters.

THE MATRIX OF OUR IRISH CHRISTIAN HERITAGE

After his death, Patrick's children in the faith consolidated his great missionary initiative. His writings became the matrix of our Irish Christian heritage. Consequently, 'the island of saints and scholars' became the light of barbarian Europe for almost another thousand years, and thus saved Western civilisation.

The effectiveness of Patrick's mission has come ringing down the centuries to find an echo in Irish hearts from generation to generation and has found unfailing expression in the great missionary thrust of the Irish nation, his children in the faith.

In the Penal Days (1695-1829) in particular, the Irish Catholics, who were outlawed, 'illegal aliens' in their own country because of their religious convictions, were mirror-images of Patrick, the stranger and sojourner for Christ '*in the land of my captivity*'. Among those oppressed 'secret people' of 'the Hidden Ireland' were the poets and scribes who toiled as slaves by day, and in the misery of their cold, dimly-lit cabins, faithfully copied manuscripts by night for the spiritual nourishment of their kith and kin and for posterity, in Ireland's darkest hour. Among them was the poet, mystic and catechist, Tadhg Gaelach Ó Súilleabháin (1715-1795).

THE PRECIOUS LIFE-BLOOD OF A MASTER-SPIRIT

'A good book', someone whose name I cannot now recall once said, 'is the precious life-blood of a master-spirit.' Patrick, our father in the faith, is surely that 'master-spirit', and his 'precious life-blood', flowing down to us through his writings, continues to nourish us Irish wherever and in whatever circumstances we may find ourselves.

PATRICK, THE PILGRIM APOSTLE OF IRELAND

Patrick, the Pilgrim Apostle of Ireland has been chosen as the title for this book because of the many references in his writing to his being an illegal alien on foreign soil, and of God's fatherly care of him during that pilgrimage for Christ (C 12:45; 26:5; 37:9; 59:20; E 1:4; 17:172). Moreover, *peregrinatio pro Christo*, called the *glasmartra* or green martyrdom, because it involved leaving Ireland forever for the sake of Christ, is one of the great traditions of Patrick's children in the faith. The title is meant to honour those who passed on the faith to us, and who shared in the suffering and the humiliation which Patrick endured during their pilrimage down through the centuries, but more particularly during the Penal Days. It commemorates the 'coffin-ships' of a century and a half ago. But, above all else, the title has been chosen so that this book may be a source of comfort for the youth of Ireland who are leaving our shores today, and, in particular, for those among you who, like Patrick, are 'illegal aliens' on foreign soil. May this lonely exile be the point of departure for your inner, spiritual renewal as it was for Patrick, so that our pilgrimage, like his, 'may not be in vain' (E 17).

THE TEXT OF SAINT PATRICK'S WRITINGS

In this edition of Patrick's *Confessio* and *Epistola* a few changes have been made in Bieler's text, all of which are attested among the variant readings and editorial conjectures recorded in the apparatus of Bieler's *Liber Epistolarum Sancti Patricii Episcopi I (LE, I)*, 1952, pp. 57-97, except where otherwise indicated. References, e.g. (LE 58:8) below, indicate the pages and line numbers in *LE, I*.

CONFESSIO

(1)   for +*bannavem taburniae*+ read *Bannaventa Berniae*

(1)   omit Bieler's <*nos*> (LE 57:11).

(1)   for *villulam* read *villam* (LE 56:5).

(4)   for *nec umquam fuit nec ante nec erit post haec* read *nec umquam fuit ante nec erit post haec* (LE 58;8).

(4)   omit Bieler's <*et*> (LE 59:12).

(4)   for *habunde* read *abunde* (LE 60:20).

(9)   for *incederem* read *inciderem* (LE 61:14).

(10) for *desertis* read *disertis* (LE 62:4).

(11) for *deserta sed 'ratum et fortissimum' scripta* read *diserta sed rata et fortissima scripta* (LE 63:11-12).

(13) for *ammiramini* read *admiramini* (LE 64:23)

(13) for *dominicati rethorici audite* read *domini cati rethorici audite ergo* (LE 64:24).

(14) for *exaga*<*e*>*llias* read *exagallias* (65:8).

(18) for *tegoriolum* read *teguriolum* (LE 66:8).

(19) for *habundabat* read *abundabat* (LE 68:3).

(19) for *habundanter* read *abundanter* (LE 68:10).

(23) for *Victoricus* read *Victoricius* (LE 70:17).

(24) for *peritissime* read *peritissimis* (LE 71:5).

(24) for *expertus sum* read *expergefactus sum* (LE 73:7).

(25) for *ammirabam* read *admirabam* (LE 72:10-11).

(26) after *peccata mea contra laboriosum episcopatum meum* supply *obiecerunt* (Howlett, BLSPB, 16).

(29) for '*vidi scriptum erat...* read *vidi quod scriptum erat...*' (LE 74:13).

(29) for *quasi sibi se iunxisset* read *quasi sibi me iunxisset* [Howlett, ibid, 16] (LE 74:16).
(34) for *cooperasti* read *comparuisti* (LE 76:17-18).
(35) for *pupillum ideo tamen responsum divinum creber admonere* read *pupillum idiotam responsum divinum crebre admonere* (LE 77:7-8).
(37) for *aliquantis* read *aliquantos* (LE 77:13).
(39) for *Abraam* read *Abraham* (LE 79:5).
(40) for *ammonet* read *admonet* (LE 80:14).
(42) for *Sed ex illis...* read *Sed et illae...* (LE 82:20).
(43) for *frates* read *fratres* (LE 82:25).
(46) for *pos* read *post* (LE 84:24).
(57) for *scrutator* read *scrutatur* (LE 88:5).

Epistola (2) for *in numero* read *innumerum numerum* (LE 92:15).
(7)   omit <*per*> (LE 94:15).
(10) for *decorione* read *decurione* (LE 96:12).

Biblical quotations are enclosed within single inverted commas. Direct discourse is enclosed within double inverted commas.
The Latin 'u' is modernized to 'v' throughout, e.g. *uico* and *custodiuimus* become *vico* and *custodivimus*, to facilitate readers.

INCLUSIVE LANGUAGE
In translating Patrick's writings I have endeavoured to use inclusive language as far as possible, at the request of many readers who wish to compare this English version with that of its Gaelic counterpart. Here an effort has been made to demonstrate the relative inclusiveness of the Gaelic language in which Patrick preached the Word of God; thus:

filius, filii (E 1:8; 4:8; 8:59; 9:77; 12:116; 13:125; 15:143, 149; 16:157; 21:222; C 1:5; 2:28; 4:31; 14:77; 23:112; 40:34,48,57; 41:11, 12; 47:152; 52:197; 59:31), 1. mac, mic; *son, sons;* 2. clann, *descendants, children.*
frater, fratres, (C 6, 14, 32, 43, 47, 49; E 9,16,21), bráthair, bráithre; *brother, brethren.*
gens (E 10:82; C 15:83; 61:6) (depending on the context), 1. cine; *a pagan people.*
2. *gentes,* (E 1:10; 10:90; 14:132; C 1:18; 13:67; 18:48; 34:9, 27; 37:7; 38:11, 14; 40:33,44; 48:157), ginte; *pagans.*
homo, homines (E 5:32; 8:66; 15:153; 16:160; C 1:12; 4:16; 7:7; 9:3; 12:56; 14:78; 17:23; 18:40; 19:60; 22:106, 109; 30:6; 33:10; 40:24; 48:163; 50:178; 53:211) is rendered, duine, *a person*; daoine, *people.*
natio-ionis (E 19:199; C 3:10) (nation), 1. cine. 2. ginte like *gens,* and the Greek *éthnos,* opp. to Christian, *the pagans.*

patria (E 1:9: 11:94; C 17:16; 36:7; 43:88), tír dúchais, one's native land or country.

plebs (E 5:36; 21:213; C 38:8; 40:54, 57; 41:60; 58 :12), pobal, muintir na tíre, treibh [a community of unpretentious people, rendered 'people' in this text to avoid the pejorative 'plebs.'

populus (C 38:5; 40:30; 51:192), pobal; a people, a great multitude, a throng.

vir-i (E 13:126; 14:130), fear, fir; a male, man, men; opp. *femina-ae*, bean, mná, a female, woman, women. 2. fear céile; husband.

WORDS CLOSELY RELATED IN MEANING:

alienigena C 1:19), coimthíoch; an alien people.

alienus (E 5:34), *a me alieni sunt*, níl aon pháirt acu liomsa; they are estranged from me.

peregrinus/peregrina (C 26:5), 1. deoraí, 2. deoraí Dé, 3. oilithreach; an exile, an alien, a pilgrim. Syn. *advena, hospes, peregrinator, alienus, alienigena,* externus; opp. *indigena, civis,* saoránach, a citizen.

perigrinatio (E 17:172; C 37:9), oilithreacht; *exile,* pilgrimage.

profuga (E 1:4; C 12:45) deoraí, dídeanaí; a banished person, *a refugee,* a fugitive.

proselitus (E 1:4: C 26:5; 59:20) (Gr. *proselutos*), coimhthíoch; a stranger in the land, *a sojourner.*

THE PLAN OF THE CONFESSIO

The following outline of the concentric structure of the *Confessio* is adapted from Dr David Howlett's version with his kind permission. Parts **I-V** marked in boldface and the chapter numbers in plain roman numerals **I-XXVI** are David Howlett's and putatively Patrick's. Upper case A-P-A', which are in the Gaelic alphabet for ease of comparison with the Gaelic version of this book, represent the concentric and parallel pairings of the twenty-six chapters. Arabic numbers enclosed in round brackets (1-62) are the traditional chapter numbers used by all modern editors and commentators. The arabic numbers without brackets are the line numbers. Words *italicised* in the text and marked by lower case letters and lower case roman numerals ai-ii-bi-ii-b'i-ii-a'i-ii in the third column show parallel and concentric connections within chapters. Small capitals indicate parallel lines and phrases between inverted parallel passages, e.g. C 1-2 A and C 62 A'. Using the traditional chapter numbers (1-62), chapter and line are indicated in the commentary as (3:23), meaning chapter 3 line 23 and so on. The cross-headings for the *Epistola* are mine, those for the *Confessio* are adapted from Dr Howlett's version.

THE CONCENTRIC PLAN OF THE CONFESSIO

PART I

Patrick's testimony of his trust in the true God

(1-2)	I	A	Prologue. Author's identification
(3)	II	B	Statement of reasons for writing echoing Psalm 88(89):6
(4)	III	C	Creed, quoting Rm 8:16-17
(5)	IV	D	Trust in God, quoting Psalm 50(49):14-15
(6)	V	E	Confession of unworthiness
(7-8)	VI	F	On truthfulness
(9-15)	VII	X	Apologia

PART II

(16-25)	VIII	G	**Patrick's testimony of his sacred calling**
(16-18)		1	Arrival in Ireland. Dreams concerning his return to Britain
(19)		2	Twenty-eight-day journey and near-starvation
(19 end)		3	God's providence. Supplying of food
(20)		4	Vision of Helias (Elijah)
(21-22)		3'	God's providence. Supplying of food
(22 end)		2'	Twenty-eight-day journey and near-starvation
(23-25)		1'	Arrival in Britain. Visions concerning his return to Ireland

PART III   **Patrick's testimony of his rejection and betrayal**

(26-27)	IX	H	Rejection by elders
(28)	X	L	Blessings which resulted from his abduction
(29)	XI	M	*The divine answer; (pupillam) pupil of eye*
(30)	XII	N	Gratitude to God
(31)	XIII	O	*I say boldly*
(32)	XIV	P	Elevation to the episcopate
(33)	XV	O'	*Again I say boldly*
(34)	XVI	N'	Gratitude to God
(35)	XVII	M'	*The divine answer; (pupillum) pupil*
(36)	XVIII	L'	Blessings which resulted from loss of homeland and parents
(37)	XIX	H'	Refusal to defer to elders

PART IV

(37end-53)	XX G'	**Patrick's testimony of his mission to the Irish**
(37-end)	1	There [in Ireland] I desire to spend [my life], quoting 2 Co 12:15
(38)	2	If the Lord should grant to me
(38)	3	What God has given to Patrick
(38-40)	4	Baptisms, ordinations, and confirmations in remote places
(41-42)	5	*Monks and virgins of Christ*
(43)	6	New Christians with whom Christ commanded him to stay in Ireland, echo of Psalm 119(118):60 influence of the holy Spirit
(44-45)	7	Total commitment to mission in Ireland
(46)	6'	Former willingness to go to Ireland echo of Psalm 119(118):60 influence of the Holy Spirit
(47-49)	5'	*Christian brethren and virgins of Christ*
(49-51)	4'	Baptisms, ordinations, and confirmations in remote places
(52-53)	3'	What Patrick has given God's people
(53)	2'	*The Lord is powerful to give me afterwards,* echo of Rm 25:24
(53 end)	1'	*That I may spend myself for your souls,* echoing 2 Co 12:15

PART V

CONFESSIO

PART I

(1-2) I A

a	i	*Ego*, PATRICIUS, PECCATOR, rústicíssimus,
		Et minimus ómnium fidélium,
		Et contemptibilissimus ápud plúrimos,
	ii	*patrem* habui Calpórnium, diaconum,
5	iii	*filium* quendam Potíti, presbyteri,
		qui fuit vico Bánnaventa Bérniae,
		Villam enim própe hábuit,
		ubi égo CAPTURAM DEDI.
b	i	*Annorum eram tunc fére sédecim.*
10	ii iii	*Deum* enim vérum *ignorábam*,
	iv	et HIBERIONE *IN CAPTIVITÁTE ADDÚCTUS SUM*
		Cum tot milia hominum secundum mérita nóstra,
		quia 'a Deo recessimus',
	v	et praecepta eius non *custodivimus*,
15	c	*Et sacerdotibus nostris non oboediéntes fúimus,*
		qui nostram salútem admonébant,
	d	i	Et Dominus *'induxit super nos iram animationis suae*
	ii	*et dispersit nos in gentibus' multis etiam 'usque ad ultimum terrae',*
	ii'	*ubi nunc parvitas mea esse videtur inter álienígenas.*
(2)	i'	*Et IBI Dominus aperuit sensum incredulitatis meae*
	c'	ut, vel, sero, *rememorárem delîcta méa,*
	b'	ii	et ut 'converterem toto corde ad Dominum *Deum* meum',
	iv	qui 'respexit HUMILITATEM MEAM'
	i iii	et *misertus est adolescentiae et IGNORÁNTIAE méae*
25	v	Et *custodivit* me ántequam scírem éum
		Et antequam saperem vel distinguerem inter bónum et
		málum,
		Et munívit me
28	a'	i ii iii	et consolatus est *me* ut *páter fílium.*

(3) II B

		Unde autem tacére non póssum,
		'neque expedit quidem',
		tanta bénefícia
		et tántam grátiam,
5		quam mihi Dominus praestáre dignátus est
		'IN TERRA CAPTIVITATIS MEAE',
		quia haec est retribútio nóstra
		ut post correptionem vel ágnitiònem Déi
		'EXÁLTARE ET CONFITERI MIRABILIA EIUS
10		coram omni natione

PART I

(1-2) I A

I PATRICK, 'A SINNER,' very rustic,
and the least of all the faithful,
and very contemptible in the estimation of most people,
had as *father* a deacon named Calpornius,

5   *the son* of Potitus, a priest
who was in the town Bannaventa Berniae;
he had an estate nearby,
where I WAS CAPTURED.
I was then almost sixteen years of age.

10   *I was indeed ignorant of the true God,*
and *I* WAS TAKEN IN CAPTIVITY to IRELAND
with so many thousands of people, and deservedly so,
because 'we turned away from God',
and *'we did not keep watch over* his precepts',

15   and *we did not obey our priests,*
who kept warning us about our salvation;
and The Lord *'poured down upon us the heat of his anger*
'and dispersed us among' many *'pagans'* even *'to the ends of the earth',*
where now my littleness is seen to be among an alien people.

(2)   *And* THERE *'the Lord opened my heart to an awareness of my unbelief'*
so that, perhaps, *I might* at last *remember my sins,*
and that *'I might turn with all my heart to the Lord my God,'*
who *'turned his gaze round on* MY LOWLINESS'
and *had mercy on my youth and* IGNORANCE

25   and *kept watch over* me before I knew him
and before I was wise or could distinguish between good
        and evil,
and he protected me

28   and comforted *me* as *a father* [comforts] a son.
(3) II B

Whence moreover I cannot remain silent,
'nor indeed is it expedient' [that I should],
concerning such great benefits
and the great grace

5   which the Lord has been pleased to bestow on me
'IN THE LAND OF MY CAPTIVITY',
because this is what we can give in return
after God corrects us and brings us to know him:
'TO EXALT AND CONFESS HIS WONDROUS DEEDS

10   before every nation

quae est sub omni caelo.'

(4) III C

Quia non est álius Déus,
nec úmquam fuit ánte
néc erit póst haec,
praeter Deum Pátrem ingénitum
5   síne princípio,
a quo est ómne princípium,
ómnia tenéntem,
út didícimus,
et huius fílium Ièsum Chrístum,
10   quem cum Pátre scílicet,
semper fuísse testámur
ante oríginem saéculi,
spiritaliter apud Patrem inenarrabíliter génitum,
ante ómne princípium,
15   et per ipsum facta sunt, visibilia et ínvisibília,

hóminem fáctum,
morte devicta, in caelis ad Pátrem recéptum.

'Et dedit illi omnem potestatem super omne nomen
caelestium
20   et terrestrium
et infernorum,
et omnis lingua confiteatur ei
quia Dominus et Deus est Iesus Christus',
Quem credimus,
25   et expectamus adventum ípsius, mòx futúrum,
'Iudex vivorum atque mortuorum,
Qui reddet unicuique secundum facta sua,'
ET 'EFFUDIT IN NOBIS ABUNDE SPÍRITUM SÁNCTUM,
DONUM' ET 'PIGNUS' ÍMMORTALITÁTIS,
30   qui facit credentes ét oboediéntes
ut sint 'FILII DEI' ET 'COHEREDES CHRISTI,'

Quem confitémur et àdorámus,
unum Deum in Trinitate sácri nóminis.

(5) IV D

Ipse enim díxit per prophétam,
'INVOCA ME IN DIE TRIBULATIONIS TUAE
ET LIBERABO TE
ET MAGNIFICABIS ME.'

which is under every heaven.'

(4) III C

Because there is no other God,
nor was there ever before,
nor will there be hereafter,
besides God the Father, unbegotten,
5 without beginning,
from whom is all beginning,
containing all things,
as we have been taught;
and his Son Jesus Christ,
10 whom we testify
to have always existed with the Father
before the beginning of the world,
spiritually and ineffably begotten by the Father,
before all beginning.
15 and through him all things have been made, visible and
  invisible.
He was made man,
and having conquered death, he was received into heaven
  by the Father.
'And he has given him all power above every name
in heaven,
20 and on earth,
and under the earth,
and every tongue should confess to him
that Jesus Christ is Lord and God',
in whom we believe,
25 and we look for his coming, soon to be,
'the judge of the living and the dead,
who will repay each one according to his own deeds,'
AND 'HE POURED OUT ON US ABUNDANTLY THE HOLY SPIRIT
AS THE GIFT' AND 'PLEDGE' OF IMMORTALITY,
30 who makes believers and listeners
so that they may be 'CHILDREN OF GOD' AND 'JOINT HEIRS
  WITH CHRIST',
whom we confess and adore,
one God in the Trinity of the Sacred Name.

(5) IV D

For he himself has said through the prophet,
'CALL ON ME IN THE DAY OF YOUR TROUBLE
AND I WILL DELIVER YOU
AND YOU WILL GLORIFY ME.'

5   Et íterum ínquit,
'Opera autem Dei revelare et confiteri
honorificum est.'

(6) V E
1   Tamen etsi IN MULTIS ÍMPERFÉCTUS SUM,
opto 'fratribus et cognatis' meis scire quálitátem
     méam,
ut possint perspicere votum ánimae méae.

(7-8) VI F

NON IGNORO 'TESTIMONIUM DOMINI MEI',
qui in psálmo testátur,
'Perdes eos qui loquuntur mendacium.'
Et íterum ínquit,
5   'OS QUOD MENTITUR OCCIDIT ANIMAM.'
Et idem Dominus in evangélio ínquit,
'Verbum otiosum quod locuti fuerint homines
reddent pro eo rationem in die iudicii.'
(8)   Unde, autem, veheménter debúeram
10   'cum timore et tremore' metuere hánc senténtiam
in die illa ubi nemo se poterit subtrahere vél abscóndere,
sed omnes omnino 'reddituri sumus rationem',

etiam minimórum peccatórum,
'ante tribunal Domini Christi'.

(9-15) VII X   **APOLOGIA**
       1
           a   Quapropter olim *cogitávi* scríbere,
sed et 'usque núnc' haesitávi;
           b   Timui enim ne *'inciderem in línguam'* hóminum,

quia *non didici* 'sícut' et 'céteri'
5   qui optime, itaque, *iura* et sácras lítteras,

utraque pari módo *combibérunt*,
           c   et sermones illorum ex infantia númquam mutárunt,
sed magis 'ad perfectum' sémper addidérunt.
           d   Nam 'sermo et loquela' nostra *translata est in línguam*
     aliénam,
10   sicut facile potest probari ex salíva scriptùrae méae
qualiter 'sum ego' in sermonibus instructus átque
     'erudítus',

5
 and again he says,
 'To reveal and confess, moreover, the works of God,
 is an honourable thing.'

(6) V E

 Nevertheless, though I AM IMPERFECT IN MANY RESPECTS,
 I wish 'my brethren and relatives' to know what kind of
   person I am,
 that they may be enabled to discern 'the vow of my soul'.

(7-8) VI F

 I AM NOT IGNORANT OF 'THE TESTIMONY OF MY LORD,'
 Who testifies in the psalm:
 'You destroy those who speak a lie.'
 And again he declares,
5 'THE MOUTH WHICH LIES DESTROYS THE SOUL.'
 And the same Lord affirms in the Gospel
 'The idle word which people will have spoken
 they will have to account for on the day of judgment.'
(8) Whence, moreover, I ought exceedingly
10 to dread this sentence 'with fear and trembling'
 on that day when no person will be able to withdraw or hide,
 but when all of us, without exception, 'shall render an
   account',
 of even the smallest sins,
 'before the judgment-seat of the Lord Christ'.

(9-15) X **APOLOGIA**

1 On which account *I have* long since *thought* about writing,
 but 'until now' I hesitated;
 for I feared lest *'I should fall under the censure of the tongue'*
   of people,
 because *I have not learned* 'just as others',
5 who, most thoroughly, then *have absorbed laws* and sacred
   letters,
 both in equal measure,
 and never changed their styles of speech from infancy,
 but rather were always bringing them 'towards perfection'.
 For our 'speech and spoken language' *has been translated*
   into an alien language,
10 as it can easily be proved from the flavour of my writing
 how 'I have been' taught and 'educated' in styles of
   speech,

quia, inquit, 'sapiens per línguam dinoscétur,

et sensus et scientia et doctrína veritátis'.

(10)   e   Sed quid prodest excusatio 'iúxta veritátem',

15   praesertim cúm praesumptióne,
                         quatenus modo ipse adpeto 'in sénectute' méa
                         quod *'in iuventute' nón comparávi,*
                         quod obstiterunt peccata méa ut cònfirmárem
                         quod ánte perlégeram?
20   Sed quis me credit etsi dixero quod ánte praefátus
                              sum?

        2
              a   Adolescens, immo *paene púer ínverbis,*
              b   CAPTÚRAM DÉDI
              c   *antequam scirem quíd adpétere*
                         vel quid vitáre debúeram.
25   d   Unde ergo hódie èrubésco
                         et veheménter pertímeo
                         denudare imperítiam méam,
                         quia disertis brevitate 'sermone explicáre' néqueo

                         Sicut, enim, spiritus géstit et ánimus,
30   et sensus mónstrat adféctus.
(11)   e   Sed si, itaque, datum mihi fuisset 'sícut' et 'céteris',
                         tamen non silerem *'propter retributionem'.*

        3
                         Et si forte videtur apud aliquantos me in hóc
                              praepónere,
                         Cum mea inscientia et 'tardiori lingua',
35   sed etiam, scríptum ést, enim:
                         'Linguae balbutientes velociter discent loqui pacem.'
                         Quanto magis nos adpetere debémus, qui sùmus,
                              ínquit:
                         'Epistola* Christi in salutem usque ad ultimum terrae,'
                         Et si non diserta sed rata ét fortíssima,

40   'scripta in cordibus vestris
                         non atramento sed Spiritu Dei vivi',

---

* The book of Armagh reads *Aepistola.*

because [Scripture] says, 'Through the tongue shall the
    wise man be recognised,
also his understanding and knowledge and teaching of the
    truth'.

(10)   But of what avail is an excuse, even when it is 'close to the
    truth,'

15   particularly [when it is attended] with obstinacy,
seeing that now 'in' my 'old age' I seek
what '*I did not accomplish in' my 'youth*',
because my sins prevented me from mastering
what I had read through before?

20   But who will believe me even if I shall say what I
    mentioned before?

2

As an adolescent, indeed, *as an almost speechless boy,*
I WAS CAPTURED
before I knew what I should seek
or what to avoid.

25   Whence therefore I blush for shame today
and I greatly fear
to expose my unlearnedness,
because I am unable 'to unfold in speech' to those trained
    in concise expression
in the way my spirit and mind desire,

30   and my heart's feelings suggest.
(11)   But if, then, I had been gifted 'just as others,'
I truly would not have remained silent '*because of the return
    due*' [from me to God].

3

And if by chance it may appear to some people that I am
    putting myself forward in this,
with my lack of knowledge and my 'rather slow tongue',

35   but even so it is written
'Stammering tongues will quickly learn to speak peace.'
How much more ought we to seek [to speak], we who are,
    he affirms,
'A letter of Christ bearing salvation to the ends of the earth'.
And though not an eloquent one, yet valid and very
    compelling,

40   'written in your hearts
not with ink but by the Spirit of the living God',

Et iterum Spiritus testatur
'Et rusticationem ab Altissimo Creatam.'

2'

(12)	a	Unde ego, *prímus rusticus,*
45	b	*profuga, indóctus,* scílicet,
	c	*'qui nescio* in posterum *providere,'*

Sed illud *'scio* certissime quia' utique 'PRIUSQUAM
    HUMILIARER'
ego eram velut lapis qui iacet in 'luto profundo',

	d	et vénit 'qui pótens est'
50		et in 'sua misericórdia' sustúlit me

Et quidem scilicet súrsum adlevávit
et collocavit me in súmmo paríete.

	e	Et inde fortiter *debúeram èxclamáre*
		'ad retribuendum' quoque áliquid *'Dómino'*
55		pro tantis beneficiis eius híc et in aetérnum,

quae mens hominum aestimáre nón potest.

1'

(13)	a	i	*Unde, autem, admirámini,* ítaque,
		ii iii iv	*'magni et pusilli qui timetis Deum',*
		iii' ii'	*et vos domini cáti rethórici,*
60		i'	*audite ergo ét scrutámini*
	b		*quis me, stultum, excitavit de médio eórum*
			qui videntur esse sapientes *et légis períti*
	c		et 'potentes *in sermone'* ét in ómni re
	d	i a	Et me quidem detestabilis huius mundi prae céteris
			ìnspirávit
65			*si talis essem –* dúmmodo aútem –
		b	*ut* 'cum metu et reverentia'
			et 'sine querella' fideliter prodéssem *génti*

ad quam 'caritas Christi' *transtúlit*

		c	*et donavit me* in vita mea, si dígnus fúero,
70		ii	denique *ut* CUM HUMILITATE et veraciter *déservirem íllis.*
(14)		iii a	In 'mensura,' itaque, 'fidei' Trinitatis óportet
			distínguere,
			sine reprehensióne perículi
		b	*notum fácere* 'DÒNUM DÉI'
		iv	et 'consolationem aeternam',
75		iii'a	*'síne timóre,'*
		b	fiducialiter *Dei* nomen *úbique expándere,*

and again the Spirit testifies:
'even rustic work was ordained by the Most High'.

2'

(12)   Whence I, *the genuine rustic,*
              a refugee, untaught, doubtless,
              'who *does not know how to provide* for the future',

              but that 'I do *know* most surely', that, indeed
              'BEFORE I WAS HUMBLED'
              I was like a stone lying in 'deep mire',
              and he 'who is mighty' came
50   and 'in his mercy' lifted me up;
              and, more than that, truly raised me aloft
              and placed me on the highest wall.
              And therefore *I ought to cry out* aloud
              in order *'to make'* some *'return'* to the Lord' also
55   for his great benefits here and in eternity,
              [benefits] which the human mind is unable to appraise.

1'

(13)   *Whence, moreover, be astonished* therefore,
              'you great and small who fear God',
              and you, lords, clever rhetoricians,
60   *hear therefore and consider* [what I am about to say];
              who was it that stirred me up, a fool, from the midst of those
              who seem to be wise and *learned in law*
              and 'powerful *in speech*' and in everything?
              And inspired even me, beyond the others of this
                  detestable world,
65   *if I should be such* [a person] – if only moreover [I were] –
              that 'with awe and reverence'
              and 'without complaint' I would faithfully be of service to
                  that pagan people
              to whom 'the love of Christ' *translated me;*
              and granted me [this flock], as long as I live, if I should be
                  worthy;
70   that at last WITH HUMILITY and in truth *I might serve them.*
(14)   And so, 'according to the measure of the faith' of the
                  Trinity it is my duty,
              without fear of the censure [I may incur],
              to make known 'THE GIFT OF GOD'
              and [his] 'eternal consolation';
75   *without fear*
              faithfully *to expound everywhere the name of God,*

ii'   ut etiam 'post obitum meum' *exagallias relinquere*
                fratribus et fíliis méis
             quos in Domino ego baptizavi tot mília hóminum.

(15)   i' a   *Et non eram* dígnus neque *tális*
80   b   *ut* hoc Dominus servulo súo concéderet,
                       post aerúmnas et tàntas móles,
                       PÓST CAPTIVITÁTEM,
                       post annos múltos *in gèntem íllam*,
                c   tantam gratiam *míhi donáret,*
85   a'   quod ego aliquando *in iuventute* mea *numquam speravi*
                          néque cogitávi.

PART II

(16-25) VIII G

(16-18) G¹   Sed postquam Hiberióne devéneram,
                        cotidie itaque pécora pascébam,
                        et frequens in díe ORÁBAM,
        a b   magis ac magis accedebat amor Dei et *tímor* ípsius,
5   c   et *fides* augebatur, et SPÍRITUS àgebátur,

                        ut in die una usque ad céntum ORATIONES,

                        et in nocte própe simíliter,
                        ut etiam in silvis et mónte manébam,
                        et ante lucem excitabar ád ORATIONEM,
10   per nivem, per gélu, per plúviam,
                        et nihil máli sentiébam,
                        neque ulla pigrítia èrat ín me,
                        sicut modo video, quia tunc spiritus ín me fervébat,
(17)   Et ibi, scilicet, quadam nócte in sómno
15   d   i   *audivi* vócem dicèntem míhi,
             ii   'Bene ieiunas cito *iturus* ad pátriam túam.'

             iii   Et iterum post paúlulum témpus
             iv   audivi 'respónsum' dicèntem míhi,
        e   'Ecce navis túa paráta est.'
20   f   Et *nón erat própe*,
                        sed forte habebat ducenta mília pássus
                        et ibi númquam fúeram,
                        nec ibi notum quemquam de homínibus habébam,
        g   *et deinde postmodum convérsus sum in fúgam,*

so that even 'after my death' *I may leave behind a legacy to my brethren and children,*

whom I have baptized in the Lord, so many thousands of people.

(15)   *And I was not* worthy nor *such* [a person]

80   *that* the Lord should concede this to his little servant,

that after troubles and such great difficulties,

AFTER CAPTIVITY,

after many years among *that pagan people,*

that *he should grant me* such great grace,

85   which, at anytime *in* my *youth, I never hoped for nor thought about.*

PART II

(16-25) VIII G

(16-18) G¹   But after I had come to Ireland,

I was herding flocks daily,

and many times a day I WAS PRAYING.

More and more the love of God and fear of him came to me,

5   and my *faith* was being increased, and THE SPIRIT was being moved,

so that in one day I would say as many as a hundred PRAYERS,

and at night nearly the same,

even while I was staying in woods and on the mountain;

and before daybreak I was roused up to PRAYER,

10   in snow, in frost, in rain;

and I felt no ill-effects from it,

nor was there any sluggishness in me,

as I see now, because the spirit was fervent in me then.

(17)   And there one night in a dream

15   *I heard* a voice saying to me,

'It is well that you are fasting, soon *you will go* to your own country.'

And again after a short time

I heard the answer saying to me:

'Look, your ship is ready.'

20   And *it was not nearby,*

but was at a distance of perhaps two hundred miles;

and I had never been there,

nor did I know anybody there,

and then later I took to flight,

25   h   *et intermisi hominem cum quo fúeram sex ánnis,*
     h'   *et veni ín virtute Déi,*
     g'   *qui viam meam ad bónum dirigébat,*
     f'e'   *et nihil metuebam donec pervéni ad nàvem íllam,*
(18)   Et illa die qua perveni profecta est návis de lòco súo,

30   et locutus sum ut haberem *unde navigáre cum íllis,*
                    et gubernator, displícuitílli,
                    et acriter cum indignatióne respóndit,
     d'   ii   'Nequaquam tu nobiscum ádpetes *íre.*'
             i   Et cum haec *audiissem* separávi me ab íllis,
35   ut venirem ad teguriolum úbi hospitábam,
                    et in itinere coépi ORARE,
             iii   *Et antequam ORATIONEM consummárem*
             iv   *audivi únum ex íllis,*
                    et fortiter éxclamabat póst me,
40   'Veni cito, quia vocant te hómines ísti,'
                    et statim ad íllos revérsus sum,
                    et coeperunt míhi dícere,
     c'   'Veni, quia ex *fide* recipimus te,
                    fac nobiscum amicitiam quo módo volúeris,'
45   Et in illa die, itaque, reppuli 'sugere mammellas eorum'

     b'a'   própter *timòrem Déi,*
                    sed verumtamen ab illis speravi venire in fídem Iesu
                        Chrísti,
                    quía géntes érant,
                    et ob hoc obtínui cum íllis,
50   et protinus *návigávimus.*
(19) G 2
                    Et post triduum térram cépimus,
                    et viginti octo dies per desertum íter fécimus,

     a   i   *et cibus défuit íllis,*
             ii   *et 'fames invaluit super eos',*
55   et alio die coepit gubernator míhi dícere,
                    'Quíd est, Christiáne?
     b   i ii iii iv *Tu dicis Deus tuus magnus et omnipotens est?*
                    Quare ergo non potes pro nóbis ORARE?
     c   *Quia nos a fame péríclitámur?*
60   Difficile est enim ut aliquem hominem úmqua
                        videámus.'
     b'   i ii   Ego enim confidénter *dixi* íllis,

25	*and I abandoned the person with whom I had stayed for six years,*
	and I came in the power of God,
	who was directing my way unto good,
	and I was fearing nothing until I reached that ship.
(18)	And on that day on which I arrived the ship had set out from its anchorage,
30	and I said that I had *the wherewithal to take passage with them;*
	but the captain was not pleased,
	and answered sharply with indignation:
	'By no means will you try *to go* with us.'
	And when *I heard* these things I left them,
35	in order to return to the little hut where I was staying.
	And on the way back I began TO PRAY;
	and before I had finished MY PRAYER,
	I heard one of them,
	shouting out vigorously after me,
40	'Come quickly because these people are calling you.'
	And I returned immediately to them,
	and they began to say to me:
	'Come, because we are receiving you *on faith,*
	make friends with us in whatever way you wish.'
45	And so on that day, accordingly, I refused 'to suck their breasts'
	because of *the fear of God,*
	but rather I hoped to come by them to the faith of Jesus Christ,
	because they were pagans;
	and thus I got my way with them,
50	and *we set sail* at once.
(19) G 2	
	And after three days we reached land,
	and for twenty-eight days we travelled through deserted country,
	and food failed them,
	and 'hunger overcame them',
55	and on the next day the captain began to say to me:
	'How is this, Christian?
	You say your God is great and all-powerful?
	Why then can you not PRAY for us?
	because we are in danger of starving?
60	It is indeed doubtful that we may ever see a human being again.'
	But *I said* to them with confidence:

	iii	'"Convertemini" ex fide "ex toto corde ad Dóminum
		Dèum méum,
	iv	*quia nihil est impossíbile ílli,"*
a'	i	*ut hodie cibum mittat vobis* in viam vestram usque dúm
		satiámini,
65	ii	*quia ubique ábundábat ílli."'*

(19end) G 3

a		Et[2] adiuvante Deo 'íta fáctum est'.
b	i	Ecce *grex porcorum in via ante oculos nóstros appáruit,*[3]
	ii	*et multos ex illis ínterfecérunt,*
c		*et ibi duas noctes manserunt et béne refécti,*
70		et canes eórum repléti sunt,
		quia multi ex íllis 'defecérunt',
		et secus viam 'semivívi relícti' sunt,
d		*et post hoc summas gratias egerunt Deo,*
d'		*et ego honorificatus sum sub oculis eorum,*
75 c'		*et ex hac die cibum abundánter habuérunt;*
b'	i	etiam *'mel silvéstre' invenérunt,*
	ii	et *'mihi partem obtulerunt',*
		et unus ex illis dixit, 'Ímmolatícium est'.
a'		*Deo gratias,*
80		exinde níhil gustávi.

(20) G 4

a		*Eadem vero nocte éram dórmiens,*
b		*et fortiter temptavit me Satanas,*
		quod memorero 'quamdiu fuero in hoc corpore',
c		*et cecidit super me véluti sàxum íngens,*
85		*et nihil membrorum meórum praévalens.*
d	i	Sed unde me venit ignaro in spiritu ut *Héliam vocárem?*

	ii	Et inter haec *vidi in caelum sólem oríri,*
d'	i	*et dum clamarem 'Helia, Helia' víribus méis,*
	ii	*ecce, splendor solis illius decídit súper me,*
90 c'		*et statim discussit a me omnem grávitúdinem,*
b'		*et credo quod a Christo Domino méo subvéntus sum,*
		et SPIRITUS eius iam túnc clamábat pró me,
		et spero quod sic erit 'in díe pressùrae' méae,
a'		sicut in evangelio ínquit, *'In ìlla díe,'*
95		Dominus testatur, *'non vos estis qui loquimini,*
		sed SPIRITUS Patris vestri qui loquitur in vobis.'

(21-22) G 3'

| | | Et iterum post annos multos adhúc CAPTURAM DEDI. |
| a | | *Ea nocte prima itaque mánsi cum íllis* |

'"Be converted' in faith 'with all your heart to the Lord *my God,*

because nothing is impossible to him',

so that today he may send food to you until you have sufficient
on your way,

'*because for him there was abundance everywhere*'"

65
(19end) G 3

And, with the help of God it so came to pass.

Look, *a herd of pigs appeared on the road before our eyes,*

and they killed many of them,

and there they remained for two nights and were well fed,

70 and their hounds received their fill,

because many of them had 'fainted away',

and were left behind 'half-alive by the wayside',

and after this they rendered the highest thanks to God,

and I became honourable in their eyes,

75 *and from that day on they had food in abundance;*

they even *found 'wild honey',*

and '*offered a part to me',*

and one of them said: 'This is a [pagan] sacrifice',

Thanks be to God,

80 I tasted none of it.

(20) G 4

Now on that same night, when I was sleeping,

Satan vigorously put me to the test,

in a way I shall remember 'as long as I shall be in this body';

and he fell upon me like a huge rock,

85 *and I had no power over my limbs.*

But whence did it occur to my ignorant spirit to call upon
Elijah *(Helias)?*

And meanwhile *I saw the sun rise into the heavens,*

and while I was shouting 'Elijah, Elijah' with all my might,

lo, the splendour of his sun [helios] fell on me,

90 *and immediately freed me of all oppressiveness,*

and I believe that I was sustained by Christ my Lord,

and that his SPIRIT *was even then crying out on my behalf,*

and I trust that it will be so 'on the day of' my 'pressing need',

as he affirms in the Gospel, '*On that day',*

95 the Lord testifies: '*It is not you who speak*

but the SPIRIT *of your Father is speaking in you.'*

(21-22) G 3'

And again many years later I WAS CAPTURED.

And *on that first* night I stayed with them

		'*Responsum*' autem '*divinum*' audívi dicèntem míhi,
100	b	'*Duobus mensibus* éris cum íllis,'
	c	*Quod 'íta fáctum est'.*
	b'	*nocte illa séxagésima*
		'liberavit me Dominus de manibus eorum'.
(22)		Etiam in itinere praevídit nobis cíbum
105		et ignem et siccitátem cotídie,
	a'	donec *decimo die* pervénimus hómines.
(22end) G 2'		

Sicut superius ínsinuávi,
Viginti et octo dies per desertum íter fécimus,
et ea nocte qua pervenimus homines *de cibo vero níhil habúimus.*

(23-25) G 1'		
110		Et iterum post paucos annos in Brittánniis éram
		cum paréntibus méis,
		qui me ut fílium sùscepérunt,
	a i	et ex fíde *rogavérunt me*
	ii	*ut* vel modo ego, post tantas tribulationes quas égo pertúli,
115	iii	*nusquam ab íllis discéderem.*
		Et ibi scilicet 'vidi in visu noctis' virum venientem quasi

dé Hiberióne,
cui nómen Victóricius,
cum epistolis innúmerabílibus,
et dedit míhi únam éx his,

120a iv bi ii		*et legi principium epistolae continentem*
		'*Vox Hibérionácum*',
	c b' i	Et cum recitabam princípium epístolae
	ii	putabam ipso momento audire vócem ipsórum
		qui erant iuxta sílvam Voclúti,
		quae est prope mare óccidentále,
125		et sic exclamaverunt 'quasi ex uno ore,'
	a' i	'*Rogámus te,* sàncte púer,
	ii iii	*ut venias et adhuc ámbulas ínter nos.'*
		Et valde 'compunctus sum corde',
	iv	*et amplius non pótui légere.*
130	a" i	*et síc expértus sum,*
		Déo grátias,
		quia post plurimos annos praestitit íllis Dóminus
		secundum clamórem illórum.
(24)		Et alia nocte, nescio Deus scit,'

I heard moreover *'a divine answer'* saying to me,
100 'For *two months* you will be with them',
which was what came to pass.
On the sixtieth night thereafter
'the Lord delivered me out of their hands'.
(22) He even provided us on the journey with food
105 and fire and dry weather every day,
until, *on the tenth day,* we encountered people.
(22end) G 2'

As I have indicated above,
we travelled through deserted country for eight and twenty days,
and on the night on which we encountered people *we had*
    indeed no food left.
(23-25) G 1'
110 And once again, after a few years, I was in the Britains
with my people,
who received me as a son,
and in faith *besought me*
that now, at least, after all the many hardships which I had
    endured,
115 *I should not ever depart from them.*
And there indeed 'I saw in a vision of the night' a man
    coming
as if from Ireland,
whose name [was] Victoricius,
with countless letters,
and he gave me one of them,
120 *and I read the beginning of the letter containing 'the Voice of the*
    Irish',
and as I was reading the beginning of the letter aloud
I imagined I heard, at that moment, the voice of those very
    people who lived beside the Wood of Fochoill,
which is near the Western Sea,
125 and thus they cried out 'as if from one mouth',
'We request you, holy boy,
that you come and walk once more among us.'
And 'I was' truly 'cut to the heart',
and I could read no further.
130 *And thus I have learned by experience,*
thanks be to God,
that after very many years the Lord has given them
according to their cry.
(24) And on another night, 'I do not know, God knows',

135   utrum ín me an iúxta me,
              ii   *verbis peritissimis quos égo audívi*
                            et non potui íntellégere,
      b"   *nisi ad postremum* ORATIONIS *síc effitiátus est:*
      c"   *"'Qui dedit animam suam pro te'*
140   ipse est qui lóquitur ín te,"
                            et sic expergefactus súm gaudibúndus.
(25) d"   Et iterum vidi in me ípsum ORANTEM,
                            et eram quasi íntra corpus méum,
                            Et audivi super me, hoc est, super 'interiorem
                                hominem',
145   et ibi fortiter ORABAT gemítibus,
                            et inter haec 'stupebam et admirabam et cogitabam'
      c'''   *quis esset quí in me* ORABAT,
      b'''   *Sed ad postremum orationis sic effitiatus est* út sit
                                SPIRITUS.
      a''' i   *Et síc expértus sum*
150   et recordatus sum, apóstolo dicénte,
                            'SPIRITUS adiuvat infirmitates ORATIONIS nostrae.
                            nam, quod OREMUS, sicut oportet, nescimus,
                            sed ipse SPIRITUS postulat pro nobis gemitibus
                                inenarrabilibus
              ii   *quae verbis exprimi non possunt.'*
155   Et iterum: 'Dominus advocatus noster postulat pro
                                nobis.'

PART III

(26-27) IX H
              a   Et quando *temptatus sum* ab aliquantis senioribus
                                meis qui venérunt
                            et peccata mea contra laboriosum episcopatum méum
                                obiecérunt,
              b   utique illo die fortiter '*impulsus sum*
                            ut caderem' híc et in aetérnum,
      5   sed Dominus pepercit proselíto et pèregríno
                            propter nomen súum benígne,
                            et valde mihi subvenit in hac cónculcatióne,

                            Quod in labe et in obprobrium non mále devéni.
              c   *Deum* oro ut 'non illis in peccatum reputetur'.
(27)   d   *'Occasionem' post annos triginta 'invenerunt me adversus',*
              e   *verbum quod confessus fueram antequam éssem diaconus.*
              f   *Propter anxietatem maesto animo insinuavi amicissimo meo*

135   whether within me or beside me,
             in most learned words I heard those whom
             I could not understand,
             except that at the end of THE PRAYER *one spoke out thus:*
             "'He who has laid down his own life for you
140   *he it is who is speaking in you'";*
             and I was thus awakened rejoicing greatly.
(25)   And again I saw him PRAYING within me,
             and I was, as it were, inside my body,
             and I heard [him] over me, this is [to say], over 'the interior
                  person',
145   and there HE WAS PRAYING earnestly with groans,
             and amidst these things 'I was astonished
                  and I kept wondering and thinking'
             who he might be who WAS PRAYING *in me,*
             but at the end of the PRAYER *he declared* that he was the SPIRIT.
             And thus I have learned by experience
150   and recalled to mind, as the apostle says,
             'The SPIRIT helps the weaknesses of our PRAYER.
             for we do not know what to PRAY for as we ought,
             but the SPIRIT himself intercedes for us with unspeakable
                  groanings
             [*things*] *which cannot be expressed in words.'*
155   And again: 'The Lord our advocate intercedes for us.'

PART III

(26-27) IX H

             And when *I was tried* by a number of my elders who came
             and cast up my sins as a charge against my laborious
                  episcopate,

             on that day, assuredly, '*I was* vigorously *overwhelmed*
             to the point of falling' here and for eternity,
5   but the Lord spared the sojourner an exile
             because of his own kindly name,
             and he came powerfully to my support in this crushing
                  under heel,
             so that, in disgrace and in shame, I did not come out badly.
             I pray *God* that 'it may not be reckoned to them as sin'.
(27)   *After thirty years* 'they invented an occasion against me',
             a word which I had confessed before I was a deacon.
             In the anxiety of my troubled mind I disclosed to my dearest friend

	e'	*quae in pueritia mea una díe gésseram,*
		ímmo in ùna hóra,
15		quia nécdum praevalébam.
		'Nescio Deus scit,'
	d'	*si habebam tunc ánnos quíndecim,*
	c'	et *Deum* vívum non credébam,
		neque ex infántia méa,
20		sed in morte et in incredúlitáte mánsi
	b'	donec valde *cástigátus sum*,
	a'	'et in veritate HUMÍLIÁTUS SUM
		fáme et nùditáte', ét cotídie.

(28) X L

Contra Hiberione non spónte pergébam

'donec' prope 'deficiebam.'
Sed hoc potius béne mihi fúit,
qui ex hoc emendátus sum a Dómino,
5   et *'aptavit me'* ut hódie éssem
quod aliquando lónge a mé erat,
ut ego cúram habérem
aut satagerem pro salúte aliórum,
quando autem *tunc* etiam de me ipso nón cogitábam.

(29) XI M

Igitur in illo die quo 'reprobatus sum'
a memorátis supradíctis,
ad noctem illam 'vidi *in visu noctis'*
quod scriptum erat contra faciem meam síne honóre,
et inter haec audivi *'responsum divínum'* dicèntem míhi:
'Male vidimus faciem designati nudáto nómine',
nec sic praedixit, 'Mále vidísti',
sed *'Mále vídimus',*

quasi síbi me iunxísset,
10   sicut dixit, *'Qui vos tangit*
quasi qui tangit pupillam oculi mei.'
(30) XII N

Idcirco 'gratias ago ei
qui me' in omnibus 'confortavit,'
ut non me impediret a profectione quám statúeram,

Et de mea quoque opera quod a Christo Domino méo
        didíceram,

what *I had done in my boyhood on one day,*
more precisely in one hour,
15 because I had not yet gained self-control.
'I do not know, God knows'
if I was then fifteen years old;
and I did not believe in the living *God,*
nor [had I believed in him] from my infancy,
20 but I remained in death and in unbelief
until the time *I was* indeed *castigated,*
'and truly HUMILIATED
by hunger and nakedness', and that daily.

(28) X L

On the other hand I did not set out for Ireland of my own
    accord
'until the time' I had nearly 'perished'.
But this was rather to my advantage,
since because of this I have been freed from fault by the Lord,
5 and *'he has fitted me'* so that today I may be
what once was far beyond me,
that I may be concerned
or rather be labouring for the salvation of others,
whereas, *at that time,* I was not thinking even about
    myself.

(29) XI M

So then on that day when 'I was reproved'
by those remembered and above-mentioned,
on that night 'I saw in *a vision of the night*'
what had been written against my face without honour,
5 and meanwhile I heard *'the divine answer'* saying to me,
'We have seen with disapproval the face of the designated man
with his name stripped naked',
and he did not say, 'You have seen with disapproval',
but *'We have seen with disapproval',*
as if he had joined me to himself,
10 just as he has said, *'He who touches you*
[is] *as he who touches the pupil of my eye.'*

(30) XII N

Therefore 'I give thanks to him
who has strengthened me' in all things
so that he did not impede my setting out [on the journey]
    on which I had decided,
nor also from my task which I had learned from Christ my
    Lord,

5   sed magis ex eo 'sensi in me virtútem' non párvam,

        et fides mea probata est coram Déo et homínibus.

(31) XIII O

        Unde autem *'audenter dico'*
        non me reprehendit consciéntia méa
        híc et in futúrum,
        'Teste Déo' hábeo
5   *'quia non sum mentitus'*
        in sermonibus quos égo retùli vóbis.

(32) XIV P

        Sed magis doleo pro amicissimo meo,
        cur hoc meruimus audire tále respónsum,
        Cui ego credidi étiam ánimam.
        Et comperi ab aliquantis fratribus
5   *ante defénsiónem íllam,*
        quod ego nón intérfui,
        nec in Brittánniis éram,
    a nec *a me* óriebátur,
    bc ut et *ille in mea absentiá* pulsáret pró me.
10   d etiam mihi *ipse ore súo* díxerat,
    d' *'Ecce, dandus es tu ad grádum episcopatus',*
    c' *quod nón eram dígnus.*
    b' Sed unde venit *ílli* póstmodum
        ut coram cunctis, bónis et mális,
15   a' et *me* publice déhonestáret
        quod ante sponte et laétus indúlserat,
        et Dominus, qui 'maior omnibus est'.

(33) XV O'

        Satis *'dico'*.
        Sed tamen non debeo abscóndere 'DÒNUM DÉI',
        quod largitus est nobis 'IN TERRA CAPTIVITATIS MEAE',
        quia tunc fortiter ínquisivi éum,
5   et íbi invèni íllum,
        et servavit me ab omnibus iníquitátibus,
        Sic credo 'propter inhabitantem Spíritum' eíus,
        qui 'operatus est' usque in hánc diem ín me.
        'Audénter' rúrsus.
10   Sed scit Deus si mihi homo hoc effátus fuísset,

        forsitan tacuissem propter 'caritatem Christi'.

5
    but rather 'I sensed within myself' not a little 'power'
      coming from him,
    and my faith was approved before God and people.

(31) XIII O

    Whence moreover *'I say boldly'*
    that my conscience does not reprove me
    here and in the future.
    'God is my witness'
5
    'that I have not lied'
    in the speeches which I have recounted to you.

(32) XIV P

    But I grieve the more for my dearest friend,
    because we merited to hear such a response from this man,
    to whom I had entrusted my very soul.
    And I have learned from some of the brethren
5
    before that defence,
    at which I was not present,
    nor was I in the Britains,
    nor did it *arise from me,*
    that, *in my absence, he would also plead for me.*
10
    He himself had even *said* to me *from his own mouth,*
    'Look, you are to be granted the order of the episcopate,'
    of which I was not worthy.
    But whence did it occur *to him* afterwards
    that in the sight of everyone, good and bad,
15
    he should put *me* to shame even publicly
    over something which before he had conceded [to me]
      joyfully and of his own accord,
    and the Lord, 'who is greater than all?'

(33) XV O'

    'I say' enough.
    But nevertheless I must not hide 'THE GIFT OF GOD',
    which has been lavished on us 'IN THE LAND OF MY CAPTIVITY',
    because then I earnestly sought him,
5
    and there I found him,
    and he kept me from all iniquities, this is my belief,
    'because of his indwelling Spirit',
    who 'has worked' in me up to this day.
    'Boldly' again [am I speaking].
10
    But, God knows, if a human being had said this to me,

    I would perhaps have remained silent about 'the charity of
      Christ'.

(34) XVI N'

	a	*Unde ergo indefessam gratiam ágo Deo méo,*
	b	*qui me fidelem servavit 'in die temptátiónis' méae,*
	c	*ita ut hodie confidenter offeram illi sácrifícium,*
	c'	*ut 'hostiam viventem' animam meam Christo Dómino méo,*
5	b'	*qui me 'servavit ab omnibus angustiis meis,'*

ut et dicam, 'Quis ego sum, Domine',
vel quae est vocátio méa,
qui mihi tanta divinitate cómparuísti,
ita ut hódie 'in géntibus'

10   constánter 'exaltárem
et magnificárem nomen túum'
ubicumque lóco fúero
Nec nón in secúndis,
sed étiam ìn pressúris,

15   ut quicquid míhi evénerit,
sive bónum sive málum,

       a'   *Aequaliter débeo suscípere,*
et Deo gratias sémper ágere,

       b"   *qui míhi osténdit*

20   ut indubitabilem eum sine fíne créderem,
Et qui mé audíerit,
ut ego inscius et 'in novissimis diebus'

       c"   hoc opus tam pium et tam mirificum audérem adgrédere,
ita ut imitarem quíppiam íllos

25   quos ante Dominus iam ólim praedíxerat
praenuntiaturos evangélium súum,
'in testimonium omnibus gentibus' ánte 'finem
       múndi',
quod ita ergo vidimus ítaque supplétum est.
Ecce, testes sumus quia evangelium praédicátum est

30   usque ubi némo últra est.

(35) XVII M'

Longum est autem totum per singula, enarrare laborem
       méum, vel per pártes.
Breviter dicam qualiter piissimus Deus de servitute
       saépe liberávit
et de periculis duodecim qua periclitata est ánima méa,
praeter insídias múltas

5   *Et 'quae verbis exprimere non valeo'.*
Nec iniuriam legéntibus fáciam,
sed Deum auctórem hábeo,
qui novit omnia etiam ántequam fíant,

(34) XVI N'

Whence therefore I give unwearied thanks to my God,
who kept me faithful 'in the day of my trial',
so that today I may confidently offer in sacrifice to him
my life as 'a living host' to Christ my Lord,

5 *who 'has saved me from all my troubles',*
so that I also may say, 'Who am I, Lord?'
or 'What is my calling?'
[You] who have appeared to me with such divinity,
so that today 'among pagans'

10 'I may' steadfastly 'exalt
and glorify your name'
wherever I may be;
and that not only in favourable circumstances,
but also in pressing need,

15 so that 'whatever may happen to me,
be it good or bad',
I ought to accept with equanimity,
and always give thanks to God,
who has shown to me

20 that I should always believe in him without any hesitation,
and who must have heard me,
so that I unknowingly and 'in the final days'
may dare to undertake this work so holy and so wondrous;
so that I to some degree may imitate those

25 whom the Lord long ago had foretold
would proclaim his Gospel,
'as a testimony to all the pagans' before 'the end of the
world'.
So we have have seen it, and so it has been fulfilled.
Behold, we are witnesses that the Gospel has been proclaimed

30 to the limit beyond which nobody dwells.

(35) XVII M'

Now it is too tedious to give an account of my labours, in
whole or in part.
Let me relate briefly how the most holy God has often
freed [me] from slavery
and from *twelve perils whereby my soul was endangered,*
besides numerous treacheries

5 *and 'things which I am unable to express in words'.*
Nor shall shall I bore my readers,
but I have God as my authority,
who knows all things even before they come to pass,

ut me, paupérculum pupíllum,
10   idiotam '*responsum divinum*' crébre admonére.

(36)   XVIII L'

'*Unde mihi haec sapientia',*
quaé in me nón erat,
qui nec 'numerum dierum noveram',
neque Déum sapiébam.
5   *Unde mihi postmodum donum tam mágnum tam*
salúbre,
Deum agnoscere vél dilígere,
sed ut patriam et paréntes amítterem.

(37)   XIX H'

Et munera multa mihi offerebantur cum flétu et
lácrimis,
ét offendi íllos,
nec non contra votum *aliquantos de* SENIORIBUS MEIS,
sed gubernante Deo nullo modo consensi neque
ádquievi íllis,
5   non mea gratia, sed Déus qui vìncit ín me,
et resistit íllis ómnibus,
ut ego veneram ad Hibernas gentes evangélium
praèdicáre,
et ab *incredulis* contumélias perférre,
ut 'audirem *obprobrium* PEREGRINATIONIS MEAE',
10   et persecutiones multas '*usque ad vincula',*
et ut darem ingenuitatem meam pro utilitáte aliórum,

Et, si dignus fúero, '*prómptus' sum,*
ut etiam '*animam meam',*
incunctanter et 'libentissime' *pro nómine eíus.*

PART IV

(37end-53) XX G'
(37end)   G'1   Et ibi opto 'impendere' eam 'usque ad mortem',

(38)   G'2   si Dominus míhi indulgéret,
(38)   G'3   quia valde 'débitor sum' Déo,
qui mihi tantam grátiam donávit,

that me, a poor little pupil,

10 an ordinary person, [his] *'divine answer'* would frequently warn.

(36) XVIII L'

'Whence did this wisdom [*come*] *to me',*
which was not in me,
who knew neither 'the number of my days',
nor did I have any discernment about God.

5 *Whence* [*was given*] *to me afterwards the gift so great, so salutary,*
to know or to love God wholeheartedly,
but at the loss of country and kindred?

(37) XIX H'

And many gifts were offered to me with weeping and tears,

and I offended [the donors],

and also, against [my] wish, *a certain number of* MY ELDERS;

but, with God as my pilot, in no way did I consent nor acquiesce,

5 not by my grace but God who conquers in me,

and I stood firm against them all,

so that I might come to the Irish pagans to proclaim the Gospel,

and to endure insults from *unbelievers,*

'so that I might hear about the *shame of my* EXILE',

10 and [endure] many persecutions *'even unto chains',*

and so that I might surrender my freeborn status for the benefit of others;

and if I should be worthy, *I am 'prepared',*

[to give up] 'even *my life'*

unhesitatingly and 'most gladly' *for his name.*

PART IV

(37end-53) XX G'

(37end)   G'1   And there [in Ireland] I choose 'to spend' it [my life] 'until I die',

(38)   G'2   if the Lord should grant [that] to me,

(38)   G'3   BECAUSE 'I AM' VERY MUCH GOD'S 'DEBTOR',

WHO HAS GRANTED TO ME SUCH GREAT GRACE,

(38-40) G'4 ab   UT *POPULI* MULTI PER ME IN DÉUM *RENÀSCERÉNTUR*,
                    ET POSTMODUM CÓNSUMMARÉNTUR,
          c   ET UT *CLERICI* UBIQUE ILLIS ÓRDINARÉNTUR,
          d   i   AD PLEBEM NUPER *VENIENTEM ÁD CREDULITÁTEM*,
               ii   QUAM SUMPSIT *DOMINUS* 'AB EXTREMIS TERRAE',
10   iii sicut olim *promiserat pér prophétas* súos:
               iv   'Ad te gentes venient ab extremis terrae et dicent,
                    "Sicut falsa comparaverunt patres nostri idola,
                    et non est in eis utilitas."'
                    Et iterum: 'Posui te lumen in gentibus,

15   ut sis in salutem usque ad extremum terrae.'

(39)   e   Et ibi volo 'expectare promíssum' ípsius,
                    qui útique nùmquam fállit,
                    sicut in evangélio pòllicétur,
                    'Venient ab oriente et occidente
20   et recumbent cum Abraham et Isaac et Iacob,'
          d'   i   sicut credimus ab omni mundo *ventúri sunt credéntes*.

(40)   Idcirco itaque oportet quidem bene et diligénter
                        piscáre
               ii   sicut *Dominus* praemonet ét docet dícens:
                    'Venite post me et faciam vos fieri piscatores hominum';
25   iii Et iterum *dícit per prophétas*,
               iv   'Ecce mitto piscatores et venatores multos dicit Déus', et
                        cétera.
                    Unde autem valde oportebat retia nóstra tendére,
                    ita ut 'multitudo copiosa et turba' Déo caperétur

          c'b'   et ubique essent *clerici quí baptizárent*,
30   a'   et exhortarent *populum* indigentem ét desiderántem,
                    sicut Dominus inquit in évangélio,
                    admonet ét docet dícens,
                    'Euntes ergo nunc docete omnes gentes,
                    baptizantes eas in nomine Patris et Filii et Spiritus
                        Sancti,
35   docentes eos observare omnia quaecumque mandavi
                        vobis,
                    Et ecce, ego vobiscum sum omnibus diebus,
                    usque ad consummationem saeculi.'
                    Et iterum dicit, 'Euntes ergo in mundum universum,
                    praedicate evangelium omni creaturae.

(38-40) G'4   THAT *A MULTITUDE* THROUGH ME *SHOULD BE REBORN* TO GOD,
AND AFTERWARDS BE CONFIRMED,
AND THAT *CLERGY* EVERYWHERE SHOULD BE ORDAINED FOR THEM,
FOR A PEOPLE *COMING* RECENTLY *TO BELIEF*,
WHOM *THE LORD* HAS TAKEN UP 'FROM THE ENDS OF THE EARTH',

10 just as he had in times past *promised through his prophets:*
'To you will the pagans come from the ends of the earth, and say:*
"Our ancestors established idols as worthless things,
and there is no benefit in them."'
And again: 'I have placed you as a light among the pagans,

G'3

15 so that you may bring salvation to the ends of the earth';

G'4

(39) *and there I wish 'to wait in hope for the promise' of him,*
who assuredly never deceives.
Just as he guaranteed in the Gospel,
'They will come from the east and the west,

20 and they will recline with Abraham and Isaac and Jacob',
just as we believe that *believers will come* from all parts of the
world.

(40) For that reason, consequently, it is indeed our duty to fish
well and diligently,
as *the Lord* admonishes in advance and teaches, saying,
'Come after me and I will make you fishers of people',

25 and again he says through the prophets,
'Look, I am sending fishers and many hunters says God', and so
forth.
Whence moreover, it was especially fitting to spread our nets,
so that 'a copious multitude and throng' should be taken
for God,
and that everywhere there should be *clergy to baptize,*

30 and exhort a needy and desiring *people,*
as the Lord affirms in the Gospel,
he admonishes and teaches, saying,
'Go therefore and teach all the pagans now,
baptizing them in the name of the Father and of the Son
and of the Holy Spirit,

35 teaching them to observe everything that I have
commanded you;
and behold, I am with you all days,
to the end of time.'
And again he says: 'Go therefore into the entire world,
proclaim the Gospel to every creature.

40   Qui crediderit et baptizatus fuerit salvus erit,
        Qui vero non crediderit condempnabitur.'
        et iterum, 'Praedicabitur hoc evangelium regni in
             universo mundo,
        in testimonium omnibus gentibus,
        et tunc veniet finis.'
45   Et item Dominus per prophetam praenúntiat ínquit,

        'Et erit in novissimis diebus, dicit Dominus,
        effundam de Spiritu meo super omnem carnem,
        et prophetabunt filii vestri et filiae vestrae,
        et iuvenes vestri visiones videbunt,
50   et seniores vestri somnia somniabunt,
        et quidem super servos meos
        et super ancillas meas in diebus illis,
        effundam de Spiritu meo et prophetabunt.'
        Et 'in Osee dicit: Vocabo "non plebem meam"
             "plebem meam"
55   et "non misericordiam consecutam" "misericordiam
             consecutam",
        Et erit in loco ubi dictum est: '"Non plebs mea vos",
        ibi vocabuntur filii Dei vivi.'

(41-42)   G'5

        Unde autem Hiberione qui numquam notitiam Déi
             habuérunt,
        nisi idola et inmunda usque nunc sémper coluérunt,

60   quomodo 'nuper facta est plebs Domini,'
        et filii Déi nuncupántur.
        Filii Scottorum et fíliae règulórum
        monachi et virgines Christi ésse vidéntur,
(42)   Et etiam una benedicta Scotta, genetíva nóbilis,
65   pulcherrima adúlta érat,
        quam égo baptizávi,
        Et post paucos dies una caúsa vénit ád nos,
        insinuavit nobis responsum accepisse a núntio Déi,

        et monuit eam ut ésset virgo Chrísti,
70   et ipsa Déo proximáret.
        Deo gratias,
        sexta ab hac die optime et avidissime arrípuit íllud,

40   The one who believes and is baptized will be saved;
but the one who does not believe will be condemned.'
And again: 'Proclaim this Gospel of the Kingdom
throughout the whole world,
as a testimony to all pagans,
and then the end will come.

45   And similarly the Lord announces beforehand through the
        prophet, he affirms,
'And in the last days it will be, the Lord declares,
I will pour out from my Spirit over all flesh,
and your sons and your daughters will prophesy,
and your youths will see visions,

50   and your elders will dream dreams,
and assuredly over my slaves
and over my handmaids in those days,
I will pour out from my Spirit and they will prophesy.'
And in Hosea he says, 'Those who were "not my people"
        I will call "my people",

55   and "her who has not obtained mercy as her who has
        obtained mercy",
and in the very place where it was said to them,
"you are not my people", there they will be called
        children of the living God.'

(41-42)   G'5

(41)   Whence moreover in Ireland those who never had a
        knowledge of God,
up to now they always worshipped nothing except idols
        and 'unclean things',
have recently 'been made a people of the Lord',
and they are called children of God.
The sons and daughters of the petty Irish kings
are seen to be monks and virgins of Christ.

(42)   and there was even one blessed Irishwoman, of noble birth,

65   most beautiful as a grown woman,
whom I baptized,
and after a few days she came to us for one cause,
she confided to us that she had received an answer from a
        messenger of God,
and he advised her that she should be a virgin of Christ,

70   and that she should draw close to God.
Thanks be to God,
six days later she most laudably, most ardently laid hold of
        that [way of life],

quod etiam omnes virgines Dei íta hoc fáciunt,
non sponte pátrum eárum,
75   sed et persecutiónes patiúntur
et improperia falsa a paréntibus súis,
et nihilominus plus augétur númerus,
et de genere nostro qui íbi náti sunt,
nescimus númerum eórum,
80   praeter viduas ét continéntes.

Sed et illae maxime laborant quae servítio dètinéntur;
usque ad terrores et minas assídue pérferunt,

sed Dominus gratiam dedit multis éx ancillis súis,
nam etsi vetantur, tamen fórtiter ìmitántur.

(43)   G'6

Unde autem etsi voluero amíttere íllas,
et ut pérgens in Brittánniis,
et libentissime 'paratus eram',
quasi ad pátriam èt paréntes,
non id solum,
90   sed etiam usque ad Gallias vísitáre frátres,
a   et ut viderem faciem sanctorum *Dómini méi.*
b   i   Scit Deus quod *ego* válde optábam,
      ii   sed *'alligatus Spiritu',*
      iii *qui mihi 'protestatur' sí hoc fécero,*
95   iv   *ut futurum reum me ésse désignat,*
c   *et timeo perdere laborem quém inchoávi,*
b'   i   et non *ego,*
      ii   *sed Chrístus Dóminus*
      iii *qui mé imperávit*
100   iv   *ut venirem esse cum illis residuum aetátis méae,*
a'   *'si Dominus* voluerit,'
           et custodierit me ab ómni via mála,
           ut non 'peccem coram illo'.
(44-45)   G'7

Spero autem hóc debúeram,

105   sed memet ípsum nón credo,
'quamdiu fuero in hoc corpore mortis',
a   *quia fortis est, qui cotidie nititur subvértere mè a fíde*
b   *et praeposita castitate religiónis non fíctae,*

because all virgins of God do this even now,
not with their fathers' consent

75 but they even suffer persecutions
and false reproaches from their own parents,
and nevertheless their number ever increases,
and those who have been born from our begetting,
we do not know their number,

80 apart from widows and married persons who live a life of
continence.
But among them slave girls are in greatest trouble;
they suffer continually even to the extent of terrors and
threats.
But the Lord has given grace to many of his own handmaids,
because even if they are forbidden, they nevertheless continue
steadfast in their imitation of him.

(43)   G'6

Whence moreover even if I wished to leave them,
and make a journey to the Britains –
and 'I was' most willingly 'prepared' [to make that journey]
in order to see my homeland and family;
not only that,

90 but even [to travel] as far as the Gauls to visit the brethren
and 'that I might see the face' of the saints *of my Lord.*
God knows *I* greatly desired it;
but 'I am bound by the Spirit',
who 'protests' to me that if I do this,

95 *he will pronounce me guilty;*
and I am afraid of losing the labour which I have begun,
and not I,
but Christ the Lord
who has commanded me

100 *to come to stay with them for the rest of my life,*
'if the Lord' wills it',
and he will keep watch over me 'from every evil way',
so that I do not 'sin in his sight'.

(44-45)   G'7

(44)   I hope moreover that I ought to do this,

105 but I do not trust myself,
'as long as I am in this body of death',
because he is strong who strives daily to turn me away from the faith
and from that chastity of an unfeigned religion which I have
proposed to keep,

	cd	*usque in finem vitae meae Christo Dómino méo.*
110	e	*Sed 'caro inimica' semper tráhit ad mórtem,*
	f	*id est ad inlecebras inlicitate pérficiéndas,*
	e'	Et 'scio ex parte' quare vitam perfectam *égo non égi*,
		'sicut et céteri' credéntes,
	d'	sed confiteor *Dómino méo,*
115		et non erubesco in conspéctu ípsius,
		'quia non mentior',
	c'	ex quo cognovi eum '*a iuventute mea*',
	b'	*crevit in me amor Dei et tímor ípsius,*
	a'	'*et usque nunc', favente Domino, 'fidem servavi'.*
(45)		Rideat autem et insúltet qui volúerit,
		ego non silebo neque abscondo signa et mírabília,
		quae mihi a Dómino monstráta sunt
		ante multos ánnos quam fíerent,
		quasi qui novit omnia etiam 'ante tempora saecularia'.
(46)		G'6'
	ab	*Unde autem debueram* sine cessatione *Deo grátias ágere,*
	c	qui saepe indulsit *insipiéntiae méae,*
		neglegéntiae méae,
		et de loco, nón in uno quóque,
		ut non mihi vehementer írascerétur,
130		qui ádiutor dátus sum,
		et non cito adquievi secundum quod mihi osténsum fúerat,
		et sicut 'Spiritus suggerebat',
		et 'misertus est' mihi Dominus in milia milium,
	d	*quia vidit in me quod 'paratus eram',*
135	d'	*sed quod mihi pro hís nesciébam,*
		de statu méo quid fácerem,
		quia multi hanc legatiónem prohibébant.
		Etiam inter se ipsos post tergum méum narrábant
		et dicebant: 'Iste quare se mittit ín perículo
140		inter hostes qui Déum non novérunt?'
		Non ut caúsa malítiae,
		sed nón sapièbat íllis,
		sicut et égo ipse téstor,
	c'	intellige propter *rustícitátem méam,*
145	b'	et non cito agnovi *gratiam* quae túnc erat ín me.
	a'	Nunc mihi sapit *quod ánte debúeram.*
(47-49)		G'5'

to the end of my life for Christ my Lord.

110 *But 'the hostile flesh' is always dragging toward death,*
that is, toward allurements to do that which is forbidden;
and 'I know in part' wherein *I have not lived a perfect life,*
'just as the others' also believing.
But I confess *to my Lord,*

115 and 'I do not blush for shame' in his presence,
'because I do not lie',
from the time I came to know him *'from my youth',*
there grew in me the love of God and fear of him,
'and up to now', with God's grace, 'I have kept the faith'.

(45) Let who will, moreover, laugh and insult,
I shall not be silent, nor do I conceal the signs and wonders,
which have been shown to me by the Lord
many years before they may come to pass,
since he knows all things even 'before the ages began'.

(46)   G'6'

(46) *Whence moreover, I ought to give* unceasing *thanks to God,*
Who has often pardoned *my lack of wisdom,*
and my negligence,
and who, on more than one occasion,
refrained from growing vehemently angry with me,

130 who had been chosen as his helper;
and yet was slow to act in accordance with what I had
        been shown,
and as 'the Spirit was suggesting to me';
and the Lord 'has shown mercy' to me 'thousands and
        thousands of times'
because he saw in me that 'I was ready',

135 *but that I did not know what to do in these circumstances,*
what I should do about my own position,
because many were trying to hinder my embassy.
They were even talking among themselves behind my back
and saying, 'Why does this man throw himself into danger

140 among enemies who do not know God?'
Not out of malice,
but it did not seem wise to them,
– as I myself testify –
because of *my rusticity,*

145 and I myself was slow to recognise *the grace* which was
        then in me.
Now I understand *what I ought* [*to have understood*] *earlier.*

(47-49)   G'5'

(47)   Nunc ergo simpliciter insinuavi fratribus ét conservis
                             méis,
                        qui mihi crediderunt propter quod 'praedixi et
                        praedico,'
                        ad roborandum et confirmándam fidem véstram.
150   Utinam ut et vos imitemini maiora et potióra faciátis.

                        Hoc erit glória méa,
                        quia 'filius sapiens
                        gloria patris est.'
(48)   Vos scitis, et Deus, qualiter inter vos cónversátus sum
155   'a iuventute mea'
                        in fide veritatis 'et in sinceritate cordis'.
                        Etiam ad gentes illas ínter quas hábito
                        ego fidem illis praestávi et praestábo.
                        Deus scit 'neminem' illórum 'circumvéni',
160   nec cogito, propter Deum et ecclésiam ípsius,

                        ne 'excitem' illis et nobis omnibus 'persecutionem',
                        et ne per me blasphemaretur nómen Dómini,

                        quia scriptum est: 'Vae homini
                        per quem nomen Domini blasphematur.'
(49)   Nam 'etsi imperitus sum in omnibus,'
                        tamen conatus sum quíppiam serváre me,
                        etiam et frátribus Chrìstiánis
                        et virginibus Christi et mulieribus relígiósis,
                        quae mihi ultronea munúscula donábant,
170   et super altare iactabant ex órnaméntis súis,
                        et iterum reddébam íllis,
                        et adversus me scandalizabantur cur hóc faciébam.

(49end-51)   G'4'
                        Sed ego propter spém perennitátis,
                        ut me in omnibus caute proptérea cònservárem,
175   ita ut non me in aliquo titulo infidéli cáperent

                        vel ministerium sérvitútis méae,
                        nec etiam in minimo incredulis locum darem infamare
                             síve detractáre.

(50)   1   Forte autem quando baptizavi tot mília hóminum

(47)   Now therefore I have frankly made known to my brethren and fellow slaves,

who have believed in me because of what 'I have proclaimed and am proclaiming',

in order to strengthen and confirm your faith.

150   Would that you too would strive for greater things and perform more excellent deeds.

This will be my glory,

because 'a wise son

is the glory of a father'.

(48)   You know, God also, how I have lived among you

155   'from my youth'

in purity of faith and in sincerity of heart.

Even these pagans among whom I dwell

I have kept and I will keep my word to them.

God knows 'I have not taken advantage of any' of them,

160   nor do I think [of doing so], on account of God and his Church,

lest 'I should stir up persecution' against them and all of us,

and lest the name of the Lord should be blasphemed through me;

because it is written: 'Woe to the person

through whom the name of the Lord is blasphemed.'

(49)   For 'even if I am unlearned in all things',

I have, nevertheless, tried in some measure to save myself,

even also from the Christian brethren

and virgins of Christ and devout women,

who of their own accord kept giving me little gifts, and who

170   kept casting some of their own ornaments on the altar,

and I kept returning them again to them,

and they in turn were annoyed with me because I kept doing this.

(49-51)   G'4'

But I [did it] because of the hope of eternal life,

that for the sake of it I should act with caution in all things,

175   so that they would not on any legal charge of unfaithfulness seize upon me

or the ministry of my slavery,

nor would I give an opportunity even in the smallest matter to unbelievers to defame or detract.

(50-53)   G'3'

(50) 1   Perhaps moreover when I baptized so many thousands of people

speraverim ab aliquo illorum vel dimídio scríptulae.

180   'Dicite mihi et reddam uobis.'
       2   Aut quando ordinavit ubique Dóminus cléricos
                     per modicitatem meam et ministerium gratis distríbui
                          íllis,
                     si poposci ab aliquo illorum vel pretium vel 'cálciamènti'
                          méi,
                     'dicite adversus me et réddam vobis' mágis.
(51)   Ego 'impendi pro' vóbis ut me 'cáperent',
                     et inter vos et ubique pergebam causa vestra in
       3   múltis perículis,
                     etiam usque ad éxteras pártes,
                     ubi némo ultra érat,
                     et ubi numquam áliquis pervénerat,
190   1'   quí baptizáret
       2'   aut cléricos òrdináret
       1"   aut pópulum cònsummáret.
                     Donánte Dómino,
                     diligenter et líbentíssime,
195   pro salute vestra ómnia gènerávi.
(52-53)   G'3'
(52)   Interim praemia dábam régibus,
                     praeter quod dabam mercedem fíliis ipsórum,
                     qui mécum ámbulant,
                     et nihilominus comprehenderunt me cum comítibus
                          méis,
200   et illa die avidissime cupiebant interficere me,
                     sed tempus nóndum vénerat.
                     Et omnia quaecumque nobiscum invenerunt,
                          rápuérunt íllud,
                     et me ipsum férro vinxérunt,
                     Et quartodecimo die absolvit me Dominus de potestáte
                          eórum,
205   et quicquid nostrum fuit redditum est nóbis propter
                          Déum,
                     et 'necessarios amicos' quos ánte praevídimus.
(53)   Vos aútem expèrti éstis
                     quantum ego érogavi íllis
                     qui iudicabant 'per omnes regiones'
210   quos ego frequéntius vìsitábam.
                     Censeo enim non minimum quam pretium quindecim
                          hominum distríbui íllis

did I expect even half a scruple* from any of them.
    [* 1/576th of a unit]

180   'Tell me, and I will restore it to you.'
Or when the Lord ordained clergy everywhere
through my insignificant person and I shared the ministry
    with them free,
if I asked any of them for even the price even of my 'shoe',

(51)   'tell me to my face and I will restore' more 'to you'.
I 'have spent, for you that they might receive' me,
and both among you and wherever I journeyed for your
    sake in many perils,
even to the remotest regions,
beyond which there lived no one,
and where no one had ever come,

190   to baptize
or ordain clergy
or to confirm the people in the faith.
With the Lord's grace,
with loving care and most willingly,

195   I have done everything for your salvation.

(52-53)   G'3'

(52)   Meanwhile I kept giving presents to the kings,
besides the fee which I paid to their sons,
who travel with me,
and none the less they seized me with my companions,

200   and on that day they most eagerly desired to kill me,
but my time had not yet come,
and everything they discovered with us, they seized it,

and me they fettered in iron;
and on the fourteenth day the Lord delivered me from
    their power,

205   and our belongings were given back to us because of God,

and the 'close friends' whom we had seen to before.

(53)   You furthermore have known by experience
how much I have paid out to those
who judged [i. the brehons] 'throughout all the districts'

210   which I more frequently visited.
For I reckon that I distributed to them not less than 'the
    price of fifteen people'

                          ita ut mé 'fruámini',
                          et ego 'vobis' semper 'frúar' in Déum.
                          Non me paenitet
215   nec sátis est míhi
                          adhuc 'impendo et superimpendam'.
(53end)   G'2'   Potens est Dominus ut det míhi póstmodum,
(53end)   G'1'   ut meipsum 'impendar pro animabus vestris'.
218

                          PART V

(54) XXI F'
             a   i   Ecce, '*TESTEM DEUM INVOCO* IN ANIMAM MEAM
                    ii   *QUIA NON MENTIOR*',
                          Neque ut sit 'occasio adulationis'
                          vel 'avaritiae' scrípserim vóbis,
5   b   *neque ut honorem spero ab áliquo véstro,*
             b'   *sufficit enim honor* qui nondum videtur sed córde
                          créditur.
             a'   i   '*Fidelis*' autem '*qui promisit,*
                    ii   *numquam mentitur*'.
(55) XXII E'

                          Sed video iam 'in praesenti saeculo'
                          me supra modum exaltátum a Dómino,
                          et NON ERAM DÍGNUS NEQUE TÁLIS
                          UT HOC MÍHI PRAESTÁRET,
5   dum scío certíssime,
                          quod mihi melius convenit paupertas ét calámitas
                          quam divitiae ét dilíciae.
                          Sed et 'Christus Dominus pauper' fúit 'pro nóbis,'
                          ego vero, míser et ínfelix,
10   Etsi opes voluero iám non hábeo,
                          'neque me ipsum iudico',
                          quia cotídie spéro
                          aut internicionem aut círcumveníri
                          aut redigi in servitutem sive occásio cùiuslíbet.
15   'Sed nihil horum vereor' propter promíssa caelórum,

                          quia iactavi meipsum in manus Dei ómnipoténtis,
                          qui úbique dòminátur.
(55end-56) XXIII D'

                          SICUT PROPHETA DICIT,
                          'IACTA COGITATUM TUUM IN DEUM,

so that 'you might enjoy' me,
and that 'I might' always 'enjoy you' in God.
I do not regret it
nor is it enough for me
that 'I still spend and shall spend more'.

(53end)   G'2'   The Lord is mighty to grant me afterwards,
(53end)   G'1'   that 'I may spend' myself 'for your souls'.
218

PART V

(54) XXI F'

Look, '*I CALL ON GOD AS WITNESS* UPON MY SOUL
THAT *I DO NOT LIE*'.
Neither, I hope, is it to provide 'an occasion of flattery'
or a pretext 'for covetousness' that I have written to you;

5   *nor that I hope for honour from any of you;*
    the honour which is not yet seen, but is believed in the
        heart *suffices for me.*
    'He' moreover *'who has promised, is faithful;*
    he never lies.'

(55) XXII E'

But I see even 'in this present world'
that I am exalted beyond measure by the Lord,
and *I WAS NOT WORTHY* OF IT, NOR WAS I OF THE SORT
THAT HE SHOULD BESTOW IT ON ME,

5   because I know most certainly,
    that poverty and adversity are better for me
    than riches and luxury.
    But 'Christ the Lord' too, was 'poor for our sakes',
    for I, wretched and unhappy,

10 have no resources now, even if I wished for them,
    'nor do I judge myself'
    because I expect daily
    either that I be massacred, or defrauded,
    or reduced to slavery or to any sort of condition whatsoever.

15 'But I fear none of these things' because of the promises
        of heaven,
    because I have cast myself into the hands of almighty God,
    who rules everywhere.

(55end-56) XXIII D'

JUST AS THE PROPHET SAYS,
'CAST YOUR CARES UPON GOD,

ET IPSE TE ENUTRIET'

(56)   Ecce, nunc 'commendo animam meam fidelíssimo
              Dèo' méo,

5   'pro quo legationem fungor' in ignobílitáte méa,
          sed quia 'personam non accipit',
          et elegit mé ad hoc offícium,
          ut 'unus' essem 'de suis mínimis' mínister.

(57) XXIV C'

          Unde autem 'retribuam illi
          pro omnibus quae retribuit mihi'?
          Sed quid dicam,
          vel quid promittam Dómino méo?
5   Quia níhil váleo
          nisi ipse míhi déderit,
          Sed 'scrutatur corda et renes',
          quia satis et nimis cupio, et 'paratus eram'
          ut donaret mihi 'bibere cálicem' eíus,
10   sicut indulsit et ceteris amantibus se.
(58)   Quapropter non contingat míhi a Dèo méo
          ut numquam amíttam 'plebem' súam
          'quam adquisivit' in últimis térrae.
          Oro Deum ut det mihi pérseverántiam
15   et dignetur ut reddam illi téstem fidélem
          usque ad transitum meum própter Deum méum.
(59)   Et si aliquid boni úmquam imitátus sum
          propter Deum méum quem díligo,
          peto ílli det míhi
20   ut cum illis proselitis et captivis pro nómine súo
          effundam sánguinem méum,
          etsi ipsam etiam cáream sèpultúram,
          Aut miserissime cadaver per singula membra dividátur
              cánibus
          aut béstiis ásperis
25   Aut 'volucres caeli comederent illud'.
          Certíssime réor,
          si mihi hóc incurrísset,
          lucratus sum animam cum córpore méo,
          quia 'sine ulla dubitatione' in die illa 'resurgemus' in
              cláritáte sólis,
30   hoc est, 'in gloria' Christi Iesu redémptoris nóstri,
          quasi 'FILII DEI' VIVI ET 'COHEREDES CHRISTI',

AND HE WILL SUSTAIN YOU.'

(56) Behold, then, 'I commend my soul to my most faithful God',

5 'for whom I am an ambassador' in my obscurity,

but 'he is no accepter of persons',

and, for this office, he chose even me

'from among his least ones' that I should be one of his ministers.

(57) XXIV C'

Whence moreover 'shall I return to him

for all his bounty to me?'

But what shall I say,

or what shall I promise to my Lord?

5 For I can do nothing

unless he himself enables me;

but 'he tests the hearts and minds',

and 'I have eagerly desired', and 'I was ready'

that he should grant to me 'to drink his cup',

10 just as he granted to others who loved him.

(58) Wherefore 'may it never happen to me' from my God

that I should ever lose his own 'people'

'whom he has formed' [for himself] at the ends of the earth.

I pray God that he may give me perseverance

15 and to grant that I may be a faithful witness to him

up to the point of death for the sake of my God.

(59) And if I ever imitated anything good

for the sake of my God whom I love dearly,

I pray him to grant to me

20 that with those sojourners and captives for his name's sake

I may shed my blood,

even if I should lack even burial itself,

or my corpse, in most wretched fashion, be divided limb by limb for dogs

or for savage beasts

25 or 'the birds of the air eat it up'.

I am firmly convinced,

that if this should happen to me,

I will have gained my soul along with my body,

because 'without any doubt we will rise again' on that day in the brightness of the sun,

30 this is [to say], 'in the glory' of Christ Jesus our Redeemer,

as 'CHILDREN OF' THE LIVING 'GOD' AND 'JOINT HEIRS WITH CHRIST',

et 'conformes futuri imaginis ipsius',

Quoniam 'ex ipso et per ipsum et in ipso' régnatúri súmus.

(60)   Nam sol iste quem videmus ipso iubente propter nos cotídie óritur,

35   sed numquam regnabit, neque permanébit splendor eíus,

sed et omnes qui adorant eum in poenam miseri mále devénient.

Nos autem qui credimus et adoramus sólem verum Chrístum,

qui númquam interíbit,

neque 'qui fecerit voluntátem' ípsius,

40   sed 'manebit in aeternum,

quomodo et Christus manet in aeternum',

qui regnat cum Deo Pátre omnìpoténte,

et cum Spiritu Sancto ánte saécula,

et nunc et per omnia saécula saèculórum. Amen.

(61) XXV B'

Ecce, iterum iterumque breviter exponam Verba Conféssiónis méae.

'TESTIFICOR' IN VERITATE ET IN 'EXULTATIONE CORDIS CORAM DEO ET SANCTIS ANGELIS eius'

quia numquam habui aliquám occásiónem

praeter évangélium

5   et promíssa íllius

ut umquam redírem ad gèntem íllam

Unde prius víx eváseram.

(62) XXVI A'

Sed précor credéntibus

et timéntibus Déum,

Quicumque dignatus fúerit inspícere

vel recípere hànc scriptúram,

5   quam PATRICIUS, PECCATOR, indoctus, scilicet, HIBERIONE conscrípsit,

ut nemo umquam dicat quod MEA ÍGNORÁNTIA,

Si aliquid pusillum egi vel démonstráverim

secundum Déi plácitum,

Sed arbitramini et veríssime credátur

10   quod 'DONUM DÉI' fuísset.

Et haec est Conféssio méa

antequam moriar.

and 'about to be conformed to his image',
since 'from him and through him and in him we are to
    reign'.

(60)   For this sun which we behold, rises daily at God's
    command for us;

35   but it will never reign, nor will its splendour endure;

all wretched people who adore it will, moreover, come to
    a wretched punishment.
We, however, who believe and adore the true sun, Christ,

who will never die;
nor will he 'who does his will':

40   but 'he will live forever,
as Christ also lives for ever',
he who reigns with God the Almighty Father,
and with the Holy Spirit before the ages,
and now and for ever and ever. Amen.

(61) XXV B'

Look, again and again I will briefly set out the words of my
    Confession.
'I TESTIFY' IN TRUTH AND 'IN EXULTATION OF HEART BEFORE
    GOD AND HIS ANGELS'
that I never had any reason
besides the Gospel

5   and his promises
for ever returning to that pagan people
whence before I had barely escaped.

(62) XXVI A'

But I beseech those who believe in
and fear God,
whoever is pleased to look at
or receive this writing,

5   which PATRICK, A SINNER, untaught, to be sure, has
    composed in IRELAND,
that no one should ever say that [it was] by MY IGNORANCE,
if I have accomplished or demonstrated any small thing
according to God's good pleasure;
but let this be your conclusion and it must be most truly
    believed

10   that it was 'THE GIFT OF GOD'.
And this is my Confession
before I die.

BIBLICAL REFERENCES IN THE CONFESSIO

1:10, 2:21, 3:6, etc. designate traditional chapter numbers and lines of text

PART I

(1-2) I A	1:1	cf 1 Tm 1:15-16
	1:2	1 Co 15:8-10; cf Ep 3:8-9
	1:10	Jb 18:21; Tb 8:5;13:4,7; Ws 12:27; cf Ga 4:8-9; 1 Th 1:9; 4:3-5
	1:12	cf Ps 119(118):67
	1:13	Dt 32:15; Is 59:13
	1:14	Gn 26:5; Dn 9:4-6; Ex 20:6
	1:17	2 Ch 29:10 (LXX); Is 42:25; cf Ps 78(77):49
	1:18	Ac 13:47; Is 49:6; Jr 9:16; Tb 13:4 [C 11:38; 38:15; E 6:45; 9:78]
	1:19	cf Is 61:1-4,7; cf Lk 1:48,52; cf Ph 2:5-11; cf Ps 34(33):5-8
(2)	2:20	Ac 16:14; Ba 1:22; Heb 3:12; Jr 4:19; Lk 24:45
	2:21	cf Pss 25(24):16-18; 69(68):6; 119(118)
	2:22	Jl 2:12-13
	2:23	Lk 1:48, 52; Mt 11:29; cf Ph 2:3; cf Ep 4:2; cf Jm 4:6,10; cf
	2:24	Ps 25(24):7
	2:25	Pss 25(24):20; 116(114-115):6; 121(120):7 Jn 8:19; cf 1 S 3:7
	2:26	Gn 3:5; cf 1 K 3:9 f
	2:27	cf Ws 4:7
	2:28	Pss 94(93):19; 119(118):76-78; 126(125); Mt 5:4; cf Lk 15; 2 Co 1:4,7; 2 Th 2:16-17
(3) II B	3:2	2 Co 12:1
	3:3-5	cf 1 Ch 17:16,26
	3:6	2 Ch 6:37; Tb 13:7 [C 33:3; 61:6-7]
	3:7	Ps 116(114-115):12; 1 Th 3:9
	3:8	Ep 1:17; cf Ho 4:1,13; 6:6; Jb 5:17-18; 2 M 6:12 f; 2 P 1, 2, 3, 8 cf Pr 1:23, 28-30; 28:15; Ws 1:9; 3:10; 16:16
	3:9	Ep 1:12; Is 25:1; Ps 89(88):6; Tb 12:7

	3:10-11	Ac 2:5; Dn 9:12
(4) III C	4:1-5	cf Is 43:10-11
	4:13-16	Col 1:16; cf Jn 1:3
	4:17	Mk 16:19
	4:18-23	Ep 1:21; Jn 20:28; cf Mt 28:18; Ph 2:9-11
	4:25	cf Tt 2:13
	4:26	Ac 10:42
	4:27	Mt 16:27 (VL); Rm 2:6
	4:28-29	Ac 2:38; 8:20; Ep 1:14; cf Ep 2:8; cf Jn 4:10; Tt 3:5-6 [C 14:73; 33:2; 62:10; 36:5]
	4:31	Rm 8:16-17
(5) IV D	5:2-4	Ps 50(49):15 [C 20:93; 34:14]
	5:6-7	Tb 12:7
(6) V E	6:2	Lk 2:44; 21:16
	6:3	Pss 57(56):12; 116(114-115):18
(7-8) VI F	7:1	2 Tm 1:8
	7:3	Ps 5:6
	7:5	Ws 1:11
	7:7-8	Mt 12:36
(8)	8:10	Ep 6:5; Ph 2:12; cf Tb 13:6
	8:11	Mt 7:22; 24:36; Rv 16:16; Si 16:16
	8:12	Mt 12:36; Rm 14:12 [C 7:7-8]
	8:14	2 Co 5:10; Rm 14:10
(9-15) VII X	9:2	Mk 13:19-20
	9:3	Si 28:23-27
	9:4	1 Th 5:6
	9:5	2 Tm 3 14:15
	9:8	Heb 7:19
	9:9	Jn 8:43-44; Ps 19(18):3-4
	9:11	2 Tm 3:16-17
	9:12-13	Jn 1:11; Ph 2:5-11; Rm 11:34-36; Si 4:29; cf. Ws 9:1-18
(10)	10:14	Ac 22:3; 2 Co 9:10; Pr 14:25
	10:16-17	Ps 71:17-18; Si 25:5; Ws 8:2
	10:28	Qo 1:8
(11)	11:31	1 Th 5:6
	11:32	Pss cf 116(114-115):12; 119(118):112

	11:34	Ex 4:10
	11:36	Is 32:4
	11:38	Ac 13:47 (Is 49:6); 2 Co 3:3 [C 1:18; 38:9; E 6:45]
	11:40-1	2 Co 3:2-3
	11:43	Si 7:15
	11:45	2 P 3:16; Pr 1:24; Qo 2:16
(12)	12:46	Qo 4:13-14
	12:47	Ps 119(118):67; 2 S 24:20
	12:48	cf Ac 4:11; Pss 40(39):2; 69(68):14; 119(118):22;124
	12:49	1 K 2:24; Lk 1:49-54; Rm 4:21; 1 Tm 6:15
	12:50	cf Pss 25(24):6; 69(68):14; 86(85):5,13,15,16; 94(93):18; 103(102):8, 11, 17; 118(117):1-4, 29; 123(122):2-3; 130(129):7; 136(135):1-26; 138(137):8; 145(144):8; 147(146-147):11; cf Mt 5:7; cf Lk 1:50, 58, 78; Ep 2:4; Tt 3:5 (C 40:55; cf E 10:82]
	12:51	cf Ps 145 (144):14
	12:52	cf Ps 113(112):7-8
	12:54	Ps 116 (114-115):12; 1 Th 3:9 [C 3:7; 57:1-2]
(13)	13:58	Ps 114(113):21; Rv 19:5
	13:61	1 S 24:21
	13:62	Heb 7:19
	13:63	cf Ac 7:22; 18:24; Lk 24:19
	13:66	Heb 12:28
	13:67	Lk 1:6; 1 Th 2:10; 3:13; 5:23
	13:68	2 Co 5:14 [C 33:11]
(14)	14:71	Rm 12:3; cf 12:6
	14:73	Jn 4:10; Ac 8:20; Ep 2:8; [C 33:2; 62:10; cf C 4:28-31; 36:5-6]
	14:74	2 Th 2:16-17
	14:77	2 P 1:10-15
	14:79	Mt 10:37-9; 8:8

PART II

| (16) VIII G | 16:5 | Lk 17:5; Rm 8:14 |

	16:9	cf Ps 9-10:3
	16:13	Ac 18:25; Rm 12:11
(17)	17:15	Ac 9:4; 11:7; 26:14
	17:18	Rm 11:4. [C 21,29,35]
	17:26	1 Co 2:3-5; 2 Co 6:7; 1 P 1:5
	17:27	Ps 5:9; Tb 4:20; 1 Th 3:11
(18)	18:45	cf Is 60:16
	18:47	cf Ga 3:26
(19)	19:54	Gn 12:10
	19:57	Cf Dt 10:17
	19:62	Ho 14:1; Jl 2:12-13 [C 1]
	19:63	Lk 1:37; (Gn 18:14); Mt 17:20
	19:66	Gn 1:7,11,24,30 [C 21:101]
	19:71	Mt 15:32
	19:72	Lk 10:30
	19:76	cf Ex 3:8; Mk 1:61; Mt 3:4; S 14:26
	19:77	Lk 24:42
	19:78	1 Co 10:28
(20)	20:82	Ac 5:3; 1 Co 7:5
	20:83	2 P 1:13
	20:88-9	Ml 4:2-6
	20:93	Mt 27:45-51; cf Ps 50(49):15 [C 34:14]
	20:95-6	Mt 10:19-20
(21)	21:99	Rm 11:4 [C 17:18; 21:3; 29:5; 35:10]
	21:101	Gn 1:7,11, 24, 30 [C 19:66]
	21:103	Gn 37:21
(23)	23:116	Dn 7:13; cf Jb 4:13 [C 29:3]
	23:125	Dn 3:5 (VL)
	23:128	Ac 2:37; Ps 109(108):17
(24)	24:134	2 Co 12:2-3 [C 27:16]
	24:139	1 Jn 3:16
	24:140	cf 2 Co 13:3; Jn 4:26; 9:37; Mt 10:19
(25)	25:144	Ep 3:16; Rm 7:22
	25:146	Ac 2:12; 8:13; cf Dn 8:37; Hab 1:5; Is 29:9,14 cf Lk 1:29

| | 25:151-4 | Rm 8:26 |
| | 25:155 | 1 Jn 2:1; cf Rm 8:27, 34 [cf C 35:5] |

PART III

(26-27) IX H	26:3-4	Ps 118(117):13
	26:9	cf 1 Ch 21:3; Dt 23:21; 24:15; 2 Tm 4:16
(27)	27:10	Dn 6:5; cf 6:13
	27:16	2 Co 12:2-3 [C 24:134]
	27:21	Cf Ps 118(117):18
	27:22	2 Co 11:27; Ps 119(118):75
	27:23	2 Co 11:27; Dt 28:48
(28) X L	28:1	Heb 13:21; Pss 18(17):38; 71(70):9
(29) XI M	29:1	cf 1 P 2:7; Ps 118(117):22,39
	29:3	Dn 7:13-14; cf Jb 4:13 [C 23:116]
	29:5	Rm 11:4; [C 21:99; 35:10; cf 17:18]
	29:10-11	Zc 2:8
(30) XII N	30:1-2	Ph 4:13; 1 Tm 1:12; cf 2 Tm 4:17
	30:4	Jn 6:45; Mt 11:29
	30:5	Lk 8:46; Mk 5:30
	30:6	cf 1 P 1:7; Si 25:1
(31) XIII O	31:1	Ac 2:29 [C 33:1,9]
	31:2	cf Jb 27:7
	31:4	2 Co 1:23
	31:5	Ga 1:20 [C 44:116; 54:8]
(32) XIV P	32:5	cf 2 Tm 4:16
	32:15	Pr 25:8
	32:17	Jn 10:29; cf 1 Jn 3:20
(33) XV O'	33:1	cf Ac 2:29
	33:2	Jn 4:10; Ac 8:20; Ep 2:8
		[C 14:73; 62:10; cf C 4:28-31; 36:5-6]
	33:3	2 Ch 6:37 [C 3:6; cf 61:6-7]
	33:4	cf 2 Ch 15:2; cf Dt 4:29-31; cf Is 30:15,18;
		55:6-7; cf Jn 1:38; 6:24; 18:7-8; 20:15
	33:5	Sg 3:4; Lk 2:46; Jn 1:41; 6:25

	33:6	Rm 8:11; Si 33:1; 2 Tm 1:12
	33:7-8	1 Co 6:19; cf 12:3b-12; Ph 2:13
	33:9	Ac 2:29
	33:10	2 Co 1:23 [cf C 20:91-92; 23:130; 25:149; 29:3-11]
	33:11	cf 2 Co 1:23; 5:14 [C 13:68]
(34) XVI N'	34:2	Ps 95(94):9
	34:3	Heb 9:23-28; 10:5
	34:4	Heb 13:5; Rm 12:1
	34:5	Col 2:9; Ps 34(33):7; cf Ps 33(34):5
	34:6	Ex 3:11; 2 S 7:18
	34:9	Ps 46(45):11
	34:10-11	Ps 34(33):4; 46(45):11; 99(98):9; 119(118):28; Si 33:10; cf Is 25:1; Ac 10:46 [C 3:9-11; 61:2-3]
	34:14	Mt 27:45-51; cf Ps 50(49):15 [C 20:93]
	34:15-17	Jb 2:10
	34:22	Ac 2:17 [C 40:46]
	34:27	Ac 13:47; Jm 2:23; Mt 24:14 [C 40:42-43]
(35) XVII M'	35:1	Ac 21:19
	35:5	Rm 8:26 [C 25:154]
	35:8	Dn 13:42
	35:9	Is 66:2
	35:10	Rm 11:4 [C 21:99; 29:5; cf 17:18; 42:68] 1 K 19:20, 29-34
(36) XVIII L'	36:1	Mt 13:54
	36:3	Jb 38:21; Ps 39(38):5
	36:5	1 Co 2:12; Ep 2:8; cf Jn 3:16; 4:10; 10:4; 17:3; Ac 8:20 [cf C 4:29; 14:73; 33:2; 62:10]
(37) XIX H'	37:9	Si 29:30
	37:10	2 Tm 2:9
	37:12	Rm 1:15
	37:13	Jn 13:37; Ph 2:8, 30
	37:14	2 Co 12:15 [cf C 51:187-188]

PART IV

(37end-53) XX G'

	37:1	2 Co 12:15; Ph 2:8, 30 [C 51:185]
	37:2	cf Is 26:15
(38)	38:3	Rom 1:14
	38:9,13	Jr 16:19
	38:10	Rm 1:2
	38:14-15	Ac 13:47 (Is 49:6) [C 1:18; 11:38]
(39)	39:16	Ac 1:4; 2 P 3:13; cf Rm 4:20-21
	39:19-20	Mt 8:11
(40)	40:24	Mt 4:19; Mk 1:17
	40:26	Jr 16:16
	40:28	Lk 6:17; cf Lk 5:6
	40:33-7	Mt 28:19-20
	40:38-41	Mk 16:15-16
	40:42-4	Mt 24:14
	40:46-53	Ac 2:17-18 (Jl 2:28-29)
	40:54-57	cf Ho 2:23; 2:1; 1:10; 1 P 2:10; Rm 9:25-26 [C 24; E 20]
(41)	41:58	2 Co 2:14; Heb 10:26; cf Rm 1:28
	41:59	2 K 17:12
	41:60	Lk 1:17
(42)	42:68	Ac 10:22; 2 Ch 36:15-16; Lk 2:26; cf Mt 2:12; Is 42:19
	42:72	cf Mt 11:12
(43)	43:87	Ps 119(118):60 [C 46:134; 57:8-9]
	43:90	Ac 7:23; 15:36
	43:91	cf Ac 20:25, 38; Col 2:2; 1 Th 3:10
	43:93	Ac 20:22
	43:94	Ac 20:23
	43:101	Jm 4:15
	43:102	Ps 119(118):101
	43:103	Lk 15:18, 21
(44)	44:106	2 P 1:13; Rm 7:24. [C 20]
	44:110	Ga 5:17; cf Pr 24:11; Rm 8:7

	44:112	cf 1 Co 13:9
	44:113	1 Th 5:6
	44:115	Ps 25(24):1, 20
	44:116	Ga 1:20 [C 31:5; 54:2]
	44:117-118	Ps 71(70):5,17; Ps 88(87):16; Ws 8:2 [C 10:17]
	44:119	2 Tm 4:7
(45)	45:121	Dn 3:99; 6:27
	45:124	Ac 15:18 (Is 45:21); 2 Tm 1:9; Tt 1:2
(46)	46:125	Ep 1:16; 1 Tm 2:13
	46:126	Ps 69(68):6
	46:129	2 K 17:18; Lm 5:22
	46:130	cf 1 Co 3:9
	46:132	Jn 14:26
	46:133	Dt 5:10; 7:9-10; Ex 20:6; Rv 5:11
	46:134	Ps 119(118):60 [C 43:87; 57:8-9]
	46:140	2 Th 1:8
	46:145	1 Tm 4:14
(47)	47:148	2 Co 13:2
	47:149	cf Jb 4:3-4
	47:150	cf Jn 14:12
	47;152-3	cf Jn 17:1-26: Pr 10:1; 15:20; Si 3:13
(48)	48:154	cf Ac 20:18; 1 S 12:21; Th 2:10
	48:155	Pss 71(70):17; 88(87):16; Ws 8:2 [C 10,44]
	48:156	1 Co 5:82; 2 Co 1:12; Th 2:14 [cf C 44:107-108,119]
	48:159	2 Co 7:2
	48:160	1 P 2:13
	48:161	Ac 13:50
	48:163	Mt 18:17
	48:164	Rm 2:24
(49)	49:165	2 Co 11:6
	49:174	cf Ep 5:15
	49:177	1 P 2:12
(50)	50:180	cf 1 S 12:3 (VL)
	50:183-4	cf 1 S 12:3 (VL)
(51)	51:185	2 Co 12:15; cf 2 Co 7:2 [C 53:216-218]

(52)	52:201	Jn 7:6
	52:205	1 P 2:13
	52:206	Ac 10:24
(53)	53:209	cf Ne (2 Ezr) 11:25; cf Gn 41:34
	53:212-13	cf Rm 15:24
	53:216,218	2 Co 1:15; cf 2 Co 7:2 [C 51:185]

PART V

(54) XXI F'	54:1-2	2 Co 1:23; Ga 1:20 [C 31:5-6]
	54:3-5	1Th 2:5
	54:6-8	Heb 10:23; cf 2 Co 4:18; Rm 10:10; Tt 1:2

(55) XXII E'	55:1	Ga 1:4
	55:8	2 Co 8:9
	55:11	1 Co 4:3
	55:15	Ac 20:24
	55:17	1 Ch 29:12; 2 Ch 20:6; Dn 4:14,22

(55end-56)XXIII D'		
	55:2-3	Ps 55(54):23
(56)	56:4	Lk 23:46; 1 P 4:19; cf Ps 31(30):6
	56:5	2 Co 5:20; Ep 6:20 [C 46:137; E 5:35]
	56:6	Ga 2:6; Dt 10:17
	56:7	Jn 15:16
	56:8	Mt 25:40

(57-60)XXIV C'		
	57:1-2	Ps 116(114-115):12 [C 3:7; 11:32; 12:54]
	57:6	cf Ws 9:17; 8:21
	57:7	Ps 7:9-10; Rv 2:23
	57:8	Ps 119(118):60
	57:9	cf Mt 20:20-28; Mk 10:35-11:11; Lk 22:24-27 [cf C 43:87-88; 46:134-135]

| (58) | 58:11 | 1 M 13:15 |
| | 58:12-13 | Is 43:21 (LXX); cf. Dt 7:2-9 |

(59)	59:20-23	cf Dt 28:26; Ps 79(78):2-3
	59:24-25	Ezk 29:5; Jr 7:33; 1 K 14:11; 16:4; Lk 8:5
	59:29-30	1 Co 15:43; Ph 3:20-21; Rt 3:13 (Ml 4:2)
	59:31	Rm 8:16; 9:26 (Ho 1:10)

	59:32	Rm 8:17
	59:33	Rm 8:29; Rm 11:36 (cf Rm 5:17)
		1 Co 4:8; Rv 22:5; 2 Tm 2:12
(60)	60:34	cf Mt 5:45
	60:35	cf Ps 72(71):5
	60:39	1 Jn 2:17
	60:40-1	Ps 89(88):37
	60:44	cf Rv 11:15
(61) XXV B'	61:2-3	1 Tm 5:21 cf Mt 16:27; 2 Tm 4:1;
		Ps 119(118):111 Mk 8:38 [C 34:10-11;
		cf E 20:200]
	61:6-7	cf 2 Ch 6:37 [C 3:6; 33:3]
(62) XXVI A'	62:10	Jn 4:10; Ac 8:20; Ep 2:8
		[C 14:73; 33:2 cf 4:28-31; 36:5-6]

PLAN OF EPISTOLA TO COROTICUS

Paragraph I

(1:1-12)	A		Patrick's divine call to mission
(1:1)		1	A bishop in Ireland
(1:2)		2	God's gift
(1:3-8)		3	A sojourner and a refugee
(1:9)		4	An exile for Christ
(1:10)		5	I live for my God
(1:10)		6	To teach pagans
(1:11)		7	I am despised
(2:12-16)	B		Fellow-citizens of demons
(2:17)	C		Comrades of Scots and Picts and apostates
(2:18)	D		Weltering in the blood of innocent Christians
(2:19)	E		A countless number
(3:20-25)	F		of martyred neophytes
(4-5:26-36)	G	1-3	Church mourns captives, martyrs, murderers, murderers are estranged from me, the ambassador of Christ. Parricide, fratricide, rapacious wolves...
(5:37)	H		The unjust have destroyed your Law, O Lord
(5:38)	L		Fruitful mission in Ireland [destroyed]
(5:39)	M		Fruitful mission in Ireland favoured by God

Paragraph II

(6:40-49)	N		Patrick's divine inheritance
(7:5O-53)	O		Excommunicate Coroticus and his minions
(7:54)	P		until they repent and do penance
(7:55-56)	R		Release slaves and captive Christian women

Paragraph III

(10:79-110)	A'		Patrick's divine call to mission
(10:79)		1'	I came to Ireland
		2'	Bound by the Spirit never to see my kindred again
(10:82-83)		3'	Mercy towards a pagan people once my captors

(10:84)	4'	Slaves and handmaids of my father's house slain
(10:85-89)	5'	I have sold my noble rank to benefit others
(10:90-92)	6'	A slave in Christ for that remote pagan people
(11-12:93-110)	7'	My own do not recognise me
(12:111-112)	B'	Betrayer of Christ and Christians
(12:113-115)	C'	Rapacious wolves
(12:116-117)	D'	White martyrdom
(12-15:118-141)	E'	An innumerable multitude
(15:142-147)	F'	of martyred neophites and white slaves
(15-16:148-160)	G'	Church mourns captives, martyrs, murderers
(16:161-164)	H'	Injustice of unjust men has prevailed
(16:165)	L'	Despised Christian Irish
(16:166-167)	M'	abandoned by British Church

Paragraph IV

(18:188-190)	N'	Murderers' evil inheritance
(19-20:191-208)	O'	Rebels against Christ, fraudulent sinners...
(20-21:209-217)	P'	Repent
(21:218-222)	R'	Release captive, Christian women

COMBINED THEMES IN THE *EPISTOLA* TO COROTICUS

Paragraphs I and III

(1:1-12; 10:79-110)			
	AA'		Patrick's divine call to mission
(1:1; 10:79)	AA'	1	A bishop in Ireland
(1:2; 10:80-81)	AA'	2	Bound by the Spirit, the Gift of God
(1:3-8; 10:82-83)			
	AA'	3	A sojourner and refugee
(1:9; 10:84)	AA'	4	An exile for Christ
(1:10; 10:85-89)	AA'	5	I live for my God
(1:10; 10:90-92)	AA'	6	A slave in Christ to teach pagans
(1:11; 11-12:93-110)			
	AA'	7	I am despised by my own

(2:12-16; 12:111-112)
              BB'   Betrayer of Christ and Christians
(2:17; 12:113-114) CC'   Rapacious wolves
(2:18; 12:116-117) DD'   Red martyrdom; white martyrdom

(2:19; 12-15:118-141)
              EE'   A countless number of

(3:20-25; 15:142-147)
              FF'   Martyred neophytes and white slaves

(4-5:26-36; 15-16:148-160)
              GG'   Church mourns captives, martyrs, murderers

(5:37; 16:161-164)
              HH'   Injustice of unjust men has prevailed over us
(5:38; 16:165)   LL'   For them it is a disgrace that we are Irish

(5:39; 16:166-167)
              MM'   Irish mission favoured by God rejected by Church
                              in Britain

Paragraphs II and IV

(6:40-49; 18:188-190)
              NN'   Eternal reward and punishment

(7:50-53; 19-20:191-208)
              OO'   Rebels against Christ

(7:54; 21:209-217)
              PP'   Excommunicate Coroticus. Repent, do penance

(7:55-56; 21:218-222)
              RR'   Release captive, Christian women

EPISTOLA

EPISTOLA AD MILITES COROTICI

PARAGRAPH I

(1)	A	a	Patricius peccator indoctus scilicet *Hiberione constitutus*, episcopum mé esse fáteor.
			Certissime reor *a Deo* 'accepi id quod sum'.

Inter barbaras itaque géntes hábito
proselitus et profuga ób amórem Déi.
5   testis est ílle si íta est.
Non quod optabam tam dure et tam aspere aliquid ex
    ore méo effúndere,

bc   *sed cogor zelo Dei, et veritas Chrísti* excitávit,
d   *pro dilectione proximorum átque filiórum,*
           pro quibus 'tradidi' patriam et parentes et 'animam
              meam usque ad mortem'.

10   ef   Si dignus sum, vivo *Deo* méo *docère* géntes.
                etsi contémpnor alíquibus.

(2)   g   Manu mea scripsi atque cóndidi *vèrba ísta,*
      B   h   danda et tradenda, *militibus mitténda* Corotici,
          l   non dico *civibus meis*, neque *civibus sanctórum*
                  Romanórum,

15   m   sed civibus daemoniorum *ob mala ópera ipsórum.*
          n   *Ritu hostíli in mòrte vívunt,*
      C   *socii Scottorum atque Pictorum apóstatarúmque,*
      D   n`   *Sanguilentos sanguinare de sanguine innocentium Chrístianórum,*
      E   'quos' ego innumerum numerum Deo 'genui' atque 'in
                  Chrísto' confirmávi,

(3) F   m'   Postera die qua *crismati neophyti* in véste cándida,

l'   flagrabat in fronte ipsorum dum crudeliter trucidati atque
              mactati gládio *sùpradíctis,*
h'g'   *misi epistolam* cum sáncto presbitero,
f'   quem ego ex infantia *dócui,* cum cléricis,
            ut nobis aliquid indulgerent de praeda vel de captivis
              baptizátis quos cepérunt:

25   cachinnos fecérunt de íllis.
(4) G   Idcirco nescio quid mágis lúgeam,
         a   an qui interfécti vel quòs cepérunt,

b   vel quos graviter zabulus ínlaqueávit.
            Perenni poena gehennam pariter cum ípso mancipábunt,

THE EPISTLE TO THE SOLDIERS OF COROTICUS

Paragraph I

(1)   A   I, Patrick, a sinner, manifestly untaught, *established in Ireland,*
profess that I am a bishop.
I most certainly believe that 'I have received' *from God* 'that which
   I am'.
And therefore I live in the midst of barbarian pagans,
a sojourner and a refugee for the love of God.

5   He is my witness that this is so.
Not that I chose to utter anything in so harsh and unpleasant a
   manner;
but I am compelled *by the zeal of God; and the truth of Christ* roused
   [me] up *for love of* [my] *nearest neighbours and children,*
for whom 'I have given up' country and parents and 'my life up to
   the point of death'.

10   If I am worthy I live for my *God to teach* the pagans,
even if I am despised by some [people].

(2)   With my own hand I have written and composed *these words,*

       B   to be given and handed over, *dispatched to the soldiers* [*of Coroticus*],
I do not say to *my fellow citizens,* [*nor*] *to fellow citizens of the holy
   Romans,*

15   but to fellow citizens of demons *because of their evil works.*
By hostile behaviour they live in death,

       C   *allies of the Scots and Picts and apostates.*

       D   *Blood-stained people who are weltering in the blood of innocent Christians,*

       E   'whom I have begotten' for God, a countless number, and confirmed
   'in Christ'.

(3)   F   On the day following that on which *the newly baptized* in white
      clothing were anointed with chrism,
it was still shining on their foreheads while they were cruelly
      slaughtered and slain with the sword by the *abovesaid people,*
I dispatched an epistle with a holy presbyter,
whom *I taught* from his infancy, with clerics,
so that they might return something to us from the booty or from the
      baptized captives whom they had captured:

25   they only jeered about them.

(4)   G   Therefore I do not know what I should lament more,
whether those who have been slain, or those whom they have
      captured,
or those whom the devil has gravely ensnared.
In eternal punishment they shall inherit hell equally with him,

30   quia utique 'qui facit peccatum servus est',
                            et 'filius zábuli' nùncupátur.
(5)   e'   Quapropter resciat omnis hómo timens *Déum*
                 d'   quod *a mé aliéni sunt*
                 c'b'   et a *Chrísto Deo méo*,
35   '*pro quo legationem fungor*'.
                            Patricida, fratricida, 'lupi rapaces devorantes plebem
                                Domini ut cibum panis',
        H   sicut ait, 'Iniqui dissipaverunt legem tuam, Domine',

        L   a'   quam in supremis temporibus *Hiberione* optime,
                                benígne *plantáverat*,
39   M   atque *instructa érat favènte Déo*.

PARAGRAPH II

(6)   Non usurpo.
        N   Pártem hábeo
                 a   cum hís '*quos advocávit*
                            et praedestinavit' evangélium *praèdicáre*
                            in persecutiónibus non *párvis*
45   '*usque ad extremum terrae,*'
                 b   Etsi invidet inimicus per tyránnidem Corotici,
                            qui Deum non veretur nec sacerdótes ipsíus,
                 c   quos elegit *et indulsit illis summam divinam sublímam*
                                potestátem,
                            '*quos ligarent super terram ligatos esse et in caelis*'.
(7) O   Unde ergo quaeso plurimum 'SANCTI ET HUMILES
                                CORDE',
                            adulari tálibus nón licet,
                            'nec cibum' nec potum 'súmere' cum ípsis,
                            nec elemosinas ipsorum récipi débeat
        P   donec crudeliter paenitentiam effusis lacrimis satis Déo
                                fáciant
55 R   d   et liberent servos Dei et ancillas *Chrísti* baptizátas,
                 e   pro quibus mortuus est ét crucifíxus.
(8)   'Dona iniquorum reprobat Altissimus.'
                            'Qui offert sacrificium ex substantia pauperum
                            quasi qui victimat filium in conspectu patris sui.'
60   f   'Divitias', inquit, 'quas congregavit iniuste' evomentur
                                de ventre eius.
                 g   trahit illum angelus mortis.
                 h   *ira draconum mulcabitur.*

30		because truly 'he who commits sin is a slave,'
		and is called 'a child of the devil'.
(5)		Wherefore let every *God*-fearing person learn
		that *they are estranged from me*
		and from *Christ my God,*
35		*'for whom I am an ambassador'.*
		Parricide, fratricide, 'rapacious wolves devouring the people of the Lord as a meal of bread'.
	H	Just as [Scripture] declares: 'The unjust have utterly destroyed your Law, O Lord',
	L	which in these last times he had most excellently [and] kindly *planted in Ireland,*
39	M	and *it had been established [taught] with God's favour.*

Paragraph II

(6)		I make no false claim.
	N	I have a part
		with those whom he has called to [*him*]
		and predestined to proclaim the Gospel
		amidst no *small* persecutions
45		*'to the ends of the earth',*
		even if the enemy shows his jealousy through the tyranny of Coroticus,
		who has reverence for neither *God* nor his priests,
		whom he has chosen *and to whom he has granted the highest divine sublime power,*
		that *'those whom they may bind on earth are bound also in the heavens'.*
(7)	O	Whence therefore I beseech most of all, [you] 'holy and HUMBLE OF HEART,'
		that it be not permissible to flatter such people,
		'to take food' or drink with them,
		nor ought one be obliged to accept their alms
	P	until, with tears poured out to God, they perform penance rigorously enough
55	R	and liberate the slaves of God and the baptized handmaids *of Christ,*
		for whom he died and was crucified.
(8)		'The Most High is not pleased with the offerings of unjust people.'
		'He who offers sacrifice from the property of the poor
		[is] like one who makes a victim of a son before his father's eyes.'
60		'The riches,' [Scripture] affirms, 'which he gathered unjustly', will be vomited from his belly;
		the angel of death drags him away;
		with the fury of dragons he shall be mutilated.

	h'	Interficiet illum lingua colubris.
	g'	*comedit autem eum ignis inextinguibilis.'*
65	f'	Ideoque, *'Vae qui replent se quae non sunt sua,'*
		vel, 'Quid prodest homini ut totum mundum lucretur
		et animae suae detrimentum patiatur?'
(9)		Longum est per singula discutere vel ínsinuáre,
		per totam legem carpere testimonia de táli cupìditáte.
70		Avaritia mortále crímen.
		'Non concupisces rem proximi tui.'
	e'	*'Non occides.'*
	d'	Homicida non potest ésse cum *Chrísto.*
	c'	'Qui odit fratrem suum homicída' *adscríbitur,*
75		vel 'Qui non diligit fratrem suum in morte manet'.
	b'	Quanto mágis *réus est*
		qui manus suas coinquinavit in sanguine fíliórum *Déi,*
	a'	*quos nuper 'adquisivit' in ultimis terrae per exhortationem*
		párvitátis nóstrae.

Paragraph III

(10) A'	ab		Numquid sine Deo vel 'secundum carnem' *Híberiòne véni?*
80			Quís me cómpulit?
			'Alligatus' sum 'Spiritu' ut non videam aliquem 'de
			cognatione mea.'
			Numquid a me piam misericordiam quod ago érga
			gentem íllam
			qui me aliquándo cepérunt
			et devastaverunt servos et ancillas dómus patris méi?
85			Ingenuus fui 'secundum carnem'.
			decurióne patre náscor.
			Vendidi enim nobílitátem méam,
			non erubesco néque me paénitet,
			pro utilitáte aliórum.
90			Denique servus sum in Christo génti éxterae
			ob gloriam ineffabilem 'perennis vitae
			quae est in Christo Iesu Domino nostro'.
(11)			Et si mei mé non cognóscunt,
			'propheta in patria sua honorem non habet'.
95	c	i	*Forte non sumus 'ex uno ovili',*
		ii	neque *'unum Deum pátrem'* habémus.
			sicut ait 'Qui non est mecum contra me est,
			et qui non congregat mecum spargit.'

The serpents' tongue shall slay him.
'unquenchable fire', moreover, 'devours him'.
65   And therefore, *'Woe to those who fill themselves with what is not their own';*
      or, 'What does it profit a person that he should gain the whole
      world and suffer the loss of his own soul?'
(9)   It is tedious to set forth or make known from single cases,
      to gather from the whole Law testimonials against such greed.
70   Avarice [is] a deadly crime.
      'You shall not covet your neighbour's possessions.'
      'You *shall* not *kill.'*
      A murderer cannot be with *Christ.*
      'He who hates his own brother' *is ascribed* 'a murderer',
75   or, *'Whoever does not love his own brother remains in death'.*
      How much more *guilty is he*
      who has stained his own hands with the blood of the children *of God,*
      whom 'he has' recently 'acquired at the ends of the earth' through the
        exhortation of our *littleness.*

PARAGRAPH III

(10)   A'   Was it that *I came to Ireland* without God's [inspiration] or
        'according to the flesh'?
80   Who compelled me?
      I am 'bound by the Spirit' not to see any 'of my kindred'.
      Could it be by myself alone that I exercise a pious act of mercy
        toward that pagan people
      who once took me captive
      and wreaked havoc on the slaves and handmaids of my father's
        house?
85   I was freeborn 'according to the flesh';
      I am born of a decurion father.
      But I have, in fact, sold my noble rank,
      I do not blush nor does it cause me regret,
      for the benefit of others.
90   In short I am a slave in Christ for that remote pagan people
      because of the unspeakable glory 'of eternal life
      in Christ Jesus our Lord'.
(11)   Even if my own people do not recognise me,
      'a prophet has no honour in his own country'.
95   *Perhaps we are not 'from the one sheepfold',*
      nor *'do we have one God as Father';*
      just as [Scripture] declares: 'He who is not with me is against me,
      and he who does not gather with me scatters.'

Non convenit:
100   'Unus destruit;
alter aedificat.'
'Non quaero quae mea sunt.'
Non méa grátia,
sed Deus 'qui dedit hanc sollicitudinem in corde meo',
105   ut unus essem de 'venatoribus sive piscatoribus'
quos olim Deus 'in novissimis diebus' ánte praenùntiávit.

(12)   Ínvidetur míhi.

               d   i   *Quid fáciam Dómine?*
                    ii   *Válde despícior.*

110   iii *Ecce oves tuae circa me laniantur átque depraedántur,*
      B'   et supradictis latrunculis iubente Corotico hostìli
                                 ménte.

                    iv ei *Longe est a caritate Dei traditor Christianórum*
      C'   e   ii   *in manus* Scottorum átque *Pictórum.*
                              'Lupi rapaces' deglutierunt gregem Domini,
115   qui utique Hiberione cum summa diligentia óptime
                                   crescébat.

      D'   iii *et filii Scottorum et fíliae règulórum*
                           monachi et vírgines Chrísti,
      E'   iv   *enumeráre néqueo.*
               f   *Quam ob rem 'iniuria iustorum non te placeat',*
120   *etiam 'usque ad inferos non placebit'.*

(13)   Quis sanctorum non hórreat iòcundáre
                                  vel convivium frúere cum tálibus?
               g   De spoliis *defunctorum* Christianorum replevérunt
                                   domos súas?
                             Dé rapínis vívunt.

125   h   *Nesciunt* miseri venenum letale cibum porrigunt ad
                                 amicos et fílios súos,
             l   i   sicut Eva non intellexit quod utique mortem *trádidit*
                                 vìro súo.
                    ii   *Sic sunt ómnes qui màle águnt;*
                    iii *'mortem' perennem poénam 'operántur'.*

(14)   m   Consuetudo *Romanorum Gallorum Chrístianórum:*
130   mittunt viros sanctos idoneos *ad Francos et céteras géntes.*
                           cum tot milia solidorum *ad redimendos captívos baptizátos.*
            m'   *Tu* potius interficis et *vendis illos genti exterae* ignoranti
                           Deum.
            l'   i   quasi in lupanar *trádis* 'membra Chrísti'.

		It does not come together:
100		'One destroys;
		another builds.'
		'I do not seek the things that are mine.'
		Not by my grace,
		but God 'who has put this eagerness into my heart',
105		so that I should be one 'of the hunters or fishers'
		whom God foretold once before 'for the last days'.
(12)		Jealousy is shown to me.
		What shall I do, Lord?
		I am greatly despised.
110		*Look, around me are your sheep torn to pieces and looted,*
	B'	and that by the aforesaid wretched little thieves, at the behest
		of the hostile-minded Coroticus.
		Far from the love of God is the betrayer of Christians
	C'	*into the hands* of Scots and *Picts.*
		'Rapacious wolves' have swallowed up the flock of the Lord,
115		which was indeed growing excellently in Ireland with the
		greatest loving care.
	D'	*Both sons and daughters of the petty Irish kings*
		[were] monks and virgins of Christ,
	E'	*I cannot count [their number].*
		Wherefore, may 'the injustice done to the righteous not please you',
120		*even 'as far as the lowest depths it will not please'.*
(13)		Which of the saints would not be horrified to make merry
		or to enjoy a feast with such people?
		They have filled their houses with the spoils of *deceased* Christians.
		They live by plunder.
125		They *do not know*, wretched people, that they offer poison, a
		deadly food to their own friends and children,
		just as Eve did not understand that she truly *handed over* death to
		her own husband.
		So are all who do evil;
		'they work death' as an eternal punishment.
(14)		[This is] the custom *of the Christian Roman Gauls:*
130		they dispatch holy and competent people *to the Franks and other pagans*
		with so many thousands of *solidi to redeem baptized captives;*
		you rather kill and *sell them to a remote pagan people* ignorant of God;
		you are handing over, as it were, 'the members of Christ' into a brothel.*

(* lit. 'house of she-wolves,' Howlett, *BLSPB*, 33)

			Qualem spem hábes in Déum,
135			vel quí te conséntit,
			aut qui te communicat verbis ádulatiónis?
			Déus iudicábit?
		ii	Scriptum est enim. *'Non solum facientes mala,*
		iii	*sed etiam consentientes damnandi sunt.'*
(15)	h'		Néscio 'quid dícam'
			vel 'quid lóquar' ámplius
F'	g'		de *defunctis*
	f'	ia	*fíliórum Déi*
		b	*quos gladius supra modum dúre tétigit.*
145		ii	Scriptum est enim. *'Flete cum flentibus,'*
		iii	Et iterum *'Si dolet unum membrum*
		iii'	*condoleant omnia membra.'*
G'		ii'	*Quapropter* ecclesia *'plorat et plangit*
		i'a	*filios' et fílias 'súas'*
150		ab	*quas adhuc gladius nóndum interfécit.*
			sed prolongati et exportati in lónga terrárum
		b	ubi 'peccatum' manifeste graviter impudénter 'abúndat'.
			ibi venundati ingénui hómines;
	e'	i	*Christiani in servitúte redácti sunt,*
155		ii	Praesertim indignissimorum pessimorum apostatarúmque
			Pictórum.
(16)			Idcirco cum tristitia et maerore vóciferábo.
		iii	O speciosissimi atque *amantissimi fratres et filii* 'quos in
			Christo genui,'
		iv	*enumeráre néqueo,*
	d'	i	*quid fáciam vóbis?*
160		ii	*Non sum dignus Deo neque homínibus sùbveníre.*
H'		iii	*'Praevaluit iniquitas iniquorum super nos.'*
		iv	*Quasi 'extranei facti sumus'.*
	c'	i	*Forte non credunt :'unum báptismum' percépimus*
		ii	*vel 'unum Deum pátrem' habémus.*
165 L'	b'		Indignum est illis *Hibérionàci* súmus.
M'			Sicut ait, 'Nonne unum *Deum* habetis'?
			'Quid dereliquistis unusquisque proximum suum'?

PARAGRAPH IV

(17)			Idcirco dóleo pro vóbis,
			doleo caríssimi míhi,
170			sed iterum gaudeo íntra meípsum.
			Non grátis 'laborávi'

What hope in God have you,
135   or anyone who concurs with you,
or who converses with you in words of flattery?
God will judge.
For it is written: *'Not only those who commit evil deeds,*
but also those who agree with them are to be condemned.'

(15)   I do not know 'what I shall say'
or 'what' more 'I shall speak'
   F' *about the deceased [ones]*
of the children of God
whom the sword has stricken with dire harshness.

145   For it is written, 'Weep with those who weep',
and again, *'If one member grieves*
all members should grieve together with it.'

   G' *Therefore* the Church *'bewails and laments*
her own sons' and daughters
150   *whom so far the sword has not yet killed,*
but who are banished and deported to distant lands
where 'sin' openly, gravely, shamelessly 'abounds';
there citizens are put up for sale;
Christians are reduced to slavery,
155   particularly among the most degraded, most vile apostates and *Picts.*

(16)   Therefore I shall cry aloud in sadness and grief:
O most beautiful and *most beloved brethren and children 'whom I have*
*   begotten in Christ',*
I cannot count them,
what can I do for you?
160   *I am not worthy to come to the aid of either God or humans.*
   H' *'The injustice of the unjust has prevailed over us',*
'we have been made', as it were, 'remote outsiders'.
Perchance they do not believe that we have received 'one baptism'
or that we have 'one God as Father'.
165 L' For them it is a disgrace that we are *Irish.*
Just as [Scripture] declares: 'Have you not one *God?'*
   M' 'Why has each one of you abandoned his own neighbour?'

PARAGRAPH IV

(17)   Therefore I grieve for you
I grieve, my dearest ones,
170   but then again I rejoice within myself.
'I have not laboured' for nothing,

vel peregrinatio mea 'in vácuum' nón fuit.

Et contigit scelus tam horréndum ineffábile.

a   Deo gratias créduli *bàptizáti*

175   De saeculo recessistis ad pàradísum.

Cerno vos,

migrare coepistis ubi 'nox non erit' 'neque luctus
     neque mors amplius',

'sed exultabitis sicut vituli ex vinculis resoluti,

et conculcabitis iniquos,

180   et erunt cinis sub pedibus vestris'.

(18)   b   Vos ergo regnabitis cum *apostolis et prophetis átque* martyribus,

aeterna regna capietis.

c   i   sicut *ípse testátur,*

ii   *inquit,*

185   d   *'Venient ab oriente et occidente.*

et recumbent cum Abraham et Isaac et Iacob in regno
     caelorum.'

e   *'Foris canes et venefici et homicidae',*

N'   et *'Mendacibus periuris pars eorum in stagnum ignis aeterni'.*

f   Non inmerito ait apostolus, *'Ubi iustus vix salvus erit*

190   *peccator et impius transgressor legis ubi se recognoscet?'*

(19) O'   f'   *Unde enim Coroticus cum suis scéleratíssimis,*

rebellatores Christi úbi se vidébunt,

qui mulierculas baptizatas praémia distríbuunt

ob miserum regnum temporale

195   quod utique in moménto tránseat?

e'   *'Sicut nubes vel fumus qui utique vento dispergitur',*

ita 'peccatores' fraudulenti 'a facie Domini peribunt.

d'   *Iusti autem epulentur in magna constántia' cum Chrísto.*

'Iudicabunt nationes' et 'regibus' iniquis 'dominabuntur'

200   *in saecula saeculorum. Amen.*

(20)   c'   i   *'Testificor coram Deo* et angelis suis' quod ita erit,
     sicut intimavit imperítiae méae.

ii   *Nón mea vérba,*

b'   *sed Dei et apostolorum átque prophetárum,*

quod ego Latínum expósui,

205   qui numquam énim mentíti sunt,

'Qui crediderit salvus erit,

qui vero non crediderit condemnabitur.

Deus locutus est.'

(21) P'   Quaeso plurimum ut quicumque famulus Dei

or my pilgrimage has not been 'in vain'.
And there happened a crime, so horrendous and unspeakable!
thanks be to God, as *baptized* faithful people
175   you have departed from this world to paradise.
I can see you clearly;
you have begun to journey where 'there shall be no night'
    'nor lamentation nor death any more',
'but you shall leap like calves loosened from chains,
and you shall tread down the wicked underfoot,
180   and they shall be ashes under your feet.'
(18)   You therefore shall reign with *the apostles and the prophets and* the
        martyrs;
you shall gain everlasting kingdoms.
Just as he himself testifies,
[*Scripture*] *affirms*,
185   *'They shall come from the east and from the west,*
and recline [at table] with Abraham and Isaac and Jacob in the kingdom
    of heaven.'
'Outside [*are*] dogs and sorcerers and murderers',
N'   and 'their portion [*is*] with lying perjurers in the pool of eternal fire'.
Not without just cause the apostle declares, 'Where the righteous
    person shall scarcely be saved,
190   where will the sinner and the impious transgressor of the Law find himself?'
(19) O'   Whence, then, Coroticus with his accursed henchmen
rebels against Christ, where will they find themselves,
they who distribute baptized maidens as prizes
and that for a wretched temporal kingdom
195   which may indeed pass away in a moment?
'Like a cloud or smoke, which is indeed dispersed by the wind,'
so shall fraudulent 'sinners perish from the face of the Lord.
But the just shall feast in great confidence' with Christ.
'They shall judge nations, and lord it over' wicked kings
200   for ever and ever. Amen.
(20)   'I bear witness before God and his angels' that it shall be so *just as he*
    intimated to my unlearnedness.
The words are not mine,
but God's and the apostles' and prophets',
which I have set forth in Latin,
205   who of course have never lied,
'He who believes shall be saved,
but he who does not believe shall be damned.
God has spoken.'
(21) P'   I earnestly request that whatever servant of God shall volunteer

prómptus fúerit,
210   ut sit gerulus lítterárum hárum,
             ut nequáquam subtrahátur,
             vel abscondátur a némine,
             sed magis potius legatur coram cúnctis plébibus,
             et praesente ípso Corotico.
215   Quod si Deus inspirat illos 'ut quandoque Deo
                    resipiscant',
             ita ut vel sero paeniteant quod tam ímpie gessérunt,
             Homicida erga frátres Dómini,
R'   a'   et liberent captivas *baptizatas* quas ánte cepérunt,

             ita ut mereantur Déo vívere
220   et sáni efficiántur
             híc et in aetérnum.
             Pax Patri et Filio et Spiritui Sancto. Amen.

210 to be a bearer of this letter,
   that on no account it be stolen,
   or hidden by anyone,
   but rather that it be read before all the people,
   even in the presence of Coroticus himself.
215 May God inspire them, at some time or another, 'to return to
    their senses before God',
   so that they may repent [however] late of such a heinous deed,
   the murder of the brethren of the Lord,
 R' and that they may release *the baptized* captive women whom they
    previously seized,
   that they may thus deserve to live for God
220 and be made whole
   here and for eternity.
   Peace to the Father and to the Son and to the Holy Spirit. Amen.

BIBLICAL REFERENCES IN THE EPISTOLA

PARAGRAPH I

(1)   1:1   1 Tm 1:15-16
             1:2   1 Co 15:10; 4:7
             1:7   Jn 2:13-25; 1 M 2:54; Ps 69(68):9
             1:9   Ac 15:26; Jn 13:37; Ph 2:30; [C 37:1, part IV]
             1:10   Jn 14:18; Mt 8:8; 10:37-39

(2)   2:19   1 Co 4:15
             2:23   Jn 14:18

(4)   4:30   Jn 8:34,4
             4:31   cf Jn 8:44
             4:32   Si 2;7-17

(5)   5:35   Ep 6:20. [C 56:5; cf 46:138]
             5:36   Mt 7:15; Ac 20:29; Pss 14(13):4; 53(52):5
             5:37   Ps (119)118:126

PARAGRAPH II

(6)   6:42-3   Rm 8:28-30
             6:45   Ac 13:47; Is 49:6; Jr 9:16; Tb 13:4
                          [C 1:18; 11:38; 38:15; E 9:78]
             6:49   Mt 16:19; 18:18

(7)   7:50   Dn (Greek), Prayer of Azariah, 65 (Dn 3:87)
             7:52   1 Co 5:11

(8)   8:57-9   Lk 9:25; Si 34:23-24
             8:60-4   Jb 20:15-16,26
             8:65   Hab 2:6
             8:66-7   Lk 9:25; Mt 16:26

(9)   9:71-2   Dt 5, 21,17; Ex 20:17,13; Rm 13:9
             9:74   1 Jn 3:14-15; cf Rm 13:9-10
             9:75   1 Jn 3:14
             9:78   Is 43:21 (Lk 1:48,52); Ps 34(33):5-8
                         cf Is 61:1-4,7 [cf C 1:18-19]

PARAGRAPH III

(10)	10:79	2 Co 1:17
	10:81	Ac 20:22 (Gn 12:1); cf Lk 2:44 [C 43:93]
	10:85	2 Co 1:17
	10:91-2	cf Jn 4:10; 10:4; cf Rm 6:23
(11)	11:94	Jn 4:44
	11:95	Jn 10:16
	11:96	Ep 4:6
	11:97-8	cf Lk 11:23; Mt 12:30
	11:100-1	cf Ga 2:18; Si 34:28
	11:103	1 Co 13:5; cf 2 Co 12:14; Ph 2:21
	11:104	2 Co 8:16
	11:105	cf Jr 16:16 [cf C 40:24-28]
	11:106	Ac 2:17 [C 34:22; 40:46; cf 40:36-37]
(12)	12:114	Ac 20:29; Mt 7:15
	12:119-20	Si 9:17 (Vulg)
(13)	13:128	2 Co 7:10; Jude 7
(14)	14:133	1 Co 6:15
	14:138-9	Rm 1:32
(15)	15:140-1	cf Jn 12:49
	15:145	Rm 12:15
	15:147	1 Co 12:26
	15:149	cf Mt 2:18; (Jr 31:15)
	15:152	cf Rm 5:20
(16)	16:157	1 Ch 4:15; cf Phm 10
	16:161	Ezk 18:20; 33:12; Ps 65(64):4
	16:162	Ps 69(68):9
	16:163-4	Ep 4:5
	16:166	Ep 4:6
	16:167	Ml 2:10

PARAGRAPH IV

(17)	17:171	Ph 2:16
	17:177	Rv 22:5; 21:4
	17:178-80	Ml 4:2-3; cf 3:20-21

(18)   18:185-6   Mt 8:11 [C 39:19-20]
              18:187   Jm 2:11; Rv 22:15
              18:188   Ml 3:5; Rv 21:8; 1 Tm 1:10
              18:189-90   1 P 4:18; (Pr 11:31)

(19)   19:196-7   Pss 37(36):20; 68(67):3-4
              19:198   cf Ws 5:1,3,8,15
              19:199   cf 1 Co 6:2; cf Ws 3:8
              19:200   Rv 20:10
(20)   20:201   Mk 8:38; cf Mt 16:27; 1 Tm 5:21;
                            2 Tm 4:1 [C 61:2]
              20:206-7   Mk 16:15-16

(21)   21:215   cf Lk 22:32; cf 2 Tm 2:25-26

BIBLICAL ABBREVIATIONS

The following is a list of the books of the Bible in alphabetical order of abbreviation:

Ac	Acts	Lk	Luke
Am	Amos	Lm	Lamentations
Ba	Baruch	Lv	Leviticus
1 Ch	1 Chronicles	1 M	1 Maccabees
2 Ch	2 Chronicles	2 M	2 Maccabees
1 Co	1 Corinthians	Mi	Micah
2 Co	2 Corinthians	Mk	Mark
Col	Colossians	Ml	Malachi
Dn	Daniel	Mt	Matthew
Dt	Deuteronomy	Na	Nahum
Ep	Ephesians	Nb	Numbers
Est	Esther	Ne	Nehemiah
Ex	Exodus	Ob	Obadiah
Ezk	Ezekiel	1 P	1 Peter
Ezr	Ezra	2 P	2 Peter
Ga	Galatians	Ph	Philippians
Gn	Genesis	Phm	Philemon
Hab	Habakkuk	Pr	Proverbs
Heb	Hebrews	Ps	Psalms
Hg	Haggai	Qo	Ecclesiastes/Qoheleth
Ho	Hosea	Rm	Romans
Is	Isaiah	Rt	Ruth
Jb	Job	Rv	Revelation
Jdt	Judith	1 S	1 Samuel
Jg	Judges	2 S	2 Samuel
Jl	Joel	Sg	Song of Songs
Jm	James	Si	Ecclesiasticus/Ben Sirach
Jn	John	Tb	Tobit
1 Jn	1 John	1 Th	1 Thessalonians
2 Jn	2 John	2 Th	2 Thessalonians
3 Jn	3 John	1 Tm	1 Timothy
Jon	Jonah	2 Tm	2 Timothy
Jos	Joshua	Tt	Titus
Jr	Jeremiah	Ws	Wisdom
Jude	Jude	Zc	Zechariah
1 K	1 Kings	Zp	Zephaniah
2 K	2 Kings		

BIBLIOGRAPHICAL ABBREVIATIONS

ACW	*Ancient Christian Writers*, Bieler's translation of the works of St Patrick.
AOS	*Aristocracy of Soul*, O'Donoghue, N. D.
ASCC	*Age of the Saints in the Early Celtic Church*, Chadwick, N.
AVCW	*A Virgin Called Woman*, M. P. Scott.
BFFG	*Be Filled with the Fullness of God*, Maloney, G. A.
BHP	*'Bibeltext der Heiligen Patrick'*, Bieler, L.
BLSPB	*The Book of Letters of Saint Patrick the Bishop*, Howlett, D. R.
BSP	*'The Bones of St Peter'*, Smothers, E .R.
BVV	*The Boyne Valley Vision*, Brennan, M.
CC	*Libra contra Collatorem*, Prosper of Aquitaine
CD	*Constitutions and Directives of the Union of the Sisters of the Presentation of the Blessed Virgin Mary*
CIS	*The Church in Early Irish Society*, Hughes, K.
CS	*Celtic Saints*, Morris, J.
CLTBS	*The Celtic Latin Tradition of Biblical Style*, Howlett, D. R.
CPEC	*Communio, the Church and the Papacy in Early Christianity*, Hertling, L.
CR	*The Celtic Realm*, Dillon, M.
CRB	*Christianity in Roman Britain to AD 500*, Thomas, C.
CRL	*The Charism of Religious Life*, de Bhaldraithe, E.
CSEG	*Christ the Sacrament of the Encounter with God*, Schillebeeckx, E.
CSSP	*The Credal Statements of St Patrick*, Oulton. J. E. L.
DK	*The Destiny of a King* (1973), Dumézil, G.
DW	*The Destiny of a Warrior* (1970), Dumézil, G.
EIA	*The Earliest Irish Annals, their first Contemporary Entries and the Earliest Entries*, Smyth, A. P.
EIL	*Early Irish Literature*, Dillon, M.
EIP	*Early Irish Poetry*, Carney, J.
ELG	*An Eoraip agus Litríocht na Gaeilge, 1600-1650*, Ó Dúshláine, T.
EN	*Evangelii Nuntiandi (Evangelisation in the Modern World)*, Paul VI
EP	*'The Enigma of St Patrick'*, Ó Raifeartaigh, T.
ESSM	*'Ex Saliva Scripturae Meae'*, Howlett, D. R.
GEIL	*A Guide to Early Irish Law*, Kelly, F.
HE	*Historia Ecclesiastica...* the Venerable Bede
IBP	*Irish Bardic Poetry*, Bergin, O.
IER	*Irish Ecclesiastical Record*
IPM	*In Praise of Mary*, Flanagan, D.
IS	*Inward Stillness*, Moloney, G. A.

ISGB   *Irish Saints in Great Britain*, Moran P. F.
ISP   *In the Steps of St Patrick,* De Breffny, B.
JB   *The Jerusalem Bible*, 1966 edition
JBC   *The Jerome Biblical Commentary*, 1970 edition
Latin   *The Latin of St Patrick*, Mohrmann, C.
LDM   *The Lives of SS Declan & Mochuda*, Power, P.
LCA   *Les Confessions de St Augustin*, Courcelle, P.
LE   *Libri Epistolarum*, Bieler's commentary on the Latin text of St Patrick's works
LHB   *Language and History in Early Britain*, Jackson, K. H.
LL   *The Life and Legend of St Patrick*, Bieler, L.
LMB   *'Language and Mentality of the Bible Writers,'* Schokel, L.
LP   *Life of St Patrick*, Bury, J. B.
LVS   *La Vie Spirituelle* (1968), Hamman, A.
LW   *The Life and Writings of the Historical St Patrick*, Hanson, R. P. C.
MAS   *Manly Anniversary Studies*, Thrall, W. F.
MIL   *Medieval Irish Lyrics*, Carney, J.
MM   *'Mission and Monasticism in the Confession of St Patrick'*, Herren, M.
MMR   *Mary, Mother of the Redeemer*, Schillebeeckx, E.
NCE   *New Catholic Encyclopedia*
NLT   *Numerical Literary Techniques in John....* Menken, M. J. J.
OC   *St Patrick, his Origins and Career*, Hanson, R. P. C.
ÓFTO   'Ó Fochoill (Foclut) go Tobar Oghiolla, A Patrician Pilgrimage', de Paor, M. B.
PAL   *Patrizio e l'Acculturazione Latina dell'Irlanda*, Malaspina, E.
PB   'Patrick and his Biographers', Binchy, D. A.
PC   Penguin Classics
PG   *Patrologia Graeca*, Migne, J.
PHOW   *Patrick in His Own Words*, Duffy, J.
PL   *Patrologia Latina*, Migne, J.
PLG   *Poetry and Letters in Early Gaul*, Chadwick, N.
PP   *Poet and Peasant*, Bailey, K. E.
PPCP   *Pagan Past and Christian Present in Early Irish Literature*, McCone, K.
PTBA   *The Patrician Texts in the Book of Armagh*, Bieler, L.
RNU   *Rí na nUile*, O Conghaile, S. S., O Ríordáin.
RP   'The Roman Primacy in the Second Century, and the Problem of the Development of Dogma', McCue, J. F.
RRA   *La religion romaine archaique* (1966), Dumézil, G.
RRS   *Reconciliation in Religion and Society*, Hurley, M.
RVC   *The Roman Villa*, Chedworth, Goodburn, R.
SADP   *Self-Abandonment to Divine Providence*, de Caussade, J. P.
SEBH   *Studies in Early British History*, (ed.) Chadwick, N.
SCO   *Sancti Columbani Opera*, Walker, G.S.M.

SJCD   *Seeking Jesus in Contemplation and Discernment*, Faricy, R.
SP   'St Patrick', Ryan, J.
SPR   'St Patrick's Readings', Dronke, P.
SPS   'A Study of Patrick's Sources', Nerney, D.
SPW   'St Patrick's Way to Sanctity', Kinsella, N.
SSP   'The Spirituality of St Patrick's Confession', Kinsella, N.
TG   *Tadhg Gaelach Ó Súilleabháin 1715-1795,* de Paor, M. B.
TI   'Textual Integrity of St Patrick's Confession', Powell, D.
TICE   *The Irish Catholic Experience*, Corish, P. J.
TLG   *Traidisiún Liteartha na nGael*, Williams, J. E. C., & Ní Mhuiríosa, M.
TLSP   *The Letters of St Patrick*, Conneely, D.
TTP   *The Two Patricks*, O Rahilly, T. F.
TRT   *The Revelatory Text*, Schneiders, S. M.
TSP   *The Testimony of St Paul*, Martini, C. M.
TTG   *The Triune God*, Marsh, T.
TU   *The Upanishads*, Eastwaran, E.
VC   *Vita consacrata,* Pope John Paul II

APPENDIX

Biblical references to dreams

Gn 20:3, 6; 28:12; 31:10, 11, 24; 37:5-6, 8-10, 20; 40:5, 8-9, 16; 41:1, 5, 11, 15; 42:7-8, 11-12, 15, 17, 22, 25-26, 32; 41:12; 42:9. Nm 12:6. Dt 13:1, 3, 5. Jd 7:13, 15. 1 S 28:15. 1K 3:3, 5, 15. Jb 7:14; 20:8; 33:15. Ps 73:20; 126:1. Qo 5:3, 7; Is 29:7. Jr 23:25, 27-8, 32; 29:8. Dn 1:17; 2:1-7, 9, 26, 28, 36, 45; 4:4-9, 18-19; 5:12; 7:1. Jl 2:28. Zc 10:2. Mt 2:12-13, 19, 22; 27:19. Ac 2:17.

Apart from the precedent in the Bible for belief in dreams, may I say here, in passing, that Patrick's propensity towards dreams, as a literary motif, links him with fourth- and fifth-century Continental writers who were partial to this theme. Jerome's famous dream in which he saw himself castigated before the throne of God for his incurable love of Cicero's writings, immediately springs to mind. Then there are those of the pagan Ausonius of Bordeaux, hardly less terrifying, in his poem Ephemeris; those of St Martin of Tours, recorded by his biographer, Sulpicius Severus (Vita, iii, v. 1), and those of Augustine mentioned in his Confessions (111. xi; X. xxx) and the City of God (X1V. xix), Chadwick, ASCC.

SELECT BIBLIOGRAPHY

Text of Bible used in commentary: *The New Oxford Annotated Bible with Apocrypha (NRSTV)*, OUP, New York, 1991.
Biblia Sacra Iuxta Vulgatam Versionem, 4th edition, Gryson, Roger, Deutsche Bibelgesellschaft, Stuttgart, 1994.

Bailey, K. E., *Poet and Peasant* and *Through Peasant Eyes, A Literary-Cultural Approach to the Parables of Luke*, William B. Eerdmans Publishing Company, Grand Rapids, Michigan, combined edition, 1983.

Bardy, Gustave, *La Vie Spirituelle d'Après Les Pères des Trois Siècles*, A. Hamman (ed.), Desclée, Tournai, 1968.

Bede, The Venerable, *Historia Ecclesiastica...*, Plummer, C. (ed.), v. i,ii, Typographeo Clarendoniano, Oxford, 1896.

Bergin, Osborn, *Irish Bardic Poetry*, The Dublin Institute for Advanced Studies (DIAS), Dublin, 1970.

Bieler, L. (ed.), *Libri Epistolarum Sancti Patricii Episcopi, Scriptores Latini Hiberniae* (SLH), Vol. i, ii, Irish Manuscripts Commission, The Stationery Office, Dublin, 1952; *The Life and Legend of St Patrick*, Clonmore and Reynolds, Dublin, 1949; *The Patrician Texts in the Book of Armagh* (SLH), x, DIAS, Dublin, 1979.

Bonhoeffer, Dietrich, *Christology*, William Collins, Sons and Company Ltd, London/Harper and Row, New York, 1966.

Brennan, Martin, *The Boyne Valley Vision*, The Dolmen Press, Mountrath, 1980.

Brooke, Daphne, *Wild Men and Holy Places* (I: The First Bishopric, St Ninian of Candida Casa), Canongate Press, Scotland, 1994.

Brown, Raymond E., SS, *The Death of the Messiah, From Gethsemane to the Grave, A Commentary on the Passion Narratives in the Four Gospels*, vols. I & II, Geoffrey Chapman, London, 1994.

Burrows, Ruth, *Guidelines for Mystical Prayer*, Sheed & Ward, London 1976; *Interior Castle Explored*, Sheed & Ward/Veritas Publications, London and Dublin, 1981.

Bury, J.B., *The Life of St Patrick and His Place in History*, Macmillan, London, 1905.

Byrne, Francis J., *Irish Kings and High-Kings*, B.T. Batsford Ltd., London, 1973.

Cameron, Averil, *The Mediterranean World in Late Antiquity AD395-600*, Routledge, London & New York, 1993.

Cantwell, Laurence, SJ, *The Theology of the Trinity*, Mercier Press, Cork, 1969.

Carmody, Clarke, *Word and Redeemer, Christology in the Fathers*, Paulist Press, New Jersey, 1966.

Carney, James, *Studies in Irish Literature and History*, DIAS, Dublin, 1955; *The Problem of St Patrick*, DIAS, Dublin, 1961, 1973; (ed.), *Early Irish Poetry*, Mercier Press, Cork, 1965; *Medieval Irish Lyrics*, Dolmen Press, Dublin, 1967.

A Carthusian, *They Speak by Silences*, Darton, Longman & Todd, London, 1975.

Chadwick, Henry, *The Early Church*, The Pelican History of the Church: I, Penguin Books, Ltd, Harmondsworth, 1967; *Augustine*, Past Masters, OUP, Oxford & New York, 1986; *The Confessions of St Augustine*, OUP, New York, 1991.

Chadwick, H.M., *Early Scotland*, CUP, Cambridge, 1949.

Chadwick, N.K. (ed.), *Studies in Early British History*, CUP, Cambridge, 1954; *Poetry and*

Letters in Early Christian Gaul, Bowes and Bowes, London, 1955; (ed.), *Studies in the Early British Church*, CUP, Cambridge, 1958; *The Age of the Saints in the Early Celtic Church*, OUP, London, 1961; (ed.), *Celt and Saxon*, CUP, Cambridge, 1963; *Celtic Britain*, Thames & Hudson, London, 1964; *The Celts,* Pelican Books, London, 1971.

Congar, Yves, *The Mystery of the Temple*, Les Éditions du Cerf, Paris, 1958/Burns & Oates Ltd, London, 1962.

Conneely, Daniel, *The Letters of Saint Patrick*, An Sagart, Máigh Nuad, 1993.

Corish, Patrick J., *The Irish Catholic Experience, a Historical Survey*, Gill & Macmillan Ltd, Dublin, 1985.

Courcelle, P., *Les Confessions de St Augustin dans la tradition littéraire*, Paris, 1963.

Craster, O.E., *Caerwent Roman City*, National Museum of Wales, Cardiff, 1951, Twelfth impression, 1981.

Drijvers, Pius, OCist, *The Psalms, their Structure and Meaning*, Herder, Freiburg/Burns & Oates, London, 1965.

de Breffny, Brian, *In the Steps of St Patrick*, Thames & Hudson, London, 1982.

de Caussade, Jean-Pierre, *Self-Abandonment to Divine Providence*, Burns & Oates Ltd, 1933/Fontana, 1972.

de Lubac, Henri, SJ, *The Splendour of the Church*, Sheed & Ward Inc., New York, 1956/ Paulist Press, New York, 1963.

de Paor, Liam, *Saint Patrick's World*, Four Courts Press, Dublin, 1993.

de Paor, Máire B., PBVM, *Tadhg Gaelach Ó Súilleabháin 1715-1795*, Coiscéim, Baile Átha Cliath, 1995.

Devine, Kieran, *Clavis Patricii 1, A Computer-Generated Concordance to the Libri Epistolarum of Saint Patrick*, RIA, Dublin, 1989.

De Meester, Conrad, *Elizabeth of the Trinity, The Complete Works*, Paris, 1980, trans. Sister Aletheia Kane OCD, ICS Publications, Washington, 1984.

De Waal, Esther, *A World Made Whole, Rediscovering the Celtic Tradition*, HarperCollins, London, 1991.

Dillon, Myles, *Early Irish Literature*, UCP, Chicago & London, 1948; 4th impression, 1969; *The Celtic Realm,* Weidenfeld & Nicholson, London, 1967.

Dodd, C.H., *The Interpretation of the Fourth Gospel*, CUP, London & New York, 1953/ 1970; *History and the Gospel* (revised edition), Hodder & Stoughton, London, 1964.

Dudley-Edwards, Ruth, *An Atlas of Irish History,* Methuen & Co, London, 1973.

Duffy, Joseph, *Patrick in His Own Words*, Veritas, Dublin, 2nd edition, 1985.

Dulles, Avery, SJ, *Models of the Church, A Critical Assessment of the Church in all its Aspects*, Gill & Macmillan, Dublin, 1976; *The Catholicity of the Church*, Clarendon Press, Oxford, 1985, 1989 edition.

Easwaran, Eknath, *The Upanishads*, Arkana Penguin Books, London, 1987.

Ernst, Cornelius, OP, *The Theology of Grace*, Theology Today Series, n. 17, Paulist Press, Notre Dame, Indiana, 1974.

Fallon, Francis T., *2 Corinthians*, New Testament Message Series 11, Veritas, Dublin, 1980.

Faricy, Robert, SJ, *Seeking Jesus in Contemplation and Discernment*, Collins, London, 1983.

Flanagan, Donal, *In Praise of Mary*, Veritas, Dublin, 1975.

Flannery, Austin, OP (ed.), *Vatican Council II, The Conciliar and Post Conciliar Documents*, Dominican Publications and the Talbot Press, Dublin, 1975.

Flower, Robin, *The Irish Tradition*, Clarendon Press, Oxford, 1947.

Frend, W.H.C., *Martyrdom and Persecution in the Early Church*, Clarendon Press, Oxford, 1965.

Freyne, S., Wansbrough, H., *Mark and Matthew*, Scripture Discussion Commentary 7, Sheed & Ward, London and Sydney, 1971.

Getty, Mary Ann, RSM, *Philippians and Philemon*, New Testament Message Series 14, Veritas, Dublin, 1980.

Goodburn, Roger, *The Roman Villa, Chedworth*, The National Trust, 1979.

Gwynn, J. (ed.), *Liber Ardmachanus, The Book of Armagh*, M.H. Gill & Fealy Bryers & Walker, Dublin, 1913.

Hanson, R.P.C., *St Patrick, His Origins and Career*, Clarendon Press, Oxford, 1968; *The Life and Writings of the Historical St Patrick*, Seabury Press, New York, 1963.

Healy, J., *Life and Writings of Saint Patrick*, Hodges Figgis, Dublin/Williams and Norgate, London, for RIA, 1905.

Henry, Françoise, *Irish Art in the Early Christian Period to AD 800*, Methuen, London, 3rd edition,1966.

Hertling, Ludwig, SJ, *Communio, Church and Papacy in Early Christianity* (1892), Loyola University Press, Chicago 1972.

Hood, A.B.E., *St Patrick, His Writings and Muirchú's Life*, ix, of Arthurian Period Sources, Phillimore, London, 1978.

Hopkins, Alannah, *The Living Legend of St Patrick*, Grafton Books, London, 1990.

Howlett, D.R., *The Book of Letters of St Patrick the Bishop*, Four Courts Press, Dublin, 1993; *The Celtic Latin Tradition of Biblical Style*, Four Courts Press, Dublin, 1995.

Hughes, Kathleen, *Early Christian Ireland, Introduction to the Sources*, CUP, Cambridge 1972; *The Church in Early Irish Society*, Methuen & Co. Ltd, London, 1966.

Hunter, A.M., *According to John*, SCM Press, London, 1968/72.

Jackson, Kenneth H., *Language and History in Early Britain*, Edinburgh University Press, Edinburgh, 1953; *The Oldest Irish Tradition: A Window on the Iron Age*, CUP, Cambridge, 1964.

Jalland, T.G., *The Life and Times of St Leo the Great*, SPCK, London, 1941.

Jeremias, Joachim, *New Testament Theology, I: The Proclamation of Jesus*, SCM Press, London, 1971/75.

John Paul II, *Crossing the Threshold of Hope*, Jonathan Cape, London, 1994; *Redemptoris Mater*, *Mary Mother of the Redeemer*, Veritas, Dublin, 1987; *Dives in Misericordia*, Encyclical Letter on the Mercy of God, CTS, London, 1980; *Dominum et Vivificantem*, Encyclical Letter on the Holy Spirit in the Life of the Church and World, CTS, London, 1986; *Redemptionis Donum*, To Men and Women Religious on their Consecration in the Light of the Mystery of the Redemption, CTS, London, 1984; *Vita Consecrata,* on the consecrated life and its mission in the Church and in the world, CTS, London, 1996.

Jones, A.H.M., *The Later Roman Empire*, 3 v., Blackwell, Oxford 1964.

Kavanaugh & Rodriguez, ODC, *The Collected Works of St John of the Cross*, ICS Publications, Washington, DC, 1979; *St Teresa of Avila, Collected Works*, i, 1976; ii, 1980, ICS Publications, Washington, DC.

Kelly, Fergus, *A Guide to Early Irish Law*, DIAS, Dublin, 1988.

Kenney, J.F., *Sources for the Early History of Ireland*, Columbia University Press, New York, 2nd edition, 1968.

Laing, Lloyd, *The Archaeology of Late Celtic Britain and Ireland, 400-1200 AD*, Methuen, London, 1975.

Lewry, Osmond, OP, *The Theology of History*, Mercier Press, Cork, 1969.

Louf, André, OCist, *Teach Us to Pray*, Darton, Longman & Todd, London, 1974.

Lussier, Ernest, SSS, *God is Love, According to John*, Alba House, New York, 1976.

Mackey, James P. (ed.), *An Introduction to Celtic Christianity*, T. & T. Clark, Edinburgh, 1993.

Maher, Michael (ed.), *Irish Spirituality*, Veritas, Dublin, 1981.

Malaspina, Elena, *Patrizio e l'Acculturazione Latina dell'Irlanda*, vol. i,ii, Japadre Editore L'Aquila, Roma, 1984.

Maloney, George A., SJ, *Inward Stillness*, Dimension Books, Denville, New Jersey, 1976; *Singers of the New Song, A Mystical Interpretation of the Song of Songs*, Ave Maria Press, Notre Dame, Indiana, 1985; *Be Filled with All the Fullness of God, Living in the Indwelling Trinity*, New City Press, New York, 1993.

Marmion, Dom Columba, OSB, *Christ the Life of the Soul*, Sands and Company, London and Edinburgh, 1922; *Christ in His Mysteries*, Sands and Company, London and Edinburgh, 1924.

Marsh, Thomas, *The Triune God: A biblical, historical and theological study*, Maynooth Bicentenary Series, Columba Press, Dublin, 1994.

Martini, Carlo M., *Ministers of the Gospel, Meditations on St Luke's Gospel*, Milan, 1981, St Pauls Publications, Slough, 1983; *The Testimony of St Paul*, Milan, 1981, St Pauls Publications, Slough, 1983; *Women and Reconciliation*, Cathedral Series 3, Veritas, Dublin, 1987.

Mascaró, Juan, *The Bhagavad Gita*, Penguin Books, London, 1962.

Menken, M.J.J., *Numerical Literary Techniques in John, The Fourth Evangelist's Use of Numbers of Words and Syllables*, Supplement to *Novum Testamentum*, Vol. LV, E.J. Brill, Leiden, 1985.

Migne, *Celestinus Papa, Epistola iv* (PL 50. 430, 431); *Prosper, Liber contra Collatorem* (PL, Vol. LI, col.271; *Victricius of Rouen, De Laude Sanctorum* (PL 20.443-4).

Mohrmann, Christine, *The Latin of St Patrick,* DIAS, Dublin, 1961.

Monden, Louis, SJ, *Sin, Liberty and Law*, Sheed & Ward, New York, 1965.

Moran, Patrick F., Cardinal, *Irish Saints in Great Britain*, Gill, Browne & Nolan, Dublin, 1879.

Moynihan, Anselm, OP, *The Lord is Within You, A Book on the Presence of God*, Dominican Publications, Dublin, 1979.

Murphy, Gerard, *Early Irish Lyrics, Eighth to Twelfth Century*, Clarendon Press, Oxford, 1956.

Murray, Donal, *Jesus is Lord*, Veritas, Dublin, 1975.

MacNéill, Eóin, *St Patrick, Apostle of Ireland*, Sheed & Ward, London, 1934.

Mac Philibín, Liam, Easpag, *Mise Pádraig*, FÁS, Baile Átha Cliath, 1960, 1961, 1982.

MacQueen, John, *St Nynia, with a translation of The Miracles of Bishop Nynia by Winifred MacQueen*, Polygon Books, Edinburgh, 1990.

Macquarrie, John, *Principles of Christian Theology*, study edition, SCM Press, London, 1966.

McCone, Kim, *Pagan Past and Christian Present in Early Irish Literature*, Maynooth Monographs 3, An Sagart, Máigh Nuad, 1990.

McNamara, Kevin, *Sacrament of Salvation, Studies in the Mystery of Christ and the Church*, The Talbot Press, Dublin, 1977.

McNamara, Martin, MCS (ed.), *Biblical Studies, The Medieval Irish Contribution*, Irish Biblical Association/Dominican Publications, Dublin, 1976.

McNamara, William, OCD, *Christian Mysticism, The Art of the Inner Way*, Element, Rockport, MA, and Dorset, 1991.

McPolin, James, SJ, *John,* New Testament Message Series 6, A Biblical-Theological Commentary, Veritas, Dublin, 1979.

Ó Conghaile and Ó Ríordáin, *Rí na nUile*, Sáirséal agus Dill, Baile Átha Cliath, 1964/1966.

O Donoghue, N.D., ODC, *Aristocracy of Soul, Patrick of Ireland*, Michael Glazier Inc., Wilmington, Delaware/Darton, Longman & Todd, London, 1987.

Ó Dúshláine, Tadhg, *An Eoraip agus Litríocht na Gaeilge 1600-1650*, An Clóchomhar, Baile Átha Cliath, 1987.

O'Dwyer, Peter, OCarm, *Mary, A History of Devotion in Ireland*, Four Courts Press, Dublin, 1988.

Ó Fiaich, Tomás, *Gaelscrínte san Eoraip*, FÁS, Baile Átha Cliath, 1986.

Ó Laoghaire, Diarmuid, SJ, *Ár bPaidreacha Dúchais*, FÁS, Baile Átha Cliath, 1975.

O'Rahilly, T.F., *The Two Patricks*, DIAS, Dublin, 1942; *Early Irish History and Mythology*, DIAS, Dublin, 1946.

Oulton, J.E.L., *The Credal Statements of St Patrick*, Hodges Figgis, Dublin/OUP, London, 1940.

Palmer, Sherrard, Ware (ed.), *The Philokalia*, 3 vols., Faber & Faber, London-Boston, 1986 edition.

Pannenberg, Wolfhart (ed.), *Jesus – God and Man* (study edition), SCM Press, London, 1968; *Revelation as History*, The Macmillan Company, London, 1968.

Paul VI, Pope, *Paenitemini/Penitence, Apostolic Constitution of Paul VI*, CTS, London, 1973; *Evangelium Nuntiandi*, Evangelization Today, Flannery, Austin, OP (ed.), Northport, New York, 1977.

Philipon, M.M., OP, *The Spiritual Doctrine of Dom Marmion*, Sands, London, 1956; *The Spiritual Doctrine of Sister Elizabeth of the Trinity*, Mercier Press, Cork, 1947.

Plummer, Charles, *Vitae Sanctorum Hiberniae*, i-ii, OUP, Oxford, 1910.

Power, David N., OMI, *The Eucharistic Mystery, Revitalizing the Tradition*, Gill & Macmillan, Dublin, 1992.

Power, P., *Lives of Declan and Mochuda*, ITS, xvi, London, 1914.

Rahner, Karl, SJ, *Encounters with Silence*, The Newman Press, Westminster, Maryland, USA, 1965; *Mary, Mother of the Lord, Theological Meditations*, Herder, Freiburg, Nelson, Edinburgh and London, 1963; *Mission and Grace I, Essays in Pastoral Theology*, Sheed & Ward, London, Melbourne and New York, 1963.

Rand, Edward Kennard, *Founders of the Middle Ages*, Harvard University Press, Cambridge, 1928.

Redknap, Mark, *The Christian Celts, Treasures of Late Celtic Wales*, National Museum of Wales, Cardiff, 1991.

Rees, Alwyn & Brinley, *Celtic Heritage, Ancient Tradition in Ireland and Wales*, Thames & Hudson, London, 1961.

Ryan, John, SJ, *Irish Monasticism*, The Talbot Press, Dublin, 1931; (ed.), *St Patrick, Thomas Davis Lectures*, Mercier Press, Cork and Dublin, 1958.

Schillebeeckx, E., OP, *Christ, the Sacrament of the Encounter with God*, Sheed & Ward, London, 1963; *Mary, Mother of the Redemption*, Sheed & Ward, London, 1964.

Schneiders, Sandra M., IHM, *New Wine-Skins, Re-imagining Religious Life Today*, Paulist Press, New York, 1966; *The Revelatory Text, Interpreting the New Testament as Sacred Scripture*, Harper, San Francisco, 1991.

Scott, M. Philip, OCist, *A Virgin called Woman, Essays on New Testament Marian Texts*, Bethlehem Abbey Press, Portglenone, 1986.

Schoof, Mark, OP, *Breakthrough, Beginnings of the New Catholic Theology*, Gill & Macmillan, Dublin, 1970.

Simpson, W.D., *St Ninian and the Christian Church in Scotland*, Edinburgh, 1940.

Smyth, Alfred P., *The Earliest Irish Annals, their first Contemporary Entries, and the Earliest Entries*, RIA Proceedings, Dublin, 1972.

Stokes, Whitley (ed.), *The Tripartite Life of Patrick with other documents relating to that saint*, Rerum Britannicarum Medii Albi Scriptores, London, 1887.

Stokes and Strachan, *Thesaurus Palaeohibernicus,* i, ii, CUP, Cambridge, 1901, 1903.

Surlis, Paul (ed.), *Faith: its Nature and Meaning,* Gill & Macmillan, Dublin 1972.

Thomas, Charles, *The Early Christian Archaeology of North Britain*, OUP, London, for Glasgow University, 1971; *Christianity in Roman Britain to AD500*, Batsford, London, 1981; *Britain and Ireland in Early Christian Times*, Thames & Hudson, London, 1971.

Todd, J.H., *St Patrick, Apostle of Ireland*, Hodges, Smith and Co, Dublin, 1864.

Thrall, W.F., *Manley Anniversary Studies*, UCP, Chicago, 1923.

Tucker, Gene M., *Form Criticism of the Old Testament*, Fortress Press, Philadelphia, 1971.

Ussher, James, *Antiquities of the British Churches,* XVII, Dublin, 1639.

Von Balthasar, Hans Urs, *Prayer*, Paulist Press, New York, 1967.

Vonier, Dom Anscar, OSB, *The Personality of Christ*, Longman, Green & Co Ltd, London, 1928.

Walker, G.S.M., *Sancti Columbani Opera, Scriptores Latini Hiberniae,* ii, DIAS, Dublin, 1970.

Wand, J.W.C., *A History of the Early Church to AD500*, Methuen & Co. Ltd, London, 1937/77.

Wansbrough, Henry, OSB, *The Theology of St Paul*, Mercier Press, Cork, 1968.

Ware, Sir James, *De Hibernia et Antiquitatibus Eius*, Grismond, J., London, 1654; *Sancto Patricio...adscripta opuscula*, 1656.

White, Newport, J.D., *A Translation of the Latin Writings of St Patrick*, vol. 5 of texts for students, London, 1918.

Williams, Mhuiríosa, *Traidisiún Liteartha na nGael*, An Clóchomhar, Baile Átha Cliath, 1979.

Woodcock, George, *Thomas Merton, Monk and Poet, A Critical Study*, Farrar, Straus, Giroux, New York, 1978.

Yarnold, Edward, SJ, *The Theology of Original Sin*, Mercier Press, Cork, 1971.

Articles, pamphlets and periodicals

Bieler, L., 'The Problem of Silva Focluti', in *Irish Historical Studies,* iii, 351-64, Dublin, 1943; 'Der Bibeltext des Heiligen Patrick', in *Biblica*, xxviii, 1, 31-58, 235-63, 1947; Binchy, D.A., 'The Fair of Tailtu and the Feast of Tara', in *Eriu,* xvii, 113-38, Dublin, 1958; 'Patrick and His Biographers, Ancient and Modern', in *Studia Hibernica*, ii, 7-123, Dublin, 1962.

Brock, Sebastian, OCist, *'The Luminous Eye, The Spiritual Vision of St Ephrem'*; *'The Ascetical Ideal: St Ephrem and proto-monasticism',* Cistercian Studies Series, 124, Roma, 1992.

Carney, James, 'Three Old-Irish Accentual Poems', in *Eriu*, xxii, 23ff.

Dronke, Peter, 'St Patrick's Reading', in *Cambridge Medieval Celtic Studies* 1, summer 1981.

Evans, R.F., 'Pelagius, Fastidius and the Pseudo-Augustinian De Vita Christiana' in *Journal of Theological Studies*, n.s. xiii, pp. 72-98, April 1962.

Esposito, M., 'The Patrician Problem and a Possible Solution', in *IHS,* x, no. 38, September 1956, 129-56.

de Bháldraithe, Eoin, OCist, 'The Charism of Religious Life', in *Religious Life Review,* V. 32, September/October 1993, 263-7.

de Paor, Liam, 'The Aggrandisement of Armagh', in *Historical Studies,* viii, Dublin, 1979.

de Paor, Máire. B., PBVM, 'Ó Fochoill go Tobar Óghiolla – A Patrician Pilgrimage' (1990), in *Comhdháil an Chraoibhín,* Roscomán, 1994, 49-76.

Dumézil, Georges, *La religion romaine archaique,* 1966; *The Destiny of the Warrior,* 1970; *The Destiny of a King,* 1973.

Grosjean, Paul, SJ, 'Sainte Patrice d'Irlande et quelques homonymes dans les anciens martyrologes', in *Journal of Ecclesiastical History,* i, 151-71, 1950; 'Notes d'Hagiographie Celtique', in *Analecta Bollandiana,* lxiii, 65-119, 1945; lxx, 317-26, 1951; lxxv, 158-226, 1957; 'Les Pictes apostats dans l'épitre de S. Patrice' in ibid., lxxvi, 354-78, 1958.

Herren, Michael, 'Mission and Monasticism in the Confessio of St Patrick' in *Sages, Saints and Storytellers* (ed.), O Corráin, D., Breathnach, L., McCone, K., *Maynooth Monograph* 2, 1989, 76-85.

Hill, Peter & Pollock, Dave, *The Whithorn Dig,* Whithorn Board of Management, Scotland, 1992.

Howlett, David, 'Ex Saliva Scripturae Meae', in ibid., 86-101.

Kinsella, Nivard, OCist, 1. 'The Spirituality of St Patrick's Confession', in *IER,* 91, 1959 A; 2. 'St Patrick's Way to Sanctity', in ibid., 95, 1961 A.

Marsh, Thomas, 'A Study of Confirmation', in *The Irish Theological Quarterly,* 39 (1972), 149-63; 319-36; 40 (1973),125-147.

McCue, James F., 'The Roman Primacy in the Second Century and the Problem of the Development of Dogma', in *Theological Studies,* n. xxv, 1964.

Morris, J., 'Pelagian Literature', in *Journal of Theological Studies,* n. xvi, 26-60, April 1965; 'The Dates of the Celtic Saints', in ibid., xvii, 342-91, October 1966.

Murphy, Gerard, 'The Origins of Irish Nature Poetry', in *Studies,* xx, 87 ff; 'Bards and Filidh', in *Éigse,* ii, 200ff; 'St Patrick and the Civilizing of Ireland', in *IER* v. Ser., lxxix, 194ff, 1953.

Nerney, D.S., 'A Study of St Patrick's Sources', in *IER,* 5th series lxxi-lxxii (1-1V), 1949.

Neilsen, Mark, *Fasting, a Positive Approach,* Ligouri Publications, Missouri, USA, 1987.

Ó Cróinín, Dáibhí, 'New Light on Palladius', in *Peritia,* 5, 1986, 276-283.

Ó Fiaich, Tomás, 'St Patrick and Armagh', in *IER,* 153-70, 1958.

O'Meara, John J., 'The Confession of St Patrick and the Confessions of St Augustine', in *IER,* 1956.

Ó Raifeartaigh, Tarlach, 'Misplacings in the Text of St Patrick's Confession', in *The Maynooth Review* x, May 1984; 'The Enigma of St Patrick', in *Seanchas Ard Mhacha,* 1-60, 1989.

Powell, Douglas, 'The Textual Integrity of St Patrick's Confession', in *Acta Bolla,* 89, 1969, pp. 387-407.

Schokel, Luis, SJ, 'Language and Mentality of the Bible Writers', in *Understanding the Bible, The Old Testament,* v. 1, 61-99, Gastonia, N.C., 1970.

Shaw, Francis, SJ, *The Real St Patrick,* CTS, Dublin, 1932.

Smothers, Edgar R., 'The Bones of St Peter', in *Theological Studies,* n. xxvii, 1966.

Thomas, Charles, *Whithorn's Christian Beginnings,* First Whithorn Lecture, 19 September 1992, Whithorn Trust, Whithorn, Scotland, 1992.

Toynbee, Jocelyn, 'Christianity in Roman Britain', in *Journal of the British Archaeological Association,* 3rd series, xvi, 1-24, 1953.

Wright, R.P., 'Roman Britain in 1963: 11 Inscriptions', in ibid., liv, p. 182, 1964.

INDEX OF NAMES AND PLACES